ISBN 978-1-397-30567-1
PIBN 11375332

SMITHSONIAN MISCELLANEOUS COLLECTIONS.
478

CATALOGUE OF PUBLICATIONS

OF THE

SMITHSONIAN INSTITUTION,

(1846–1882,)

WITH AN

ALPHABETICAL INDEX OF ARTICLES

IN THE

SMITHSONIAN CONTRIBUTIONS TO KNOWLEDGE, MISCELLANEOUS COLLECTIONS, ANNUAL REPORTS, BULLETINS AND PROCEEDINGS OF THE U. S. NATIONAL MUSEUM, AND REPORT OF THE BUREAU OF ETHNOLOGY.

BY WILLIAM J. RHEES,
CHIEF CLERK OF THE INSTITUTION.

WASHINGTON:
SMITHSONIAN INSTITUTION.
1882.

JUDD & DETWEILER, PRINTERS,
WASHINGTON, D. C.

CONTENTS.

		Page.
1.	Smithsonian Contributions	v
2.	Miscellaneous Collections	vi
3.	Annual Reports	vii
4.	Bulletins of the U. S. National Museum	viii
5.	Proceedings of the U. S. National Museum	ix
6.	Report of Bureau of Ethnology	ix
7.	Copyright	ix
8.	Use of illustrations	x
9.	Size of editions	x
10.	Distribution of publications	xi
11.	Rules of distribution	xii
12.	Form of application for publications	xiii
13.	Price list of publications	xiv
List of Publications, A to Q		1
List of Publications, Regular Series, 1–478		3
Classified List of Separate Publications		91
	Anatomy, Physiology, Medicine, and Surgery	92
	Anthropology	92
	Architecture	94
	Astronomy	94
	Bibliography	95
	Biography	95
	Biology	96
	Botany	96
	Chemistry and Technology	97
	Electricity and Magnetism	97
	Geology	98
	Mathematics	98
	Meteorology	99
	Microscopy	100
	Mineralogy	100
	Miscellaneous	100
	Palæontology	102
	Philology	102

Page.

CLASSIFIED LIST OF SEPARATE PUBLICATIONS—Continued.
- Physical Geography 103
- Physics 103
- Terrestrial Physics 104
- Zoölogy—Birds 104
  - Fishes 105
  - Insects 105
  - Mammals 106
  - Mollusks 106
  - Radiates 107
  - Reptiles 107

SMITHSONIAN CONTRIBUTIONS TO KNOWLEDGE—
- Table showing date, number of pages, illustrations, &c. . . 108

MISCELLANEOUS COLLECTIONS—
- Table showing date, number of pages, illustrations, &c. . . 109

ANNUAL REPORTS OF THE INSTITUTION—
- Table showing date, number of pages, illustrations, &c. . . 110

PUBLICATIONS OF THE U. S. NATIONAL MUSEUM—
- Table showing titles, number in Smithsonian series, &c. . . 111

BULLETINS OF THE U. S. NATIONAL MUSEUM—
- Table showing date, number of pages, illustrations, &c. . . 112

BULLETINS OF THE U. S. NATIONAL MUSEUM, collected in volumes—
- Table showing date, number of pages, illustrations, &c. . . 112

PROCEEDINGS OF THE U. S. NATIONAL MUSEUM—
- Table showing date, number of pages, illustrations, &c. . . 113

PUBLICATIONS OF THE BUREAU OF ETHNOLOGY—
- Table showing date, number of pages, illustrations, &c. . . 113

Publications having separate numbers in the Smithsonian series but included in the Annual Reports of the Institution . . 114

Publications not included in regular series of "Contributions," "Collections," or "Reports" 116

List of papers published in the Contributions to Knowledge, giving authors, titles, and commissions of reference 117

ALPHABETICAL INDEX of all articles in Smithsonian publications . 121

PREFACE.

The present catalogue embraces all the articles published by the Smithsonian Institution from its organization in 1846 to the first of July, 1882, a period of thirty-six years.

At the beginning nothing was issued but pamphlets explanatory of the plan of the Institution and brief annual reports of the proceedings of the Board of Regents, indicated in the catalogue by the letters A, B, C, D, E, F, G, H, I, J, K, L, M, N, O, Q. An elaborate work, (P in the catalogue), by ROBERT DALE OWEN, on public architecture, with special reference to the plans of the Smithsonian Institution, prepared on behalf of the Building Committee, was printed at the expense of the Institution in 1849, but did not form part of the regular series organized by the Secretary of the Institution, Prof. Henry.

1. SMITHSONIAN CONTRIBUTIONS TO KNOWLEDGE.

The series entitled "Smithsonian Contributions to Knowledge," in quarto form, was commenced in 1848 by the publication of Squier and Davis' Ancient Monuments of the Mississippi Valley. The following "Advertisement" of the first volume, prepared by Prof. Henry, has been inserted in every succeeding volume to indicate the character and design of the series:

"This volume is intended to form the first of a series of volumes, consisting of original memoirs on different branches of knowledge published at the expense and under the direction of the Smithsonian Institution. The publication of this series forms part of a general plan adopted for carrying into effect the benevolent intentions of James Smithson, Esq., of England. This gentleman left his property in trust to the United States of America to found at Washington an institution which should bear his own name, and have for its objects 'the *increase* and *diffusion* of knowledge among men.' This trust was accepted by the Government of the United States, and an act of Congress was passed August 10, 1846, constituting the President and the other principal executive officers of the General Government, the Chief Justice of the Supreme Court, the Mayor of Washington, and such other persons as they might elect honorary members, an establishment under the name of the 'Smithsonian Institution, for the increase and diffusion of knowledge among men.' The members and honorary members of this establishment are to hold stated and special meetings for the supervision of the affairs of the Institution and for the advice and instruction of a Board of Regents, to whom the financial and other affairs are entrusted.

"The Board of Regents consists of three members *ex-officio* of the establishment, namely, the Vice-President of the United States, the Chief Justice of the Supreme Court, and the Mayor of Washington, together with twelve other members, three of whom are appointed by the Senate from its own body, three by the House of Representatives from its members, and six citizens appointed by a joint resolution of both houses. To this Board is given the power of electing a Secretary and other officers, for conducting the active operations of the Institution.

"To carry into effect the purposes of the testator, the plan of organization should evidently embrace two objects, one, the increase of knowledge by the addition of new truths to the existing stock; the other, the diffusion of knowledge thus increased among men. No restriction is made in favor of any kind of knowledge, and hence each branch is entitled to and should receive a share of attention.

"The act of Congress, establishing the Institution, directs, as part of the plan of organization, the formation of a Library, a Museum, and a Gallery of Art, together with provisions for physical research and popular lectures, while it leaves to the Regents the power of adopting such other parts of an organization as they may deem best suited to promote the objects of the bequest.

"After much deliberation, the Regents resolved to divide the annual income, thirty thousand nine hundred and fifty dollars, into two equal parts, one part to be devoted to the increase and diffusion of knowledge by means of original research and publications, the other half of the income to be applied in accordance with the requirements of the act of Congress to the gradual formation of a Library, a Museum, and a Gallery of Art."

(The Programme of Organization, adopted December 8, 1847, follows.)

"In accordance with the rules adopted in the Programme of Organization, each memoir in this volume has been favorably reported on by a Commission appointed for its examination. It is however, impossible, in most cases, to verify the statements of an author; and, therefore, neither the Commission nor the Institution can be responsible for more than the general character of a memoir."

The total number of papers published in the 23 volumes of "Contributions" is 119, with an aggregate of 12,456 pages, 1,567 wood cuts, 523 plates, and 16 maps, each volume averaging 541½ pages.

2. Miscellaneous Collections.

In the year 1862, another series was instituted, entitled "Smithsonian Miscellaneous Collections" each volume of which has the following preface:

"The present series, entitled "Smithsonian Miscellaneous Collections," is intended to embrace all the publications issued directly by the Smithsonian

Institution in octavo form; those in quarto constituting the "Smithsonian Contributions to Knowledge." The quarto series includes memoirs, embracing the records of extended original investigations and researches, resulting in what are believed to be new truths, and constituting positive additions to the sum of human knowledge. The octavo series is designed to contain reports on the present state of our knowledge of particular branches of science; instructions for collecting and digesting facts and materials for research; lists and synopses of species of the organic and inorganic world; museum catalogues; reports of explorations; aids to bibliographical investigations, etc.; generally prepared at the express request of the Institution and at its expense.

"The position of a work in one or the other of the two series will sometimes depend upon whether the required illustrations can be presented more conveniently in the quarto or the octavo form.

"In the Smithsonian Contributions to Knowledge, as well as in the present series, each article is separately paged and indexed, and the actual date of its publication is that given on its special title page, and not that of the volume in which it is placed. In many cases works have been published and largely distributed years before their combination into volumes.

"While due care is taken on the part of the Smithsonian Institution to insure a proper standard of excellence in its publications, it will be readily understood that it cannot hold itself responsible for the facts and conclusions of the authors, as it is impossible in most cases to verify their statements."

The total number of papers published in the 23 volumes of "Miscellaneous Collections" is 122, each volume averaging 882½ pages, with an aggregate of 20,299 pages, 2,868 wood cuts, and 43 plates.

3. Annual Reports.

By the act of Congress organizing the Institution it was made the duty of the "Board of Regents to submit at each session a report of the operations, expenditures, and condition of the Institution." These Annual Reports form a third series of Smithsonian publications. They consist of the reports of the Secretary to the Board of Regents of the operations and condition of the Institution; the reports of committees of the Board; reports of lectures; extracts from correspondence; original or translated articles relating to the history and progress of science, etc.

The first report was submitted by the Board to the second session of the 29th Congress, 1847, and formed an octavo pamphlet of 38 pages. A similar report was presented annually thereafter, varying in size from 64 pages to 326, printed in pamphlet form with paper covers up to 1853, when Congress ordered the report to be bound in cloth. In the volume for that year the essential portion of the contents of the preceding seven reports was reprinted, and this is now considered as the first of a set of Smithsonian Reports. The number of pages was limited between 1854 and 1876 to 400. In the latter year this restriction was removed, and since then the average number of pages has been 600.

The number of copies of these reports for general distribution ordered by Congress has been very variable, the largest being 7,500 in 1874 and 1875, and the smallest 150 in 1847. The number of copies granted the Institution each year is shown in the following table:

Number of extra copies furnished the Institution by Congress for distribution.

For the Year.	No. of Copies.	For the Year.	No. of Copies.	For the Year.	No. of Copies.
1847	150	1859	2,000	1871	5,000
1848	1,000	1860	2,000	1872	5,000
1849	500	1861	2,000	1873	6,000
1850	1,000	1862	2,000	1874	7,500
1851	2,000	1863	2,000	1875	7,500
1852	2,000	1864	2,000	1876	6,500
1853	3,000	1865	2,000	1877	6,500
1854	2,500	1866	2,000	1878	6,500
1855	2,500	1867	2,000	1879	7,000
1856	2,500	1868	2,000	1880	7,000
1857	5,000	1869	3,000		
1858	5,000	1870	5,000		

The total number of pages in the 35 volumes of Annual Reports is 14,419, average 412 pages; total number of woodcuts, 1,898.

4. Bulletins of the U. S. National Museum.

In the year 1875 a fourth series of publications (octavo) was commenced, entitled "Bulletins of the National Museum," intended to illustrate the collections of natural history and ethnology belonging to the United States, constituting the National Museum, of which the Smithsonian Institution is the custodian.

Twenty of these Bulletins have been published, with an aggregate of 3,103 pages, 45 plates, and 1 map.

5. Proceedings of the U. S. National Museum.

In imitation of the practice of those learned societies which publish periodically descriptions of new species, &c., in the form of proceedings of weekly or monthly meetings, and thus present to the world the discoveries connected with the establishment at the earliest practicable moment, it appeared to be very desirable that the National Museum should have some medium of prompt publication for announcing descriptions of specimens received, (many of which are new species,) as well as other interesting facts relative to natural history furnished by correspondents of the Institution. To meet this want a fifth series of publications, (octavo,) entitled "Proceedings of the National Museum," was commenced in 1880. They are printed in successive signatures as fast as material sufficient for 16 pages is prepared, and distributed at once to scientific societies and leading active working naturalists in this country and in Europe,* each signature having printed at the bottom of its first page the date of actual issue, for settling any questions as to priority of publication. Of this series four volumes have been published, comprising 2,221 pages, with 28 cuts and 19 plates.

6. Reports of the Bureau of Ethnology.

The sixth series of publications is the annual report (in Imperial octavo) of the Bureau of Ethnology, placed by Congress in charge of the Smithsonian Institution. The first volume of this series was issued in 1881, and consists of 638 pages, with 343 cuts, 54 plates, and 1 map.

The distribution of this volume to individuals is wholly by Members of Congress and the Director of the Bureau, Major J. W. Powell—the Institution having copies at its disposal only for the libraries on its regular list of distribution for its own full series.

7. Copyright.

No copyright has ever been secured on the publications of the Institution. They are left free to be used by compilers of books without any restrictions, except that full credit shall be given to the name of Smithson for any extracts which may be made from them.

---

* Prof. Baird's report for 1880.

8. Use of Illustrations.

Copies of the wood cuts used by the Institution are granted to authors or publishers on payment of the actual cost of production of electrotypes, and promise to give proper reference to the article in which they originally appeared.

9. Size of Editions.

In the first experiments of the Smithsonian system of publication, the proper magnitude of the editions necessary to meet the immediate and future demand could not be accurately ascertained. The number of copies of the Contributions then fixed upon, has since been found inadequate, although it was larger than that usually issued by other institutions. The edition has, therefore, been augmented, until at the present time 1,000 copies of each article are set aside to be combined into volumes, and an extra number, varying with the probable demand, struck off for separate distribution, and for sale.

Each article is complete in itself, with separate paging, title, and index, and without any necessary relationship to others combined with it in the same volume.

Of the early volumes of Smithsonian Contributions, the edition, for reasons already explained, was less than of the succeeding ones, so that complete sets cannot now be furnished.

In the year 1862, the plan of stereotyping every article printed by the Institution was adopted, the plates being carefully preserved, thus making it practicable at any time to issue new editions except where expensive lithographic plates were used, a limited number, only, of impressions from these having been taken.

A number of the earlier articles in octavo were out of print before the commencement of the series of "Miscellaneous Collections," and consequently are not included in them.

The printing of the "Bulletins" and "Proceedings" is authorized by the Department of the Interior and paid for out of its fund. An edition of 1,000 copies is published, of which one-half is distributed by the Department of the Interior and one-half by the Institution. As the pages are stereotyped, the cost of additional copies is slight; and for the purpose of making sure that a sufficient number of sets will be accessible forever to students in all parts of the world, it has been considered expedient to print 1,500 additional copies of each for incorporation in the Miscellaneous Collections.*

10. Distribution of Publications.

The distribution of the publications of the Institution is a matter which requires much care and judicious selection, the great object being to make known to the world the truths which may result from the expenditure of the Smithson fund. For this purpose the Contributions are so distributed as to be accessible to the greatest number of readers; that is, to large central libraries.

The volumes of Contributions are presented on the express condition that, while they are carefully preserved, they shall be accessible at all times to students and others who may desire to consult them, and be returned to the Institution in case the establishments to which they are presented at any time cease to exist.

These works, it must be recollected, are not of a popular character, but require profound study to fully understand them; they are, however, of importance to the professional teacher and the popular expounder of science. They contain the materials from which general treatises on special subjects may be elaborated.†

Full sets of the publications cannot be given to all who apply for them, since this is impossible with the limited income of the Institution, and, indeed, if care be not exercised in the distribution, so large a portion of the income will be annually expended on the production of copies for distribution of what has already been published that nothing further can be done in the way of new publications. It must be recollected that every addition to the list of distribution not only involves the giving of the publications which have already been made, but also of those which are to be made hereafter.‡

The rules governing the distribution of the Smithsonian publications are appended. To enable institutions not coming within their provisos, as well as individuals, to procure copies of such as may be desired, a small number is set aside and sold by the Institution at a price which is intended merely to cover the actual cost of their publication.

---

* Prof. Baird's report for 1880.

† Prof. Henry's report for 1876.

‡ Prof. Henry's report for 1873.

11. Rules for Distribution of the Publications of the Smithsonian Institution.

To Institutions.

The publications of the Smithsonian Institution are furnished:

1st. To learned societies of the first class, which present complete series of their publications to the Institution.

2d. To libraries of the first class, which give in exchange their catalogues and other publications; or an equivalent, from their duplicate volumes.

3d. To colleges of the first class, which furnish catalogues of their libraries and of their students, and all publications relative to their organization and history.

4th. To public libraries containing 25,000 volumes.

5th. To smaller public libraries, where a large district would be otherwise unsupplied.

6th. Institutions devoted exclusively to the promotion of particular branches of knowledge may receive such Smithsonian publications as relate to their respective objects.

To Individuals.

The gratuitous distribution to *individuals*, of the publications of the Institution, is restricted:

1st. To those who are engaged in original research in the branch of science to which the book asked for pertains.

2d. To those who require it in the business of instruction.

3d. To donors to the museum or library of the Institution.

12. Form of Application for Publications.

To the Smithsonian Institution, Washington, D. C.

Date, 18

In behalf of the , we respectfully apply for the publications of the Smithsonian Institution, on condition that all volumes received shall be carefully preserved, be accessible to any person who may wish to consult them, and be returned to the Smithsonian Institution in case the establishment at any time ceases to exist.

1. Name of Establishment ----------------
2. Location—Town ----------------

   State ----------------
3. When established ----------------
4. Character ----------------
5. Buildings and property ----------------
6. Permanent fund ----------------
7. Annual income ----------------
8. Volumes in library ----------------
9. Number of persons having use of books ----------------
10. Date of last catalogue of library ----------------
11. What publications made ----------------

    (Send printed list if possible.)
12. Names of Officers: President ----------------

    Secretary ----------------

    Librarian ----------------
13. Addresses of principal scientific men connected with the Establishment and subjects in which specially interested ----------------

I recommend the above application.

---------------- *Member of Congress,*

---------------- *District* ---------------- *State.*

13. Price List of Smithsonian Publications.

Where no price is given the work is out of print, and cannot be furnished. Of those marked "free" the edition is limited, and copies are only given to those specially interested in the subjects to which they pertain, who are collaborators of the Institution or contributors to its library or museum.

P	$10 00	60	$1 00	120	$1 00	180	$1 00	240		300	$0 25	360	free.	420	free.
1		61	1 00	121	25	181	2 00	241	$7 50	301		361		421	free.
2		62	2 00	122	6 00	182	2 50	242	7 50	302	25	362	free.	422	$0 25
3		63	1 00	123	6 00	183	25	243	free.	303	50	363	free.	423	6 00
4		64	free.	124		184	12 00	244	1 00	304	50	364	free.	424	6 00
5		65		125	6 00	185	free.	245	free.	305	50	365	free.	425	2 00
6		66		126	1 25	186	50	246	12 00	306	50	366	free.	426	free.
7		67		127	1 25	187	50	247	50	307		367	free.	427	free.
8		68		128	25	188	50	248		308	50	368		428	free.
9		69		129	1 00	189	1 00	249		309	free.	369		429	free.
10		70	6 00	130	1 50	190	free.	250		310	25	370	free.	430	free.
11		71		131	1 25	191		251	free.	311	50	371	free.	431	free.
12	4 00	72	3 00	132	25	192	5 00	252		312		372	free.	432	free.
13	2 00	73	25	133	2 00	193	free.	253		313	50	373	free.	433	free.
14	1 00	74		134		194		254	2 00	314	6 00	374	free.	434	free.
15	4 00	75		135		195		255		315	6 00	375	free.	435	free.
16		76	12 00	136		196		256	2 00	316	free.	376	free.	436	free.
17	50	77		137		197	1 00	257		317	3 00	377	free.	437	free.
18		78	12 00	138	free.	198		258	2 00	318	2 00	378	free.	438	free.
19		79	1 00	139	free.	199	2 00	259	3 00	319	free.	379	free.	439	35
20	1 00	80	1 00	140	75	200	25	260		320	free.	380	free.	440	50
21	1 00	81		141	1 50	201	50	261	free.	321	25	381	free.	441	1 50
22		82	1 50	142	3 00	202	3 50	262	3 00	322	6 00	382	free.	442	50
23	2 00	83	1 25	143	1 25	203		263		323		383	$2 50	443	1 00
24		84	1 50	144	1 00	204	1 00	264		324	free.	384	free.	444	50
25	50	85	25	145	75	205	free.	265		325	free.	385	free.	445	free.
26		86		146	1 50	206	12 00	266	25	326	50	386	free.	446	free.
27	50	87	25	147		207	free.	267	1 00	327	75	387	free.	447	free.
28	1 00	88	1 00	148	free.	208	50	268		328	5 00	388	free.	448	free.
29		89	5 00	149		209		269		329		389	free.	449	free.
30		90	5 00	150		210	25	270	2 00	330		390	free.	450	free.
31		91		151	12 00	211	12 00	271		331	2 00	391	free.	451	free.
32		92	12 00	152		212	6 00	272	12 00	332	2 00	392	free.	452	free.
33	75	93		153		213	6 00	273	6 00	333	2 00	393	free.	453	free.
34	free.	94	50	154		214	1 00	274	6 00	334	25	394	free.	454	free.
35		95	6 00	155		215		275	50	335	free.	395	free.	455	free.
36	1 00	96	20 00	156	50	216	25	276	50	336	6 00	396	free.	456	free.
37		97	1 00	157		217		277	3 00	337	6 00	397	free.	457	free.
38		98	4 00	158		218		278	free.	338		398	free.	458	free.
39		99	12 00	159	1 00	219	2 00	279	25	339		399	free.	459	free.
40		100	50	160		220		280	1 00	340	12 00	400	free.	460	free.
41	1 00	101	free.	161	50	221	1 00	281	75	341	50	401	free.	461	free.
42		102		162	1 00	222	3 00	282	25	342	50	402	free.	462	free.
43		103	2 00	163	free.	223	1 00	283	25	343	free.	403	free.	463	50
44		104		164	50	224		284	12 00	344	free.	404	free.	464	free.
45		105	50	165		225		285	12 00	345	50	405	free.	465	free.
46		106	50	166	1 00	226	free.	286	50	346	12 00	406	free.	466	free.
47	50	107		167	1 00	227	25	287	2 00	347	free.	407		467	2 00
48		108	25	168	free.	228	50	288	50	348		408	free.	468	6 00
49	1 00	109		169	6 00	229	12 00	289	50	349	25	409	free.	469	free.
50	1 50	110		170	free.	230	25	290	free.	350	free.	410	free.	470	50
51		111	12 00	171		231		291	25	351		411	free.	471	free.
52	5 00	112	12 00	172		232	2 00	292	50	352	free.	412	50	472	free.
53	50	113	25	173	2 50	233	25	293	50	353	3 00	413	50	473	free.
54	50	114	1 25	174	2 00	234	free.	294	50	354	free.	414	15	474	free.
55		115	free.	175	1 00	235	free.	295	50	355		415	free.	475	6 00
56		116		176	free.	236	free.	296	50	356	50	416	6 00	476	
57	1 00	117	2 00	177	25	237	free.	297	50	357	2 50	417	free.	477	free.
58	5 00	118	1 00	178	free.	238	free.	298	50	358	1 00	418	free.	478	75
59	25	119	1 00	179	3 00	239	2 00	299		359	free.	419	free.		

LIST OF PUBLICATIONS

OF THE

SMITHSONIAN INSTITUTION.

NOTE.—A to Q indicate early publications not embraced in the regular series.

A. Journal of Proceedings of the Regents of the Smithsonian Institution, at the city of Washington, beginning on the first Monday of September, 1846. 1846. 8vo., pp. 32.

B. Report of the Organization Committee of the Smithsonian Institution, with the resolutions accompanying the same and adopted by the Board of Regents; also, the Will of the testator, the Act accepting the bequest, and the Act organizing the Institution. 1847. 8vo., pp. 32.

C. Digest of the Act of Congress establishing the Smithsonian Institution. August 10, 1846. 8vo., pp. 8.

D. Address delivered on occasion of laying the Corner Stone of the Smithsonian Institution, May 1, 1847. By GEORGE M. DALLAS, Chancellor of the Institution. 1847. 8vo., pp. 8.

E. Smithson's Bequest. Professor HENRY'S exposition before the New Jersey Historical Society, at its meeting in Princeton, on Wednesday, September 27. 1847. 8vo., pp. 8.

F. First Report of the Secretary of the Smithsonian Institution to the Board of Regents; giving a Programme of Organization, and an account of the operations during the year. Presented December 8, 1847. 1848. 8vo., pp. 48.

G. [First] Report from the Board of Regents, submitted to Congress, of the operations, expenditures, and condition of the Smithsonian Institution. Senate Doc. 211; 29th Congress, 2d Session. 1847. 8vo., pp. 38.

H. Second Report of the Board of Regents of the Smithsonian Institution, to the Senate and House of Representatives, showing the operations, expenditures, and condition of the Institution during the year 1847. 30th Congress, 1st Session. Senate Miscellaneous No. 23. 1848. 8vo., pp. 208.

H. Report for 1847—Continued.

CONTENTS.

Report of Prof. J. Henry, and Proceedings of the Board.

Gallatin, A.; Robinson, E.; Bartlett, J. R.; Turner, W. W.; Morton, S. G.; Marsh, G. P. On publication of Squier & Davis's Ancient Monuments.

Jewett, C. C. Report on plan of library.

Loomis, E. Report on meteorology of the United States.

Espy, J. P. On meteorology.

I. Third Annual Report of the Board of Regents of the Smithsonian Institution, for the year 1848. 30th Congress, 2d Session. H. R. Miscellaneous, No. 48. 1849. 8vo., pp. 64.

CONTENTS.

Report of Prof. J. Henry, and Proceedings of the Board.

Jewett, C. C. Report on library.

Stevens, H. Prospectus of a Bibliographia Americana.

Hare, R. Letter relative to gift of apparatus.

Guyot, A. On metric system for scientific observations.

J. Programme of organization of the Smithsonian Institution. Presented in the first annual report of the Secretary, and adopted by the Board of Regents, December 13, 1847. 1847. 4to., pp. 4.

K. Correspondence relative to the acceptance for publication of the ethnological memoir of Messrs. Squier and Davis. 1847. 8vo., pp. 8.

L. [First] Report of the Organization Committee of the Smithsonian Institution. Reprinted from the National Intelligencer, December 8, 1846. 8vo., pp. 8.

M. Reports, etc., of the Smithsonian Institution, exhibiting its plans, operations, and financial condition up to January 1, 1849. From the third annual report of the Board of Regents. Presented to Congress February 19, 1849. 1849. 8vo., pp. 72.

N. Officers and Regents of the Smithsonian Institution, with the act of Congress accepting the bequest, and the act incorporating said Institution. 1846. 8vo., pp. 14.

O. An Act to establish the Smithsonian Institution. Approved Aug. 10, 1846. pp. 8.

P. Hints on Public Architecture, containing, among other illustrations, views and plans of the Smithsonian Institution; together with an appendix relative to building materials. Prepared on behalf of the Building Committee of the Smithsonian Institution, by Robert Dale Owen, chairman of the committee. 1849. 4to., pp. 140, 99 woodcuts, 15 plates.

Q. Check list of periodical publications received in the reading-room of the Smithsonian Institution, for the year 1853. 1853. 4to., pp. 28.

REGULAR SERIES.

1. Ancient Monuments of the Mississippi Valley; comprising the results of extensive original surveys and explorations. By E. G. SQUIER and E. H. DAVIS. 1848. 4to., pp. 346, 207 woodcuts, 48 plates. (S. C. I.)

2. Smithsonian Contributions to Knowledge. Vol. I. 1848. 4to., pp. 360, 207 woodcuts, 48 plates.

CONTENTS.

SQUIER and DAVIS. Ancient Monuments, Mississippi Valley. No. 1.

3. Researches relative to the Planet Neptune. By SEARS C. WALKER. 1849. 4to., pp. 60. (S. C. II.)

4. Ephemeris of the Planet Neptune for the Opposition of 1848. By SEARS C. WALKER. 1848. 4to, pp. 8. (S. C. II.)

5. Ephemeris of the Planet Neptune from the date of the Lalande Observations of May 8 and 10, 1795, and for the Opposition of 1846, '47, '48, and '49. By SEARS C. WALKER. April, 1849. 4to., pp. 32. (S. C. II.)

6. Ephemeris of the Planet Neptune for the year 1850. By SEARS C. WALKER. April, 1850. 4to., pp. 10. (S. C. II)

7. Ephemeris of the Planet Neptune for the year 1851. By SEARS C. WALKER. December, 1850. 4to., pp. 10. (S. C. II.)

8. *Occultations visible in the United States during the year 1848. By JOHN DOWNES. 1848. 4to., pp. 12.

9. *Occultations visible in the United States during the year 1849. By JOHN DOWNES. 1848. 4to., pp. 24.

10. *Occultations visible in the United States during the year 1850. By JOHN DOWNES. 1849. 4to., pp. 26.

11. Occultations visible in the United States during the year 1851. By JOHN DOWNES. October, 1850. 4to., pp. 26. (S. C. II.)

12. On the Vocal Sounds of Laura Bridgman, the Blind Deaf Mute at Boston; compared with the Elements of Phonetic Language. By FRANCIS LIEBER. 1850. 4to., pp. 32, one plate. (S. C. II.)

13. Contributions to the Physical Geography of the United States. Part I. On the physical geography of the Mississippi valley, with suggestions for the improvement of the navigation of the Ohio and,

---

*These three papers by Mr. Downes, Nos. 8, 9, 10, were not published in the series of Contributions.

other rivers. By CHARLES ELLET, JR. 1850. 4to., pp. 64, 2 woodcuts, 1 plate. (S. C. II.)

14. A Memoir on *Mosasaurus*, and the three Allied New Genera, *Holcodus*, *Conosaurus*, and *Amphorosteus*. By ROBERT W. GIBBES. November, 1850. 4to., pp. 14, 3 plates of 28 figures. (S. C. II.)

15. Aboriginal Monuments of the State of New York. Comprising the results of original surveys and explorations; with an illustrative appendix. By E. G. SQUIER. 1850. 4to., pp. 188, 79 woodcuts, 14 plates of 33 figures. (S. C. II.)

16. The Classification of Insects from Embryological Data. By LOUIS AGASSIZ, 1850. 4to., pp. 28, 8 woodcuts, one plate of 23 figures. (S. C. II.)

17. Memoir on the Explosiveness of Nitre, with a view to elucidate its agency in the tremendous explosion of July, 1845, in New York. By ROBERT HARE. 1850. 4to., pp. 20. (S. C. II.)

18. Report on the History of the Discovery of Neptune. By BENJAMIN APTHORP GOULD, JR. 1850. 8vo., pp. 56.

19. Directions for Meteorological Observations, intended for the first class of observers. By ARNOLD GUYOT. 1850. 8vo., pp. 40, 9 woodcuts.

20. Microscopical Examination of Soundings, made by the United States Coast Survey off the Atlantic coast of the United States. By J. W. BAILEY. January, 1851. 4to., pp. 16 and 1 plate of 68 figures. (S. C. II.)

21. Fourth Annual Report of the Board of Regents of the Smithsonian Institution, for the year 1849. 31st Congress, 1st Session. Senate Miscellaneous No. 120, 8vo., pp. 64, with appendix of 207 pp. House of Representatives Miscellaneous No. 50. 1850. 8vo., pp. 272.

CONTENTS.

Report of Prof. J. HENRY, and Proceedings of the Board.

GRAY, ASA. Account of Lindheimer's, Fendler's and Wright's botanical explorations in New Mexico and California.

AGASSIZ, LOUIS. On the formation of a museum.

List of meteorological observers.

JEWETT, C. C. Report on library and catalogue system.

JEWETT, C. C. Report on public libraries of the United States.

22. Plantæ Wrightianæ Texano-Neo-Mexicanæ. By ASA GRAY. Part I. March, 1852. 4to., pp. 146, 10 plates of 127 figures. (S. C. III.)

An account of a collection of plants made by Charles Wright in Western Texas, New Mexico, and Sonora, in the years 1851 and 1852.

23. Microscopical Observations made in South Carolina, Georgia, and Florida. By J. W. BAILEY. 1851. 4to., pp. 48, 3 plates of 83 figures. (S. C. II.)

24. Ephemeris of the Planet Neptune for the year 1852. By SEARS C WALKER. 1853. 4to. pp. 10. (S. C. III.)

25. Notices of Public Libraries in the United States of America. By CHAS. C. JEWETT. Printed by order of Congress as an appendix to the Fourth Annual Report of the Board of Regents of the Smithsonian Institution. 1851. 8vo., pp. 210.

26. Smithsonian Contributions to Knowledge. Vol. II. 1851. 4to., pp. 572, 89 woodcuts, 24 plates.

CONTENTS.

WALKER, S. C. Researches relative to Neptune. No. 3.
LIEBER, F. Vocal sounds of Laura Bridgman. No. 12.
BAILEY, J. W. Microscopical soundings off Atlantic Coast. No. 20.
ELLET, C. Physical geography of the Mississippi Valley. No. 13.
GIBBES, R. W. Mosasaurus and three allied genera. No. 14.
AGASSIZ, L. Classification of insects from embryological data. No. 16.
HARE, R. Explosiveness of nitre. No. 17.
BAILEY, J. W. Microscopical observations in S. C., Ga., Fla. No. 23.
SQUIER, E. G. Aboriginal monuments of State of New York. No. 15.
WALKER, S. C. Ephemeris of Neptune for 1848. No. 4.
WALKER, S. C. Ephemeris of Neptune for 1846, '47, '48, '49. No. 5.
WALKER, S. C. Ephemeris of Neptune for 1850. No. 6.
WALKER, S. C. Ephemeris of Neptune for 1851. No. 7.
DOWNES, J. Occultations visible in the United States in 1851. No. 11.

27. On Recent Improvements in the Chemical Arts. By JAMES C. BOOTH and CAMPBELL MORFIT. 1852. 8vo., pp. 216. (M. C. II.)

28. Fifth Annual Report of the Board of Regents of the Smithsonian Institution, for the year 1850. Special session, March, 1851. Senate Miscellaneous No. 1. 1851. 8vo., pp. 145. (Extra edition of 326 pp.)

CONTENTS.

Report of Prof. J. HENRY, and Proceedings of the Board.
JEWETT, C. C. General catalogue system for libraries.
BAIRD, S. F. Report on museum, and statistics of British Museum.
Memorial of the Regents to Congress, relative to the Smithson Fund.
SQUIER, E. G. Antiquities of Nicaragua.
Report of Commission on General Stereotype Catalogue of Pub. Libraries.
CULBERTSON, T. A. Expedition to the Mauvaises Terres and Upper Missouri.
PORTER, T. C. List of plants of Upper Missouri.
HARRIS, E. List of birds and mammalia of Missouri river.
CULBERTSON, T. A. Indian tribes of the Upper Missouri.
JEWETT, C. C. Copyright books from 1846–1849.

29. Occultations visible in the United States during the year 1852. By JOHN DOWNES. 1851. 4to., pp. 34. (S. C. III.)

30. Contributions to the Natural History of the Fresh Water Fishes of North America. By CHARLES GIRARD. Part I.—A monograph of the Cottoids. December, 1851. 4to., pp. 80, 3 plates of 48 figures. (S. C. III.)

31. A Collection of Meteorological Tables, with other tables useful in Practical Meteorology. By ARNOLD GUYOT. 1852. 8vo., pp. 212.

32. Nereis Boreali-Americana: or, Contributions to a History of the Marine Algæ of North America. By WILLIAM HENRY HARVEY. Part I.—Melanospermeæ. January, 1852. 4to., pp. 152, 12 colored plates of 29 figures. (S. C. III.)

33. The Law of Deposit of the Flood Tide: its Dynamical Action and Office. By CHARLES HENRY DAVIS. 1852. 4to., pp. 14. (S. C. III.)

34. Directions for Collecting, Preserving, and Transporting Specimens of Natural History. March, 1859. 8vo., pp. 40, 6 woodcuts. (M. C. II.)

35. Observations on Terrestrial Magnetism. By JOHN LOCKE. April, 1852. 4to., pp. 30. (S. C. III.)

36. Researches on Electrical Rheometry. By A. SECCHI. May, 1852. 4to., pp. 60, 3 plates of 15 figures. (S. C. III.)

37. Descriptions of Ancient Works in Ohio. By CHAS. WHITTLESEY. 1851. 4to., pp. 20, 7 plates of 18 figures. (S. C. III.)

38. Smithsonian Contributions to Knowledge. Vol. III. 1852. 4to., pp. 562, and 35 plates.

CONTENTS.

LOCKE, J. Terrestrial magnetism. No. 35.
SECCHI, A. Electrical rheometry. No. 36.
GIRARD, C. Monograph of the cottoids. No. 30.
HARVEY, W. H. Marine algæ of North America. Part I. No. 32.
GRAY, A. Plantæ Wrightianæ Texano-Neo-Mexicanæ. Part I. No. 22.
DAVIS, C. H. Law of deposit of the flood tide. No. 33.
WHITTLESEY, C. Descriptions of ancient works in Ohio. No. 37.
WALKER, S. C. Ephemeris of the planet Neptune for 1852. No. 24.
DOWNES, J. Occultations visible in United States during 1852. No. 29.

39. Smithsonian Contributions to Knowledge. Vol. IV. 1852. 4to., pp. 426.

CONTENTS.

RIGGS, S. R. Dakota Grammar and Dictionary. No. 40.

40. Grammar and Dictionary of the Dakota Language. Collected by the members of the Dakota mission. Edited by S. R. RIGGS. 1852. 4to., pp. 414. (S. C. IV.)

41. Memoir on the Extinct Species of American Ox. By JOSEPH LEIDY. December, 1852. 4to., pp. 20, 4 plates of 15 figures. (S. C. v.)

42. Plantæ Wrightianæ Texano-Neo-Mexicanæ. By ASA GRAY. Part II. February, 1853. 4to., pp. 120, 4 plates of 39 figures. (S. C. v.)

43. Nereis Boreali-Americana; or, Contributions to a History of the Marine Algæ of North America. By W. H. HARVEY. Part II.—Rhodospermeæ. March, 1853. 4to., pp. 262, 24 plates, colored, of 64 figures. (S. C. v.)

44. A Flora and Fauna within Living Animals. By JOSEPH LEIDY. April, 1853. 4to., pp. 68, 10 plates of 140 figures. (S. C. v.)

45. Anatomy of the Nervous System of *Rana pipiens*. By JEFFRIES WYMAN. March, 1853. 4to., pp. 52, 4 woodcuts, 2 plates of 29 figures. (S. C. v.)

46. Plantæ Frémontianæ: or, Descriptions of Plants collected by J. C. Frémont in California. By JOHN TORREY. 1853. 4to., pp. 24, 10 plates of 89 figures. (S. C. VI.)

47. On the Construction of Catalogues of Libraries, and their publication by means of separate stereotyped titles. With rules and examples. By CHARLES C. JEWETT. 1852. 8vo., pp. 78. 1853. 8vo., pp. 108.

48. Bibliographia Americana Historico-Naturalis; or Bibliography of American Natural History for the year 1851. 1851. By CHARLES GIRARD. December, 1852. 8vo., pp. 64.

49. Catalogue of North American Reptiles in the Museum of the Smithsonian Institution. By S. F. BAIRD and C. GIRARD. Part I.—Serpents. January, 1853. 8vo., pp. 188. (M. C. II.)

50. Synopsis of the Marine Invertebrata of Grand Manan: or the region about the mouth of the Bay of Fundy, New Brunswick. By WM. STIMPSON. March, 1853. 4to., pp. 68, 3 plates of 37 figures. (S. C. VI.)

51. Sixth Annual Report of the Board of Regents of the Smithsonian Institution, for the year 1851. 32d Congress, 1st session, Senate Mis. No. 108. 1852. 8vo., pp. 104.

CONTENTS.

Report of Prof. J. HENRY, and Proceedings of the Board.
JEWETT, C. C. Smithsonian library and copyright system.
BAIRD, S. F. Natural history explorations in the United States in 1851.
FOREMAN, E. Meteorological system and correspondence.
LEIDY, J. Report on fossils from Nebraska.
TURNER, W. W. Indian philology.

51. Report for 1851—Continued.

Report of Committee of American Association for Promotion of Science, on a system of combined meteorological observations for North America.

52. Winds of the Northern Hemisphere. By JAMES H. COFFIN. November, 1853. 4to., pp. 200, 6 woodcuts, 13 plates of 238 figures. (S. C. VI.)

53. Catalogue of Portraits of North American Indians, and Sketches of Scenery, etc., painted by J. M. STANLEY. Deposited with the Smithsonian Institution. December, 1852. 8vo., pp. 76. (M. C. II.)

54. Occultations of Planets and Stars by the Moon, during the year 1853. By JOHN DOWNES. 1853. 4to., pp. 36. (S. C. VI.)

55. Smithsonian Contributions to Knowledge. Vol. V. 1853. 4to., pp. 538, 4 woodcuts, 45 plates.

CONTENTS.

LEIDY, J. Flora and fauna within living animals. No. 44.
LEIDY, J. Extinct species of American ox. No. 41.
WYMAN, J. Anatomy of the nervous system of Rana pipiens. No. 45.
HARVEY, W. H. Marine algæ of North America. Part II. No. 43.
GRAY, A. Plantæ Wrightianæ. Part II. No. 42.

56. Smithsonian Contributions to Knowledge. Vol. VI. 1854. 4to., pp. 484, 9 woodcuts, 53 plates.

CONTENTS.

TORREY, J. Plantæ Frémontianæ. No. 46.
TORREY, J. Batis maritima. No. 60.
TORREY, J. Darlingtonia californica. No. 61.
STIMPSON, W. Marine invertebrata of Grand Manan. No. 50.
COFFIN, J. H. Winds of the Northern Hemisphere. No. 52.
LEIDY, J. Ancient fauna of Nebraska. No. 58.
DOWNES, J. Occultations during the year 1853. No. 54.

57. Seventh Annual Report of the Board of Regents of the Smithsonian Institution, for the year 1852. 32d Congress, 2d Session, Senate Mis. No. 53. 1853. 8vo., pp. 96.

CONTENTS.

Report of Prof. J. HENRY, and Proceedings of the Board.
JEWETT, C. C. Report on library and the Halliwell manuscripts.
BAIRD, S. F. Scientific explorations in America in 1852.
FOREMAN, E. Report on meteorological system.

58. The Ancient Fauna of Nebraska: or, a Description of Remains of Extinct Mammalia and Chelonia, from the Mauvaises Terres of Nebraska. By JOSEPH LEIDY. June, 1853. 4to., pp. 126, 3 woodcuts, 25 plates of 126 figures. (S. C. VI.)

59. Account of a Tornado near New Harmony, Indiana, April 30, 1852,

with a map of the track, etc. By JOHN CHAPPELSMITH. April, 1855. 4to., pp. 12, 2 woodcuts, 1 map, 1 plate. (S. C. VII.)

60. Observations on the *Batis maritima* of Linnæus. By JOHN TORREY. April, 1853. 4to., pp. 8, 1 plate of 21 figures. (S. C. VI.)

61. On the *Darlingtonia Californica;* a new pitcher-plant from Northern California. By JOHN TORREY. April, 1853. 4to., pp. 8, 1 plate of 9 figures. (S. C. VI.)

62. Catalogue of the Described Coleoptera of the United States. By F. E. MELSHEIMER. July, 1853. 8vo., pp. 190.

63. Notes on New Species and Localities of Microscopical Organisms. By J. W. BAILEY, February, 1854. 4to., pp. 16, 7 woodcuts, 1 plate of 39 figures. (S. C. VII.)

64. List of Foreign Institutions in Correspondence with the Smithsonian Institution. 1856. 8vo., pp. 16.

65. Registry of Periodical Phenomena. Folio, pp. 4.

66. The Annular Eclipse of May 26, 1854. 1854. 8vo., pp. 14, 1 map.

67. Eighth Annual Report of the Board of Regents of the Smithsonian Institution for the year 1853. 33d Congress, 1st Session, Senate Doc. No. 73, pp. 269. House of Representatives, Mis. Doc. No. 97. 1854. 8vo., pp. 310.*

CONTENTS.

Report of Prof. J. HENRY, and Proceedings of the Board.
JEWETT, C. C. Report on library.
BAIRD, S. F. Report on publications, exchanges, museum, and explorations.
BLODGET, L. List of meteorological observers.
PEARCE, J. A. Report of Committee of Regents on distribution of Smithsonian income.
MEACHAM, J. Minority report of Committee on income.
SMITHSON, J. Will of
RUSH, R. Letter from, relative to James Smithson.
GILBERT, D., President of the Royal Society. Notice of Smithson.
SMITHSON, J. List of papers presented by, to the Royal Society.
SMITHSON, J. Contributions to the Annals of Philosophy.
Act of Congress accepting Bequest, July 1, 1836.
Act of Congress to establish the Smithsonian Institution, August 10, 1846.
BERRIEN, J. McP. Construction of the Act establishing the Smithsonian Institution.
HENRY, J. Address on the Smithsonian Institution.

* This is the first of the series of annual reports published by Congress as a bound volume.

67. Report for 1853—Continued.

EVERETT, E.; SPARKS, J.; PIERCE, B.; LONGFELLOW, H. W.; GRAY, A. Report of American Academy of Arts and Sciences on Organization of Smithsonian Institution.

HENRY, J. First Report of the Secretary, Dec. 8, 1847. (Reprint.)
" Second Report of the Secretary for 1848. "
" Third Report of the Secretary for 1849. "
" Fourth Report of the Secretary for 1850. "
" Fifth Report of the Secretary for 1851.
" Sixth Report of the Secretary for 1852. "

68. Vocabulary of the Jargon or Trade Language of Oregon. By B. RUSH MITCHELL, with additions by W. W. TURNER. April, 1853. 8vo., pp. 22.

69. List of Domestic Institutions in correspondence with the Smithsonian Institution. 1853. 8vo., pp. 16.

70. The Antiquities of Wisconsin, as Surveyed and Described, by I. A. LAPHAM. May, 1855. 4to., pp. 108, 65 woodcuts, one map, 54 plates of 112 figures. (S. I. VII.)

71. Archæology of the United States; or Sketches, Historical and Bibliographical, of the progress of information and opinion respecting Vestiges of Antiquity in the United States. By SAMUEL F. HAVEN. July, 1856. 4to., pp. 172. (S. C. VIII.)

72. A Memoir on the Extinct Sloth tribe of North America. By JOSEPH LEIDY. June, 1855. 4to., pp. 70, 16 plates of 139 figures. (S. C. VII.)

73. Publications of Learned Societies and Periodicals in the Library of the Smithsonian Institution. December 31, 1854. Part 1. 1855. 4to., pp. 40. (S. C. VII.)

74. Catalogue of Publications of the Smithsonian Institution. Corrected to June, 1862. 8vo., pp. 52. (M. C. V.)

75. Ninth Annual Report of the Board of Regents of the Smithsonian Institution, for the year 1854. Senate Mis. Doc. No. 24, 33d Congress, 2d session. House of Representatives, Mis. Doc. No. 37. 1855. 8vo., pp. 464, 4 woodcuts.

CONTENTS.

Report of Prof. J. HENRY, and Proceedings of the Board.

BAIRD, S. F. Report on publications, exchanges, museum, and explorations in the years 1853 and 1854.

ALEXANDER, B. S. Report of architect.

List of meteorological stations and observers.

MARSH, G. P. Lecture on the camel.

BRAINARD, D. Lecture on nature and cure of bites of serpents and the wounds of poisoned arrows.

LOOMIS, E. Lecture on the zone of small planets between Mars and Jupiter.

75. Report for 1854—Continued.

CHANNING, W. F. Lecture on the American fire alarm telegraph.

REED, H. Lectures on the Union.

RUSSELL, R.; HENRY, J. Lectures and notes on meteorology.

HARE, R. On John Wise's observation of a thunderstorm.

GIBBONS, H. Climate of San Francisco.

LOGAN, T. M. Meteorological observations at Sacramento, California.

HATCH, F. W. Meteorological observations at Sacramento, California.

FROEBEL, J. Remarks contributing to the physical geography of the North American Continent.

STRANG, J. J. Natural history of Beaver Island, Michigan.

EOFF, J. Habits of the black bass of the Ohio.

HEAD, J. E. Natural history of the country about Fort Ripley, Minn.

PARVIN, J. B. Habits of the gopher of Illinois.

MANN, C. Habits of a species of salamander.

HOY, P. R. On the amblystoma luridum, a salamander inhabiting Wis.

CARLETON, J. H. Diary of an excursion in New Mexico.

BAIRD, S. F. Fishes on the coast of New Jersey and Long Island.

JACKSON, C. T. Catalogue of rocks, minerals, and ores collected on geological survey in Michigan.

LOCKE, J. Catalogue of rocks, minerals, ores, and fossils.

FOSTER, J. W. Catalogue of rocks, minerals, etc.

WHITNEY, J. D. Catalogue of rocks, minerals, etc.

OWEN, D. D. Catalogue of geological specimens.

BERLANDIER, L. Catalogue of collection of historical and geographical manuscripts, maps, etc.

HENRY, J. Circular respecting new report on libraries.

HENRY, J. Circular respecting copyrights.

76. Smithsonian Contributions to Knowledge. Vol. VII. 1855. 4to., pp. 260, 74 woodcuts, 72 plates, two maps.

CONTENTS.

CHAPPELSMITH, J. Tornado near New Harmony, Indiana. No. 59.

BAILEY, J. W. New species and localities of microscopic organisms. No. 63.

LAPHAM, I. A. Antiquities of Wisconsin. No. 70.

LEIDY, J. Extinct sloth tribe of North America. No. 72.

Publications of societies and periodicals in Smithsonian Library. Part I. No. 73.

77. Tenth Annual Report of the Board of Regents of the Smithsonian Institution, for the year 1855. 34th Congress, 1st session, Senate Mis. Doc. 73. House of Representatives Mis. Doc. 113. 1856. 8vo., pp. 440, 79 woodcuts.

CONTENTS.

Report of Prof. J. HENRY, and Proceedings of the Board.

BAIRD, S. F. Report on publications, exchanges, museum, and explorations.

List of meteorological observers.

Correspondence:

HAMILTON COLLEGE, Clinton, N. Y. Examination of Spencer's Telescope.

77. Report for 1855—Continued.

American Academy of Arts and Sciences, Boston, Mass. Thanks to Smithsonian Institution for Exchanges.

Stone, Wm. J. On plaster casts of antique and modern statues, etc.

Illinois State Board of Education. Meteorological system for every State.

Butler, A. P. Report of Senate Judiciary Committee on the Management of the Smithsonian Institution, Feb. 6, 1855.

Harvey, W. H. Lecture on marine algæ.

Morris, J. G. Lecture on natural history as applied to farming and gardening.

Morris, J. G. Lecture on insect instincts and transformations.

Chace, G. I. Lecture on oxygen and its combinations.

Smith, J. L. Lecture on meteoric stones.

Snell, E. S. Lecture on planetary disturbances.

Logan, T. M. On the climate of California.

Morris, O. W.; Henry, J. Quantity of rain at different heights.

Guyot, A.; Henry J. Directions for meteorological observations.

Henry, J. Earthquake directions.

Henry, J. Aurora directions.

Green, J. Account of a new barometer.

Henry, J. Registration of periodical phenomena.

Masterman, S. Observations on thunder and lightning.

Letterman, J. Sketch of the Navajo Indians.

Clingman, T. L. Topography of Black Mountain, North Carolina.

Robinson, E.; Ludewig, H. E.; Squier, E. G.; Murphey, H. C.; Hodgson, W. B.; Irving, W.; Prescott, W. H.; Sparks, J.; Bancroft, G.; Hawks, F. L. Communications relative to publication of Spanish works on New Mexico, by Buckingham Smith.

Müller, J. Report on recent progress in physics—Galvanism.

78. Smithsonian Contributions to Knowledge. Vol. VIII. 1856. 4to., pp. 564, 52 woodcuts, 9 plates.

CONTENTS.

Haven, S. F. Archæology of the United States. No. 71.

Olmsted, D. Recent secular period of aurora borealis. No. 81.

Alvord, B. Tangencies of circles and of spheres. No. 80.

Jones, J. Chemical and physiological investigations relative to vertebrata. No. 82.

Force, P. Auroral phenomena in higher northern latitudes. No. 84.

Publications of societies and periodicals in Smithsonian Library. Part II. No. 85.

79. New Tables for determining the Values of the Coefficients in the Perturbative Function of Planetary Motion, which depend upon the ratio of the mean distances. By John D. Runkle. November, 1856. 4to., pp. 64. (S. C. IX.)

80. The Tangencies of Circles and of Spheres. By Benjamin Alvord. January, 1856. 4to., pp. 16, 25 woodcuts, 9 plates of 20 figures. (S. C. VIII.)

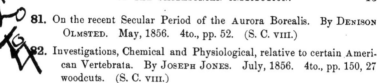

81. On the recent Secular Period of the Aurora Borealis. By DENISON OLMSTED. May, 1856. 4to., pp. 52. (S. C. VIII.)

82. Investigations, Chemical and Physiological, relative to certain American Vertebrata. By JOSEPH JONES. July, 1856. 4to., pp. 150, 27 woodcuts. (S. C. VIII.)

83. On the Relative Intensity of the Heat and Light of the Sun upon Different Latitudes of the Earth. By L. W. MEECH. November, 1856. 4to., pp. 58, 5 woodcuts, 6 plates of 9 figures. (S. C. IX.)

84. Record of Auroral Phenomena observed in the higher Northern Latitudes. By PETER FORCE. July, 1856. 4to., pp. 122. (S. C. VIII.)

85. Publications of Learned Societies and Periodicals in the Library of the Smithsonian Institution. Part II. May, 1856. 4to., pp. 38. (S. C. VIII.)

86. Observations on Mexican History and Archæology, with a special notice of Zapotec Remains, as delineated in Mr. J. G. Sawkins's drawings of Mitla, etc. By BRANTZ MAYER. November, 1856. 4to., pp. 36, 17 woodcuts, 4 plates of 6 figures. (S. C. IX.)

87. Psychrometrical Table for Determining the Elastic Force of Aqueous Vapor, and the Relative Humidity of the Atmosphere from indications of the Wet and the Dry Bulb Thermometer, Fahrenheit. By JAMES H. COFFIN. 1856. 8vo., pp. 20. (M. C. I.)

88. Researches on the Ammonia-cobalt Bases. By WOLCOTT GIBBS and FREDERICK AUG. GENTH. December, 1856. 4to., pp. 72, 21 woodcuts. (S. C. IX.)

89. North American Oölogy. By THOMAS M. BREWER. Part I. Raptores and Fissirostres. 1857. 4to., pp. 140, 5 plates of 193 figures. (S. C. XI.)

90. Illustrations of Surface Geology. By EDWARD HITCHCOCK. April, 1857. 4to., pp. 164, 2 woodcuts, 12 plates of 89 figures. (S. C. IX.)

91. Annual Report of the Board of Regents of the Smithsonian Institution, for the year 1856. 34th Congress, 3d session, Senate, No. 54, House of Representatives, Mis. Doc. No. 55. 1857. 8vo., pp. 468, 69 woodcuts.

CONTENTS.

Report of Prof. J. HENRY, and Proceedings of the Board.

BAIRD, S. F. Report on publications, exchanges, museum, and explorations.

List of meteorological stations and observers.

KOHL, J. G. On a collection of the charts and maps of America.

REID, D. B. Architecture in relation to ventilation, warming, lighting, fire-proofing, acoustics, and the general preservation of health.

91. Report for 1856—Continued.

HENRY, J. Syllabus of a course of lectures on physics.

HENRY, J. Acoustics applied to public buildings.

BAIRD, S. F. Directions for collecting, preserving, and transporting specimens of natural history.

GILL, T. Fishes of New York.

GUEST, W. E. Ancient Indian remains near Prescott, Canada West.

SHARPLESS, T., and PATTERSON, R. Phonography.

Institutions in which phonography is taught.

WALL, G. P., and SAWKINS, J. G. Report on the survey of the economic geology of Trinidad.

BABBAGE, C. On tables of the constants of nature and art.

HENRY, J. On the mode of testing building materials, and an account of the marble used in the extension of the United States Capitol.

SMALLWOOD, C. Description of the observatory at St. Martin, Isle Jesus, Canada East.

MEECH, L. W. Relative intensity of the heat and light of the sun.

MÜLLER, J. Report on recent progress in physics—electricity.

92. Smithsonian Contributions to Knowledge. Vol. IX. 1857. 4to., pp. 480, 45 woodcuts, 22 plates.

CONTENTS.

MEECH, L. W. Intensity of heat and light of sun upon different latitudes. No. 83.

HITCHCOCK, E. Illustrations of surface geology. No. 90.

MAYER, B. Mexican history and archæology, and Zapotec remains. No. 86.

GIBBS, W. and GENTH, F. A. Researches on ammonia-cobalt bases. No. 88.

RUNKLE, J. D. New tables, planetary motion. No. 79.

RUNKLE, J. D. Asteroid supplement to new tables. No. 94.

93. Smithsonian Meteorological Observations for the year 1855. (Printed for examination by the observers.) 1857. 8vo., pp. 118.

94. Asteroid Supplement to New Tables for determining the Values of $b_s^{(i)}$ and its derivatives. By JOHN D. RUNKLE. May, 1857. 4to., pp. 72. (S. C. IX.)

95. Nereis Boreali-Americana: or, Contributions to the History of the Marine Algæ of North America. By WILLIAM HENRY HARVEY. Part III.—Chlorospermeæ. March, 1858. 4to., pp. 142, 14 plates of 44 figures. (S. C. X.)

96. Nereis Boreali-Americana: or, Contributions to a History of the Marine Algæ of North America. By WILLIAM HENRY HARVEY. Three parts in one vol., with 50 plates. May, 1858. 4to., pp. 568. [Nos. 32, 43, 95.]

97. Magnetical Observations in the Arctic Seas. By ELISHA KENT KANE. Made during the Second Grinnell Expedition in search of Sir John

Franklin, in 1853–'54–'55, at Van Rensselaer Harbor, and other points on the west coast of Greenland. Reduced and discussed by Charles A. Schott. 1859. 4to., pp. 72, 1 woodcut, 2 plates. (S. C. x.)

98. Grammar and Dictionary of the Yoruba Language. With an introductory description of the country and people of Yoruba. By T. J. Bowen. June, 1858. 4to., pp. 232, 1 map. (S. C. x.)

99. Smithsonian Contributions to Knowledge. Vol. X. 1858. 4to., pp. 462, 1 woodcut, 16 plates, 1 map.

CONTENTS.

Harvey, W. H. Marine algæ. Part III. Chlorospermeæ. No. 95.
Kane, E. K. Magnetical observations in the Arctic seas. No. 97.
Bowen, T. J. Grammar and dictionary of the Yoruba language. No. 98.

100. An Account of the Total Eclipse of the Sun on September 7, 1858, as observed near Olmos, Peru. By J. M. Gilliss. April, 1859. 4to., pp. 22, 1 woodcut, 1 plate. (S. C. xi.)

101. Map of the Solar Eclipse of March 15, 1858. By Thomas Hill. January, 1858. 8vo., pp. 8, 1 plate.

102. Catalogue of the described Diptera of North America. By R. Osten Sacken. January, 1858. 8vo., pp. 116. October, 1859. (M. C. iii.)

103. Meteorological Observations made at Providence, Rhode Island, from December, 1831, to May, 1860. By A. Caswell. October, 1860. 4to., pp. 188. (S. C. xii.)

104. Meteorological Observations in the Arctic Seas. By E. K. Kane. Made during the Second Grinnell Expedition in search of Sir John Franklin, in 1853–'54–'55, at Van Rensselaer Harbor, and other points on the west coast of Greenland. Reduced and discussed by Charles A. Schott. November, 1859. 4to., pp. 120, 10 woodcuts. (S. C. xi.)

105. Catalogue of North American Mammals, chiefly in the Museum of the Smithsonian Institution. By Spencer F. Baird. July, 1857. 4to., pp. 22.

106. Catalogue of North American Birds, chiefly in the Museum of the Smithsonian Institution. By Spencer F. Baird. October, 1858. 4to., pp. 42.

107. Annual Report of the Board of Regents of the Smithsonian Institution, for the year 1857. 35th Congress, 1st Session, Senate Mis. Doc. No. 272, House of Representatives, No. 135. 1858. 8vo., pp. 438, 100 woodcuts.

107. Report for 1857—Continued.

CONTENTS.

Report of Prof. J. HENRY, and Proceedings of the Board.
BAIRD, S. F. Report on publications, exchanges, museum, and explorations.
List of meteorological stations and observers.
STANLEY, J. M. Report of Committee of Regents on gallery of Indian portraits.
CONTAXAKI, MISS ELIZA B. Present of ornamental album from Greece.
CHASE, S. P. On telegraph.
GALE, L. D. On telegraph.
HALL, J. On telegraph.
MASON, C. On telegraph.
HENRY, J. On telegraph.
HENRY, J. On telegraph, deposition of, Sept. 1849.
HENRY, J. Communication relative to a publication by Prof. Morse.
FELTON, C. C. Report of special committee of Board of Regents on the communication of Prof. Henry relative to the electro-magnetic telegraph.
HENRY, J. History of the electro-magnetic telegraph.
LECONTE, J. Lecture on coal.
ALEXANDER, S. Lecture on vastness of the visible creation.
FENDLER, A. Meteorology and ethnology, Colonia Tovar, Venezuela, S. A.
LOGAN, T. M. Meteorology of Sacramento, California.
DEWEY, C. On best hours to find mean temperatures.
WISSNER, J. Meteorology of the District of Columbia.
MASTERMAN, S. Observations on natural phenomena, shooting stars, aurora, etc.
MÜLLER, J. Report on recent progress in physics. (Electricity, galvanism.)

108. Catalogue of North American Birds, chiefly in the Museum of the Smithsonian Institution. BY SPENCER F. BAIRD. 1859. 8vo. pp. 24. (M. C. II.)

108*. Same Title, (printed for labelling, with one side of each leaf blank.)

109. Annual Report of the Board of Regents of the Smithsonian Institution, for the year 1858. 35th Congress, 2d Session, Senate Mis. Doc. No. 49. House Rep., No. 57. 1859. 8vo., pp. 448, 48 woodcuts.

CONTENTS.

Report of Prof. J. HENRY, and Proceedings of the Board.
Correspondence:
SCHLEIDEN, R. Free freight between Germany and United States to Smithsonian Institution by the North German Lloyd.
SABINE, E. On continuance of magnetic observations.
BAIRD, S. F. Report on publications, exchanges, museum, and explorations.
List of meteorological stations and observers.
CASWELL, A. Lecture on astronomy.
CUVIER, M. Memoir of Priestley.
BAIRD, S. F. Instructions for collecting nests and eggs of American birds.
BAIRD, S. F. Instructions for collecting insects.

109. Report for 1858—Continued.

LeConte, J. L. Instructions for collecting coleoptera.
Clemens, B. Instructions for collecting hymenoptera.
Uhler, P. R. Instructions for collecting orthoptera.
Uhler, P. R. Instructions for collecting hemiptera.
Uhler, P. R. Instructions for collecting neuroptera.
Loew, H.; Osten Sacken, R. Instructions for collecting diptera.
Clemens, B. Instructions for collecting lepidoptera.
Taylor, A. S. Grasshoppers and locusts of America.
Motschulsky, V. On means of destroying the grasshopper.
Martins, C. Vegetable colonization of the British Isles of Shetland, Faroe, and Iceland.
DeCandolle, A. Causes which limit vegetable species towards the north in Europe and similar regions.
Cooper, J. G. Distribution of the forests and trees of North America, and catalogue of the native trees of the United States.
Blackiston; Bland; Willis, J. R. Birds of Nova Scotia.
Bland; Willis J. R. Birds of Bermuda.
DuPrez, M. F. Atmospheric electricity.
Müller, J. Recent progress in physics. (Galvanism.)
Henry, J. Meteorological stations, cost of establishment of.
Hodgins, J. G. Meteorological stations of Upper Canada.
Dudley, T. Earthquake at New Madrid, Missouri.
Naill, D. W. Dispersion of a cloud by an electrical discharge.
Hare, R. Method of forming small weights.
Friedländer, J. Plan of a Bibliography.
Lyon, S. S. Antiquities from Kentucky.
Gardiner, R. H. Barometer, rain and snow gauges.
Guest, W. E. Snow gauge.
Gardiner, R. H. Opening and closing of Kennebec river, Maine.
Canudas, A. Earthquakes in Guatemala.
Humphreys, A. A. Method of ascertaining the amount of water in rivers.

110. Annual Report of the Board of Regents of the Smithsonian Institution, for the year 1859. 36th Congress, 1st Session, House of Representatives, Mis. Doc. No. 90. 1860. 8vo., pp. 450, 57 woodcuts.

CONTENTS.

Report of Prof. J. Henry, and Proceedings of the Board.
Baird, S. F. Report of publications, exchanges, museum, and explorations.
List of meteorological stations and observers.
Pearce, J. A. Notice of Richard Rush.
Felton, C. C. Notice of W. W. Turner.
Felton, C. C. Notice of Washington Irving.
Bache, A. D. Notice of James P. Espy.
Bache, A. D. Notice of G. Würdemann.
Henry, J. Notice of Parker Cleaveland.
Correspondence:
Duke of Northumberland. Presentation of books.
Henry, J. Account of Priestley's lens.

110. Report for 1859—Continued.

CUNARD, E. Free freight to Smithsonian Institution, between United States and England.

LOGAN, W. E. Request for duplicate shells.

ROSS, B. R. Observations in Hudson's Bay Territory.

JOHNSON, S. W. Lectures on agricultural chemistry.

CARPENTER, P. P. Lectures on the shells of the Gulf of California.

MÆDLER, M. Movement of the stars around a central point.

DE LA RIVE, A. Report on the transactions of the Society of Physics and Natural History of Geneva, from July, 1858, to June, 1859.

RETZIUS, A. Present state of ethnology in relation to the form of the human skull.

FLOURENS, M. Memoir of Pyramus de Candolle.

AIRY, G. B. On the means which will be available for correcting the measures of the sun's distance in the next twenty-five years.

POWELL, B. Report on the state of knowledge of radiant heat, made to the British Association in 1832, 1840, and 1854.

HILGARD, J. E. Description of the magnetic observatory at the Smithsonian Institution.

POGGENDORFF, J. C. On the use of the galvanometer as a measuring instrument.

MALLET, R. On observations of earthquake phenomena.

CASELLA, L. Description of meteorological instruments.

GREEN, J.; WÜRDEMANN, W. On filling barometer tubes.

WELSH, J. The construction of a standard barometer, and apparatus and processes employed in the verification of barometers at the Kew Observatory.

111. Smithsonian Contributions to Knowledge. Vol. XI. 1859. 4to., pp. 502, 20 woodcuts, 23 plates.

CONTENTS.

BREWER, T. M. North American Oölogy. Part 1. Raptores and Fissirostres. No. 89.

GILLISS, J. M. Total eclipse of the sun, September 7, 1858, in Peru. No. 100.

BACHE, A. D. Magnetic and meteorological observations. Part I. No. 113.

KANE, E. K. Meteorological observations in the Arctic seas. No. 104.

LECONTE, J. L. Coleoptera of Kansas and Eastern New Mexico. No. 126.

SONNTAG, A. Observations on terrestrial magnetism in Mexico. No. 114.

LOOMIS, E. On certain storms in Europe and America, December, 1836. No. 127.

112. Smithsonian Contributions to Knowledge. Vol. XII. 1860. 4to., pp. 538, 15 woodcuts, 3 plates.

CONTENTS.

KANE, E. K. Astronomical observations in the Arctic seas. No. 129.

WHITTLESEY, C. Fluctuations of level in North American lakes. No. 119.

112. Contributions to Knowledge. Vol. XII—Continued.

CASWELL, A. Meteorological observations at Providence, Rhode Island, 28½ years. No. 103.

SMITH, N. D. Meteorological observations near Washington, Arkansas, 20 years. No. 131.

MITCHELL, S. W. Researches upon venom of the rattlesnake. No. 135.

113. Discussion of the Magnetic and Meteorological Observations made at the Girard College Observatory, Philadelphia, in 1840–'41–'42–'43–'44–'45. Part I. Investigation of the eleven year period in the amplitude of the solar-diurnal variation and of the disturbances of the magnetic declination. By A. D. BACHE. November, 1859. 4to., pp. 22, 5 woodcuts. (S. C. XI.)

114. Observations on Terrestrial Magnetism in Mexico. Conducted under the direction of Baron VON MÜLLER, with notes and illustrations of an examination of the volcano Popocatepetl and its vicinity. By AUGUST SONNTAG. February, 1860. 4to., pp. 92, 4 woodcuts, one plate. (S. C. XI.)

115. Proceedings of the Board of Regents of the Smithsonian Institution, in relation to the Electro-Magnetic Telegraph. 1861. 8vo., pp. 40, 7 woodcuts. (M. C. II.)

116. List of Public Libraries, Institutions, and Societies in the United States and British Provinces of North America. By WILLIAM J. RHEES. 1859. 8vo., pp. 84.

117. Catalogue of Publications of Societies and of other Periodical Works in the Library of the Smithsonian Institution, July 1, 1858. Foreign Works. 1859. 8vo., pp. 264. (M. C. III.)

118. Catalogue of the Described Lepidoptera of North America. By JOHN G. MORRIS. May, 1860. 8vo., pp. 76. (M. C. III.)

119. On Fluctuations of Level in the North American Lakes. By CHARLES WHITTLESEY. July, 1860. 4to., pp. 28, 2 plates of 4 figures. (S. C. XII.)

120. Results of Meteorological Observations made at Marietta, Ohio, between 1826 and 1859, inclusive. By S. P. HILDRETH. To which are added results of observations taken at Marietta, by JOSEPH WOOD, between 1817 and 1823. Reduced and discussed by Charles A. Schott. September, 1867. 4to., pp. 52, 14 woodcuts. (S. C. XVI.)

121. Discussion of the Magnetic and Meteorological Observations made at the Girard College Observatory, Philadelphia, in 1840–'41'–42'–43–'44–'45. By A. D. BACHE. Part II.—Investigation of the solar-diurnal variation in the magnetic declination and its annual inequality. June, 1862, 4to., pp. 28, 8 woodcuts. (S. C. XIII.)

122. Smithsonian Miscellaneous Collections. Vol. I. 1862. 8vo., pp. 738, 23 woodcuts.

CONTENTS.

Directions for meteorological observations. No. 148.
COFFIN, J. H. Psychrometrical tables. No. 87.
GUYOT, A. Meteorological and physical tables. No. 153.

123. Smithsonian Miscellaneous Collections. Vol. II. 1862. 8vo., pp. 714, 33 woodcuts.

CONTENTS.

BOOTH, J. C.; MORFIT, C. Recent improvements in chemical arts. No. 27.
Proceedings of Board of Regents in relation to the electro-magnetic telegraph. No. 115.
STANLEY, J. M. Catalogue of portraits of North American Indians. No. 53.
BAIRD, S. F. Catalogue of North American birds. No. 108.
BAIRD, S. F.; GIRARD, C. Catalogue of North American reptiles. Serpents. No. 49.
Check-list shells North America. No. 128.
Directions for collecting specimens of natural history. No. 34.
HENRY, J. Circular to officers Hudson Bay Company. No. 137.
Instructions for collecting nests and eggs. No. 139.
North American grasshoppers. No. 163.
North American shells. No. 176.
MORGAN, L. H. Circular respecting relationship. No. 138.

124. Smithsonian Miscellaneous Collections. Vol. III. 1862. 8vo., pp. 776, 49 woodcuts.

CONTENTS.

OSTEN SACKEN, R. Catalogue diptera North America. No. 102.
MORRIS, J. G. Catalogue described lepidoptera North America. No. 118.
LE CONTE, J. L. Classification coleoptera. I. No. 136.
Catalogue publications of societies in Smithsonian library. No. 117.

125. Smithsonian Miscellaneous Collections. Vol. IV. 1862. 8vo., pp. 762, 30 woodcuts.

CONTENTS.

HAGEN, H. Synopsis of North American neuroptera. No. 134.
MORRIS, J. G. Synopsis of North American lepidoptera. No. 133.

126. The Coleoptera of Kansas and Eastern New Mexico. By JOHN L. LE CONTE. December, 1859. 4to., pp. 64, 2 plates of 33 figures, 1 map. (S. C. XI.)

127. On Certain Storms in Europe and America, December, 1836. By ELIAS LOOMIS. February, 1860. 4to., pp. 28, 13 plates. (S. C. XI.)

128. Check-lists of the Shells of North America. By ISAAC LEA, P. P. CARPENTER, WM. STIMPSON, W. G. BINNEY, and TEMPLE PRIME. June, 1860. 8vo., pp. 52. (M. C. II.)

129. Astronomical Observations in the Arctic Seas. By E. K. KANE. Made during the Second Grinnell Expedition in search of Sir John Franklin, in 1853, 1854, and 1855, at Van Rensselaer Harbor, and other points in the vicinity of the northwest coast of Greenland. Reduced and discussed by Charles A. Schott. May, 1860. 4to., pp. 56, 3 woodcuts, 1 map. (S. C. XII.)

130. Tidal Observations in the Arctic Seas. By E. K. KANE. Made during the Second Grinnell Expedition in search of Sir John Franklin, in 1853, 1854, and 1855, at Van Rensselaer Harbor. Reduced and discussed by Charles A. Schott. October, 1860. 4to., pp. 90, 3 woodcuts, 4 plates. (S. C. XIII.)

131. Meteorological Observations made near Washington, Arkansas, from 1840 to 1859, inclusive. By NATHAN D. SMITH. October, 1860. 4to., pp. 96. (S. C. XII.)

132. Discussion of the Magnetic and Meteorological Observations made at the Girard College Observatory, Philadelphia, in 1840–'41–'42–'43–'44–'45. By A. D. BACHE. Part III.—Investigation of the influence of the moon on the magnetic declination. June, 1862. 4to., pp. 16, 3 woodcuts. (S. C. XIII.)

133. Synopsis of the Described Lepidoptera of North America. By JOHN G. MORRIS. Part I.—Diurnal and crepuscular lepidoptera. February, 1862. 8vo., pp. 386, 30 woodcuts. (M. C. IV.)

134. Synopsis of the Neuroptera of North America. With a list of the South American species. By HERMANN HAGEN. July, 1861. 8vo., pp. 368. (M. C. IV.)

135. Researches upon the Venom of the Rattlesnake. With an investigation of the anatomy and physiology of the organs concerned. By S. WEIR MITCHELL. December, 1860. 4to., pp. 156, 12 woodcuts. (S. C. XII.)

136. Classification of the Coleoptera of North America. By JOHN L. LE CONTE. Part I. March, 1862. 8vo., pp. 312, 49 woodcuts. (M. C. III.)

137. Circular to Officers of the Hudson's Bay Company. 1860. 8vo., pp. 6. (M. C. II; M. C. VIII.)

138. Circular in reference to the Degrees of Relationship among different Nations. By LEWIS H. MORGAN. January, 1860. 8vo., pp. 34. (M. C. II.)

139. Instructions in reference to Collecting Nests and Eggs of North American Birds. January, 1860. 8vo., pp. 22, 20 woodcuts. (M. C. II.)

140. List of the Coleoptera of North America. Prepared for the Smithsonian Institution. By JOHN L. LE CONTE. Part I. April, 1866. 8vo., pp. 82. (M. C. VI.)

141. Monographs of the Diptera of North America. By H. LOEW. Part I. Edited, with additions, by R. OSTEN SACKEN. April, 1862. 8vo., pp. 246, 15 woodcuts, 2 plates of 42 figures. (M. C. VI.)

142. Bibliography of North American Conchology, previous to the year 1860. By W. G. BINNEY. Part I.—American Authors. March, 1863. 8vo., pp. 658. (M. C. V.)

143. Land and Fresh-Water Shells of North America. By W. G. BINNEY. Part II.—Pulmonata Limnophila and Thalassophila. September, 1865. 8vo., pp. 172, 372 woodcuts. (M. C. VII.)

144. Land and Fresh-Water Shells of North America. By W. G. BINNEY. Part III.—Ampullariidæ, Valvatidæ, Viviparidæ, fresh-water Rissoidæ, Cyclophoridæ, Truncatellidæ, fresh-water Neritidæ, Helicinidæ. September, 1865. 8vo., pp. 128, 253 woodcuts. (M. C. VII.)

145. Monograph of American Corbiculadæ, (recent and fossil.) By TEMPLE PRIME. December, 1865. 8vo., pp. 92, 86 woodcuts. (M. C. VII.)

146. Meteorological Observations in the Arctic Seas. By FRANCIS LEOPOLD McCLINTOCK. Made on board the Arctic searching yacht "Fox," in Baffin Bay and Prince Regent's Inlet, in 1857, 1858, and 1859. Reduced and discussed by Charles A. Schott. May, 1862. 4to., pp. 164, 15 woodcuts, 1 map. (S. C. XIII.)

147. Annual Report of the Board of Regents of the Smithsonian Institution, for the year 1860. 36th Congress, 2d Session. Senate Mis. Doc., No. 21, 1861. 8vo., pp. 448, 73 woodcuts.

CONTENTS.

HENRY, J. Secretary's report of operations.
BOARD OF REGENTS, Proceedings of
BAIRD, S. F. Report on publications, exchanges, museum, and explorations.
List of meteorological stations and observers.
List of meteorological material contributed to Smithsonian Institution.

147. Report for 1860—Continued.

Correspondence:

CITIZENS OF PHILADELPHIA. Memorial relative to Lowe's aeronautic voyages across the Atlantic.

LEPSIUS, R. Presentation of books on Egypt.

MÜLLER, F. On Smithsonian exchanges.

HINCKS, WM. On Smithsonian exchanges.

HENRY, J. Reply to memorial on Lowe's aeronautic voyage.

HENRY, J. On currents of the atmosphere and aerial navigation.

ROGERS, F. Lectures on roads and bridges.

CARPENTER, P. P. Lectures on mollusca, or shell fish, and their allies.

MORLOT, A. General views on archæology.

The microscope.

NICKLÈS, M. J. Scientific Congress of Carlsruhe, 1858.

CUVIER, M. Memoir of René Just Haüy.

SABINE, E. Magnetic storms.

GARDINER, R. H. Disappearance of ice.

FENDLER, A. Temperature of St. Louis, Missouri.

DEWEY, C. Best hours for temperature observations.

HENRY, J. Description of Smithsonian anemometer.

NEWTON, A. Suggestions for saving parts of the skeleton of birds.

VOLLUM, E. P. On the wingless grasshopper of California.

WURDEMAN, G. Specimens of flamingo, etc., from South Florida.

GESNER, W. Habits of pouched rat, or salamander of Georgia.

BARNARD, V. Birds of Chester county, Pennsylvania.

COOPER, J. G. Forests and trees of Florida and the Mexican Boundary.

148. Directions for Meteorological Observations and the Registry of Periodical Phenomena. 1860. 8vo., pp. 72, 23 woodcuts. (M. C. I.)

149. Annual Report of the Board of Regents of the Smithsonian Institution, for the year 1861. 37th Congress, 2d Session, House of Representatives Mis. Doc., No. 77. 1862. 8vo., pp. 464, 25 woodcuts.

CONTENTS.

HENRY, J. Secretary's report of operations.

BOARD OF REGENTS, Proceedings of

BAIRD, S. F. Report on publications, exchanges, museum, and explorations.

List of meteorological stations and observers.

List of meteorological material contributed to Smithsonian Institution.

KING, C. B. Catalogue of engravings presented to the Smithsonian Institution.

Correspondence:

FLADGATE, CLARKE, and FINCH. Smithson's residuary legacy.

KUNHARDT & Co. Free freight to Smithsonian Institution, between United States and Germany.

TROYON, F. Lacustrian habitations.

MORLOT, A. Archæology.

HILL, A. J. Map of antiquities of United States.

ROYAL ACADEMY OF SCIENCE, MADRID. Exchanges.

149. Report for 1861—Continued.

MEXICAN SOC. OF GEOG. AND STATISTICS. Exchanges.
HAGEN, H. Neuroptera.
HAMILTON COLLEGE, CLINTON, N. Y. Exchange of specimens.
CODD, J. A. Acknowledgment for books.
SHEPARD, C. U. Arrangement of mineralogical collection.
UNIVERSITY OF TORONTO. Scientific co-operation.
ROYAL HORTICULTURAL SOCIETY, LONDON. Exchange of publications.
BETHUNE, C. J. Acknowledgment for books.
PEASE, W. H. Acknowledgment for shells, etc.
Circular of the Institute of Rupert's Land.
CRUMMELL, A. Facts respecting Liberia College.
GIBBS, G.; AND OTHERS. Recommendation of Shea's Indian linguistics.
SHEA, J. G. Account of library of Indian linguistics.

WOOLSEY, T. D. Eulogy on Cornelius C. Felton.
COX, S. S. Eulogy on Stephen A. Douglas.
ROGERS, F. Lecture on bridges.
ALEXANDER, S. Lecture on the relations of time and space.
HAYES, I. I. Lecture on Arctic explorations.
FLOURENS, M. Memoir of Geoffroy Saint Hilaire.
LAUGEL, A. The sun, its chemical analysis.
LEE, DR. Progress of astronomical photography.
LESPIAULT, PROF. Small planets between Mars and Jupiter.
DUFOUR, C.; KÄMTZ. Scintillation of the stars.
DAUBRÉE, M. Metamorphism and the formation of crystalline rocks.
CRAIG, B. F. Nitrification.
HUNT, T. S. History of petroleum or rock-oil.
ALLEN, Z. Explosibility of coal oils.
Destructive effect of iron-rust.
TROYON, F. Lacustrian cities of Switzerland.
RUTIMEYER, A. Fauna of Middle Europe during the Stone Age.
TROYON, F. Report on ethnological collections of Museum at Lausanne.
TROYON, F. Archæological researches made at Concise.
PEALE, T. R. Ancient mound in St. Louis, Missouri.
GIBBS, G. Instructions for archæological investigations
HENRY, J. Circular, ancient mining in Lake Superior Copper Region.
MORGAN, L. H. Suggestions relative to ethnological map of North America.
COUES, E.; PRENTISS, S. S. List of birds of the District of Columbia.
PRIZE QUESTIONS:

Holland Society of Science, Harlem.
Batavian Society of Experimental Philosophy of Rotterdam.
Society of Arts and Sciences of Utrecht.
Royal Academy of Netherlands.

150. Annual Report of the Board of Regents of the Smithsonian Institution, for the year 1862. 37th Congress, 3d session, House of Representatives Mis. Doc., No. 25. 1863. 8vo., pp. 446, 94 woodcuts.

62

150. Report for 1862—Continued.

CONTENTS.

HENRY, J. Secretary's report of operations.
BOARD OF REGENTS, Proceedings of
BAIRD, S. F. Report on publications, exchanges, museum, and explorations.
List of meteorological stations and observers.
List of meteorological material contributed to Smithsonian Institution.
Correspondence :
STANTON, E. M. Deposit of Beaufort library.
CANBY, E. Deposit of Bishop Johns' library.
SIBLEY, H. Meteorological telegrams.
ENGLEMANN, G. Heights of mountains in Colorado.
GUYOT, A. On mountain measurements.
HUBBARD, J. S. Investigations of Biela's comet.
DARLINGTON, W. History of Chester county, Pa.
LYMAN, THEODORE. Ethnographical collections.
DE SCHLAGINTWEIT, H. Ethnographical collections,
DAA, L. K. Ethnological Museum of Norway.
DILLE, I. Antiquities in Missouri and Tennessee.
REID, A. Skulls and mummy from Patagonia.
GIBBS, G. Philological circular.
GIBBS, G. Ethnological map of United States.
GIBBS, G. Indian vocabularies.
WATKINS, E. A. Systems of relationship of Cree Indians.
FLACHENECKER, G. Indian languages.
PEASE, W. H. Natural history of Pacific islands.
WIRTZ, H. R. Herbarium captured in Tennessee.
METTENIUS, G. Acknowledgment for ferns.
DE SAUSSURE, H. Hymenoptera.
ROMERO, M. Explorations of John Xantus in Mexico.
BACHE, A. D. Eulogy on James A. Pearce.
BARNARD, F. A. P. Lectures on the undulatory theory of light.
WILSON, D. Lectures on physical ethnology.
MORLOT, A. Lecture on the study of high antiquity.
LUBBOCK, J. North American archæology.
FLOURENS, M. Historical sketch of the Academy of Science of Paris.
FLOURENS, M. Memoir of Leopold von Buch.
FLOURENS, M. Memoir of Louis Jacques Thenard.
QUATREFAGES, M. Memoir of Isidore Geoffroy St. Hilaire.
PHIPSON, T. L. The catalytic force, or studies on the phenomena of contact.
HERSCHEL, J. On atoms.
LESLEY, J. P. On the classification of books.
RIED, A. Human remains from Patagonia.
PRIZE QUESTIONS
London Institution of Civil Engineers.
Provincial Society of Arts and Sciences, Utrecht.
Royal Danish Society of Science.
Academy of Sciences of the Institute of Bologna.

151. Smithsonian Contributions to Knowledge. Vol. XIII. 1863. 4to., pp. 558, 80 woodcuts, 4 plates, 3 maps.

CONTENTS.

KANE, E. K. Tidal observations, Arctic seas. No. 130.
McCLINTOCK, F. L. Meteorological observations, Arctic seas. No. 146.
WHITTLESEY, C. Ancient mining on shores of Lake Superior. No. 155.
BACHE, A. D. Discussion, Girard College observations. Part II. No. 121.
BACHE, A. D. Discussion, Girard College observations. Part III. No. 132.
BACHE, A. D. Discussion, Girard College observations. Parts IV, V, VI. No. 162.
BACHE, A. D. Magnetic survey of Pennsylvania, &c. No. 166.
MITCHELL, S. W.; MOREHOUSE, G. R. Researches upon anatomy and physiology of chelonia. No. 159.

152. Lectures on Mollusca or "Shell-fish," and their Allies. Prepared for the Smithsonian Institution. By PHILIP P. CARPENTER. 1861. 8vo., pp. 140.

153. Tables, Meteorological and Physical, Prepared for the Smithsonian Institution. By ARNOLD GUYOT. Third edition, revised and enlarged. 1859. 8vo., pp. 638. (M. C. I.)

CONTENTS.

I. Thermometrical tables, A.
II. Hygrometrical tables, B.
III. Barometrical tables, C.
IV. Hypsometrical tables, D.
V. Meteorological corrections, E.
VI. Miscellaneous tables, F.

154. List of Foreign Correspondents of the Smithsonian Institution. Corrected to January, 1862. May, 1862. 8vo., pp. 56. (M. C. V.)

155. Ancient Mining on the Shores of Lake Superior. By CHARLES WHITTLESEY. April, 1863. 4to., pp. 34, 30 woodcuts, 1 map. (S. C. XIII.)

156. Catalogue of Minerals, with their Formulas, etc. By T. EGLESTON. June, 1863. 8vo., pp. 56. (M. C. VII.)

157. Results of Meteorological Observations made under the direction of the United States Patent Office and the Smithsonian Institution, from the year 1854 to 1859, inclusive, being a Report of the Commissioner of Patents made at the first session of the 36th Congress. Vol. I. 1861. 36th Congress, 1st session, Senate Ex. Doc. 4to., pp. 1270.

158. Smithsonian Miscellaneous Collections. Vol. V. 1864. 8vo., pp. 774.

158. Miscellaneous Collections. Vol. V—Continued.

CONTENTS.

BINNEY, W. G. Bibliography of North American conchology. No. 142.
Catalogue of publications of the Smithsonian Institution to June, 1862. No. 74.
List of foreign correspondents of the Smithsonian Institution to January, 1862. No. 154.

159. Researches upon the Anatomy and Physiology of Respiration in the Chelonia. By S. WEIR MITCHELL and GEORGE R. MOREHOUSE. April, 1863. 4to., pp. 50, 10 woodcuts. (S. C. XIII.)

160. Instructions for Research Relative to the Ethnology and Philology of America. By GEORGE GIBBS. March, 1863. 8vo., pp. 56. (M. C. VII.)

161. A Dictionary of the Chinook Jargon or Trade Language of Oregon. By GEORGE GIBBS. March, 1863. 8vo., pp. 60. (M. C. VII.)

162. Discussion of the Magnetic and Meteorological Observations made at the Girard College Observatory, Philadelphia, in 1840–'41–'42–'43–'44–'45. Second section, comprising Parts IV, V, and VI. Horizontal force. Investigation of the eleven (or ten) year period and of the disturbances of the horizontal component of the magnetic force, with an investigation of the solar diurnal variation, and of the annual inequality of the horizontal force, and of the lunar effect on the same. By A. D. BACHE. November, 1862. 4to., pp. 78, 11 woodcuts. (S. C. XIII.)

163. Circular in Reference to the History of North American Grasshoppers. January, 1860. 8vo., pp. 4. (M. C. II.)

164. Smithsonian Museum Miscellanea. 1862. 8vo., pp. 88. (M. C. VIII.)

CONTENTS.

Abbreviations of names of States and Territories of North America, for labelling insects, shells, &c.
A series of small figures, from 1–1643.
A series of medium figures, from 1–2747.
A series of large figures, from 1–2599.
Blank check-list of specimens.
No. 5. consists of columns of figures from 1 to 1,000, and of two series, 25 and 50, to the 8vo. column. All these are stereotyped and printed with from one to eight columns on each page, with blank spaces of greater or less extent, as may be required.

165. Monograph of the Bats of North America. By H. ALLEN. June, 1864. 8vo., pp. 110, 73 woodcuts. (M. C. VII.)

166. Records and Results of a Magnetic Survey of Pennsylvania and parts of Adjacent States, in 1840 and 1841, with some additional records and Results of 1834, 1835, 1843 and 1862, and a map. By A. D. BACHE. October, 1863. 4to., pp. 88, 1 map. (S. C. XIII.)

167. New Species of North American Coleoptera. By JOHN L. LE CONTE. Part I. March, 1863. April, 1866. 8vo., pp. 180. (M. C. VI.)

168. Circular Relative to Collections of Birds from Middle and South America. December, 1863. 8vo., pp. 2. (M. C. VIII.)

169. Smithsonian Miscellaneous Collections. Vol. VI. 1867. 8vo., pp. 888. 15 woodcuts, 7 plates of 106 figures.

CONTENTS.

LOEW, H. Monograph of diptera. Part I. No. 141.
LOEW, H. Monograph of diptera. Part II. No. 171.
LE CONTE, J. L. List of coleoptera of North America. No. 140.
LE CONTE, J. L. New species of North American coleoptera. No. 167.

170. Comparative Vocabulary. May, 1863. 4to., pp. 20.

171. Monographs of the Diptera of North America. By H. LOEW. Part II. Edited by R. Osten Sacken. January, 1864. 8vo., pp. 372, 5 plates of 44 figures. (M. C. VI.)

172. Palæontology of the Upper Missouri; a Report upon Collections made principally by the Expeditions under command of Lieutenant G. K. Warren, United States Topographical Engineers, in 1855 and 1856. Invertebrates. By F. B. MEEK and F. V. HAYDEN. Part I. April, 1865. 4to., pp. 158, 48 woodcuts, 5 plates of 41 figures. (S. C. XIV.)

173. The Gray Substance of the Medulla Oblongata and Trapezium. By JOHN DEAN. February, 1864. 4to., pp. 80, 5 woodcuts, 16 plates of 65 figures. (S. C. XVI.)

174. Bibliography of North American Conchology previous to the year 1860. By W. G. BINNEY. Part II. Foreign authors. June, 1864. 8vo., pp. 302. (M. C. IX.)

175. Discussion of the Magnetic and Meteorological Observations made at the Girard College Observatory, Philadelphia, in 1840, 1841, 1842, 1843, 1844 and 1845. Third section, comprising Parts VII, VIII, and IX. Vertical force. Investigations of the eleven (or ten) year period and of the disturbances of the vertical component of the magnetic force, and appendix on the magnetic effect of the aurora bore-

annual inequality of the vertical force; and of the lunar effect on the vertical force, the inclination, and total force. By A. D. BACHE. April, 1864. 4to., pp. 72, 14 woodcuts. (S. C. XIV.)

176. Circular in Reference to Collecting North American Shells. January, 1860. 8vo., pp. 4. (M. C. II.)

177. Check-list of the Invertebrate Fossils of North America. Cretaceous and Jurassic. By F. B. MEEK. April, 1864. 8vo., pp. 42. (M. C. VII.)

178. Circular to Entomologists. 1860. 8vo., pp. 2. (M. C. VIII.)

179. Catalogue of Publications of Societies and of Periodical Works, belonging to the Smithsonian Institution, January 1, 1866. 1866. 8vo., pp. 596. (M. C. IX.)

180. On the Construction of a Silvered Glass Telescope, fifteen and a half inches in aperture, and its use in Celestial Photography. By HENRY DRAPER. July, 1864. 4to., pp. 60, 53 woodcuts. (S. C. XIV.)

181. Review of American Birds in the Museum of the Smithsonian Institution. By S. F. BAIRD. Part I.—North and Middle America. June, 1864—June, 1866. 8vo., pp. 484, 80 woodcuts. (M. C. XII.)

182. Results of Meteorological Observations made under the Direction of the United States Patent Office and the Smithsonian Institution, from the year 1854 to 1859, inclusive, being a Report of the Commissioner of Patents made at the first session of the 36th Congress. Vol. II. Part I. 36th Congress, 1st session. Senate Ex. Doc. 1864. 4to., pp. 546.

183. Check-list of the Invertebrate Fossils of North America. Miocene. By F. B. MEEK. November, 1864. 8vo., pp. 34. (M. C. VII.)

184. Smithsonian Contributions to Knowledge. Vol. XIV. 1865. 4to., pp. 490, 158 woodcuts, 25 plates.

CONTENTS.

BACHE, A. D. Discussion Girard College observations. Parts VII, VIII, IX. No. 175.

BACHE, A. D. Discussion Girard College observations. Parts X, XI, XII. No. 186.

DRAPER, H. Construction of silvered glass telescope and its use in celestial photography. No. 180.

MEEK, F. B.; HAYDEN, F. V. Palæontology of the Upper Missouri. No. 172.

LEIDY, J. Cretaceous reptiles of the United States. No. 192.

185. List of the Described Birds of Mexico, Central America, and the West Indies not in the Collection of the Smithsonian Institution. January 1, 1863. 8vo., pp. 8.

186. Discussion of the Magnetic and Meteorological Observations made at the Girard College Observatory, Philadelphia, 1840–'41–'42–'43–'4-4 '45. Fourth section, comprising Parts X, XI and XII. Dip and total force; analysis of the disturbances of the dip and total force; discussion of the solar diurnal variation and annual inequality of the dip and total force; and discussion of the absolute dip, with the final values for declination, dip and force between 1841 and 1845. By A. D. BACHE. April, 1865. 4to., pp. 42, 8 woodcuts. (S. C. XIV.)

187. Annual Report of the Board of Regents of the Smithsonian Institution, for the year 1863. 38th Congress, 1st Session. House of Representatives, Mis. Doc. No. 83. 1864. 8vo., pp. 420, 56 woodcuts.

CONTENTS.

HENRY, J. Secretary's report of operations.
BOARD OF REGENTS, Proceedings of
BAIRD, S. F. Report of publications, exchanges, museum, and explorations.
List of meteorological stations and observers.
Meteorological material contributed to Smithsonian Institution.
Correspondence:
- GOULD, B. A. Discussion of Piazzi's astronomical observations.
- PACKARD, F. A. Project of an outline history of education in the United States.
- CHAMBER OF COMMERCE OF BORDEAUX. Exchange of publications.
- AGRICULTURAL ASSOCIATION OF MILAN. Exchange of publications.
- IRWIN, B. J. D. Tucson meteorite.
- SANTIAGO AINSA. Tucson meteorite.
- POOLE, H. Cone-in-cone.
- HUNGARIAN NATIONAL MUSEUM. Acknowledgment for birds.
- UNIVERSITY OF CHRISTIANIA, NORWAY. Ethnological specimens presented.
- IMP. GEOLOG. INSTITUTE, VIENNA. Tertiary fossils presented.
- BRITISH MUSEUM. Electrotypes of engravings of shells granted.
- FISHER, J. G. Acknowledgment of perrennibranchiates.
- HAIDINGER, W. Honorary medal to Von Martius.
- HUDSON'S BAY CO. Kennicott's explorations.

WHITNEY, W. D. Lectures on the principles of linguistic science.
DEBEAUMONT, ELIE. Memoir of C. F. Bautemps-Beaupré.
ALEXANDER, C. A. Origin and history of the Royal Society of London.
WETHERILL, C. M. Modern theory of chemical types.
DE LA RIVE, A. Phenomena which accompany the propagation of electricity in highly rarefied elastic fluids.
MARCET, PROF. Report on Society of Physics and Natural History of Geneva, from July, 1862, to June, 1863.

187. Report for 1863—Continued.

PLATEAU, J. Experimental and theoretical researches on the figures of equilibrium of a liquid mass withdrawn from the action of gravity. Part I.

History of discovery relative to magnetism.

GAUTIER, PROF. Researches relative to the nebulæ.

MERINO, St. M. Figure of the earth.

ARAGO, F. Æronautic voyages, etc.

GLAISHER, JAS. Account of balloon ascensions.

BAEGERT, JAC. Aboriginal inhabitants of the California peninsula.

JONES, J. M. Kjœkken-mœdding in Nova Scotia.

MORLOT, A. Abstract of Dr. Keller's report on lacustrian settlements.

RAU, C. Agricultural implements of the North American stone period.

TROWBRIDGE, D. Ancient fort and burial ground in Tompkins county, New York.

KELLEY, O. H. Ancient town in Minnesota.

FOSTER, J. W. Ancient relics in Missouri.

DANILSEN, A. F. Mound in East Tennessee.

Purple dyeing, ancient and modern.

PEALE, T. R. Method of preserving lepidoptera.

FIGANIERRE, M. Account of remarkable accumulation of bats.

Tables of English and French weights and measures.

Table for conversion of centigrade degrees to Fahrenheit's scale.

188. Annual Report of the Board of Regents of the Smithsonian Institution, for the year 1864. 38th Congress, 2d Session. House of Representatives, Mis. Doc. 1865. 8vo., pp. 450, 50 woodcuts.

CONTENTS.

HENRY, J. Secretary's report of operations.

BOARD OF REGENTS, Proceedings of

WEBB, T. W. Account of Prof. Henry Draper's telescope.

LEIDY, JOS. Review of "Cretaceous reptiles of United States."

BAIRD, S. F. Report on publications, exchanges, museum, and explorations.

List of foreign institutions from which donations to the library have been received in exchange. 1860–64.

List of meteorological stations and observers.

Meteorological material contributed to Smithsonian Institution.

WALLACH, R.; HENRY, J. Report of Committee of Regents in relation to the fire, January, 1865.

FOURIER, JOS. Memoir of Delambre.

DELAUNAY, M. Essay on the velocity of light.

WETHERILL, C. M. Ozone and antozone.

JAMIN, J. Vegetation and the atmosphere.

BECQUEREL, M. Preservation of copper and iron in salt water.

Preservation of wood.

Caoutchouc and gutta percha.

VON KAROLYI; CRAIG, B. F. Products of the combustion of gun-cotton and gun-powder.

PETTENKOFER, MAX. Apparatus for testing the results of perspiration and respiration.

LAMONT, J. The solar eclipse of July 18, 1860.

188 Report for 1864—Continued.

DEPRADOS, M. LE BARON. Eclipse of the sun, April 25, 1865.

DUBY, M. Report on the transactions of the Society of Physics and Natural History of Geneva, 1861.

DECANDOLLE, A. Report on the transactions of the Society of Physics and Natural History, 1862.

TROYON, FRED. On the crania helvetica.

PLATEAU, J. Experimental and theoretical researches on the figures of equilibrium of a liquid mass withdrawn from the action of gravity, etc. Parts II, III, IV.

RAU, C. Artificial shell deposits in New Jersey.

GIBBS, G. The intermixture of races.

BAEGERT, J. Aboriginal inhabitants of the California peninsula. Part II.

MORLOT, A. The study of high antiquity in Europe.

PRIZE QUESTIONS:

Holland Society of Sciences at Harlem.

Imperial Society of Natural Sciences of Cherbourg.

Royal Prussian Academy of Sciences.

Imperial Academy of Sciences at Vienna.

EXPLORATIONS:

Scientific expedition to Mexico. A report addressed to the Emperor of France by the Minister of Public Instruction.

KIRBY, W. W. A journey to the Yukon, Russian America.

FEILNER, J. Explorations in Upper California in 1860.

HOY, P. R. Journal of an exploration of Western Missouri in 1854.

Tables of English and French weights and measures.

Table of chemical equivalents of sixty-three elements.

189. Catalogue of the Orthoptera of North America described previous to 1867. By SAMUEL H. SCUDDER. October, 1868. 8vo., pp. 110. (M. C. VIII.)

190. Queries Relative to Tornadoes. By JOSEPH HENRY. 8vo., pp. 4, 1 woodcut. (M. C. X.)

191. Smithsonian Miscellaneous Collections. Vol. VII. 1867. 8vo., pp. 878, 813 woodcuts.

CONTENTS.

ALLEN, H. Monograph of bats of North America. No. 165.

BINNEY, W. G. Land and fresh-water shells of North America. Part II. No. 143.

BINNEY, W. G. Land and fresh-water shells of North America. Part III. No. 144.

STIMPSON, W. Hydrobiinæ. No. 201.

PRIME, T. Monograph of American corbiculadæ. No. 145.

CONRAD, T. A. Check-list of fossils—eocene and oligocene. No. 200.

MEEK, F. B. Check-list of fossils—miocene. No. 183.

MEEK, F. B. Check-list of fossils—cretaceous and jurassic. No. 177.

EGLESTON, T. Catalogue of minerals. No. 156.

GIBBS, G. Dictionary of Chinook jargon. No. 161.

GIBBS, G. Instructions for ethnological and philological research. No. 160.

List of works published by the Smithsonian Institution to January, 1866. No. 203.

192. Cretaceous Reptiles of the United States. By JOSEPH LEIDY. May, 1865. 4to., pp. 142, 35 woodcuts, 20 plates of 309 figures. (S. C. XIV.)

193. Duplicate Shells Collected by the United States Exploring Expedition under Captain C. Wilkes. 8vo., pp. 4.

194. Land and Fresh-water Shells of North America. Part I.—Pulmonata geophila. By W. G. BINNEY and T. BLAND. February, 1869. 8vo., pp. 328, 723 woodcuts. (M. C. VIII.)

195. Discussion of the Magnetic and Meteorological Observations made at the Girard College Observatory, Philadelphia, in 1840–'41–'42–'43–'44–'45. Parts I to XII inclusive. (Nos. 113^{XI}, 121^{XIII}, 132^{XIII}, 162^{XIII}, 175^{XIV}, 186^{XIV}.) 4to., pp. 262, 49 woodcuts.

196. Physical Observations in the Arctic Seas. By ISAAC I. HAYES. Reduced and discussed by Charles A. Schott. June, 1867. 4to., pp. 286, 15 woodcuts, 3 maps, 3 plates. (S. C. XV.)

197. On the Fresh-water Glacial Drift of the Northwestern States. By CHARLES WHITTLESEY. May, 1866. 4to., pp. 38, 14 woodcuts, 1 map, 1 plate. (S. C. XV.)

198. Physical Observations in the Arctic Seas. By ELISHA KENT KANE. Made during the Second Grinnell Expedition in Search of Sir John Franklin, in 1853, 1854, and 1855, at Van Rensselaer Harbor and other points on the West Coast of Greenland. Reduced and discussed by Charles A. Schott. Part I.—Magnetism. II.—Meteorology. III.—Astronomy. IV.—Tides. (Nos. 97^{X}, 104^{XI}, 129^{XII}, 130^{XIII}.) 1859–'60. 4to., pp. 340, 17 woodcuts, 1 map, 6 plates.

199. An Investigation of the Orbit of Neptune, with General Tables of its Motion. By SIMON NEWCOMB. January, 1866. 4to., pp. 116. (S. C. XV.)

200. Check-list of the Invertebrate Fossils of North America, Eocene and Oligocene. By T. A. CONRAD. May, 1866. 8vo., pp. 46. (M. C. VII.)

201. Researches upon the Hydrobiinæ and Allied Forms; chiefly made upon materials in the Museum of the Smithsonian Institution. By WILLIAM STIMPSON. August, 1865. 8vo., pp. 64, 32 woodcuts. (M. C. VII.)

202. Geological Researches in China, Mongolia, and Japan, during the years 1862 to 1865. By RAPHAEL PUMPELLY. August, 1866. 4to., pp. 173, 18 woodcuts, 3 plates of 10 figures, 6 plates of 15 maps. (S. C. XV.)

203. List of Works published by the Smithsonian Institution. January, 1866. 8vo., pp. 12. (M. C. VII.)

204. Results of Meteorological Observations made at Brunswick, Maine, between 1807 and 1859. By PARKER CLEAVELAND. Reduced and discussed by Charles A. Schott. May, 1867. 4to., pp. 60, 8 woodcuts. (S. C. XVI.)

205. Circular Relating to Collections in Archæology and Ethnology. By JOSEPH HENRY. January, 1867. 8vo., pp. 2. (M. C. VIII.)

206. Smithsonian Contributions to Knowledge. Vol. XV. 1867. 4to., pp. 620, 47 woodcuts, 13 plates, 4 maps.

CONTENTS.

NEWCOMB, S. Orbit of Neptune. No. 199.
WHITTLESEY, C. Fresh-water glacial drift of Northwestern States. No. 197.
PUMPELLY, R. Geological researches in China, Mongolia, and Japan. No. 202.
HAYES, I. I. Physical observations in the Arctic seas. No. 196.

207. Suggestions Relative to Objects of Scientific Investigation in Russian America. By JOSEPH HENRY. May, 1867. 8vo., pp. 10. (M. C. VIII.)

208. The Gliddon Mummy Case in the Museum of the Smithsonian Institution. By CHARLES PICKERING. June, 1867. 4to., pp. 6, 1 plate. S. C. XVI.)

209. Annual Report of the Board of Regents of the Smithsonian Institution, for the year 1865. 39th Congress, 1st Session, House of Representatives Mis. Doc. No. 102. 1866. 8vo., pp. 496, 139 woodcuts.

CONTENTS.

HENRY, J. Secretary's report of operations.
BOARD OF REGENTS. Proceedings of
BAIRD, S. F. Report of publications, exchanges, museum, and explorations.
List of addresses of foreign institutions since 1862.
List of meteorological stations and observers.
List of meteorological material contributed.
Correspondence:
  HENRY, J. Letter to Secretary of Treasury on payment of interest in coin.
  LEIDY, J.; TRYON, G. W. Report on shells presented to Academy of Natural Sciences.
  MEXICAN SOC. OF GEOG. AND STATISTICS. Exchange system.

209. Report for 1865—Continued.

EVANS, J. Climate of Colorado.
GIVEN, W. F. Remarkable electric phenomenon.
HALE, C. Explorations of the Nile.
MINING DEPT., MELBOURNE. Exchange system.
CARLETON, J. H. Meteorites in Mexico.
CONRAD, T. A. Chalk found in United States.
REGENTS OF UNIVERSITY OF STATE OF NEW YORK. Acknowledgment for specimens.
McMASTERS, S. Y. Language of Navajos said to resemble the Welsh.
GIBBS, G. Indian languages.
LISBOA, M. M. Books on Brazil presented.
BRAZILIAN NAT. HIST. MUSEUM. Specimens from Brazil presented.
BERN MUSEUM. Request for Bison.
IMPERIAL LIBRARY OF VIENNA. Books presented.
BRUCE, F. W. A., British Minister. Introducing and recommending Dr. Berendt.
DE IRISARRI, A. T., Guatemalan Minister. Introducing and recommending Dr. Berendt.
MOLINA, L., Costa Rican Minister. Introducing and recommending Dr. Berendt.
ROSING, J. Exchange system.
GOVERNMENT OF BREMEN. Exchange system.
HODGINS, J. G. Meteorological system of Canada.
BRITISH MUSEUM. Acknowledgment of specimens.
TORONTO UNIVERSITY. Objects of the Museum.
PETITOT, E. Account of the Indians of British America.

Act of Congress to transfer Smithsonian Library to Library of Congress.
BARNARD, J. G. Eulogy on Gen. Jos. G. Totten.
FLOURENS, M. Memoir of Ducrotay de Blainville.
CHOSSAT, DR. Report on the transactions of the Society of Physics and Natural History of Geneva, from July, 1863, to June, 1864.
PLANTAMOUR, M. E. Report on the transactions of the Society of Physics and Natural History of Geneva, from July, 1864, to June, 1865.
LOOMIS, E. Aurora Borealis, or Polar Light; its phenomena and laws.
THE SENSES. Sense of feeling; sense of smell.
MATTEUCCI, C. Lectures on electro-physiology.
DESOR, E. Palafittes or Lacustrian constructions of the Lake of Neuchatel.
PLATEAU, J. Experimental and theoretical researches on the figures of equilibrium of a liquid mass withdrawn from the action of gravity, etc. Part V.
LILLJEBORG, W. Outline of a systematic review of the classification of birds.
PRIZE QUESTIONS:

Royal Danish Society of Sciences.
Imperial Academy of Sciences of Vienna.
Pontifical Academy of the Nuovi Lincei.
Royal Scientific and Literary Institute of Lombardy.
Imperial Society of Science, Agriculture, and Arts of Lille.
Dunkirk Society for the encouragement of sciences, letters, and arts.

NEWTON, H. A. Metric system of weights and measures, with tables.

210. Arrangement of Families of Birds, adopted provisionally by the Smithsonian Institution. By S. F. BAIRD. June, 1866. 8vo., pp. 8. (M. C. VIII.)

211. Smithsonian Contributions to Knowledge. Vol. XVI. 1870. 4to., pp. 498, 76 woodcuts, 18 plates.

CONTENTS.

DEAN, J. Gray substance of the medulla oblongata and trapezium. No. 173.

CLEAVELAND, P. Meteorological observations, Brunswick, Maine, 53 years. No. 204.

HILDRETH, S. P. Meteorological observations, Marietta, O. No. 120.

PICKERING, C. Gliddon mummy case. No. 208.

COFFIN, J. H. Orbit and phenomena of a meteoric fire ball. No. 221.

GOULD, B. A. Transatlantic longitude. No. 223.

SWAN, J. G. Indians of Cape Flattery. No. 220.

212. Smithsonian Miscellaneous Collections. Vol. VIII. 1869. 8vo., pp. 921, 730 woodcuts, 4 plates.

CONTENTS.

OSTEN SACKEN, R. Monograph of the diptera of North America. Part IV. No. 219.

SCUDDER, S. H. Catalogue of the orthoptera of North America. No. 189.

BINNEY, W. G.; BLAND, T. Land and fresh-water shells of North America. Part I. No. 194.

BAIRD, S. F. Arrangement of families of birds. No. 210.

HENRY, J. Circular to officers of the Hudson's Bay Company. No. 137.

HENRY, J.; GIBBS, G.; BAIRD, S. F. Suggestions relative to scientific investigations in Russian America. No. 207.

HENRY, J. Circular relative to archæology and ethnology. No. 205.

HENRY, J. Circular to entomologists. No. 178.

HENRY, J. Circular relative to collections of birds from Middle and South America. No. 168.

BAIRD, S. F. Smithsonian Museum miscellanea. No. 164.

213. Smithsonian Miscellaneous Collections. Vol. IX. 1869. 8vo., pp. 914.

CONTENTS.

BINNEY, W. G. Bibliography of North American conchology. Foreign authors. Part II. No. 174.

Catalogue of publications of societies and of periodicals in Smithsonian Library, 1866. No. 179.

214. Annual Report of the Board of Regents of the Smithsonian Institution, for the year 1866. 39th Congress, 2d Session, House of Representatives, Mis. Doc. No. 83. 1867. 8vo., pp. 470, 70 woodcuts.

CONTENTS.

HENRY, J. Secretary's report of operations.

BOARD OF REGENTS. Proceedings of

214. Report for 1866—Continued.

BAIRD, S. F. Report on publications, exchanges, museum, and explorations.

List of meteorological stations and observers.

Act of Congress to receive into the United States Treasury the residuary legacy of Smithson, etc.

Memorial of Board of Regents to Congress relative to the fund.

HENRY, J. Memoir of W. W. Seaton.

Report on system of accounts.

FLOURENS, M. Memoir of Magendie.

THE SENSES. Sense of taste; sense of hearing; sense of sight.

HUGGINS, W. Results of spectrum analysis applied to the heavenly bodies.

External appearance of the sun's disk.

MOIGNO, ABBE. Accidental or subjective colors: Persistence of images, contrast, irradiation, daltonism, etc.

PLATEAU, J. Figures of equilibrium of a liquid mass withdrawn from the action of gravity. Part VI.

GOSSE, DR. Report on the transactions of the Society of Physics and Natural History of Geneva, from July, 1865, to June, 1866.

GIBBS, G. Notes on the Tinneh or Chepewyan Indians of British and Russian America. 1. The Eastern Tinneh, by Bernard R. Ross, Esq. 2. The Loucheux Indians, by William L. Hardisty. 3. The Kutchin Tribes, by Strachan Jones, Esq.

VON HELLWALD, F. The American migration, with notes by Prof. Henry.

RAU, C. Indian pottery.

BRINTON, D. G. Artificial shell deposits of the United States.

DILLE, I. Sketch of ancient earth-works of Ohio.

Pile-work antiquities of Olmutz.

ESTES, L. C. Antiquities on the banks of the Mississippi river and Lake Pepin.

GIBBS, G. Physical Atlas of North America.

DAVIS, E. H. On ethnological research.

SCHERZER; SCHWARZ. Table of anthropological measurements.

International Archæological Congress, organized by the Archæological Academy of Belgium, in concert with the French Society of Archæology. Antwerp, 1866.

HIGGINS, H. H. On vitality, with notes by Prof. Henry.

LEWIS, J. Instructions for collecting land and fresh-water shells.

WOOD, H. C. Instructions for collecting myriapods, phalangidæ, etc.

WETHERILL, C. M. Plan of a research upon the atmosphere.

LEWIS; QUALE. Account of the cryolite of Greenland.

EXTRACTS FROM THE METEOROLOGICAL CORRESPONDENCE OF THE INSTITUTION.—

HENRY, J. Remarks by

DENNIS, W. C. Evaporation in Florida.

DENNIS, W. C. Fresh-water in the ocean.

DEWEY, C. The winds.

BALTZELL, J. Winds in Florida.

WARD, L. F. Barometer tube breaking suddenly.

ANDREWS, S. L. Meteors.

214. Report for 1866—Continued.

BALFOUR, J. The wind and fog.
HUNTINGTON, G. C. Climate of Kelley's Island, Ohio.
MALLINIKROOT, C. Changes of wind.
CAPEN, F. L. Meteorological discovery.
FENDLER, A. Meteorology of Colonia Tovar.
HILLIER, S. L. Effect of lightning.
BANNISTER, H. M. Formation of clouds over Gulf stream.
BANNSSTER, H. M. Climate of Alaska.

VAILLANT, M. Horary variations of the barometer, with notes by Prof. Henry.
ENGLEHARDT, M. Formation of ice at the bottom of water.
SARTORIUS, C. Earthquake in Eastern Mexico, January, 1866.
DREUTZER, O. E. Statistics relative to Norwegian mountains, lakes, and the snow-line.

215. Annual Report of the Board of Regents of the Smithsonian Institution, for the year 1867. 40th Congress, 2d Session, Senate Mis. Doc. No. 86. 1868. 8vo., pp. 506, 10 woodcuts.

CONTENTS.

HENRY, J. Secretary's report of operations.
BOARD of REGENTS. Proceedings of
BAIRD, S. F. Report of exchanges and museum.
BAIRD, S. F. List of expeditions and other sources from which the specimens in the Government Museum have been mainly derived.
List of meteorological stations and observers.
Meteorological material contributed in addition to the regular observations.
CLUSS, A. Report of the architect.
Correspondence:

AMER. ACAD. OF ARTS AND SCIENCES. Exchange system.
KNIGHT, G. H. New system of weights and measures with 8 as the metrical number.
BOLLES, E. C. Account of Portland Society of Natural History.
BATH AND WEST OF ENG. SOC. FOR ENCOUR. OF AGRIC., ARTS, ETC. Exchange system.
HAMBURG ZOOL. GARDENS. Exchange of specimens.
CHICAGO ACAD. OF SCIENCES. Acknowledgment for specimens.
TAYLOR, W. B. Report on improved system of numeration.
ST. PETERSBURG ACAD. OF SCIENCES. Exchange system.
ZISGENBALS, H. Schlagintweit ethnographic collection.
LLOYD, W. A. Sparrows sent to United States.
LLOYD, W. A. Exchange of specimens.
MUSEUM OF NAT. UNIV. OF GREECE. Exchange of specimens.
LABOULAYE, M. Acknowledgment for books on education.
ACAD. OF SCIENCES, STOCKHOLM. Acknowledgment of birds.
GOULD, J. Acknowledgment of birds.
MAYBERRY, S. P. Gradual approach of sea upon land.
UNIVERSITY OF COSTA RICA. Exchange of specimens.

GUILD, R. A. Biographical notice of Chas. C. Jewett.
GRAY, A, Biographical notice of W. H. Harvey.
AGASSIZ, L. Report on use of new ball in Smithsonian Building.

215. Report for 1867—Continued.

Memorial of Regents to Congress asking appropriations for Museum.
DEBEAUMONT, E. Memoir of Legendre.
PELTIER, F. A. Memoir of J. C. A. Peltier.
Scientific researches of Peltier.
MAILLY, E. History of Royal Institution of Great Britain.
DE LA RIVE, PROF. Michael Faraday, his life and works.
FLOURENS, M. The Jussieus and the natural method.
MAREY, M. Natural history of organized bodies.
MATTEUCCI, C. On the electrical currents of the earth.
Considerations on electricity.
Electricity—Account of lightning discharges, with notes by Prof. Henry. G. W. Dodge, O. M. Poe, J. C. Cresson, H. Haas, H. J. Kron, B. F. Mudge, New Haven Journal, S. D. Martin, G. Wright, C. G. Boerner, W. S. Gilman, C. W. Dean, J. A. Osborne.
DARWIN, C. Queries about expression for anthropological inquiry.
PETTIGREW, J. B. Modes of flight in relation to aeronautics.
Man as the contemporary of the mammoth and reindeer in Middle Europe.
JAMIN, M. Photo-chemistry.
ABBE, C. Description of the observatories at Dorpat and Poulkova.
TYLOR, E. B. On traces of the early mental condition of man.

ETHNOLOGY:
GUNN, D. Indian remains, Red River Settlement, Hudson's Bay Territory.
READ, M. C. Ancient mound near Chattanooga, Tenn.
PIDGEON, W. Ancient burial mound in Indiana.
BERTHOUD, E. L. Ancient remains in Colorado.
AGNEW, S. A. Mounds in Mississippi.
WHITNEY, J. D. Cave in Calaveras county, California.
Ethnological Department of the French Exposition, 1867.
HAYDEN, F. V. Notes on Indian history.
MEIGS, J. A. Description of a human skull from Rock Bluff, Ill.
KABIS, M. Introduction to the study of the Coptic language.
SMART, C. Notes on the Tonto Apaches.
BERENDT, C. H. Explorations in Central America.
GUNN, D. Notes of an egging expedition to Shoal Lake, Lake Winnipeg.
ROTHROCK, J. T. Sketch of the flora of Alaska.

METEOROLOGY:
Hurricane in the island of St. Thomas.
LATIMER, G. A. Earthquakes in St. Thomas.
Maritime disasters of the Antilles.
DICKINSON, A. B. Eruption of a volcano in Nicaragua.
YOUNG, W. J. Cloud-bursts.
WOODWORTH, A. Meteorite in Mexico.
SIMSON, R. Meteorite in Mexico.
ERNST, G. A. Meteorology of Caracas, South America.
TUCKETT, F. F. On barometer tables.
LATIMER, G. A. Great hurricane at Tortola, St. Thomas, and Porto Rico.
PIKE, N. Cyclone in the Indian Ocean.

215. Report for 1867—Continued.

PRIZE QUESTIONS:

Royal Danish Society of Sciences.

Pontifical Academy of the Nuovi Lincei.

DE LA RUE, W. Abbreviations used in England, 1867.

216. List of Photographic Portraits of North American Indians in the Gallery of the Smithsonian Institution. 1867. 8vo., pp. 42. (M. C. XIV.)

217. Letter by M. Hoek in reference to the Meteoric Shower of November 13th, 1867. 8vo., pp. 4.

218. Systems of Consanguinity and Affinity of the Human Family. By LEWIS H. MORGAN. 1869. 4to., pp. 616, 6 woodcuts, 14 plates. (S. C. XVII.)

219. Monographs of the Diptera of North America. By R. OSTEN SACKEN. Part IV. 1869. 8vo., pp. 358, 7 woodcuts, 4 plates of 92 figures. (M. C. VIII.)

220. The Indians of Cape Flattery, at the entrance to the Strait of Fuca, Washington Territory. By JAMES G. SWAN. March, 1870. 4to., pp. 118, 44 woodcuts. (S. C. XVI.)

221. The Orbit and Phenomena of a Meteoric Fire Ball, seen July 20, 1860. By JAMES H. COFFIN. May, 1869. pp. 56, 3 woodcuts, 1 map. (S. C. XVI.)

222. Tables and Results of the Precipitation, in Rain and Snow, in the United States, and at some stations in adjacent parts of North America, and in Central and South America. By CHARLES A. SCHOTT. March, 1872. 4to., pp. 178, 8 woodcuts, 5 plates, and 3 double charts. (S. C. XVIII.)

223. The Transatlantic Longitude, as determined by the Coast Survey Expedition of 1866. By BENJAMIN APTHORP GOULD. October, 1869. 4to., pp. 110, 2 woodcuts. (S. C. XVI.)

224. Annual Report of the Board of Regents of the Smithsonian Institution, for the year 1868. 40th Congress, 3d Session. House of Representatives, Ex. Doc. No. 83. 1869. 8vo., pp. 474, 40 woodcuts.

CONTENTS.

HENRY, J. Secretary's report of operations.
BOARD OF REGENTS, Proceedings of
List of meteorological stations and observers.
List of meteorological material contributed to Smithsonian Institution.
DELAFIELD, R. Report of Committee of Regents on Washington canal.
FLOURENS, M. Memoir of Cuvier.
FLOURENS, M. History of the works of Cuvier.
DE BEAUMONT, E. Memoir of Oersted.
Notice of Christian Frederic Schœnbein, the discoverer of ozone.

224. Report for 1868—Continued.

HENRY, J. Appendix to notice of Schœnbein.
HAGEN, G. Memoir of Encke.
RAWSON, R. Memoir of Eaton Hodgkinson.
CAZIN, A. Recent progress in relation to the theory of heat.
MULLER, J. Principles of the mechanical theory of heat.
MAGRINI, L. Continuous vibratory movement of all matter, ponderable and imponderable.
TYNDALL, J. Radiation.
DAUBRÉE, M. Synthetic experiments relative to meteorites.
BRUSH, G. J. Catalogue of meteorites in the mineralogical collection of Yale College.
DE SAUSSURE, H. Observations on the electric resonance of mountains.
STEWART, B. Experiments on aneroid barometers made at the Kew Observatory.
ELLERY, R. L. J. Address of the president of the Royal Society of Victoria.
WARTMANN, E. Report on the transactions of the Society of Physics and Natural History of Geneva, from July, 1867, to June, 1868.
BROCA, P. History of the transactions of the Anthropological Society of Paris, from 1865 to 1867.
RAU, C. Drilling in stone without metal.
RAU, C. Agricultural flint implements in southern Illinois.
Notice of the Blackmore Museum, Salisbury, England.
PRIZE QUESTIONS:
Holland Society of Sciences of Harlem.
Imperial Academy of Sciences, Belles Lettres, and Arts, of Bordeaux.
POLLOCK, J. Assay of gold and silver coins at the Mint of the United States.
Table of foreign gold and silver coins.
List of publications of the Smithsonian Institution up to July, 1869, with systematic and alphabetical index.

225. List of Foreign Correspondents of the Smithsonian Institution; corrected to January, 1870. April, 1870. 8vo., pp. 56.

226. A List of the Smithsonian Publications, from 1846 to 1869. November, 1869. 8vo., pp. 34.

227. Arrangement of the Families of Mollusks. By THEODORE GILL. February, 1871. 8vo., pp. 65. (M. C. x.)

228. Annual Report of the Board of Regents of the Smithsonian Institution, for the year 1869. 41st Congress, 3d Session. House of Representatives, Ex. Doc. No. 153. 1871. 8vo., pp. 430, 38 woodcuts, 1 map.

CONTENTS.

HENRY, J. Secretary's report of operations.
BOARD OF REGENTS, Proceedings of
List of meteorological stations and observers.
List of meteorological material contributed to Smithsonian Institution.

228. Report for 1869—Continued.

Berthrand, M. Kepler: his life and works.
Arago, M. Eulogy on Thomas Young.
De Beaumont, E. Memoir of Auguste Bravais.
Rau, C. Memoir of C. F. P. Von Martius.
Matteucci, C. Life and scientific labors of Stefano Marianini.
Hunt, T. S. Chemistry of the earth.
Matteucci, C. Electrical currents of the earth.
Marey, M. Phenomena of flight in the animal kingdom.
Babinet, M. The northern seas.
Lombard, H. C. Report on the transactions of the Society of Physics and of Natural History of Geneva, July, 1868, to June, 1869.
Simpson, J. H. Coronado's march in search of the "Seven Cities of Cibola."
Lubbock, J. Social and religious condition of the lower races of man.
Huxley, T. H. Principles and methods of palæontology.
Schott, A. Remarks on the "Cara Gigantesca" of Yzamal, in Yucatan. tan.
Becquerel, M. Forests and their climatic influence.
Brenndecke, F. Meteorites.
Abich, S. Remarkable forms of hail-stones in Georgia.
Sartorius, C. Eruption of the volcano of Colima.

229. Smithsonian Contributions to Knowledge. Vol. XVII. 1871. 4to., pp. 616, 6 woodcuts, 14 plates.

CONTENTS.

Morgan. Systems of consanguinity and affinity of the human family. No. 218.

230. Arrangement of the Families of Mammals. By Theodore Gill. November, 1872. 8vo., pp. 104. (M. C. xi.)

231. Memoranda of Inquiry relative to the Food Fishes of the United States. By S. F. Baird. 1871. 8vo., pp. 8. (M. C. x.)

232. The Secular Variations of the Elements of the Orbits of the Eight Principal Planets, Mercury, Venus, the Earth, Mars, Jupiter, Saturn, Uranus, and Neptune, with tables of the same; together with the obliquity of the ecliptic and the precession of the equinoxes in both longitude and right ascension. By John N. Stockwell. 1872. 4to., pp. 220. (S. C. xviii.)

233. Converging Series expressing the Ratio between the Diameter and the Circumference of a Circle. By Wm. Ferrel. April, 1871. 4to., pp. 6. (S. C. xviii.)

234. Questions Relative to the Food Fishes of the United States. By S. F. Baird. 1871. 8vo., pp. 14. (M. C. x.)

235. Instructions for Observations of Thunder Storms. By Joseph Henry. 1871. 8vo., p. 1. (M. C. x.)

236. Circular Relative to Heights. By JOSEPH HENRY. 1871. 8vo., pp. 2. (M. C. x.)

237. Directions for constructing Lightning Rods. By JOSEPH HENRY. 1871. 8vo., pp. 4. (M. C. x.)

238. List of the Institutions, Libraries, Colleges, and other Establishments in the United States in correspondence with the Smithsonian Institution. By WM. J. RHEES. July, 1872. 8vo., pp. 256. (M. C. x.)

239. Observations on Terrestrial Magnetism, and on the Deviations of the Compasses of the United States Iron Clad Monadnock during her cruise from Philadelphia to San Francisco, in 1865 and 1866. By WM. HARKNESS. 1872. 4to., pp. 226, 2 woodcuts. (S. C. XVIII.)

240. Problems of Rotary Motion presented by the Gyroscope, The Precession of the Equinoxes, and The Pendulum. By J. G. BARNARD. 1872. 4to., pp. 56, 6 woodcuts. (S. C. XIX.)

241. A Contribution to the History of the Fresh Water Algæ of North America. By HORATIO C. WOOD, Jr. 1872. 4to., pp. 272, 21 plates of 340 figures. (S. C. XIX.)

242. Lucernariæ and their Allies. A Memoir on the Anatomy and Physiology of Haliclystus Auricula and other Lucernarians, with a Discussion of their Relations to other Acalephæ, to Beroids and Polypi. By H. J. CLARK. 1878. 4to., pp. 138, 11 plates of 149 figures. (S. C. XXII.)

243. List of Foreign Correspondents of the Smithsonian Institution; corrected to January, 1872. 1872. 8vo., pp. 66. (M. C. x.)

244. Annual Report of the Board of Regents of the Smithsonian Institution, for the year 1870. 42d Congress, 1st Session. House of Representatives, Ex. Doc. No. 20. 1871. 8vo., pp. 494, 28 woodcuts.

CONTENTS.

HENRY, J. Secretary's report of operations.
BOARD OF REGENTS, Proceedings of
List of meteorological stations and observers.
List of meteorological material contributed to Smithsonian Institution.
HENRY, J. Eulogy on Alexander Dallas Bache.
BACHE, A. D. Lecture on Switzerland.
HENRY, J. On a physical observatory.
ARAGO, M. The History of my Youth, an autobiography.
ARAGO, M. Eulogy on Herschel.
Life and labors of Henry Gustavus Magnus.
ANDERSON, M. B. Life of Prof. Chester Dewey.
TAYLOR, W. B. Thoughts on the nature and origin of force.

244. Report for 1870—Continued.

VON LIEBIG, J. Induction and deduction.

HAUGHTON, S. Relation of food to work, and its bearing on medical practice.

REYNOLDS, J. E. Hydrogen as gas and as a metal.

WISEMAN, N. Identification of the artisan and artist.

BABINET, M. The diamond and other precious stones.

ETHNOLOGY:

GIBBS, G. On the language of the aboriginal Indians of America.

WILLIAMS, H. C. On antiquities in some of the Southern States.

GARDNER, W. H. Ethnology of the Indians of the valley of the Red River of the North.

FINCK, H. Account of antiquities in the State of Vera Cruz, Mexico.

DUNNING, E. O. Account of antiquities in Tennessee.

STEPHENSON, M. F. Account of ancient mounds in Georgia.

DAYTON, E. A. Explorations in Tennessee.

HARWOOD, A. A. Account of the sarcophagus in the National Museum, now in charge of the Smithsonian Institution.

GRANT, E. M. Account of the discovery of a stone image in Tennessee, now in possession of the Smithsonian Institution.

BLYDEN, E. D. On mixed races in Liberia.

FOWLER, J. On shell-heaps.

PEALE, T. R. On the uses of the brain and marrow of animals among the Indians of North America.

LYON, S. S. Report of an exploration of ancient mounds in Union county, Kentucky.

BARRANDT, A. Sketch of ancient earthworks on the Upper Missouri.

STELLE, J. P. Account of aboriginal ruins at Savannah, Tennessee.

STELLE, J. P. Account of aboriginal ruins in Hardin Co., Tennessee.

TERRESTRIAL PHYSICS:

CAMPBELL, J. V. The earthquake in Peru, August 13, 1868.

PALMIERI, Prof. The electro-magnetic seismograph.

JOHNSON, W. W. On the distribution of forest trees in Montana, Idaho, and Washington.

SARGENT, W. D. Influence of the aurora on the telegraph.

METEOROLOGY:

POËY, A. New classification of clouds.

TACCHINI, P. On the evaporation observed at Palermo, in 1865 and 1866.

ZANTEDESCHI, F. On the electricity of induction in the ærial strata of the atmosphere, which, in the shape of a ring, surround a cloud that is resolving into rain, snow, or hail.

PALMIERI, Prof. On the presence of electricity during the fall of rain.

ELLIOTT, R. S. Climate of Kansas.

PORTER, Commodore. Account of a hail storm on the Bosphorus.

BACHE, G. M. Account of a hail storm in Texas.

245. Check List of Publications of the Smithsonian Institution to July, 1872. 1872. 8vo., pp. 21. (M. C. x.)

246. Smithsonian Contributions to Knowledge. Vol. XVIII. 1872. 4to., pp. 646, 10 woodcuts, 5 plates, 3 charts.

CONTENTS.

SCHOTT, C. A. Tables of rain and snow. No. 222.
STOCKWELL, J. N. Secular variations of the orbits of planets. No. 232.
HARKNESS, W. Observations on terrestrial magnetism. No. 239.
FERREL, W. Converging series, expressing the ratio between the diameter and the circumference of a circle. No. 233.

247. Arrangement of the Families of Fishes, or Classes Pisces, Marsipobranchii, and Leptocardii. By THEODORE GILL. November, 1872. 8vo., pp. 96. (M. C. XI.)

248. On the Geology of Lower Louisiana and the Salt Deposit on Petite Anse Island. By EUGENE W. HILGARD. June, 1872. 4to., pp. 38, 4 woodcuts, 2 plates. (S. C. XXIII.)

249. Annual Report of the Board of Regents of the Smithsonian Institution, for the year 1871. 42d Congress, 1st Session. Senate Mis. Doc. No. 149. 1873. 8vo., pp. 473, 3 woodcuts.

CONTENTS.

HENRY, J. Secretary's report of operations.
BOARD OF REGENTS, Proceedings of
List of meteorological stations and observers.
Meteorological material contributed to Smithsonian Institution.
Meteorological articles received by the Institution, and deposited in the Library of Congress. Auroras, earthquakes, etc.
DODGE, N. S. Memoir of Sir John Frederick William Herschel.
ARAGO, M. Eulogy on Joseph Fourier.
ODLING, W. Professor Thomas Graham's scientific work.
HELMHOLTZ, H. On the relation of the physical sciences to science in general.
KORNHUBER, G. A. Alternate generation and parthenogenesis in the animal kingdom.
REICHARDT, W. Present state of our knowledge of cryptogamous plants.
STOCKWELL, J. N. Recent researches on the secular variations of the planetary orbits.
DE FOREST, E. L. Methods of interpolation applicable to the graduation of irregular series, such as tables of mortality. Part I.
DE SAUSSURE, H. Report on the transactions of the Society of Physics and Natural History of Geneva, from July, 1870, to June, 1871.
Expedition toward the North Pole:
HENRY, J.; HILGARD, J. E.; NEWCOMB, S.; BAIRD, S. F.; MEEK, F. B.; AGASSIZ, L. Scientific instructions to Captain Hall.
ETHNOLOGY:
COMFORT, A. J. Indian mounds near Fort Wadsworth, Dakota.
BERTHOUD, E. L. Antiquities on the Cache la Poudre River, Weld county, Colorado Territory.
LYON, W. B. Antiquities in New Mexico.

249. Report for 1871—Continued.

SPAINHOUR, J. M. Antiquities in Lenoir county, North Carolina.

McCONNELL, E. M. Account of the old Indian village, Kushkushkee, near Newcastle, Pennsylvania.

GROSSMANN, F. E. Pima Indians of Arizona.

CROOK, G. Indian mode of making arrow-heads and obtaining fire.

PETER, R. Ancient mound near Lexington, Kentucky.

BROWN, D. Shell-heap in Georgia.

SCHOTT, A. Remarks on ancient relic of Maya sculpture.

MUCH, M. Ancient history of North America.

RŒHRIG, F. L. O. On the language of the Dakota or Sioux Indians.

METEOROLOGY, with notes by Professor Henry:

LATIMER, G. Meteorology of Porto Rico.

COLLINS, Colonel. Meteorology of the Green river country.

LAMARK. Distinction between tornadoes and tempests.

MEEK, J. B. Account of a tornado which occurred in Spruce Creek Valley, Centre county, Pennsylvania.

HENRY, J. Effect of the moon on the weather.

KNIGHT, R. T.; HENRY, J. Connection of gales of wind and appearance of the aurora.

HARRISON, W. Account of a storm in Butler county, Kansas, June 23, 1871.

250. Smithsonian Miscellaneous Collections. Vol. X. 1873. 8vo., pp. 913, 5 woodcuts.

CONTENTS.

CARPENTER, P. P. Mollusks of western North America. No. 252.

GILL, T. Arrangement of the families of mollusks. No. 227.

HENRY, J. Instructions for observations of thunder storms. No. 235.

HENRY, J. Circular relative to heights. No. 236.

HENRY, J. Directions for constructing lightning rods. No. 237.

HENRY, J. Queries relative to tornadoes. No. 190.

BAIRD, S. F. Questions relative to the food fishes of the United States. No. 234.

BAIRD, S. F. Memoranda of inquiry relative to food fishes. No. 234.

RHEES, W. J. List of institutions, etc., in the United States in correspondence with the Smithsonian Institution. No. 238.

List of foreign correspondents of the Smithsonian Institution, for 1872. No. 243.

Check list of publications of the Smithsonian Institution, 1872. No. 245.

251. Memoir of C. F. P. Von Martius. By C. RAU. 1871. 8vo., pp. 12.

252. The Mollusks of Western North America. By P. P. CARPENTER. December, 1872. 8vo., pp. 446, 4 woodcuts. (M. C. x.)

CONTENTS.

Supplementary report on the present state of our knowledge with regard to the mollusca of the west coast of North America.

Review of Professor C. B. Adams' "Catalogue of the Shells of Panama" from the type specimens.

252. Mollusks of Western America—Continued.

Diagnoses of new forms of mollusks collected at Cape St. Lucas, Lower California.

Contributions towards a monograph of the pandoridæ.

Diagnoses of new forms of mollusca from the Vancouver district.

Diagnoses of new species and a new genus of mollusks, from the Reigen Mazatlan collection; with an account of additional specimens presented to the British Museum.

Descriptions of new species and varieties of chitonidæ and acmæidæ, from the Panama collection of the late Prof. C. B. Adams.

Diagnoses of new species of mollusks from the west tropical region of North America.

Diagnoses of new forms of mollusca from the west coast of North America, first collected by Col. E. Jewett.

Diagnoses of new forms of mollusca, collected by Col. E. Jewett, on the west tropical shores of North America.

Diagnoses des mollusques nouveaux provenant de Californie et faisant partie du Musée de l'Institution Smithsonienne.

On the pleistocene fossils collected by Col. E. Jewett, at Santa Barbara, California; with descriptions of new species.

253. Land and Fresh Water Shells of North America. Part IV. Strepomatidæ (American Melanians). By GEO. W. TRYON, Jr. December, 1873. 8vo., pp. 490, 871 woodcuts. (M. C. XVI.)

254. Synopsis of American Wasps. Solitary Wasps. By HENRY DE SAUSSURE. December, 1875. 8vo., pp. 430, 4 plates of 31 figures. (M.C. XIV.)

255. The Constants of Nature. Part I. Specific Gravities: Boiling and Melting Points; and Chemical Formulæ. By FRANK WIGGLESWORTH CLARKE. December, 1873. 8vo., pp. 272. (M. C. XII.)

256. Monographs of the Diptera of North America. Part III. By H. LOEW. December, 1873. 8vo., pp. 381, 4 plates of 116 figures. (M. C. XI.)

257. Systematic Index to List of Foreign Correspondents of the Smithsonian Institution. 1872. 8vo., pp. 30. (M. C. X.)

258. Bibliographical Index to North American Botany; or, Citations of Authorities for all the recorded Indigenous and Naturalized Species of the Flora of North America; with a Chronological Arrangement of the Synonymy. Part I. Polypetalæ. By SERENO WATSON. March, 1878. 8vo., pp. 484. (M. C. XV.)

259. Explorations of the Aboriginal Remains of Tennessee. By JOSEPH JONES. October, 1876. 4to., pp. 181, 110 woodcuts. (S. C. XXII.)

260. Regulations of the Smithsonian Institution. January, 1872. 8vo., pp. 41, 1 woodcut.

261. Directions for Collecting and Preserving Insects. By A. S. PACKARD, Jr. 1873. 8vo., pp. 60, 55 woodcuts. (M. C. XI.)

262. An Investigation of the Orbit of Uranus, with General Tables of its Motion. By SIMON NEWCOMB. August, 1873. 4to., pp. 296. (S. C. XIX.)

263. Circular of Instructions to Observatories relative to Telegraphic Announcements of Astronomical Discoveries. By JOSEPH HENRY. May, 1873. 8vo., pp. 4. (M. C. XII.)

264. New Species of North American Coleoptera. Part II. By JOHN L. LE CONTE. 1873. 8vo., pp. 74. (pp. 169–240.) (M. C. XI.)

265. Classification of the Coleoptera of North America. Part II. By JOHN L. LE CONTE. June, 1873. 8vo., pp. 72. (pp. 279–348.) (M. C. XI.)

266. On the Structure of Cancerous Tumors and the mode in which Adjacent Parts are Invaded. TONER LECTURE No. I. Delivered March 28, 1873. By J. J. WOODWARD. November, 1873. 8vo., pp. 44. 5 woodcuts. (M. C. XV.)

267. The Haidah Indians of Queen Charlotte's Islands, British Columbia, with a brief description of their Carvings, Tattoo Designs, etc. By JAMES G. SWAN. July, 1874. 4to., pp. 22, 7 plates of 24 figures. (S. C. XXI.)

268. The Winds of the Globe; or, the Laws of Atmospheric Circulation over the Surface of the Earth. By JAMES HENRY COFFIN. The tables completed and maps drawn by S. J. Coffin, with a discussion and analysis of the tables and charts by Alexander Wœikof. December, 1875. 4to., pp. 781, 4 woodcuts, 26 plates of 221 figures. (S. C. XX.)

269. The Sculptures of Santa Lucia Cosumalwhuapa, in Guatemala, with an account of travels in Central America and on the Western Coast of South America. By S. HABEL. 1878. 4to., pp. 94, 8 plates of 25 figures. (S. C. XXII.)

270. Catalogue of the described Diptera of North America. By C. R. OSTEN SACKEN. 1878. 8vo., pp. 324. (M. C. XVI.)

271. Annual Report of the Board of Regents of the Smithsonian Institution, for the year 1872. 42d Congress, 3d Session. House of Representatives, Mis. Doc. No. 107. 1873. 8vo., pp. 456, 109 woodcuts.

CONTENTS.

HENRY, J. Secretary's report of operations.
BOARD OF REGENTS, Proceedings of

271. Report for 1872—Continued.

List of meteorological stations and observers.

HENRY, J. Notes relative to George Catlin.

Report of Committee of Regents on Corcoran Art Gallery.

AGASSIZ, L. Narrative of the Hassler expedition.

BACHE, A. D. Bequest to National Academy of Sciences.

CORCORAN, W. W. Deed of gift of Art Gallery.

TONER, J. M. Deed of foundation of Toner lectures.

TYNDALL, J. Trust fund for the promotion of science in the U. S.

HAMILTON, J. Bequest of $1,000 to Smithsonian Institution.

HENRY, J. Circular sent with specimens presented.

ARAGO, M. Eulogy on Ampère.

FISCHER, F. Scientific labors of Edward Lartet.

PEABODY, A. P. Scientific education of mechanics and artisans.

BAUER, A. Organic bases.

KLETZINSKY, Prof. Nitrogen bodies of modern chemistry.

EGLESTON, T. Scheme for the qualitative determination of substances by the blowpipe.

Blowpipe apparatus of Hawkins and Wale.

SUESS, E. Boundary line between geology and history.

BREZINA, A. Explanation of the principles of crystallography and crystallophysics.

WŒIKOFF, A. Meteorology in Russia.

DONATI, G. B. Phenomena in telegraphic lines during the aurora borealis.

ETHNOLOGY:

BROCA, P. The Troglodytes, or cave dwellers, of the valley of the Vézere.

RAU, C. Ancient aboriginal trade in North America.

RAU, C. North American stone implements.

BRUFF, J. G. Indian engravings on the face of rocks along Green River valley in the Sierra Nevadas.

LEE, J. C. Y. Ancient ruin in Arizona.

BARRANDT, A. Haystack mound, Lincoln county, Dakota.

BREED, E. E. Earthworks in Wisconsin.

DEAN, C. K. Mound in Wisconsin.

WARNER, J. Big elephant mound in Grant county, Wisconsin.

CUTTS, J. B. Ancient relics in northwestern Iowa.

PERRINE, T. M. Mounds near Anna, Union county, Illinois.

PETER, R. Ancient mounds in Kentucky.

STEPHENSON, M. F. Mounds in Bartow county, Georgia.

MCKINLEY, W. Mounds in McIntosh and Early counties, Georgia.

HOTCHKISS, T. P. Indian remains in Caddo parish, Louisiana.

LOCKETT, S. H. Mounds in Louisiana.

PEALE, T. R. Prehistoric remains in vicinity of City of Washington, D. C.

DEVEREUX, J. H. Catalogue of cabinet of Indian relics presented to Smithsonian Institution.

DEVEREUX, J. H. Ancient pottery from Phillips County, Arkansas.

KIPP, J. On the accuracy of Catlin's account of the Mandan ceremonies.

272. Smithsonian Contributions to Knowledge. Vol. XIX. 1874. 4to., pp. 640, 6 woodcuts, 21 plates.

CONTENTS.

BARNARD, J. G. Problems of rotary motion. No. 240.
WOOD, H. C. Fresh-water algæ of North America. No. 241.
NEWCOMB, S. Orbit of Uranus. No. 262.

273. Smithsonian Miscellaneous Collections. Vol. XI. 1874. 8vo., pp. 790, 55 woodcuts, 4 plates.

CONTENTS.

GILL, T. Arrangement of the families of mammals. No. 230.
GILL, T. Arrangement of the families of fishes. No. 247.
LOEW, H. Monograph of the diptera of North America. Part III. No. 256.
PACKARD, A. S. Directions for collecting and preserving insects. No. 261.
LE CONTE, J. L. New species of North America coleoptera. Part II. No. 264.
LE CONTE, J. L. Classification of North America coleoptera. Part II. No. 265.

274. Smithsonian Miscellaneous Collections. Vol. XII. 1874. 8vo., pp. 767, 86 woodcuts.

CONTENTS.

BAIRD, S. F. Review of American birds. Part I. No. 181.
CLARKE, F. W. The constants of nature. Part I.—Specific gravities. No. 255.
HENRY, J. Circular on Telegraphic announcements of astronomical discoveries. No. 263.

275. Annual Report of the Board of Regents of the Smithsonian Institution, for the year 1873. 43d Congress, 1st Session. Senate Mis. Doc. No. 130. 1874. 8vo., pp. 452, 33 woodcuts.

CONTENTS.

HENRY, J. Secretary's report of operations.
BOARD OF REGENTS, Proceedings of
BAIRD, S. F. Report on Museum and exchanges.
ENDLICH, F. M. List of minerals in the National Museum.
Classified record of monthly meteorological reports preserved in the Smithsonian Institution.
Classified list of meteorological publications, and meteorological articles in periodicals deposited in Library of Congress in 1873.
GARFIELD, J. A. Biographical notice of S. P. Chase and L. Agassiz.
HAMLIN, H. Biographical notice of S. P. Chase.
PARKER, P. Biographical notice of L. Agassiz.
HAMILTON, J. Bequest deposited in United States Treasury.
DODGE, N. S. Memoir of Charles Babbage.

275. Report for 1873—Continued.

HENRY, J. On the "Moon-Hoax."

BABBAGE, C. Extracts from writings of

STEBBINS, R. P. Memoir of Louis Agassiz.

GRAY, A. Memoir of John Torrey.

STEVENS, J. A. Memoir of George Gibbs.

DALTON, J. C. Origin and propagation of disease.

HELMHOLZ H.; MAXWELL, J. C. Later views of the connection of electricity and magnetism.

GOULD, B. A. Account of the astronomical observatory at Cordoba, Argentine Republic.

MAILLY, E. Estimate of the population of the world.

MORIN, A. Warming and ventilating buildings. Part I.

DEFOREST, E. Additions to a memoir on methods of interpolation. Part II.

ETHNOLOGY:

SCHUMACHER, P. Remarks on the Kjökken-Möddings on the Northwest Coast of America.

BERENDT, C. H. On a grammar and dictionary of the Carib or Karif language, with some account of the people by whom it is spoken.

GILLMAN, H. The mound-builders and platycnemism in Michigan.

MASON, O. T. The Leipsic "Museum of Ethnology."

PERRINE, T. M. Antiquities of Union county, Illinois.

PATTON, A. Antiquities of Knox county, Indiana, and Lawrence County, Illinois.

Miscellaneous Correspondence:

DALL, W. H. Explorations on the Western coast of North America.

PIERSON, W. M. Discovery of a large meteorite in Mexico.

BRUNOT, F. R. On the habits of the beaver.

JEVONS, W. S. On a national library.

PRIZE QUESTIONS OF SCIENTIFIC SOCIETIES:

Society for the Encouragement of Science, Literature, and Art, Dunkirk, France.

Society of Science, Art, and Literature of Hainaut, Mons. Belgium.

Royal Institute for the Encouragement of the Natural, Economical, and Technological Sciences, Naples, Italy.

Royal Academy of Science, Literature, and the Fine Arts, Brussels, Belgium.

Society of Sciences of Haarlem, Holland.

276. The Constants of Nature. Part II. A Table of Specific Heats for Solids and Liquids. By FRANK W. CLARKE. April, 1876. 8vo., pp. 58. (M. C. XIV.)

277. Tables, Distribution, and Variations of the Atmospheric Temperature in the United States and some adjacent parts of America. By CHARLES A. SCHOTT. April, 1876. 4to., pp. 360, 10 woodcuts, 2 plates, 3 maps. (S. C. XXI.)

278. Check-list of Publications of the Smithsonian Institution. July, 1874. 8vo., pp. 24.

279. On Strain and Over-action of the Heart. TONER LECTURE No. III. Delivered May 14th, 1874. By J. M. DA COSTA. August, 1874. 8vo., pp. 32, 2 woodcuts. (M. C. xv.)

280. Statement and Exposition of certain Harmonies of the Solar System. By STEPHEN ALEXANDER. March, 1875. 4to., pp. 104, 20 woodcuts. (S. C. XXI.)

281. On the General Integrals of Planetary Motion. By SIMON NEWCOMB. December, 1874. 4to., pp. 40. (S. C. XXI.)

282. A Study of the Nature and Mechanism of Fever. TONER LECTURE No. IV. Delivered January 20, 1872. By HORATIO C. WOOD. February, 1875. 8vo., pp. 50. (M. C. xv.)

283. Catalogue of the Fishes of the East Coast of North America. By THEODORE GILL. 1875. 8vo., pp. 56. (M. C. XIV.)

284. Smithsonian Contributions to Knowledge. Vol. XX. 1876. 4to., pp. 794, 4 woodcuts, 26 plates.

CONTENTS.

COFFIN, J. H. The winds of the globe. No. 268.

285. Smithsonian Contributions to Knowledge. Vol. XXI. 1876. 4to., pp. 543, 30 woodcuts, 9 plates, 3 maps.

CONTENTS.

ALEXANDER, S. Harmonies of the solar system. No. 280.
NEWCOMB, S. Integrals of planetary motion. No. 281.
SWAN, J. G. Haidah Indians of Queen Charlotte's Islands, British Columbia. No. 267.
SCHOTT, C. A. Tables, atmospheric temperature in the United States. No. 277.

286. Annual Report of the Board of Regents of the Smithsonian Institution, for the year 1874. 43d Congress, 2d Session. House Doc. No. 56. 1875. 8vo., pp. 416, 46 woodcuts.

CONTENTS.

HENRY, J. Secretary's report of operations.
BOARD OF REGENTS. Proceedings of
List of articles deposited by the Smithsonian Institution in the Corcoran

286. Report for 1874—Continued.

ARAGO, M. Eulogy on La Place.
MAILLY, M. Eulogy on Quetelet.
DUMAS, M. Eulogy on A. A. de la Rive.
HILGARD, J. E. Tides and tidal action in harbors.
LEMSTRÖM, S.; DE LA RIVE, A. A. Electricity of the atmosphere and the Aurora Borealis.
DE CANDOLLE, A.; GRAY, J. E. On a dominant language for science.
SCHOTT, C. A.; EVERETT, J. D. Underground temperature.
DUPRE, W.; HENRY, J. Earthquakes in North Carolina, 1874.
DE LA RIVE, A. A. Report on the transactions of the Society of Physics and Natural History of Geneva, from July, 1872, to June, 1873.
MORIN, A. Warming and ventilating buildings. Part II.
ETHNOLOGY:
SCHUMACHER, P. Ancient graves and shell-heaps of California.
KING, W. M. Account of the burial of an Indian squaw, San Bernardino county, California.
McWHORTER, T. Ancient mounds of Mercer county, Illinois.
PRATT, W. H. Antiquities of Whitesides county, Illinois.
FARQUHARSON, R. J. A study of skulls and long bones, from mounds near Albany, Illinois.
TIFFANY, A. S. The shell-bed skull.
HILL, G. W. Antiquities of northern Ohio.
ROBERTSON, R. S. The age of stone, and the troglodytes of Breckinridge county, Kentucky.
DAVIS, A. C. Antiquities of Isle Royale, Lake Superior.
SMITH, J. W. C. Antiquities of Yazoo county, Mississippi.
WRIGHT, D. F. Antiquities of Tennessee.
LAW, A. E. Antiquities of Blount county, Tennessee.
CUSHING, F. H. Antiquities of Orleans county, New York.
ROBERTSON, R. S. Antiquities of La Porte county, Indiana.
ROBERTSON, R. S. Antiquities of Allen and De Kalb counties, Ind.
HAILE, J.; McHENRY, J. W. Antiquities of Jackson county, Tennessee.
ANDERSON, W. Antiquities of Perry county, Ohio.
BRYAN, O. N. Antiquities of Charles county, Maryland.
KRON, F. J. Antiquities of Stanley and Montgomery counties, North Carolina.
MITCHELL, A. Antiquities of Florida.
BARTRAM, J. Antiquities of Florida.

287. The Archæological Collection of the United States National Museum, in charge of the Smithsonian Institution, Washington, D. C. By CHARLES RAU. 1876. 4to., pp. 118, 340 woodcuts. (S. C. XXII.)

288. The Constants of Nature. First supplement to Part I. Specific Gravities, Boiling Points, and Melting Points. By FRANK W. CLARKE. April, 1876. 8vo., pp. 62. (M. C. XIV.)

289. The Constants of Nature. Part III. Tables of Expansion by Heat for Solids and Liquids. By FRANK W. CLARKE. April, 1876. 8vo., pp. 58. (M. C. XIV.)

290. Circular for Distribution at the Centennial Exhibition, 1876, containing List of Smithsonian Publications and Rules of Distribution; List of Foreign Agents; Number of Foreign and Domestic Institutions in Correspondence; List of Regents, Officers, and Assistants of the Institution. 1876. 12mo., pp. 12.

291. Dual Character of the Brain. TONER LECTURE No. II. Delivered April 22, 1874. By C. E. BROWN-SÉQUARD. January, 1877. 8vo., pp. 26. (M. C. XV.)

292. Check-list of North American Batrachia and Reptilia; with a Systematic List of the Higher Groups, and an Essay on Geographical Distribution based on the specimens contained in the United States National Museum. By EDWARD D. COPE. 1875. 8vo., pp. 108. (M. C. XIII.) *Bulletin of the National Museum No.* 1.

293. Contributions to the Natural History of Kerguelen Island, made in Connection with the American Transit-of-Venus Expedition, 1874–'75. By J. H. KIDDER. I.—Ornithology, by Elliott Coues. 1875. 8vo., pp. 61. (M. C. XIII.) *Bulletin of the National Museum, No.* 2.

294. Contributions to the Natural History of Kerguelen Island, made in connection with the United States Transit-of-Venus Expedition, 1874–75. By J. H. KIDDER. II.—Oology, Botany, &c. 1876. 8vo., pp. 124. (M. C. XIII.) *Bulletin of the National Museum, No.* 3.

CONTENTS.

KIDDER, J. H.; COUES, E. Oology.
BOTANY:
  GRAY, ASA. A.—Phænogamia, filices, et lycopodiaceæ.
  JAMES, T. P. B.—Musci.
  TUCKERMAN, E. C.—Lichenes.
  FARLOW, W. G. Algæ.
CROZET FLORA.
ENDLICH, F. M. Geology.
KIDDER, J. H. Mammals.
GILL, T. N. Fish.
DALL, W. H. Mollusks.
INSECTS:
  OSTEN-SACKEN, C. C. Diptera.
  HAGEN, H. A. Pseudo-neuroptera.
  SMITH, S. I. Crustaceans.
  VERRILL, A. E. Annelids, echinoderms, and anthozoa.
KERSHNER, E. Collection.
KIDDER, J. H.; COUES, E. A study of chionis minor.

1875. 8vo., pp. 56. (M. C. XIII.) *Bulletin of the National Museum, No. 4.*

296. Catalogue of the Fishes of the Bermudas. Based chiefly upon the collections of the United States National Museum. By G. BROWN GOODE. 1876. 8vo., pp. 84. (M. C. XIII.) *Bulletin of the National Museum, No. 5.*

297. Classification of the Collection to illustrate the Animal Resources of the United States. A List of Substances derived from the Animal Kingdom, with Synopsis of the Useful and Injurious Animals and a Classification of Methods of Capture and Utilization. By G. BROWN GOODE. 1876. 8vo., pp. 140. (M. C. XIII.) *Bulletin of the National Museum, No. 6.*

298. Annual Report of the Board of Regents of the Smithsonian Institution, for the year 1875. 44th Congress, 1st Session. Senate Mis. Doc. No. 115. 1876. 8vo., pp. 422, 354 woodcuts.

CONTENTS.

HENRY, J. Secretary's report of operations.
BOARD OF REGENTS, Proceedings of
BAIRD, S. F. Report on Museum and explorations.
BAIRD, S. F. Report on the proposed plan of exhibit by the Smithsonian Institution at the International Centennial Exhibition at Philadelphia.
PARKER, P. Eulogy on Henry Wilson.
ARAGO, M. Eulogy on Alexander Volta.
DE CANDOLLE, A. Probable future of the human race.
DE CANDOLLE, A. Report on the transactions of the Society of Physics and Natural History of Geneva, from July, 1873, to June, 1874.
PRESTWICH, J. The past and future of geology.
WEX, H. G. Diminution of the water of rivers and streams.
TAYLOR, W. B. Refraction of sound.
HENRY, J. On the organization of local scientific societies.
ETHNOLOGY:
MORTILLET, G. DE; CHANTRE, E. International code of symbols for charts of pre-historic archæology.
GILLMAN, H. Characteristics pertaining to ancient man in Michigan.
ABBOTT, C. C. The stone age in New Jersey.

299. Annual Report of the Board of Regents of the Smithsonian Institution, for the year 1876. 44th Congress, 2d Session. Senate Mis. Doc. No. 46. 1877. 8vo., pp. 488, 73 woodcuts.

CONTENTS.

HENRY, J. Secretary's report of operations.
BOARD OF REGENTS, Proceedings of
BAIRD, S. F. Report on Museum and explorations.
BAIRD, S. F. Report on Centennial Exhibition of 1876.
Centennial awards to Smithsonian Institution.

299. Report for 1876—Continued.

GRAY, A.; SARGENT, A. A.; CLYMER, H. Report of Committee on the Museum.

BANCROFT, G. Memorial to Congress, in behalf of the Regents, for new museum.

List of collections presented by foreign commissioners to the United States.

ARAGO, M. Eulogy on Gay Lussac.

FIALHO, A. Biographical sketch of Dom Pedro II.

TAYLOR, W. B. Kinetic theories of gravitation.

PILAR, G. The revolutions of the crust of the earth.

KIRKWOOD, D. The asteroids between Mars and Jupiter.

ETHNOLOGY:

MASON, O. T. The Latimer collection of antiquities from Porto Rico in the National Museum at Washington, D. C.

ROMER, F. F. Pre-historic antiquities of Hungary.

BLONDEL, S. Jade. A historical, archæological, and literary study of the mineral called Yu by the Chinese.

WILLIAMSON, G. Antiquities in Guatemala.

BERENDT, C. H. Collection of historical documents in Guatemala.

STRONG, MOSES. Observations on the pre-historic mounds of Grant county, Wisconsin.

SNYDER, J. F. Deposits of flint implements, Illinois.

SMITH, C. D. Ancient mica mines in North Carolina.

PEET, S. D. Double-walled earthwork in Ashtabula county, Ohio.

ELLSWORTH, E. W. Ancient implement of wood, from Connecticut.

POWERS, S. Centennial mission to the Indians of Western Nevada and California.

DOYLE, W. E. Indian forts and dwellings, Indian Territory.

BRACKETT, A. G. The Sioux or Dakota Indians.

300. On the Surgical Complications and Sequels of the Continued Fevers. With a Bibliography of works on Diseases of the Joints, Bones, Larynx, the Eye, Gangrene, Haematoma, Phlegmasia, etc. TONER LECTURE No. V. Delivered February 17, 1876. By WILLIAM W. KEEN. March, 1876. 8vo., pp. 72, 5 woodcuts. (M. C. xv.)

301. List of Publications of the Smithsonian Institution, July, 1877. 1877 8vo., pp. 72. (M. C. xiv.)

302. Subcutaneous Surgery, its Principles, and its recent Extension in Practice. TONER LECTURE No. VI. Delivered September 13, 1876. By WILLIAM ADAMS. April, 1877. 8vo., pp. 20. (M. C. xv.)

303. Contributions to the Natural History of the Hawaiian and Fanning Islands and Lower California, made in connection with the United States North Pacific Surveying Expedition, 1873–'75. By THOS. H. STREETS. 1877. 8vo., pp. 172. (M. C. XIII.) *Bulletin of the National Museum, No. 7.*

303. Natural History of Hawaiian Islands—Continued.

CONTENTS.

ORNITHOLOGY.
HERPETOLOGY.
ICHTHYOLOGY:
I. Fishes of Upper and Lower California.
II. Fishes of the Hawaiian Islands.
III. Fishes of the Fanning Islands.
IV. Fishes from the Samoan Islands.
CRUSTACEA.
BOTANY.

304. Index to the Names which have been appplied to the Subdivisions of the Class Brachiopoda, excluding the *Rudistes*, previous to the year 1877. By W. H. DALL. 1877. 8vo., pp. 88. (M. C. XIII.) *Bulletin of the National Museum, No.* 8.

305. Contributions to North American Ichthyology. Based primarily on the collections of the United States National Museum. I.—Review of Rafinesque's Memoirs on North American Fishes. By DAVID S. JORDAN. 1877. 8vo., pp. 56. (M. C. XIII.) *Bulletin of the National Museum, No.* 9.

306. Contributions to North American Ichthyology. Based primarily on the Collections of the United States National Museum. II. A.—Notes on Cottidæ, Etheostomatidæ, Percidæ, Centrarchidæ, Aphododeridæ, Dorysomatidæ, and Cyprinidæ, with revisions of the genera and descriptions of new or little known species. B.—Synopsis of the Siluridæ of the Fresh Waters of North America. By DAVID S. JORDAN. 1877. 8vo., pp. 124, 45 plates of 100 figures. (M. C. XIII.) *Bulletin of the National Museum, No.* 10.

307. Report on the Centennial Exhibition, Philadelphia. By S. F. BAIRD. 1877. 8vo., pp. 22.

308. Contributions to North American Ichthyology, based primarily on the collections of the United States National Museum. III. A.—On the Distribution of the Fishes of the Alleghany Region of South Carolina, Georgia, and Tennessee, with descriptions of new or little known species. By DAVID S. JORDAN and ALEMBERT W. BRAYTON. B.—A Synopsis of the Family Catostomidæ. By DAVID S. JORDAN. 1878. 8vo., pp. 237. (M. C. XXIII.) *Bulletin of the National Museum, No.* 12.

309. List of Foreign Correspondents of the Smithsonian Institution. Corrected to January, 1878. March, 1878. 8vo., pp. 120. (M. C. XV.)

310. On the Internal Structure of the Earth, considered as affecting the Phenomena of Precession and Nutation; supplementary to article under the above head, Smithsonian Contributions to Knowledge, Vol. XIX, No. 240, being the third of the Problems of Rotary Mo-

tion. By J. G. BARNARD. August, 1877. 4to., pp. 19, 4 woodcuts. (S. C. XXIII.)

311. Index Catalogue of Books and Memoirs relating to Nebulæ and Clusters, etc. By EDWARD S. HOLDEN. November, 1877. 8vo., pp. 126. (M. C. XIV.)

312. Smithsonian Miscellaneous Collections. Vol. XIII. 1878. 8vo., pp. 982, 45 plates. *Bulletins of the National Museum, Nos.* 1–10.

CONTENTS.

COPE, E. D. North American batrachia and reptilia. No. 292.
KIDDER, J. H.; COUES, E. Birds of Kerguelen Island. No. 293.
KIDDER, J. H., and others. Oology, botany, &c., of Kerguelen Island. No. 294.
LAWRENCE, G. N. Birds of Mexico. No. 295.
GOODE, G. B. Fishes of Bermuda. No. 296.
GOODE, G. B. Classification of animal resources. No. 297.
STREETS, T. H. Natural history of Hawaiian Islands, Fanning Islands, and Lower California. No. 303.
DALL, W. H. Index of brachiopoda. No. 304.
JORDAN, D. S. North American Ichthyology. Nos. 305 and 306.

313. The Flora of St. Croix and the Virgin Islands. By Baron H. F. A. EGGERS. 1879. 8vo., pp. 139. (M. C. XXIII.) *Bulletin of the National Museum, No.* 13.

314. Smithsonian Miscellaneous Collections. Vol. XIV. 1878. 8vo., pp. 911, 4 plates.

CONTENTS.

DE SAUSSURE, H. Synopsis of American wasps. No. 254.
GILL, T. Catalogue of fishes. No. 283.
CLARKE, F. W. Specific gravity tables. Supp. I. No. 288.
CLARKE, F. W. Specific heat tables. No. 276.
CLARKE, F. W. Tables of expansion by heat. No. 289.
Catalogue of photograph portraits of North American Indians. No. 216.
Check list of Smithsonian publications to July, 1877. No. 301.
HOLDEN, E. S. Catalogue of books relative to nebulæ. No. 311.

315. Smithsonian Miscellaneous Collections. Vol. XV. 1878. 8vo., pp. 880, 53 woodcuts.

CONTENTS.

WATSON, S. Botanical index. No. 258.
WOODWARD, J. J. Toner Lecture I. Cancerous tumors. No. 266.
BROWN-SÉQUARD, C. E. Toner Lecture II. The brain. No. 291.
DA COSTA, J. M. Toner Lecture III. The heart. No. 279.
WOOD, H. C. Toner Lecture IV. Study of fever. No. 282.
KEEN, W. W. Toner Lecture V. Continued fevers. No. 300.
ADAMS, W. Toner Lecture VI. Subcutaneous surgery. No. 302.
List of foreign correspondents of the Smithsonian Institution to January, 1878. No. 309.

315. Miscellaneous Collections. Vol. XV—Continued.

Circular in reference to American archæology. No. 316.
Circular. Inquiries relative to crawfish and crustacea. No. 319.
Circular relating to collections of living reptiles. No. 320.

316. Circular in reference to American Archæology. 1878. 8vo., pp. 15, 38 woodcuts. (M. C. xv.)

317. A Classification and Synopsis of the Trochilidæ. By DANIEL GIRAUD ELLIOT. 1879. 4to., pp. 289, 127 woodcuts. (S. C. XXIII.)

318. On the Remains of Later Pre-historic Man, obtained from Caves in the Catherina Archipelago, Alaska Territory, and especially from the Caves of the Aleutian Islands. By W. H. DALL. 1878. 4to., pp. 44, 10 plates of 39 figures. (S. C. XXII.)

319. Circular of Inquiries relative to the Natural History of the American Crawfish and other Fresh Water Crustacea. 1878. 8vo., pp. 8, 2 woodcuts. (M. C. xv.)

320. Circular relating to Collections of Living Reptiles. 1878. 8vo., pp. 2. (M. C. xv.)

321. The Nature of Reparatory Inflammation in Arteries after Ligatures, Acupressure, and Torsion. TONER LECTURE No. VII. Delivered June 27, 1878. By EDW. O. SHAKESPEARE. March, 1879. 8vo., pp. 74, 7 plates of 11 figures. (M. C. XVI.)

322. Smithsonian Miscellaneous Collections. Vol. XVI. 1880. 8vo., pp. 950, 871 woodcuts, 7 plates.

CONTENTS.

TRYON, G. W. Land and fresh water shells. Strepomatidæ. No. 253.
OSTEN SACKEN, C. R. Catalogue of diptera. No. 270.
SHAKESPEARE, E. O. Nature of reparatory inflammation. No. 321.
Circular relative to scientific and literary exchanges. No. 324.
Business arrangements of the Smithsonian Institution. No. 325.
ELLIOT, D. G. List of species of humming birds. No. 334.
List of the principal scientific and literary institutions in the United States. No. 335.
List of publications of the Smithsonian Institution. No. 344.

323. Annual Report of the Board of Regents of the Smithsonian Institution, for the year 1877. 45th Congress, 2d Session. Senate Mis. Doc. No. 35. 1878. 8vo., pp. 500, 49 woodcuts.

CONTENTS.

HENRY, J. Secretary's report of operations.
BOARD OF REGENTS, Proceedings of
BAIRD, S. F. Report on Museum and explorations.
BAIRD, S. F. List of explorations furnishing collections to the National Museum, 1838 to 1877.

323. Report for 1877—Continued.

HOLMGREN, F. Color blindness in its relation to accidents by rail and sea.

HENRY, J. Color blindness.

PLANTAMOUR, E. Report on the transactions of the Geneva Society of Physics and Natural History, from June, 1874, to June, 1875.

MÜLLER, J. Report on the transactions of the Geneva Society of Physics and Natural History, from June, 1875, to June, 1876.

FAVRE, A. Report on the transactions of the Geneva Society of Physics and Natural History, from June, 1876, to June, 1877.

ETHNOLOGY:

CANNON, G. L. Antiquities of Jefferson and Clear Creek counties, Colorado.

STRONG, MOSES. Antiquities in Wisconsin.

HART, J. N. DE. The mounds and osteology of the mound builders of Wisconsin.

BREED, E. E. Pits at Embarrass, Wisconsin.

MOULTON, M. W. Mounds in Delaware county, Iowa.

KNAPP, Mrs. G. Earthworks on the Arkansas river, sixteen miles below Little Rock.

LYKINS, W. H. R. Antiquities of Kansas City, Missouri.

SHAW, J. The mound builders in the Rock river valley, Illinois.

COCHRANE, J. Antiquities of Mason county, Illinois.

HILL, G. W. Ancient earthworks of Ashland county, Ohio.

CASE, H. B. Flint implements in Holmes county, Ohio.

MILLER, F. Mound in Trumbull county, Ohio.

FRIEL, J. Antiquities of Hancock county, Kentucky.

ROBERTSON, R. S. Antiquities of Nashville, Tennessee.

CLARK, W. M. Antiquities of Tennessee.

JONES, Jr., C. C. Aboriginal structures in Georgia.

BAILEY, W. B. F. Antiquities of Spalding county, Georgia.

GAINES, A. S.; CUNNINGHAM, K. M. Shell-heaps on Mobile river.

RAU, C. The stock in trade of an aboriginal lapidary.

RAU, C. Observations on a gold ornament from a mound in Florida.

HALDEMAN, S. S. On a polychrome bead from Florida.

HARRISON, A. M. Colored bead dug from a mound on the eastern coast of Florida.

MAYBERRY, S. P. Shell-heaps at the mouth of Saint John's river, Florida.

TAYLOR, W. M. Ancient mound in western Pennsylvania.

SHEPARD, E. M. Deposit of arrow heads near Fishkill, New York.

GIBBS, G. J. Stone celts in the West Indies and Africa.

GALT, F. L. The Indians of Peru.

BOWERS, S. History and antiquities of Santa Rosa Island, California.

McPARLIN, T. A. Notes on the history and climate of New Mexico.

WEISMANN, A. On the change of the Mexican axolotl to an amblystoma.

ABBE, C. Short memoirs on meteorological subjects, translated by, viz:

HANN, J. On the diminution of aqueous vapor with increasing altitude in the atmosphere.

HANN, J. On the influence of rain upon the barometer and upon the formation of precipitation in general.

323. Report for 1877—Continued.

HANN, J. Atmospheric pressure and rain-fall.

HANN, J. The laws of the variation of temperature in ascending currents of air.

SOHNCKE, L. The law of the variation of temperature in ascending moist currents of air.

REYE, T. Rain-fall and barometric minima.

HANN, J. On the relation between the difference of pressure and the velocity of the wind according to the theories of Ferrel and Colding.

FERREL, W. Reply to the criticisms of J. Hann.

COLDING, A. Some remarks concerning the nature of currents of air.

COLDING, A. On the whirlwind at St. Thomas on the 21st of August, 1871.

PESLIN, M. On the relation between barometric variations and the general atmospheric currents.

324. Circular relative to Scientific and Literary Exchanges. 1879. 8vo., pp. 2. (M. C. XVI.) Free.

325. Business Arrangements of the Smithsonian Institution. January, 1879. 8vo., pp. 7. (M. C. XVI.) Free.

326. Catalogue of the Collection to illustrate the Animal Resources and the Fisheries of the United States, exhibited at Philadelphia, in 1876, by the Smithsonian Institution and the United States Fish Commission, and forming a part of the United States National Museum. By G. BROWNE GOODE. 1879. 8vo., pp. 367. (M. C. XXIII.) *Bulletin of the National Museum, No.* 14.

327. The Scientific Writings of JAMES SMITHSON. Edited by W. J. RHEES. 1879. 8vo., pp. 166, 32 woodcuts, 1 plate. (Portrait.) (M. C. XXI.)

CONTENTS.

SMITHSON, J. Scientific writings.

JOHNSON, W. R. Memoir on the scientific character and researches of James Smithson.

IRBY, J. R. McD. Works and character of James Smithson.

328. The Smithsonian Institution. Documents relative to its Origin and History. By WILLIAM J. RHEES. 1879. 8vo., pp. 1027. (M. C. XVII.)

CONTENTS.

SMITHSON, J. Will of

Correspondence between attorneys in England, Department of State, Richard Rush, and others relative to the bequest of Smithson.

RUSH, R. The case stated.

Opinion of English counsel.

Decree of Chancery Court awarding bequest to the United States.

Account of case of the United States.

Bill of costs of the case of the United States.

RUSH, R. Accounts of

SMITHSON, J. Schedule of personal effects.

328. Smithsonian Institution. Documents—Continued.

SMITHSON, J. Residuary legacy of

Congressional proceedings in relation to the bequest. 1835 to 1877. Twenty-fourth to Forty-fourth Congress.

HENRY, J. Digest of act of Congress to establish the Smithsonian Institution.

ADAMS, J. Q. Extracts from Memoirs of, relative to Smithson bequest.

TREASURY OF U. S. Accounts of, with Smithson fund.

Proposed applications of Smithson bequest.

Report of Organization Committee of the Board of Regents of the Smithsonian Institution.

HENRY, J. Programme of organization of Smithsonian Institution.

Letters relative to the programme of organization.

329. The Smithsonian Institution. Journals of the Board of Regents, Reports of Committees, Statistics, etc. By WILLIAM J. RHEES. 1879. 8vo., pp. 851. (M. C. XVIII.)

CONTENTS.

Journal of Proceedings of the Board of Regents from 1846 to 1876.

Report of the Special Committee of the Board of Regents on the distribution of the income.

Report of the Special Committee of the Board of Regents—Prof. Felton—on the present of the Greek album from Miss E. Contaxaki.

Report of the Special Committee of the Board of Regents—Prof. Felton—on the purchase of the Stanley Indian gallery.

HENRY, J. Communication relative to a publication by Prof. S. F. B Morse.

Report of the Special Committee of the Board of Regents on the invention of the electro-magnetic telegraph.

Report of the Special Committee of the Board of Regents relative to the Smithsonian fire of January 24, 1865.

Act of Congress to transfer custody of library to Library of Congress.

Act of Congress to receive into Treasury of the United States residuary legacy of Smithson, and to authorize increase of fund to a million dollars.

Report of the Special Committee of the Board of Regents on best use of new hall of Institution.

Report of Executive Committee of the Board of Regents on the Washington city canal.

Report of the Executive Committee of the Board of Regents relative to the Corcoran Art Gallery.

Report of the Special Committee of the Board of Regents on the museum.

EULOGIES AND BIOGRAPHICAL SKETCHES:

Agassiz, L.; Bache, A. D.; Chase, S. P.; Cleaveland, P.; Douglas, S. A.; Espy, J. P.; Felton, C. C.; Harvey, W. H.; Irving, W.; Jewett, C. C.; Pearce, J. A.; Priestley, J.; Rush, R.; Seaton, W. W.; Totten, J. G.; Turner, W. W.; Wilson, H.; Wurdeman, G.

AGASSIZ, L. Narrative of expedition through Straits of Magellan to California.

BACHE, A. D. Will of, establishing Bache Scientific Fund.

CORCORAN, W. W. Deed of gift and trust of Corcoran Art Gallery.

329. Smithsonian Institution. Journals, &c.—Continued.

TONER, J. M. Deed of, establishing Toner Lectures for advance of medical science.

TYNDALL, J. Deed of, establishing trust for promotion of science in the United States.

HAMILTON, J. Bequest of, to Smithsonian Institution.

Circular sent with specimens of natural history, etc., presented to institutions.

Journal of the Executive Committee from Sept. 12, 1846, to Dec. 21, 1849.

Report of the Executive Committee, from 1847 to 1875.

Journal of the Building Committee, from Feb. 17, 1847, to Dec. 1, 1847.

Report of the Building Committee, 1847-1867.

General financial and statistical statements, receipts and expenditures, classified, 1846 to 1877.

Statistics of literary and scientific exchanges, additions to the library, etc., 1846 to 1877.

Appropriations from National Treasury by Congress for Smithsonian Institution and National Museum, 1846-1876.

List of Regents of the Institution from 1846 to 1879, according to mode of appointment, residence, etc.

Act of Congress to establish the Smithsonian Institution, August 10, 1846.

The same, according to the Revised Statutes.

By-Laws of the "Establishment."

The "Establishment" of the Smithsonian Institution, organization and journal of proceedings, 1846 to 1877.

Examination of Professor Henry by the English Government Scientific Commission, June 28, 1870.

330. Smithson and his Bequest. By WILLIAM J. RHEES. 1880. 8vo., pp. 76, 9 plates. (M. C. XXI.)

CONTENTS.

Life of Smithson.

Legislation of Congress in relation to the bequest.

List of first Board of Regents.

Obituary notice of Smithson, March, 1830.

DUTENS, L. Account of the First Duke of Northumberland.

Notice of the First Duke in The Gentleman's Magazine, 1786.

Coffin-plate inscription of Hugh Smithson.

Account of Earl Percy.

Notice of Smithson's paper on "Tabasheer."

DAVY, SIR H. Notice of Smithson's paper on "Calamines."

Illustrations of presentations of books to Smithson.

BERZELIUS. Notice of Smithson's researches.

Extracts from Smithson's scientific writings.

Catalogue of the library of Smithson.

Notice of the city of Washington, in Harriott's travels.

Notice of the city of Washington, in Weld's travels.

331. The Palenque Tablet, in the United States National Museum, Washington, D. C. By CHARLES RAU. 1879. 4to., pp. 90, 2 plates. (S. C. XXII.)

332. Proceedings of the U. S. National Museum for 1878. Vol. I. 1879. 8vo., pp. 524, 8 cuts, 8 plates. (M. C. xix.)

CONTENTS.

Bean, T. H. Description of a new sparoid fish, *Sargus holbrookii*, from Savannah bank.

On the occurrence of *Stichæus punctatus* (Fahr.) Kröyer, at St. Michael's, Alaska.

On the identity of *Euchalarodus Putnami* Gill, with *Pleuronectes glaber* (Storer) Gill, with notes on the habits of the species.

Description of a species of *Lycodes* (*L. Turneri*) from Alaska.

See also under Goode and Bean.

Belding, L. A partial list of the birds of Central California.

Cook, C. The manufacture of porpoise-oil.

Dall, W. H. Description of new forms of mollusks from Alaska contained in the collections of the National Museum.

Postpliocene fossils in the Coast Range of California.

Fossil mollusks from later tertiaries of California.

Note on shells from Costa Rica kitchenmidden, collected by Drs. Flint and Bransford.

Distribution of Californian tertiary fossils.

Descriptions of new species of shells from California in the collections of the National Museum.

Report on the limpets and chitons of the Alaskan and Arctic regions, descriptions of genera and species believed to be new.

Edwards, V. N. On the occurrence of the Oceanic Bonito, *Orcynus pelamys* (Linné) Poey, in Vineyard Sound, Massachusetts.

Gill, T. Synopsis of the pediculate fishes of the Eastern Coast of Extratropical North America.

Note on the *Antennariidæ*.

On the proper specific name of the common pelagic antennariid *Pterophryne*.

Note on the *Ceratiidæ*.

Note on the *Maltheidæ*.

Goode, G. B. The *Clupea tyrannus* of Latrobe.

The occurrence of *Belone latimanus* in Buzzard's bay, Massachusetts.

The voices of Crustaceans.

A revision of the American species of the genus *Brevoortia*, with a description of a new species from the Gulf of Mexico.

The occurrence of *Hippocampus antiquorum*, or an allied form, on St. George's Banks.

The occurrence of the Canada porcupine in West Virginia.

On two fishes from the Bermudas mistakenly described as new by Dr. Günther.

Goode, G. B.; Bean, T. H. The Craig flounder of Europe, *Glyptocephalus cynoglossus*, on the coast of North America.

The Oceanic Bonito on the coast of the United States.

Description of *Caulolatilus microps*, a new species of fish from the Gulf coast of Florida.

332. Proceedings of National Museum. Vol. I—Continued.

GOODE, G. B.; BEAN, T. H. On a new serranoid fish, *Epinephelus Drummond-Hayi*, from the Bermudas and Florida.

Descriptions of two new species of fishes, *Lutjanus Blackfordii* and *Lutjanus stearnsii*, from the Coast of Florida.

A note upon the Black Grouper (*Epinephelus nigritus* (Holbrook) Gill) of the Southern coast.

Descriptions of two gadoid fishes, *Phycis Chesteri* and *Haloporphyrus viola*, from the deep-sea fauna of the Northwestern Atlantic.

Description of *Argentina syrtensium*, a new deep-sea fish from Sable Island Bank.

The identity of *Rhinonemus caudacuta*, (Storer) Gill with *Gadus cimbrius* Linn.

Note on *Platessa ferruginea* D. H. Storer, and *Platessa rostrata* H. R. Storer.

On the identity of *Brosmius brosme americanus* Gill, with *Brosmius brosme* (Müller) White.

JACKSON, J. B. S. Arsenic acid for protecting anatomical preparations from insects.

JEFFERSON, J. P. On the mortality of fishes in the Gulf of Mexico in 1878.

JEFFERSON, J. P.; PORTER, J. Y.; MOORE, T. On the destruction of fish in the vicinity of the Tortugas during the months of September and October, 1878.

JORDAN, D. S. Notes on a collection of fishes from Clackamas river, Oregon.

JORDAN, D. S.; GILBERT, C. H. Notes on the fishes of Beaufort harbor, North Carolina.

LAWRENCE, G. N. Catalogue of the birds of Dominica, from collections made for the Smithsonian Institution, by Frederick A. Ober, together with his notes and observations.

Catalogue of the birds of St. Vincent, from collections made by Fred. A. Ober, under the directions of the Smithsonian Institution. with his notes thereon.

Catalogue of the birds of Antigua and Barbuda, from collections made for the Smithsonian Institution, by Fred. A. Ober, with his observations.

Catalogue of the birds of Grenada, from a collection made by Fred. A. Ober for the Smithsonian Institution, including others seen by him, but not obtained.

Catalogue of the birds collected in Martinique, by Fred. A. Ober for the Smithsonian Institution.

Catalogue of a collection of birds obtained in Guadeloupe for the Smithsonian Institution, by Fred. A. Ober.

A general catalogue of the birds noted from the islands of the Lesser Antilles visited by Fred. A. Ober; with a table showing their distribution, and those found in the United States.

LUPTON, N. T. On the breeding habits of the sea-catfish (*Ariopsis milberti?*)

MERRILL, J. C. Notes on the ornithology of Southern Texas, being a list of birds observed in the vicinity of Fort Brown, Texas, from February, 1876, to June, 1878.

332. Proceedings of National Museum. Vol. I—Continued.

POEY, F. Notes on the American species of the genus *Cybium.*

PRATT, R. H. Catalogue of casts taken by Clark Mills of the heads of sixty-four Indian prisoners of various western tribes, and held at Fort Marion, St. Augustine, Florida, in charge of R. H. Pratt.

RIDGWAY, R. On a new humming bird (*Atthis Ellioti*) from Guatemala.

A review of the American species of the genus *Scops*, Savigny.

Descriptions of several new species and geographical races of birds contained in the collection of the United States National Museum.

Description of two new species of birds from Costa Rica, and notes on other rare species from that country.

Descriptions of new species and races of American birds, including a synopsis of the Genus *Tyrannus*, Cuvier.

STEARNS, S. A note on the Gulf menhaden, *Brevoortia patronus*, Goode.

STEINDACHNER, F. Note on *Perca flavescens.*

WILMOT, S. Notes on the western gizzard shad, *Dorosoma cepedianum heterurum* (Raf.) Jordan.

333. Proceedings of the U. S. National Museum for 1879. Vol. II. 1881. 8vo., pp. 503, 2 wood cuts, 7 plates. (M. C. XIX.)

CONTENTS.

BEAN, T. H. A list of European fishes in the collection of the United States National Museum.

On the species of Astroscopus of the Eastern United States.

On the occurrence of *Hippoglossus vulgaris*, Flem., at Unalashka and St. Michael's, Alaska.

Description of an apparently new species of *Gasterosteus* (*G. atkinsii*) from the Schoodic Lakes, Maine.

Description of a new fish from Alaska (*Anarrhichas lepturus*), with notes upon other species of the genus *Anarrhichas.*

Notes on collection of fishes from eastern Georgia.

Description of a new species of *Amiurus* (*A. ponderosus*) from the Mississippi river.

Descriptions of two species of fishes, collected by Prof. A. Dugès in Central Mexico.

Descriptions of some genera and species of Alaskan fishes.

See also under Goode and Bean.

BREWER, T. M. Notes on the nests and eggs of the eight North American species of empidonaces.

COOPER, J. G. On the migrations and nesting habits of west coast birds.

COUES, E. Fourth instalment of ornithological bibliography, being a list of faunal publications relating to British birds.

GÄRKE, H. On the birds of Heligoland.

GOODE, G. B. A study of the trunk fishes (*Ostraciontidæ*), with notes upon the American species of the family.

A preliminary catalogue of the fishes of the St. John's river and the east coast of Florida, with descriptions of a new genus and three new species.

Description of a new species of amber fish (*Seriola stearnsii*) obtained near Pensacola, Fla., by Mr. Silas Stearns.

333. Proceedings of National Museum. Vol. II—Continued.

GOODE, G. B.; BEAN, T. H. Description of *Alepocephalus bairdii*, a new species of fish from the deep-sea fauna of the western Atlantic.

Description of a species of *Lycodes* (*L. paxillus*), obtained by the United States Fish Commission.

Description of a new species of *Liparis* (*L. ranula*), obtained by the United States Fish Commission off Halifax, Nova Scotia.

Catalogue of a collection of fishes sent from Pensacola, Fla., and vicinity, by Mr. Silas Stearns, with descriptions of six new species.

Description of a new genus and species of fish, *Lopholatilus chamæleonticeps*, from the south of New England.

On the occurrence of *Lycodes vahlii*, Reinhardt, on La Have and Grand Banks.

Catalogue of a collection of fishes obtained in the Gulf of Mexico by Dr. J. W. Velie, with description of seven new species.

HARGER, O. Notes on New England *Isopoda*.

JORDAN, D. S. Notes on certain typical specimens of American fishes in the British Museum and in the Museum d'Histoire Naturelle, at Paris.

Description of new species of North American fishes.

Notes on a collection of fishes obtained in the streams of Guanajuato and in Chapala lake, Mexico, by Prof. A. Dugès.

KIDDER, J. H. Report of experiments upon the animal heat of fishes, made at Provincetown, Mass., during the summer of 1879, in connection with operations of the United States Fish Commission.

LOCKINGTON, W. N. Review of the *Pleuronectidæ* of San Francisco.

Descriptions of new genera and species of fishes from the coast of California.

MERRILL, J. C. On the habits of the Rocky Mountain goat.

PRATT, R. H. List of names, ages, tribe, &c., of Indian boys and girls at Hampton Normal and Agricultural Institute, Virginia, plaster casts of whose heads were taken by Clark Mills, Esq., March, 1879.

SMITH, S. I. Occurrence of *Chelura terebrans*, a crustacean destructive to the timber of submarine structures, on the coast of the United States.

Notice of a new species of the *Willemœsia* group of crustacea (recent *Eryontidæ*.)

VERRILL, A. E. Notice of recent additions to the marine invertebrata of the northeastern coast of America, with descriptions of new genera and species and critical remarks on others.

VERRILL, A. E.; RATHBUN, R. List of marine invertebrata from the New England coast, distributed by the United States Commission of Fish and Fisheries.

WHITE, C. A. Descriptions of new species of carboniferous invertebrate fossils.

Descriptions of new cretaceous invertebrate fossils from Kansas and Texas.

Note on *Endothyra ornata*.

Note on *Criocardium* and *Ethmocardium*.

334. List of described species of Humming Birds. By DANIEL GIRAUD ELLIOT. 1879. 8vo., pp. 22. (M. C. XVI.)

335. List of the Principal Scientific and Literary Institutions in the United States, May, 1879. 1879. 8vo., pp. 6. (M. C. XVI.)

336. Smithsonian Miscellaneous Collections. Vol. XVII. 1880. 8vo., pp. 1034.

CONTENTS.

Documents relative to the origin and history of the Smithsonian Institution. No. 328.

337. Smithsonian Miscellaneous Collections. Vol. XVIII. 1880. 8vo., pp. 851.

CONTENTS.

Journals of the Board of Regents, Reports of Committees, Statistics, etc. No. 329.

338. Notes on the Life and Character of Joseph Henry. Read before the Philosophical Society of Washington, October 26, 1878. By JAMES C. WELLING. 1880. 8vo., pp. 30, 1 plate. (Portrait.) (M. C. XXI.)

339. A Memoir of Joseph Henry: a Sketch of his Scientific Work. Read before the Philosophical Society of Washington, October 26, 1878. By WILLIAM B. TAYLOR. 1880. 8vo., pp. 225, 1 plate. (Portrait.) (M. C. XXI.)

340. Smithsonian Contributions to Knowledge. Vol. XXII. 1880. 4to., pp. 537, 474 woodcuts, 20 plates.

CONTENTS.

JONES, J. Explorations of aboriginal remains of Tennessee. No. 259.
HABEL, S. Sculptures of Santa Lucia Cosumaluhuapa, in Guatemala. No. 269.
RAU, C. Archæological collection of U. S. National Museum. No. 287.
RAU, C. Palenque tablet in the U. S. National Museum. No. 331.
DALL, W. H. Remains of later pre-historic man in Alaska. No. 318.

341. Annual Report of the Board of Regents of the Smithsonian Institution, for the year 1878. 45th Congress, 3d Session. Senate, Mis. Doc. No. 59. 1879. 8vo., pp. 575, 12 woodcuts.

CONTENTS.

BAIRD, S. F. Secretary's report of operations.
Report of Government explorations and surveys.
Acts and resolutions of Congress relative to the Smithsonian Institution and the National Museum. Forty-fifth Congress, 2d and 3d Sess., 1878, 1879.
BOARD OF REGENTS, Proceedings of
GRAY, A. Biographical memoir of Joseph Henry.
ARAGO, F. Biography of Condorcet.
FAVRE, E. Biographical notice of Louis Agassiz.

341. Report for 1878—Continued.

TAYLOR, W. B. Henry and the telegraph.
LAUTENBACH, B. F. Irritation of a polarized nerve.
WOOD, H. C. Researches upon fever.
LECONTE, J. Constants of nature.
List of apparatus available for scientific researches.
OBER, F. A. Ornithology of the Carribee Islands.
KUMLIEN, L. Report of explorations in Greenland.
HENRY, J. Researches in sound.

342. Contributions to the Natural History of Arctic America, made in connection with the Howgate Polar Expedition, 1877-'78. By LUDWIG KUMLIEN. 1879. 8vo., pp. 179. (M. C. XXIII.) *Bulletin of the National Museum, No.* 15.

CONTENTS.

KUMLIEN, L. Ethnology, mammals, and birds.
BEAN, T. H. Fishes.
VERRILL, A. E. Annelides, molluscoids, and radiates.
DALL, W. H. Mollusks.
INSECTS:
EDWARDS, W. H. Diurnal lepidoptera.
SCUDDER, S. H. and others. Hymenoptera, nocturnal lepidoptera, diptera, coleoptera, neuroptera, and arachnida.
GRAY, A. Plants.
TUCKERMAN, E. Lichens.
FARLOW, W. G. Algæ.

343. Annual Reports of the Secretary of the Smithsonian Institution, JOSEPH HENRY, 1865 to 1877. 1880. 8vo., pp. 548.

344. Check-list of Publications of the Smithsonian Institution, July, 1879. 1879. 8vo., pp. 16. (M. C. XVI.)

345. Annual Report of the Board of Regents of the Smithsonian Institution, for the year 1879. 1880. 46th Congress, 2d Session. Senate Mis. Doc. No. 54. 8vo., pp. 631, 216 woodcuts.

CONTENTS.

BAIRD, S. F. Secretary's report of operations.
BOARD OF REGENTS, Proceedings of
Acts and resolutions of Congress relative to the Smithsonian Institution and the National Museum. 45th Congress, 3d Session; 46th Congress, 2d Session. 1878-1880.
Report of the National Museum Building Commission.
Report of the Architects.
RHEES, W. J. James Smithson and his bequest.
KNIGHT, E. H. A study of the savage weapons at the Centennial Exhibition, Philadelphia, 1876.
ANTHROPOLOGY:
WORSAAE, J. J. A. The preservation of antiquities and national monuments in Denmark.
HAVARD, V. The French half-breeds of the Northwest.

345. Report for 1879—Continued.

NORRIS, P. W. Prehistoric remains in Montana, between Fort Ellis and the Yellowstone river.

BRACKETT, A. G. The Shoshone or Snake Indians: their religion, superstitions, and manners.

BURR, R. T. Ruins in White river cañon, Pima county, Arizona.

ARMSTRONG, T. Mounds in Winnebago county, Wisconsin.

ANDERSON, W. G. Mounds near Quincy, Ill., and in Wisconsin.

EVANS, S. B. Notes on some of the principal mounds in Des Moines valley.

DAHLBERG, R. N. and C. Composition of ancient pottery found near the mouth of Chequest creek, at Pittsburg, on the Des Moines river.

BROADHEAD, G. C. Prehistoric evidences in Missouri.

THOMPSON, T. Mounds in Muscatine county, Iowa, and Rock Island county, Illinois.

TŒLLNER, A. Antiquities of Rock Island county, Illinois.

OEHLER, A. Stone cists near Highland, Madison county, Illinois.

MITCHELL, B. Mounds in Pike county, Illinois.

ADAMS, W. H. Mounds in the Spoon River valley, Illinois.

QUICK, E. R. Mounds in Franklin county, Indiana.

JACKMAN, F. Mounds and earthworks of Rush county, Indiana.

JONES, JR., C. C. Primitive manufacture of spear and arrow points along the line of the Savannah river.

GESNER, W. Mica beds in Alabama.

HOUGH, J. Mounds in Washington county, Mississippi.

BRODNAX, B. H. Mounds in Moorehouse Parish, Louisiana.

BEAUCHAMP, W. M. Wampum belts of the Six Nations.

ANDREWS, F. D. Indian relics from Schoharie, New York.

WALKER, S. T. Preliminary explorations among the Indian mounds in Southern Florida.

WALKER, S. T. Report on the shell heaps of Tampa bay, Florida.

NUTTER, F. H. Mounds on Gideon's farm, near Excelsior, Hennepin county, Minnesota.

MASON, O. T. Summary of correspondence of the Smithsonian Institution previous to January 1, 1880, in answer to circular No. 316.

MASON, O. T. Anthropological investigations during the year 1879.

BOEHMER, G. H. Index to papers on anthropology published by the Smithsonian Institution, 1847 to 1878.

PISKO, F. J. On the present fundamental principles of physics.

VON BAUMHAUER, E. H. A universal meteorograph, designed for detached observatories.

HOLDEN, E. S. Reports of American observatories.

346. Smithsonian Contributions to Knowledge. Vol. XXIII. 1881. 4to., pp. 766, 160 woodcuts, 18 plates of 165 figures.

CONTENTS.

CLARK, H. J. Lucernariæ and their allies. No. 242.

HILGARD, E. W. Geology of Lower Louisiana and Petite Anse Island. No. 248.

BARNARD, J. G. Internal structure of the earth. No. 310.

ELLIOT, D. G. Classification and synopsis of the trochilidæ. No. 317.

WOOD, H. C. Fever; a study in physiology. No. 357.

347. Nomenclature of Clouds. Two lithographic plates. 1851. 8vo.

348. Report on the Fishes of the New Jersey Coast, as observed in the Summer of 1854. By SPENCER F. BAIRD. 1855. 8vo., pp. 40.

349. Suggestions for the Sanitary Drainage of Washington City. TONER LECTURE No. VIII. Delivered May 26, 1880. By GEORGE E. WARING, JR. June, 1880. 8vo., pp. 26.

350. A Map of the Stars near the North Pole; for observations on the Aurora. Copied from the Map used in the Toronto Observations. 1856. 15 inches by 12 inches.

351. On the Distribution of the Forests and Trees of North America; with notes on its Physical Geography. By J. G. COOPER. 1859. 8vo., pp. 36, 1 woodcut.

352. Brief Abstract of a series of six Lectures on the Principles of Linguistic Science. Delivered at the Smithsonian Institution in March, 1864. By WILLIAM D. WHITNEY. 1864. 8vo., pp. 22.

353. Tables and Results of the Precipitation, in Rain and Snow, in the United States, and at some stations in adjacent parts of North America, and in Central and South America. Collected by the Smithsonian Institution, and discussed under the direction of Joseph Henry and Spencer F. Baird, Secretaries. By CHARLES A. SCHOTT. May, 1881. 4to., pp. 269, 8 woodcuts, 5 plates, 5 charts.

354. Essay on the Velocity of Light. By M. DELAUNAY. Translated for the Smithsonian Institution by Alfred M. Mayer. 1864. 8vo., pp. 31.

355. Ozone and Antozone. By CHARLES M. WETHERILL. 1864. 8vo., pp. 12.

356. A Memorial of Joseph Henry. (Published by order of Congress.) 1880. 8vo., pp. 532, 1 plate.

CONTENTS.

INTRODUCTION. Proceedings in Congress relative to public commemoration.

PART I.—OBSEQUIES OF JOSEPH HENRY.

- WAITE, M. R. Mortuary announcement.
- Proceedings of the Board of Regents.
- The funeral, May 16, 1878.
- HODGE, C. Prayer at the funeral.
- MITCHELL, S. S. Funeral sermon.

PART II.—MEMORIAL EXERCISES AT THE CAPITOL.

- Announcement by Executive Committee of the Regents.
- McCOSH, J. Introductory prayer.
- HAMLIN, H. Address.

WITHERS, R. E. Address.
GRAY, A. Address.
CLYMER, H. Reading of telegrams.
ROGERS, W. B. Address.
GARFIELD, J. A. Address.
COX, S. S. Address.
SHERMAN, W. T. Address.
SUNDERLAND, B. Concluding prayer.

PART III.—MEMORIAL PROCEEDINGS OF SOCIETIES.
Proceedings of the Philosophical Society of Washington.
Proceedings of the Albany Institute.
MEADS, O. Memorial minute.
Proceedings of the United States Light-House Board.
DOD, S. B. Memorial discourse.
CAMERON, H. C. Reminiscences.
WELLING, J. C. Memorial address.
TAYLOR, W. B. Memorial address.
LOVERING, J. Obituary memoir.
NEWCOMB, S. Biographical memoir.
MAYER, A. M. Memorial address.

APPENDIX. Proceedings in Congress regarding the erection of a monument to Joseph Henry.

357. Fever: A Study in Morbid and Normal Physiology. By HORATIO C. WOOD. January, 1878. 8vo., pp. 263, 16 woodcuts, 5 plates of 16 figures. (S. C. XXIII.)

358. The Constants of Nature. Part IV. Atomic Weight Determinations: A Digest of the Investigations published since 1814. By GEORGE F. BECKER. August, 1880. 8vo., pp. 152.

359. A Planisphere of the Visible Heavens, extending to 40° of south declination, for observations on Meteoric displays. Prepared by a Committee of the Connecticut Academy of Arts and Sciences. 1864. 30 inches by 24½ inches.

360. Palafittes, or Lacustrian Constructions of the Lake of Neuchatel By E. DESOR. Translated for the Smithsonian Institution. 1865. 8vo., pp. 53, 118 woodcuts.

361. An account of the Aboriginal Inhabitants of the California Peninsula, as given by JACOB BAEGERT, a German Jesuit Missionary, who lived there seventeen years during the second half of the last century. Translated and arranged for the Smithsonian Institution, by CHARLES RAU. 1865. 8vo., pp. 41.

362. Artificial Shell-deposits in New Jersey. By CHARLES RAU. 1865. 8vo., pp. 6, 1 woodcut.

363. Instructions for collecting Land and Fresh Water Shells. By JAMES LEWIS. 1866. 8vo., pp. 8.

364. Outline of a Systematic Review of the Class of Birds. By W. LILLJEBORG. Translated for the Smithsonian Institution. 1866. 8vo., pp. 16.

365. Notes on the Tinneh or Chepewyan Indians of British and Russian America. 1.—The Eastern Tinneh; by BERNARD R. ROSS. 2.—The Loucheux Indians; by WILLIAM L. HARDISTY. 3.—The Kutchin Tribes; by STRACHAN JONES. Compiled by GEORGE GIBBS. 1866. 8vo., pp. 25, 11 woodcuts.

366. Directions for Collecting, Preserving, and Transporting Specimens of Diatomacea, and other Microscopic Organisms. By ARTHUR M. EDWARDS. 1867. 8vo., pp. 7.

367. Sketch of the Flora of Alaska. By J. T. ROTHROCK. 1867. 8vo., pp. 33.

368. Indian Pottery. By CHARLES RAU. 1867. 8vo., pp. 11, 9 woodcuts.

369. Dorpat and Poulkova. By CLEVELAND ABBE. 1867. 8vo., pp. 23.

370. A Deposit of Agricultural Flint Implements found in Southern Illinois. By CHARLES RAU. 1868. 8vo., pp. 9, 5 woodcuts.

371. The Metric System of Weights and Measures, with Tables. Prepared for the Smithsonian Institution. By H. A. NEWTON. 1868. 8vo., pp. 23.

372. Drilling in Stone without the use of Metal. By CHARLES RAU. 1869. 8vo., pp, 11, 12 woodcuts.

373. Meteorological Stations, and Observers of the Smithsonian Institution, in North America and adjacent Islands, from the year 1849, to the end of the year 1868. 1869. 8vo., pp. 42.

374. Three Rain-Charts of the United States, showing the distribution by Isohyetal lines of the mean precipitation in rain and melted snow. 1, for the Summer months; 2, for the Winter months; 3, for the Year. 1870. 20 inches by 14 inches.

375. Thoughts on the Nature and Origin of Force. By WILLIAM B. TAYLOR. 1870. 8vo., pp. 19.

376. On the Chemistry of the Earth. By T. STERRY HUNT. 1871. 8vo., pp. 26.

377. The Diamond and other Precious Stones. By M. BABINET. Translated for the Smithsonian Institution, by John Stearns. 1872. 8vo., pp. 33.

378. The Language of the Dakota or Sioux Indians. By F. L. O. RŒHRIG. 1872. 8vo., pp. 19.

379. Eulogy on Prof. Alexander Dallas Bache, late Superintendent of the U. S. Coast Survey, President of the National Academy of Sciences, etc. By JOSEPH HENRY. 1872. 8vo., pp. 28.

380. The Scientific Education of Mechanics and Artizans. By ANDREW P. PEABODY. 1873. 8vo., pp. 13.

381. Temperature-Chart of the United States, showing the distribution, by Isothermal lines, of the mean temperature for the Year. 1873. 16½ inches by 10½ inches.

382. North American Stone Implements. By CHARLES RAU. 1873. 8vo., pp. 16, 7 woodcuts.

383. Archæological Researches in Nicaragua. By J. F. BRANSFORD. 1881. 4to., pp. 100, 202 woodcuts, 2 plates of 40 figures.

384. Circular in reference to Shipping Fresh Fish and other Animals. By S. F. BAIRD. 1881. 8vo., pp. 4.

385. Ancient Aboriginal Trade in North America. By CHARLES RAU. 1873. 8vo., pp. 49.

386. Explanation of the Principles of Crystallography and Crystallophysics. By ARISTIDES BREZINA. Translated for the Smithsonian Institution, by T. Egleston. 1874. 8vo., pp. 36.

387. Three Temperature-Charts of the United States, showing the distribution, by Isothermal curves, of the mean temperature of the lower atmosphere. 1, for the Summer months; 2, for the Winter months; 3, for the Year. 1874. 28½ inches by 19¾ inches.

388. Temperature Chart of the United States, showing the distribution, by Isothermal lines, of the mean temperature for the year. 1874. 20 inches by 13½ inches.

389. An Account of Investigations relative to Illuminating Materials. (From the Light-House Board Report for 1875.) By JOSEPH HENRY. 1881. 8vo., pp. 25.

390. On Tides and Tidal Action in Harbors. By JULIUS E. HILGARD, 1875. 8vo., pp. 22, 15 woodcuts.

393. The Mound Builders, and Platycnemism in Michigan. By HENRY GILLMAN. 1874. 8vo., pp. 28, 12 woodcuts. Also, Certain Characteristics pertaining to Ancient Man in Michigan. By HENRY GILLMAN. 1877. 8vo., pp. 13, 13 woodcuts.

394. The Stone Age in New Jersey. By C. C. ABBOTT. 1877. 8vo. pp. 136, 58 plates of woodcuts, containing 223 figures.

395. Kinetic Theories of Gravitation. By WILLIAM B. TAYLOR. 1877. 8vo., pp. 80.

396. Notes on the History and Climate of New Mexico. By THOMAS A. MCPARLIN. 1877. 8vo., pp. 30.

397. The Latimer Collection of Antiquities from Porto Rico, in the National Museum at Washington, D. C. By OTIS T. MASON. 1877. 8vo., pp. 23. 14 plates of woodcuts, containing 60 figures.

398. Short Memoirs on Meteorological Subjects: By Julius Hann; L. Sohncke; Theodore. Reye; William Ferrel; A. Colding; and M. Peslin. Compiled and Translated for the Smithsonian Institution by CLEVELAND ABBE. 1878. 8vo., pp. 104.

399. Color Blindness in its Relation to Accidents by Rail and Sea. By FRITHIOF HOLMGREN. Translated for the Smithsonian Institution, by M. L. Duncan. 1878. 8vo., pp. 72, 5 woodcuts.

400. Aboriginal Structures in Georgia. By CHARLES C. JONES, Jr. 1878. 8vo., pp. 13, 5 woodcuts.

401. On the change of the Mexican Axolotl to an Amblystoma. By AUGUST WEISMANN. Translated for the Smithsonian Institution, by Henry M. Douglass. 1878. 8vo., pp. 29.

402. The Stock-in-Trade of an Aboriginal Lapidary. By CHARLES RAU. 1878. 8vo., pp. 9, 16 woodcuts.

403. Observations on a Gold Ornament found in a Mound in Florida. By CHARLES RAU. 1878. 8vo., pp. 6, 1 woodcut.

404. On a Polychrome Bead from Florida. By S. S. HALDEMAN. 1878. 8vo., pp. 6, 2 woodcuts.

405. An Historical Sketch of Henry's Contribution to the Electro-Magnetic Telegraph; with an account of the origin and development of Prof. Morse's invention. By WILLIAM B. TAYLOR. 1879. 8vo., pp 103.

406. Henry on Sound. A Summary of Researches in Sound conducted in the service of the United States Light-House Board, by JOSEPH HENRY, during the years 1865 to 1877. 1879. 8vo., pp. 106, 12 woodcuts.

407. Biographical Memoir of Joseph Henry. Prepared in behalf of the Board of Regents. By ASA GRAY. 1879. 8vo., pp. 35.

408. Report of the Secretary of the Smithsonian Institution, for the year 1878. By S. F. BAIRD. 1879. 8vo., pp. 60.

409. Report of the National Museum Building Commission, and of the Architects, for 1879. 1880. 8vo., pp. 18, 2 folding plates.

410. Reports of Astronomical Observatories for 1879. By E. S. HOLDEN. 1880. 8vo., pp. 60.

411. The effect of Irritation of a Polarized Nerve. By B. F. LAUTENBACH. 1880. 8vo., pp. 59.

412. On the Zoological Position of Texas. By EDWARD D. COPE. 1880. 8vo., pp. 55. *Bulletin of the National Museum No.* 17.

413. Exhibit of the Fisheries and Fish Culture of the United States of America, at the Internationale Fischerei Austsellung, at Berlin, April 20, 1880, and forming a part of the collection of the National Museum, made by the United States Fish Commission. Prepared under the direction of G. BROWN GOODE. 1880. 8vo., pp. 279. *Bulletin of the National Museum, No.* 18.

414. Base Chart of the United States. Prepared by CHARLES A. SCHOTT. 1880. (28½ x 19½ inches.)

415. A Study of the Savage Weapons at the Centennial Exhibition, Philadelphia, 1876. By EDWARD H. KNIGHT. 1880. 8vo., pp. 90, 147 woodcuts.

416. Smithsonian Miscellaneous Collections. Vol. XIX. 1880. 8vo., pp. 1034.

CONTENTS.

Proceedings of the U. S. National Museum. Vol. I. 1878. No. 332.
Proceedings of the U. S. National Museum. Vol. II. 1879. No. 333.

417. Henry as a Discoverer. A Memorial Address, delivered before the American Association for the Advancement of Science, August 26, 1880. By ALFRED M. MAYER. 1880. 8vo., pp. 36.

418. Report of the Secretary of the Smithsonian Institution, for the year 1879. By SPENCER F. BAIRD. 1880. 8vo., pp. 76.

419. Report of the Secretary of the Smithsonian Institution, for the year 1880. By SPENCER F. BAIRD. 1881. 8vo., pp. 88.

420. Anthropological Investigations in 1879. By OTIS T. MASON. 1881. 8vo., pp. 30.

421. Index to Anthropological Articles in Publications of the Smithsonian Institution. By GEORGE H. BŒHMER. 1881. 8vo., pp. 10.

422. Nomenclature of North American Birds chiefly contained in the United States National Museum. By ROBERT RIDGWAY. 1881. 8vo., pp. 94. *Bulletin of the National Museum, No.* 21.

423. Smithsonian Miscellaneous Collections. Vol. XX. 1881. 8vo. pp. 846.

CONTENTS.

Bulletin of the Philosophical Society of Washington:
- Vol. I, March, 1871, to June, 1874, pp. 218.
- Vol. II, October 10, 1874, to November 2, 1878, pp. 452.
- Vol. III, November 9, 1878, to June 19, 1880, pp. 169.

424. Smithsonian Miscellaneous Collections. Vol. XXI. 1881. 8vo., pp. 773, 42 woodcuts, 13 plates.

CONTENTS.

RHEES, W. J. James Smithson and his bequest. No. 330.
SMITHSON, J. Scientific writings. No. 327.
JOHNSON, W. R. Scientific character and researches of Smithson. No. 327.
IRBY, J. R. McD. The works and character of Smithson. No. 327.
A memorial of Joseph Henry. No. 356.

425. Proceedings of the United States National Museum for 1880. Vol. III. 1881. 8vo., pp. 595, 5 cuts, 2 plates.

CONTENTS.

BEAN, T. H. Description of a new hake (*Phycis earlii*), from South Carolina, and a note on the occurrence of *Phycis regius* in North Carolina.
Check-list of duplicates of North American fishes distributed by the Smithsonian Institution in behalf of the United States National Museum, 1877–'80.
CATTIE, S. T. On the genitalia of male eels and their sexual characters.
ENDLICH, F. M. List of species and varieties of minerals in the National Museum of the United States in 1879.
GARMAN, S. Synopsis and descriptions of the American *Rhinobatidæ*.
GILL, T. On the identity of the genus *Leurynnis* Lockington, with *Lycodopsis* Collett.
GOODE, G. B. Descriptions of seven new species of fishes from deep soundings on the Southern New England coast, with diagnoses of two undescribed genera of flounders and a genus related to *Merlucius*.
Fishes from the deep waters on the South coast of New England obtained by the United States Fish Commission in the summer of 1880.
The frigate mackerel (*Auxis Rochei*) on the New England coast.
Notacanthus phasganorus, a new species of *Notacanthidæ* from the Grand Banks of Newfoundland.
HAY, O. P. On a collection of fishes from Eastern Mississippi.

425. Proceedings of National Museum. Vol. III—Continued.

HEILPRIN, A. On some new species of eocene *mollusca* from the Southern United States.

JORDAN, D. S. Notes on a collection of fishes from East Florida, obtained by J. A. Henshall.

Notes on a collection of fishes from St. John's river, Florida, obtained by A. H. Curtiss.

Note on a forgotten paper of Dr. Ayres, and its bearing on the nomenclature of the cyprinoid fishes of the San Francisco markets.

Note on "*Sema*" and "*Dacentrus*."

Description of a new species of *Caranx* (*Caranx Beani*), from Beaufort, North Carolina.

JORDAN, D. S.; GILBERT, C. H. Notes on a collection of fishes from San Diego, California.

Description of new flounder (*Xystreurys liolepis*), from Santa Catalina Island, California.

Description of a new ray (*Platyrhina triseriata*), from the coast of California.

Description of a new species of "rock cod" (*Sebastichthys serriceps*), from the coast of California.

On the occurrence of *Cephaloscyllium laticeps* (Duméril) Gill on the coast of California.

On the oil shark of Southern California (*Galeorhinus galeus.*)

Description of a new flounder (*Pleuronichthys verticalis*), from the coast of California, with notes on other species.

Notes on sharks from the coast of California.

On the generic relations of *Platyrhina exasperata*.

Description of a new species of *Sebastichthys* (*Sebastichthys miniatus*), from Monterey bay, California.

Description of a new species of "rock fish" (*Sebastichthys carnatus*), from the coast of California.

Description of a new species of ray (*Raia stellulata*), from Monterey, California.

Description of a new species of *Xiphister* and *Apodichthys*, from Monterey, California.

Description of two new species of *Sebastichthys* (*Sebastichthys entomelas* and *Sebastichthys rhodochloris*), from Monterey bay, Cal.

Description of a new agonoid fish (*Brachiopsis xyosternus*), from Monterey bay, California.

Description of a new flounder (*Hippoglossoides exilis*), from the coast of California.

Description of a new species of ray (*Raia rhina*) from the coast of California.

Description of two new species of fishes (*Ascelicthys rhodorus* and *Scytalina cerdale*), from Neah Bay, Washington Territory.

Description of two new species of scopeloid fishes (*Sudis ringens* and *Myctophum crenulare*), from Santa Barbara channel, California.

Description of two new species of flounders (*Parophrys ischyurus* and *Hippoglossoides elassodon*), from Puget Sound.

Description of seven new species of sebastoid fishes, from the coast of California.

425. Proceedings of National Museum. Vol. III—Continued.

JORDAN, D. S.; GILBERT, C. H. Description of a new embiotocoid (*Abeona aurora*), from Monterey, California, with notes on a related species.

Description of a new flounder (*Platysomatichthys stomias*), from the coast of California.

Description of a new embiotocoid fish (*Cymatogaster rosaceus*), from the coast of California.

Description of a new species of deep-water fish (*Icichthys Lockingtoni*), from the coast of California.

Description of a new embiotocoid fish (*Ditrema atripes*), from the coast of California.

Description of a new scorpænoid fish (*Sebastichthys maliger*), from the coast of California.

Description of a new scorpænoid fish (*Sebastichthys proriger*), from Monterey Bay, California.

Description of a new agonoid (*Agonus vulsus*), from the coast of California.

Description of a new species of *Hemirhamphus* (*Hemirhamphus Rosæ*), from the coast of California.

Description of a new species of notidanoid shark (*Hexanchus corinus*), from the Pacific coast of the United States.

Description of a new species of *Nemichthys* (*Nemichthys avocetta*), from Puget Sound.

Description of a new species of *Paralepis* (*Paralepis coruscans*), from the Straits of Juan de Fuca.

List of the fishes of the Pacific coast of the United States, with a table showing the distribution of the species.

On the generic relations of *Belone exilis* (Girard).

Notes on a collection of fishes from Utah Lake.

Description of a new species of rockfish (*Sebastichthys chrysomelas*), from the coast of California.

LAWRENCE, G. N. Description of a new species of bird of the family *Turdidæ*, from the island of Dominica, W. I.

Description of a new species of parrot of the genus *Chrysotis*, from the island of Dominica.

Description of a new species of *Icterus*, from the West Indies.

LOCKINGTON, W. N. Remarks on the species of the genus *Chirus* found in San Francisco market, including one hitherto undescribed.

Description of a new fish from Alaska (*Uranidea microstoma*).

Description of a new species of *Agonidæ* (*Brachyopsis verrucosus*), from the coast of California.

Description of a new genus and some new species of California fishes (*Icosteus ænigmaticus* and *Osmerus attenuatus*).

Description of a new chiroid fish (*Myriolepis zonifer*), from Monterey Bay, California.

Description of a new sparoid fish (*Sparus brachysomus*), from Lower California.

Note on a new flat fish (*Lepidopsetta isolepis*), found in the markets of San Francisco.

Description of a new species of *Prionotus* (*Prionotus stephanophrys*), from the coast of California.

RATHBUN, R. The littoral marine fauna of Provincetown, Cape Cod, Massachusetts.

425. Proceedings of National Museum. Vol. III—Continued.

RIDGWAY, R. Revisions of nomenclature of certain North American birds.

A catalogue of the birds of North America.

Catalogue of *Trochilidæ* in the collection of the United States National Museum.

RYDER, J. A. On *Camaraphysema*, a new type of sponge.

List of the North American species of myriapods belonging to the family of the *Lysiopetalidæ*, with a description of a blind form from Luray Cave, Virginia.

SMITH, R. On the occurrence of a species of *Cremnobates* at San Diego, California.

SMITH, S. I. Preliminary notice of the crustacea dredged in 64 to 325 fathoms off the south coast of New England by the United States Fish Commission, in 1880.

SWAN, J. G. The surf smelt of the northwest coast, and the method of taking them by the Quillehute Indians, West Coast of Washington Territory.

The eulachon or candle fish of the northwest coast.

VERRILL, A. E. Notice of recent additions to the marine invertebrata of the northeastern coast of America, with descriptions of new genera and species, and critical remarks on others.

Part II.—*Mollusca*, with notes on *Annelida*, *Echinodermata*, etc., collected by the United States Fish Commission.

Part III.—Catalogue of *mollusca* recently added to the fauna of Southern New England.

WHITE, C. A. Note on the occurrence of *Productus giganteus* in Cal.

Note on *Acrothele*.

Description of a new cretaceous *Pinna* from New Mexico.

Note on the occurrence of *Stricklandia salteri* and *S. davidsoni* in Georgia.

Description of a very large fossil gasteropod, from the State of Puebla, Mexico.

Descriptions of new invertebrate fossils from the mesozoic and cenozoic rocks of Arkansas, Wyoming, Colorado, and Utah.

426. A Synopsis of the Scientific Writings of Sir William Herschel. By EDWARD S. HOLDEN and CHARLES S. HASTINGS. 1881. 8vo., pp. 118.

427. Record of Recent Progress in Science, 1879 and 1880. Astronomy. By EDWARD S. HOLDEN. 1881. 8vo., pp. 39.

428. Record of Recent Progress in Science, 1879 and 1880. Geology and Mineralogy. By GEORGE W. HAWES. 1881. 8vo., pp. 30.

429. Record of Recent Progress in Science, 1879 and 1880. Physics and Chemistry. By GEORGE F. BARKER. 1881. 8vo., pp. 65.

430. Record of Recent Progress in Science, 1879 and 1880. Botany. By WM. G. FARLOW. 1881. 8vo., pp. 19.

431. Record of Recent Progress in Science, 1879 and 1880. Zoology. By THEODORE GILL. 1881. 8vo., pp. 62.

432. Record of Recent Progress in Science, 1880. Anthropology. By OTIS T. MASON. 1881. 8vo., pp. 51.

433. Report of a visit to the Luray Cavern, in Page County, Virginia, under the auspices of the Smithsonian Institution, July 13 and 14, 1880. 1881. 8vo., pp. 12, 6 woodcuts.

434. Report of the National Museum Building Commission and of the Architects for 1880. 1881. 8vo., pp. 12.

435. Discussion of the Barometric Observations of E. S. Snell. By F. H. LOUD. 1881. 8vo., pp. 23, 7 woodcuts.

436. List of Periodicals received by the Smithsonian Institution. 1881. 8vo., pp. 9.

437. Check-list of Publications of the Smithsonian Institution to December, 1881. 1881. 8vo., pp. 22.

438. Reports of Astronomical Observatories for 1880. By E. S. HOLDEN and GEORGE H. BŒHMER. 1881. 8vo., pp. 128.

439. Warming and Ventilating Occupied Buildings. By ARTHUR MORIN. Translated for the Smithsonian Institution by Clarence B. Young. 1882. 8vo., pp. 92, 32 woodcuts.

440. Articles on Anthropological Subjects contributed to the Annual Reports of the Smithsonian Institution from 1863 to 1877. By CHARLES RAU. 1882. 8vo., pp. 180, 53 woodcuts.

CONTENTS.

RAU, C., Preface by. (February, 1882.)

BAEGERT, J. Account of the aboriginal inhabitants of the Californian peninsula. Translated and arranged for the Smithsonian by Chas. Rau. From Smithsonian Report for 1863–64. No. 361.

Agricultural implements of the North American stone period. From Report for 1863.

Artificial shell deposits in New Jersey. From Report for 1864. No. 362.

Indian pottery. From Report for 1866. No. 368.

Drilling in stone without metal. From Report for 1868. No. 372.

Deposit of agricultural flint implements in Southern Illinois. From Report for 1868. No. 370.

Memoir of C. F. P. Von Martius. From Report for 1869. No. 251.

Ancient aboriginal trade in North America. From Report for 1872. No. 385.

North American stone implements. From Report for 1872. No. 382.

ROMER, F. F. Prehistoric antiquities of Hungary. Translated by Chas. Rau. From Report for 1876. No. 392.

Stock in trade of an aboriginal lapidary. From Report for 1877. No. 402.

Observations on a gold ornament from a mound in Florida. From Report for 1877. No. 403.

441. The Constants of Nature. Part V. A Recalculation of the Atomic Weights. By FRANK WIGGLESWORTH CLARKE. 1882. 8vo., pp. 293.

442. Annual Report of the Board of Regents of the Smithsonian Institution, for the year 1880. Forty-sixth Congress, 3d Session, Senate Mis. Doc. No. 31. 1881. 8vo., pp. 782, 13 woodcuts.

CONTENTS.

BAIRD, S. F. Secretary's report of operations.
List of periodicals received by the Institution.
Rules for the examination of specimens submitted to the Institution.
TAYLOR, F. W. Report of the chemist.
Additions to the collections of the National Museum.
Additions to Museum by the Berlin International Fisheries Exhibition.
STEVENSON, J. Report of explorations in New Mexico and Arizona.
Receipts and distribution of specimens.
GOODE, G. B. The first decade of the U. S. Fish Commission.
Report of the Executive Committee on the Henry statue.
Report of the Executive Committee for 1880.
BOARD OF REGENTS; Proceedings of
Report of the National Museum Building Commission for 1880.
Report of the Superintending Architects of the Museum Building.
RECORD OF RECENT SCIENTIFIC PROGRESS:
- BAIRD, S. F. Introduction.
- HOLDEN, E. S. Astronomy.
- HAWES, G. W. Geology.
- BARKER, G. F. Physics.
- BARKER, G. F. Chemistry.
- HAWES, G. W. Mineralogy.
- FARLOW, W. G. Botany.
- GILL, T. Zoology.
- MASON, O. T. Anthropology.

MASON, O. T. Bibliography of anthropology.
MASON, O. T. Abstracts of anthropological correspondence.
MASON, O. T. Report on Luray Cavern.
LOUD, F. H. Discussion of Prof. Snell's barometric observations.
HENRY, J. Investigation of illuminating materials.
HOLDEN, E. S.; HASTINGS, C. S. Synopsis of the scientific writings of William Herschel.
HOLDEN, E. S.; BŒHMER, G. H. Reports of astronomical observatories.

443. Results of Meteorological Observations made at Providence, Rhode Island, extending over a period of forty-five years, from December, 1831, to December, 1876. By ALEXIS CASWELL. 1882. 4to, pp. 40.

444. Guide to the Flora of Washington and Vicinity. By LESTER F. WARD. 1881. 8vo., pp. 265. One map. *Bulletin of the National Museum, No. 22.*

445. Plan of Organization and Regulations of the United States National Museum. By G. BROWN GOODE. 1882. 8vo., pp. 58. Two woodcuts. (*Circular of U. S. National Museum, No.* 1.)

446. Circular addressed to Friends of the Museum. By SPENCER F. BAIRD. 1882. 8vo., pp. 2. (*Circular of U. S. National Museum, No.* 2.)

447. Circular in reference to Petroleum Collections. By SPENCER F. BAIRD. 1882. 8vo., pp. 4. (*Circular of U. S. National Museum, No.* 3.)

448. Circular concerning the Department of Insects. By SPENCER F. BAIRD. 1882. 8vo., pp. 2. (*Circular of U. S. National Museum, No.* 4.)

449. Establishment and Officers of the Smithsonian Institution and National Museum, January 1, 1882. 1882. 8vo., pp. 2. (*Circular of U. S. National Museum, No.* 5.)

450. Classification and Arrangement of the Materia Medica Collection. By JAMES M. FLINT. 1882. 8vo., pp. 2. (*Circular of U. S. National Museum, No.* 6.)

451. A Classification of the Forms in which Drugs and Medicines appear, and are administered. By JAMES M. FLINT. 1882. 8vo., pp. 8. (*Circular of U. S. National Museum, No.* 7.)

452. Memoranda for Collectors of Drugs for the Materia Medica Section of the National Museum. By JAMES M. FLINT. 1882. 8vo., pp. 2. (*Circular of U. S. National Museum, No.* 8.)

453. Circular in reference to the Building-Stone Collection. By SPENCER F. BAIRD. 1882. 8vo., pp. 6. (*Circular of U. S. National Museum, No.* 9.)

454. Two letters on the work of the National Museum. By BARNET PHILLIPS. 1882. 8vo., pp. 10. (*Circular of U. S. National Museum, No.* 10.)

455. A Provisional Classification of the Food Collections. By G. BROWN GOODE. 1882. 8vo., pp. 18. (*Circular of U. S. National Museum, No.* 11.)

456. Classification of the Collections of the U. S. National Museum to illustrate the Art of Taxidermy. By W. T. HORNADAY. 1882. 8vo., pp. 2. (*Circular of U. S. National Museum, No.* 12.)

457. Outline of a Scheme of Classification for the Collections in the United States National Museum. By G. BROWN GOODE. 1882. 8vo., pp. 4. (*Circular of U. S. National Museum, No.* 13.)

458. Circular requesting material for the Library of the United States National Museum. By SPENCER F. BAIRD. 1882. 8vo., pp. 4. (*Circular of U. S. National Museum, No.* 14.)

459. The Organization and Objects of the United States National Museum. By G. BROWN GOODE. 1882. 8vo., pp. 4. (*Circular of U. S. National Museum, No.* 15.)

460. Directions for Collecting and Preserving Plants. By LESTER F. WARD. 1882. 8vo., pp. 32.

461. Check-List. Flora of Washington and Vicinity. By LESTER F. WARD. 1882. 8vo., pp. 62.

462. Catalogue of Old World Birds in the U. S. National Museum. By ROBERT RIDGWAY. 1882. 8vo., pp. 20.

463. Bibliography of the Fishes of the Pacific Coast of the United States, to the end of 1879. By THEODORE GILL. 1882. 8vo., pp. 77. (M. C. XXIII.) *Bulletin of National Museum, No.* 11.

464. Directions for Collecting and Preserving Fish. By TARLETON H. BEAN. 1881. 8vo., pp. 6.

465. List of Marine Invertebrates, mainly from the New England Coast, distributed by the U. S. National Museum. Series II. By RICHARD RATHBUN. 1881. 8vo., pp. 6.

466. Directory of Officers, Collaborators, Employés, etc., of the Smithsonian Institution, National Museum, Geological Survey, Bureau of Ethnology, and Fish Commission. 1882. 8vo., pp. 8.

467. Proceedings of the United States National Museum for 1881. Vol. IV. 1882. 8vo., pp. 600, 13 cuts, 2 plates. (M. C. XXII.)

CONTENTS.

BAIRD, S. F. Notes on certain aboriginal shell mounds on the coast of New Brunswick and of New England.

BEAN, T. H. Descriptions of new species of fishes (*Uranidea marginata*, *Potamocottus Bendirei*) and of *Myctophum crenulare* J. and G.

Notes on some fishes from Hudson's Bay.

Descriptions of new fishes from Alaska and Siberia.

Directions for collecting and preserving fish.

A preliminary catalogue of the fishes of Alaskan and adjacent waters.

A partial bibliography of the fishes of the Pacific coast of the United States and of Alaska, for the year 1880.

Notes on a collection of fishes made by Capt. Henry E. Nichols, U. S. N., in British Columbia and Southern Alaska, with descriptions of new species and a new genus (*Delolepis*).

See also under Goode and Bean.

BENDIRE, C. Notes on *Salmonidæ* of the upper Columbia.

467. Proceedings of National Museum. Vol. IV—Continued.

BOYD, C. H. Remains of the walrus (?) in Maine.

CARLIN, W. E. Observations of *Siredon lichenoides.*

DALL, W. H. On the genera of chitons.

On certain limpets and chitons from the deep waters off the eastern coast of the United States.

ENDLICH, F. M. An analysis of water destructive to fish in the Gulf of Mexico.

FARLOW, W. G. Report on the contents of two bottles of water from the Gulf of Mexico, forwarded by the Smithsonian Institution.

GILBERT, C. H. See under Jordan and Gilbert.

GILL, T. Note on the Latiloid genera.

GLAZIER, W. C. W. On the destruction of fish by polluted waters in the Gulf of Mexico.

GOODE, G. B. The Taxonomic relations and geographical distribution of the members of the swordfish family, (*Xiphiidæ.*)

GOODE, G. B.; BEAN, T. H. Description of a new species of fish, *Apogon pandionis*, from the deep water off the mouth of Chesapeake Bay.

Benthodesmus, a new genus of deep-sea fishes, allied to *Lepidopus.*

HAWES, G. W. On the mineralogical composition of the normal mesozoic diabase upon the Atlantic border.

On the determination of feldspar in thin sections of rocks.

INGERSOLL, E. On the fish mortality in the Gulf of Mexico.

JAPANESE LEGATION, Washington. Catalogue of a collection of Japanese cotton fibre presented to the U. S. National Museum by the Government of Japan, together with the amount of the annual crop of Japan and the price of cotton.

JOHNSON, S. H. Notes on the mortality among fishes of the Gulf of Mexico.

JORDAN, D. S.; JOUY, P. L. Check-list of duplicates of fishes from the Pacific coast of North America, distributed by the Smithsonian Institution in behalf of the United States National Museum, 1881.

JORDAN, D. S.; GILBERT, C. H. Notes on the fishes of the Pacific coast of the United States.

Description of *Sebastichthys mystinus.*

Description of a new species of *Ptychochilus* (*Ptychochilus Harfordi*) from Sacramento river.

Note on *Raia inornata.*

Notes on a collection of fishes, made by Lieut. Henry E. Nichols, U. S. N., on the west coast of Mexico, with descriptions of new species.

List of fishes collected by Lieut. Henry E. Nichols, U. S. N., in the Gulf of California and on the west coast of Lower California, with descriptions of four new species.

Descriptions of thirty-three new species of fishes from Mazatlan, Mexico.

Description of a new species of *Pomadasys* from Mazatlan, with a key to the species known to inhabit the Pacific coasts of tropical America.

467. Proceedings of National Museum. Vol. IV—Continued.

Description of a new species of *Xenichthys* (*Xenichthys ocyurus*) from the west coast of Central America.

Descriptions of five new species of fishes from Mazatlan, Mexico.

JOUY, P. L. Description of a new species of *Squalius* (*Squalius aliciæ*) from Utah Lake.

LAWRENCE, G. N. Description of a new sub-species of *Loxigilla* from the island of St. Christopher, West Indies.

LOCKINGTON, W. N. Description of a new genus and species of *Cottidæ*.

LUGGER, O. The occurrence of the Canada porcupine in Maryland.

MCKAY, C. L. A review of the genera and species of the family *Centrarchidæ*, with a description of one new species.

MOORE, M. A. Fish mortality in the Gulf of Mexico.

PIRZ, A. Methods of making and preserving plaster casts.

PLATEAU, F. The rapid preparation of large myological specimens.

PORTER, J. Y. On the destruction of fish by poisonous water in the Gulf of Mexico.

RATHBUN, R. List of marine invertebrates, mainly from the New England coast, distributed by the United States National Museum. (Series II.)

List of Marine invertebrates from the New England coast, distributed by the United States National Museum. (Series III.)

RAU, C. List of anthropological publications by

RIDGWAY, R. On a duck new to the North American fauna.

On *Amazilia Yucatanensis*, (Cabot,) and *A. cerviniventris*, Gould.

A review of the genus *Centurus*, Swainson.

List of species of Middle and South American birds not contained in the United States National Museum.

List of special desiderata among North American birds.

Catalogue of Old World birds in the United States National Museum.

Notes on some Costa Rican birds.

Description of a new fly-catcher, and a supposed new petrel, from the Sandwich Islands.

Description of a new owl from Porto Rico.

Descriptions of two new thrushes from the United States.

On two recent additions to the North American bird fauna, by L. Belding.

RYDER, J. A. On Semper's method of making dry preparations.

SHUFELDT, R. W. Remarks upon the osteology of *Opheosaurus ventralis*.

SMITH, R. Description of a new Gobioid fish, (*Othonops eos*,) from San Diego, California.

Description of a new species of Gobiesox, (*Gobiesox rhessodon*,) from San Diego, California.

SMITH, S. B. On the Chinook names of the salmon in the Columbia River.

STEJNEGER, L. Description of two new races of *Myadestes obscurus*, Lafr.

TRANSLATION. Metallic castings of delicate natural objects.

TRUE, F. W. On the North American land tortoises of the genus *Xerobates*.

On the rare rodent *Cricetodipus parvus* (Baird) Coues.

467. Proceedings of National Museum. Vol. IV—Continued.

WARD, L. F. Catalogue of a collection of Japanese woods presented to the U. S. National Museum by the University of Tokio, Japan.

WHITE, C. A. On certain cretaceous fossils from Arkansas and Colorado.

ANONYMOUS. The comparative action of dry heat and sulphurous acid upon putrefactive bacteria.

APPENDICES—*Circulars of the U. S. National Museum:*

No. 1. Plan of organization and regulations of the Museum.
No. 2. Circular addressed to the friends of the Museum.
No. 3. Circular in reference to petroleum collections.
No. 4. Circular concerning the department of insects.
No. 5. Establishment and officers of the Smithsonian Institution and Museum.
No. 6. Classification and arrangement of the materia medica collection.
No. 7. A classification of the forms in which drugs and medicines appear and are administered.
No. 8. Memoranda of collectors of drugs for the materia medica section of the National Museum.
No. 9. Circular in reference to the building-stone collection.
No. 10. Two letters on the work of the National Museum.
No. 11. A provisional classification of the food collections.
No. 12. Classification of the collections to illustrate the art of taxidermy.
No. 13. Outline of a scheme of Museum classification.
No. 14. Circular requesting material for the library of the Museum.
No. 15. The organization and objects of the National Museum.
No. 16. Plans for the installation of collections.
No. 17. Contributions and their acknowledgment.
No. 18. List of publications of the United States National Museum.

468. Smithsonian Miscellaneous Collections. Vol. XXII. 1882. 8vo., pp. 1200, cuts 18, plates 4.

CONTENTS.

Proceedings of the U. S. National Museum. Vol. III. 1880. No. 425.
Proceedings of the U. S. National Museum. Vol. IV. 1881. No. 467.

469. List of Foreign Correspondents of the Smithsonian Institution. Corrected to January, 1882. 1882. 8vo., pp. 174.

470. Nomenclator Zoologicus. An Alphabetical List of all Generic Names that have been employed by Naturalists for Recent and Fossil Animals from the earliest times to the close of the year 1879. In two parts. Part I.—List of Generic Names employed in Zoology and Paleontology to the close of the year 1879, chiefly supplemental to those catalogued by Agassiz and Marschall, or indexed in the Zoological Record. By SAMUEL H. SCUDDER. 1882. 8vo., pp. 398. *Bulletin of the National Museum, No.* 19.

471. List of Marine Invertebrates from the New England Coast, distributed by the U. S. National Museum. Series III.—Educational Series. By RICHARD RATHBUN. 1881. 8vo., pp. 4.

472. Plans for the Installation of Collections in the U. S. National Museum. By G. BROWN GOODE. 1882. 8vo., pp. 2. (*Circular of U. S. National Museum, No.* 16.)

473. Contributions to the United States National Museum, and their Acknowledgement. 1882. 8vo., pp. 2. (*Circular of U. S. National Museum, No.* 17.)

474. List of Publications of the United States National Museum. 1882. 8vo., pp. 12. (*Circular of U. S. National Museum, No.* 18.)

475. Smithsonian Miscellaneous Collections. Vol. XXIII. 1882. 8vo., pp. 1003. *Bulletins of the National Museum, Nos.* 11 *to* 15.

CONTENTS.

GILL, T. Bibliography of fishes of Pacific coast. *Bulletin No.* 11. No. 463.

JORDAN, D. S.; BRAYTON, A. W. Fishes of Alleghany region of South Carolina, Georgia, and Tennessee, and synopsis of *Catostomidæ*. *Bulletin No.* 12. No. 308.

EGGERS, H. F. A. Flora of St. Croix and the Virgin Islands. *Bulletin No.* 13. No. 313.

GOODE, G. B. Catalogue of collection illustrating animal resources and fisheries of the United States. *Bulletin No.* 14. No. 326.

KUMLIEN, L. Natural history of Arctic America. *Bulletin No.* 15. No. 342.

476. First Annual Report of the Bureau of Ethnology to the Secretary of the Smithsonian Institution, 1879–80. By J. W. POWELL, Director. 1881. Royal 8vo., pp. 638. 343 cuts, 54 plates, 1 folded map.

CONTENTS.

POWELL, J. W. Report of the Director of the Bureau.

POWELL, J. W. On the evolution of language.

POWELL, J. W. Mythology of the North American Indians.

POWELL, J. W. Wyandot government.

POWELL, J. W. Limitations to the use of some Anthropological data.

YARROW, H. C. Study of the mortuary customs of the North American Indians.

HOLDEN, E. S. Studies in Central American picture-writing.

ROYCE, C. C. Cessions of land by Indian tribes to the United States.

MALLERY, GARRICK. Sign language among North American Indians, compared with that among other peoples and deaf-mutes.

PILLING, J. C. Catalogue of linguistic manuscripts in the library of the Bureau of Ethnology.

DORSEY, J. O. Illustration of the method of recording Indian languages. How the rabbit caught the sun in a trap. (An Omaha myth.)

GATSCHET, A. S. Details of an Indian conjurer's practice. (In the Klamath Lake dialect.)

GATSCHET, A. S. The relapse. (In the Klamath Lake dialect.)

RIGGS, S. R. A dog's revenge. (A Dakota Fable.)

477. Report on International Exchange, with list of Official Publications of the U. S. Government, between 1868 and 1881. By GEORGE H. BŒHMER. 1882. 8vo., pp. 113.

478. Catalogue of Publications of the Smithsonian Institution up to July 1, 1882, with Index to all Articles in the "Smithsonian Contributions to Knowledge," "Miscellaneous Collections," "Annual Reports," "Bulletins and Proceedings of the U. S. National Museum," etc. By WILLIAM J. RHEES. 1882. 8vo., 1882, pp.

Report on International Exchanges, with List of Official Publications of the U. S. Government, between 1865 and 1881. By George H. Boehmer. 1881. 8vo, pp. 118.

Catalogue of Publications of the Smithsonian Institution up to July 1, 1882, with Index to all Articles in the "Smithsonian Contributions to Knowledge," "Miscellaneous Collections," "Annual Reports," "Bulletins and Proceedings of the U. S. National Museum," etc. By William J. Rhees. 1882. 8vo, 1882, pp. [illegible]

[illegible]

378. First Annual Report of the Bureau of [illegible] of the Smithsonian Institution, 1879-80. By J. W. Powell [illegible] 1881. Royal 8vo, pp. [illegible]

CONTENTS.

[illegible]

CLASSIFIED LIST OF SEPARATE PUBLICATIONS

OF THE

SMITHSONIAN INSTITUTION.

SUBJECTS.

I. ANATOMY, PHYSIOLOGY, MEDICINE, and SURGERY.
II. ANTHROPOLOGY. (*See* also Philology.)
III. ARCHÆOLOGY. (*See* Anthropology.)
IV. ARCHITECTURE.
V. ASTRONOMY.
VI. BIBLIOGRAPHY.
VII. BIOGRAPHY.
VIII. BIOLOGY. (*See* also Anatomy, Botany, Microscopy, Palæontology, and Zoology.)
IX. BOTANY.
X. CHEMISTRY and TECHNOLOGY.
XI. ELECTRICITY and MAGNETISM.
XII. ETHNOLOGY. (*See* Anthropology, also Philology.)
XIII. GEOLOGY. (*See* also Palæontology.)
XIV. MAGNETISM. (*See* Electricity, etc.)
XV. MATHEMATICS.
XVI. MEDICINE and SURGERY. (*See* Anatomy, etc.)
XVII. METEOROLOGY.
XVIII. MICROSCOPY.
XIX. MINERALOGY.
XX. MISCELLANEOUS.
XXI. NATURAL HISTORY. (*See* Biology.)
XXII. PALÆONTOLOGY.
XXIII. PHILOLOGY.
XXIV. PHYSICAL GEOGRAPHY.
XXV. PHYSICS. (*See* also Terrestrial Physics.)
XXVI. PHYSIOLOGY. (*See* Anatomy, etc.)
XXVII. TECHNOLOGY. (*See* Chemistry, etc.)
XXVIII. TERRESTRIAL PHYSICS.
XXIX. ZOOLOGY.—*Birds.*
Fishes.
Insects.
Mammals.
Mollusks.
Radiates.
Reptiles, and Batrachians.
Shells. (See Mollusks.)

I.—ANATOMY, PHYSIOLOGY, MEDICINE, AND SURGERY.

	No. in Catalogue.
ADAMS. Subcutaneous surgery (Toner Lecture, No. 6)	302
BROWN-SÉQUARD. Dual character of the brain (Toner Lecture, No. 2)	291
DACOSTA. The heart (Toner Lecture, No. 3)	279
DEAN. Medulla oblongata (s. c.)	173
FLINT. Classification of drugs and medicines	451
FLINT. Classification of materia medica collection	450
FLINT. Memoranda for collection of drugs	452
HOLMGREN. Color-blindness	399
JONES. Chemical and physiological investigations (s. c.)	82
KEEN. Continued fevers (Toner Lecture, No. 5)	300
LAUTENBACH. Effect of irritation of a polarized nerve	411
LEIDY. Flora and fauna within living animals (s. c.)	44
MITCHELL and MOREHOUSE. Chelonia (s. c.)	159
MITCHELL. Venom of rattlesnake (s. c.)	135
SHAKESPEARE. Reparatory inflammation (Toner Lecture, No. 7)	321
WARING. Sanitary drainage of Washington (Toner Lecture, No. 8)	349
WEISMANN. Change of Mexican axolotl	401
WOOD. Morbid and normal physiology of fever (s. c.)	357
WOOD. Study of fever (Toner Lecture, No. 4)	282
WOODWARD. Cancerous tumors (Toner Lecture, No. 1)	266
WYMAN. Rana pipiens (s. c.)	45

II.—ANTHROPOLOGY. (*See also* PHILOLOGY.)

ABBOTT. Stone age in New Jersey	394
Archæology, circular on	205, 316
BÆGERT. Aboriginal inhabitants of California	361
BŒHMER. Index to archæological articles in Smithsonian publications	421
BRANSFORD. Archæological researches in Nicaragua (s. c.)	383
DALL. Prehistoric man, Aleutian Islands (s. c.)	318
DESOR. Palafittes of the Lake of Neuchatel	360
GIBBS. Ethnological and philological instructions	160
GIBBS. Tinneh, or Chepewyan Indians	365
GILLMAN. Characteristics of ancient man in Michigan	393
GILLMAN. Mound builders and platycnemism	393
HABEL. Sculptures in Guatemala (s. c.)	269
HALDEMAN. Polychrome bead from Florida	404

ANTHROPOLOGY—Continued.

	No. in Catalogue.
HARDISTY. Loucheux Indians	365
HAVEN. American archæology (s. c.)	71
Indians, photographic portraits of, list of	216
JONES. Aboriginal structures in Georgia	400
JONES. Antiquities of Tennessee (s. c.)	259
JONES. Kutchin Indians	365
KNIGHT. Savage weapons	415
LAPHAM. Antiquities of Wisconsin (s. c.)	70
MASON. Anthropological investigations in 1879	420
MASON. " " 1880	432
MASON. Latimer antiquities from Porto Rico	397
MASON. Recent progress in anthropology	432
MAYER. Mexican archæology (s. c.)	86
MORGAN. Circular relative to relationship	138
MORGAN. Systems of consanguinity (s. c.)	218
PICKERING. Gliddon mummy case (s. c.)	208
POWELL. First annual report of Bureau of Ethnology	476
RAU. Ancient aboriginal trade in North America	385
RAU. Archæological collection in Smithsonian Institution (s. c.)	287
RAU. Articles on anthropological subjects, (from Reports S. I.)	440
RAU. Artificial shell deposits in New Jersey	362
RAU. Deposit of agricultural flint implements	370
RAU. Drilling in stone without metal	372
RAU. Gold ornament in mound in Florida	403
RAU. Indian Pottery	368
RAU. North American stone implements	382
RAU. Palenque tablet (s. c.)	331
RAU. Stock-in-trade of aboriginal lapidary	402
ROMER. Prehistoric antiquities of Hungary (translated by RAU)	392
ROSS. Eastern Tinneh Indians	365
SQUIER and DAVIS. Ancient monument of Mississippi valley (s. c.)	1
SQUIER and DAVIS. Aboriginal monuments of New York (s. c.)	15
STANLEY. Catalogue of Indian Portraits	53
SWAN. Indians of Cape Flattery (s. c.)	220
SWAN. Haidah Indians (s. c.)	267
WHITTLESEY. Ancient mining at Lake Superior (s. c.)	155
WHITTLESEY. Ancient works in Ohio (s. c.)	37

III.—ARCHÆOLOGY. (*See* ANTHROPOLOGY.)

IV.—ARCHITECTURE.

	No. in Catalogue.
Building-stones, circular relative to	453
OWEN. Hints on public architecture	P
Report of National Museum building commission and architects for 1879	409
Report of National Museum building commission and architects for 1880	434

V.—ASTRONOMY.

ABBE. Observatories of Dorpat and Poulkova	369
ALEXANDER. Harmonies of the solar system (s. c.)	280
Astronomical telegram circular	263
DOWNES. Occultations 1848 (s. c.)	8
DOWNES. " 1849 (s. c.)	9
DOWNES. " 1850 (s. c.)	10
DOWNES. " 1851 (s. c.)	11
DOWNES. " 1852 (s. c.)	29
DOWNES. " 1853 (s. c.)	54
DRAPER. Silvered-glass telescope (s. c.)	180
Eclipse, annular, 1854	66
GILLISS. Solar eclipse, Peru (s. c.)	100
GOULD. History of Neptune	18
GOULD. Transatlantic longitude (s. c.)	223
HILL. Map solar eclipse	101
HOLDEN and BŒHMER. Reports of observatories for 1880	438
HOLDEN and HASTINGS. Synopsis of Sir William Herschel's writings	426
HOLDEN. Index catalogue of Nebulæ	311
HOLDEN. Recent progress in astronomy	427
HOLDEN. Reports of observatories for 1879	410
KANE. Astronomical observations arctic seas (s. c.)	129, 198
NEWCOMB. Integrals of planetary motion (s. c.)	281
NEWCOMB. Orbit of Neptune (s. c.)	199
NEWCOMB. Orbit of Uranus (s. c.)	262
RUNKLE. Planetary tables (s. c.)	79
RUNKLE. Planetary tables, supplement	94
Star-map, circumpolar	350
Star-map, of the visible heavens	359
STOCKWELL. Orbits of planets (s. c.)	232
WALKER. Researches Neptune (s. c.)	3

ASTRONOMY—Continued.

	No. in Catalogue.
WALKER. Ephemeris Neptune, 1848 (s. c.)	4
WALKER. " 1795-1849 (s. c.)	5
WALKER. " 1850 (s. c.)	6
WALKER. " 1851 (s. c.)	7
WALKER. " 1852 (s. c.)	24

VI.—BIBLIOGRAPHY.

BINNEY. Bibliography of conchology, part I	142
BINNEY. " " " II	174
Exchanges, list of Smithsonian, part I	73
Exchanges, " " " II	85
Exchanges, " " to 1858	117
GILL. Bibliography of fishes of Pacific coast	463
GIRARD. Bibliography of natural history, 1851	48
HOLDEN and HASTINGS. Synopsis of Sir William Herschel's writings	426
HOLDEN. Index catalogue of books and memoirs on Nebulæ	311
Institutions, principal literary and scientific in United States	335
JEWETT. Catalogue system	47
JEWETT. Public libraries	25
Publications, Smithsonian Institution, list of (successive issues,)	74, 203, 226, 245, 278, 290, 301, 344, 437, 478
Periodicals, received by the Institution, list of	Q, 436
Publications of learned societies in library Smithsonian Inst	73, 85, 179
RHEES. Catalogue and index of Smithsonian publications	479
RHEES. Public libraries	116, 238
WATSON. Bibliography of North American botany	258

VII.—BIOGRAPHY.

GRAY. Memoir of Joseph Henry	407
HENRY. Eulogy on Alex. Dallas Bache	379
Henry, Memorial of (By numerous contributors.)	356
HOLDEN and HASTINGS. Scientific writings of Sir William Herschel	426
MAYER. Henry as a discoverer	417
RAU. Memoir of Von Martius	251
RHEES. Life and bequest of James Smithson	330
TAYLOR. Memoir of and scientific work of Joseph Henry	339
WELLING. Life and character of Joseph Henry	338

VIII.—BIOLOGY. (*See also* Anatomy, Microscopy, Palæontology, Botany, and Zoology.)

	No. in Catalogue.
Baird. Circular for shipping fresh-fish and other animals	384
Circular for collecting birds	168
Circular for collecting craw-fish	319
Circular for collecting grasshoppers	163
Circular for collecting shells	176, 363
Circular for observations in Russian America	207
Circular to officers of the Hudson Bay Co.	137
Circular to entomologists	178
Cope. Zoology of Texas	412
Directions for collecting and preserving specimens	34
Directions for collecting and preserving specimens of nests and eggs	139
Edwards. Directions for collecting diatomacea	366
Gill. Recent progress in zoology	431
Girard. Bibliography of natural history	48
Goode. Animal resources and fisheries exhibit, 1876	326
Goode. Classification of animal resources	297
Kidder and others. Natural history of Kerguelen Island	294
Kumlien. Natural history of Arctic America	342
Leidy. Flora and fauna within animals (s. c.)	44
Museum miscellanea, numbers, labels, etc.	164
Packard. Directions for collecting insects	261
Proceedings of the U. S. National Museum	I, **332**; II, **333**; III, **425**; IV, **467**
Periodical phenomena register	65, 148
Scudder. List of genera of animals	470
Stimpson. Marine Invertebrata, Grand Manan, (s. c.)	50
Streets. Natural history of Hawaiian, Fanning Islands, etc	303
Weismann. Change of Mexican axolotl	401

IX.—BOTANY.

Cooper. Forests and trees of North America	351
Eggers. Flora of St. Croix	313
Farlow. Recent progress in botany	430
Gray. Plantæ Wrightianæ, I (s. c.)	22
Gray. " " II (s. c.)	42
Harvey. North American marine algæ, I (s. c.)	32
Harvey. " " " II (s. c.)	43
Harvey. " " " III (s. c.)	95

BOTANY—Continued.

	No. in Catalogue.
HARVEY. North American marine algæ, complete (s. c.)	96
LEIDY. Flora within animals (s. c.)	44
Periodical phenomena, register of	65, 148
ROTHROCK. Flora of Alaska	367
TORREY. Batis maritima (s. c.)	60
TORREY. Darlingtonia Californica (s. c.)	61
HARVEY. Plantæ Frémontianæ (s. c.)	46
WARD. Check list of flora of Washington	461
WARD. Directions for collecting and preserving plants	460
WARD. Guide to the flora of Washington	444
WATSON. Index to North American botany	258
WOOD. Fresh water algæ (s. c.)	241

X.—CHEMISTRY AND TECHNOLOGY.

BARKER. Recent progress in chemistry	429
BECKER. Atomic weight determinations	358
BOOTH and MORFIT. Chemical arts	27
CLARKE. Expansion tables	289
CLARKE. Recalculation of atomic weights	441
CLARKE. Specific gravity tables	255
CLARKE. " " " 1st supplement	288
CLARKE. Specific heat tables	276
GIBBS and GENTH. Ammonia-cobalt bases (s. c.)	88
HARE. Explosiveness of nitre (s. c.)	17
HENRY. Investigation of illuminating materials	389
HUNT. Chemistry of the earth	376
JONES. Chemical and physiological investigations (s. c.)	82
MORIN. Warming and ventilating occupied buildings	439
NEWTON. Metric system of weights and measures	371
SMITHSON. Scientific writings	327
TAYLOR. Henry and the telegraph	405
WETHERILL. Ozone and antozone	355

XI.—ELECTRICITY AND MAGNETISM.

BACHE. Magnetic discussion, part I (s. c.)	113
BACHE. " " part II (s. c.)	121
BACHE. " " part III (s. c.)	132

ELECTRICITY AND MAGNETISM—Continued.

	No. in Catalogue.
BACHE. Magnetic discussion, parts IV to VI (s. c.)	162
BACHE. " " parts VII to IX (s. c.)	175
BACHE. " parts X to XII (s. c.)	186
BACHE. " " parts I to XII, complete (s. c.)	195
BACHE. Magnetic survey of Pennsylvania (s. c.)	166
GOULD. Transatlantic longitude by electro-magnetic signals (s. c.)	223
HARKNESS. Magnetic observations on the iron-clad Monadnock (s. c.)	239
HAYES. Arctic observations (s. c.)	196
HENRY. Communication to Regents on the electro-magnetic telegraph	115
KANE. Arctic observations (s. c.)	97, 198
LOCKE. Observations on terrestrial magnetism (s. c.)	35
SECCHI. Researches on electrical rheometry (s. c.)	36
SONNTAG. Terrestrial magnetism, Mexico (s. c.)	114
TAYLOR. Henry and the telegraph	405

XII.—ETHNOLOGY. (*See* ANTHROPOLOGY and PHILOLOGY.)

XIII.—GEOLOGY. (*See also* PALÆONTOLOGY.)

COOPER. Physical geography of North America	351
HAWES. Recent progress in geology	428
HILGARD. Geology of lower Louisiana (s. c.)	248
HITCHCOCK. Surface geology (s. c.)	90
MASON. Luray Cavern in Virginia	433
PUMPELLY. Geology of China, Mongolia, and Japan (s. c.)	202
WHITTLESEY. Fluctuations of lakes (s. c.)	119
WHITTLESEY. Glacial drift (s. c.)	197

XIV.—MAGNETISM. (*See* ELECTRICITY.)

XV.—MATHEMATICS.

ALVORD. Tangencies of circles (s. c.)	80
FERREL. Converging series (s. c.)	233
NEWCOMB. General integrals of planetary motion (s. c.)	281

XVI.—MEDICINE. (*See* ANATOMY, etc.)

XVII.—METEOROLOGY.

	No. in Catalogue
ABBE. Meteorological memoirs	398
BACHE. Girard College observations (s. c.)	113, 121, 132, 162, 175, 186, 195
CASWELL. Observations, Providence, Rhode Island, 1831–1860 (s. c.)	103
CASWELL. Observations, Providence, Rhode Island, 1831–1876 (s. c.)	443
CHAPPELSMITH. Tornado (s. c.)	59
Clouds, nomenclature of	347
COFFIN. Meteoric fire-ball (s. c.)	221
COFFIN. Psychrometrical tables	87
COFFIN. Winds, northern hemisphere (s. c.)	52
COFFIN. Winds of the globe (s. c.)	268
COLDING. The nature of air currents	398
COLDING. The whirlwind of St. Thomas in 1871	398
COOPER, J. G. Forests and trees of North America	351
Directions for meteorological observations	19, 148
FERREL. Reply to strictures of J. Hann	398
FORCE. Record of auroras (s. c.)	84
GUYOT. Meteorological directions	19, 148
GUYOT. Meteorological and physical tables	31, 153
HANN. Diminution of vapor with altitude	398
HANN. Influence of rain on the barometer	398
HANN. Atmospheric pressure and rain-fall	398
HANN. Laws of temperature in ascending currents	398
HANN. Relation between pressure and wind	398
HAYES. Arctic observations (s. c.)	196
HENRY. Circular, altitudes	236
HENRY. " directions for constructing lightning rods	237
HENRY. " thunder-storms	235
HENRY. " tornadoes	190
HILDRETH AND WOOD. Observations, Marietta, Ohio (s. c.)	120
HOEK. Letter on meteoric shower	217
LOUD. Discussion of Snell's barometric observations	435
LOOMIS. Storms in 1836 (s. c.)	127
Map of the stars near the north pole for aurora	350
McCLINTOCK. Arctic observations (s. c.)	146
McPARLIN. Climate of New Mexico	396
MEECH. Intensity sun's heat (s. c.)	83
CLEAVELAND. Meteorological observations, Brunswick, Maine (s. c.)	204
KANE. Meteorological arctic observations (s. c.)	104, 198
Meteorological observations, 1855	93

METEOROLOGY—Continued.

	No. in Catalogue.
Meteorological results, 1854–59, vol. 1	157
Meteorological results, 1854–59, vol. 2	182
Meteorological stations and observers 1849–1868	373
Meteors, November	217
OLMSTEAD. Aurora (s. c.)	81
Periodical phenomena, registry of	65, 148
PESLIN. Relation between barometric pressure and air currents	398
Planisphere of the visible heavens, for observation of meteors	359
Rain charts for summer, winter, and year	374
REYE. Rainfall and barometric minima	398
SCHOTT. Base chart of the United States	414
SCHOTT. Tables of rain and snow in the United States (s. c.)	222, 353
SCHOTT. Tables of temperature (s. c.)	277
SMITH. Observations, Washington, Arkansas (s. c.)	131
SOHNCKE. Variation of temperature in ascending currents of moist air	398
Temperature chart of U. S. for year	381, 388
Temperature charts of the U. S. for summer, winter, and year	387

XVIII.—MICROSCOPY.

BAILEY. Microscopic observations, Southern States (s. c.)	23
BAILEY. New microscopic organisms (s. c.)	63
BAILEY. Soundings, coast survey (s. c.)	20
DEAN. Medulla oblongata (s. c.)	173
EDWARDS. Directions for collecting microscopic organisms	366
LEIDY. Flora and fauna within living animals (s. c.)	44
WOODWARD. Cancerous tumors	266

XIX.—MINERALOGY.

BABINET. Diamond and precious stones	377
BREZINA. Crystallography and crystallophysics	386
EGLESTON. Catalogue of minerals	156
HAWES. Recent progress in mineralogy	428

XX.—MISCELLANEOUS.

Relative to the Smithsonian Institution.

Act of Congress to establish the Smithsonian Institution	O, 391
BOEHMER. Report on international exchanges	477

MISCELLANEOUS—Continued.

	No. in Catalogue.
Business arrangements of the Smithsonian Institution	325
Committee on Organization, report of	B, L
Correspondence Squier and Davis	K
Circular relative to exchanges	324
Circular relative to Smithsonian Institution	290
DALLAS. Address, laying corner-stone of Smithsonian Institution	D
Digest of act of Congress relative to Smithsonian Institution	C
Directory of officers, collaborators and employés	466
Establishment and officers of Smithsonian Institution and Museum	449
HENRY. Exposition, Smithson's bequest	E
History of Smithsonian Institution	328
Institutions, list of domestic	69, 238
Institutions, list of foreign	64, 154, 225, 243, 469
Journals of the Board of Regents, statistics, etc	329
Officers and Regents and act of organization	N
PEABODY. Scientific education of mechanics	380
Proceedings, Regents, 1846	A
Programme of organization	J
Regulations of Smithsonian Institution	260

Relative to the National Museum.

BAIRD. Circular relative to petroleum collections	447
BAIRD. Circular to friends of the museum	446
BAIRD. Report on Smithsonian exhibit at Centennial, 1876	307
Circular of the United States National Museum, No. 1	445
" " " " " 2	446
" " " " " 3	447
" " " " " 4	448
" 5	449
" " 6	450
" " " " " 7	451
" " 8	452
" " 9	453
" " " " 10	454
" 11	455
" " 12	456
" " " " " 13	457
" 14	458
" " 15	459
" 16	472

MISCELLANEOUS—Continued.

	No. in Catalogue.
Circular of the United States National Museum, No. 17	473
" " " " " 18	474
Circular requesting material for Museum library	458
Classification of animal resources	297
Contributions to Museum, and acknowledgement	473
GOODE. Animal resources and fisheries	326
GOODE. Classification of Museum collections	457
GOODE. Classification of the food collections	455
GOODE. Installation of collections in Museum	472
GOODE. Organization and objects of the Museum	459
GOODE. Organization and regulations of the Museum	445
HORNADAY. Classification of the collections in taxidermy	456
Hudson's Bay circular	137
PHILLIPS. Letters on the work of the National Museum	454
Publications of National Museum, list of	474

XXI.—NATURAL HISTORY. (*See* BIOLOGY.)

XXII.—PALÆONTOLOGY.

CONRAD. Check list of eocene fossils	200
GIBBES. Mosasaurus (s. c.)	14
LEIDY. Ancient fauna, Nebraska (s. c.)	58
LEIDY. Cretaceous reptiles (s. c.)	192
LEIDY. Extinct sloths (s. c.)	72
LEIDY. Fossil ox (s. c.)	41
MEEK. Check list of cretaceous and jurassic fossils	177
MEEK. Check list of miocene fossils	183
MEEK and HAYDEN. Palæontology of Nebraska (s. c.)	172

XXIII.—PHILOLOGY.

BOWEN. Yoruba grammar and dictionary (s. c.)	98
GIBBS. Chinook jargon	161
GIBBS. Comparative Vocabulary	170
GIBBS. Ethnological and philological instructions	160
LIEBER. Vocal sounds of Laura Bridgman (s. c.)	12
MITCHELL and TURNER. Vocabulary of jargon	68

PHILOLOGY—Continued.

		No. in Catalogue.
MORGAN.	Systems of consanguinity (s. c.)	218
RIGGS.	Dakota grammar and dictionary (s. c.)	40
RŒHRIG.	Language of the Dakota or Sioux Indians	378
WHITNEY.	Lectures on Linguistics	352

XXIV.—PHYSICAL GEOGRAPHY.

COOPER.	Physical geography of North America	351
ELLET.	Physical geography of the Mississippi valley (s. c.)	13
HAYES.	Observations in the Arctic seas (s. c.)	196
HENRY.	Circular relative to heights	236
MASON.	Luray Cavern in Virginia	433

XXV.—PHYSICS. (*See also* TERRESTRIAL PHYSICS.)

BARKER.	Recent progress in physics	429
BARNARD.	Internal structure of the earth (s. c.)	310
BARNARD.	Problems of rotary motion (s. c.)	240
BREZINA.	Crystallography and crystallophysics	386
COFFIN.	Winds of the globe (s. c.)	52, 268
DAVIS.	Law of deposit of flood-tide (s. c.)	33
DELAUNAY.	Essay on velocity of light	354
DRAPER.	Telescope in photography (s. c.)	180
GOULD.	Transatlantic longitude (s. c.)	223
GUYOT.	Physical and meteorological tables	31, 153
HAYES.	Physical observations, Arctic seas (s. c.)	196
HENRY.	Electro-magnetic telegraph	115
HENRY.	Investigation of illuminating materials	389
HENRY.	Lightning rods	237
HENRY.	Researches on sound	406
HILGARD.	Tides and tidal action	390
HOLMGREN.	Color-blindness	399
HUNT.	Chemistry of the earth	376
KANE.	Physical observations, Arctic seas (s. c.)	198
MEECH.	Heat and light of the sun (s. c.)	83
NEWTON.	Metric weights and measures	371
TAYLOR.	Henry and the telegraph	405
TAYLOR.	Kinetic theories of gravitation	395
TAYLOR.	Nature and origin of force	375

PHYSICS—Continued. No. in Catalogue

SCHOTT. Base chart of the United States ---- **414**
SECCHI. Electrical rheometry (s. c.) ---- **36**
WHITTLESEY. Fluctuations, level of lakes (s. c.) ---- **119**

XXVI.—PHYSIOLOGY. (*See* ANATOMY, etc.)

XXVII.—TECHNOLOGY. (*See* CHEMISTRY, etc.)

XXVIII.—TERRESTRIAL PHYSICS.

BACHE. Discussion of magnetic observations (s. c.) ---- I, **113**; II, **121**; III, **132**; IV-VI, **162**; VII-IX, **175**; X-XII, **186**; I-XII, **195**
BACHE. Magnetic survey of Pennsylvania (s. c.) ---- **166**
BARNARD. Problems of rotary motion, and precession of equinoxes (s. c.) ---- **240**
COFFIN. Winds of the globe (s. c.) ---- **268**
COFFIN. Winds of the northern hemisphere (s. c.) ---- **52**
DAVIS. Dynamical action, etc., of the flood tide (s. c.) ---- **33**
FORCE. Record of auroral phenomena (s. c.) ---- **84**
HAYES. Physical observations in Arctic seas (s. c.) ---- **196**
HENRY. Circular relative to altitudes ---- **236**
HILGARD. Tides and tidal action in harbors ---- **390**
HUNT. Chemistry of the earth ---- **376**
KANE. Magnetical observations in the Arctic seas (s. c.) ---- **97**
KANE. Physical observations in the Arctic seas (s. c.) ---- **198**
KANE. Tidal observations in the Arctic seas (s. c.) ---- **130**
LOCKE. Observations on terrestrial magnetism in United States (s. c.) ---- **35**
MÜLLER. Observations on terrestrial magnetism in Mexico (s. c.) ---- **114**
OLMSTEAD. Secular period of the aurora (s. c.) ---- **81**
SONNTAG. Observations on terrestrial magnetism in Mexico (s. c.) ---- **114**
WHITTLESEY. Fluctuations of level in the North American lakes (s. c.) ---- **119**

XXIX.—ZOOLOGY.

Birds.

BAIRD. Arrangement of birds ---- **210**
BAIRD. Catalogue of birds, 4to ---- **106**
BAIRD. " " 8vo ---- **108**

ZOOLOGY—Continued.

	No. in Catalogue.
BAIRD. Instructions for collecting bird's nests and eggs	139
BAIRD. Review of birds, part I	181
BREWER. North American oology, part I (s. c.)	89
Circular, birds of South America	168
Desiderata of birds of Mexico, Central America, etc	185
ELLIOT. List of Trochilidæ, (humming birds)	334
ELLIOT. Monograph of Trochilidæ (s. c.)	317
KIDDER and COUES. Birds of Kerguelen Island	293
LAWRENCE. Birds of Mexico	295
LILLJEBORG. Outline of classification of birds	364
RIDGWAY. Catalogue of old world birds in Museum	462
RIDGWAY. Nomenclature of North American birds	422

Fishes.

BAIRD. Circular for shipping fresh fish	384
BAIRD. Circular relative to food fishes	234
BAIRD. Fishes of New Jersey coast	348
BAIRD. Inquiry relative to food-fishes	231
BEAN. Directions for collecting and preserving fish	464
GILL. Arrangement of fishes	247
GILL. Bibliography of fishes of Pacific coast	463
GILL. Catalogue of fishes	283
GILL. Fishes of Western North America	307
GIRARD. Monograph, cottoids (s. c.)	30
GOODE. Berlin exhibit of fisheries and fish culture	413
GOODE. Fishes of Bermuda	296
JORDAN and BRAYTON. Fishes of South Carolina, Georgia, and Tennessee	308
JORDAN. Notes on cottidæ	306
JORDAN. Notes on Rafinesque's memoirs, North American fishes	305

Insects.

AGASSIZ. Classification of insects (s. c.)	16
Circular to entomologists	178
Circular concerning department of insects	448
DE SAUSSURE. Monograph of wasps, hymenoptera	254
HAGEN. Synopsis of neuroptera	134
LE CONTE. Classification of coleoptera, part I	136
LE CONTE. " " part II	265
LE CONTE. Kansas and New Mexico coleoptera (s. c.)	126

ZOOLOGY—Continued.

	No. in Catalogue.
LE CONTE. List of coleoptera	140
LE CONTE. New species of coleoptera, part I	167
LE CONTE. " " part II	264
LOEW. Monograph of diptera, part I	141
LOEW. " " part II	171
LOEW. " " part III	256
MELSHEIMER. Catalogue of coleoptera	62
MORRIS. Catalogue of lepidoptera	118
MORRIS. Synopsis of lepidoptera	133
OSTEN SACKEN. Monograph of diptera, part IV	219
OSTEN SACKEN. Catalogue of diptera	102, 270
PACKARD. Directions for collecting insects	261
SCUDDER. Catalogue of orthoptera	189

Mammals.

ALLEN. Monograph, North American bats	165
BAIRD. Catalogue, mammals	105
GILL. List of families of mammals	230

Mollusks.

BINNEY. Bibliography North American conchology, part I	142
BINNEY. " " " " II	174
BINNEY. Land and fresh-water shells, part I. Pulmonata geophila	194
BINNEY. " " " " II. Pulmonata Limnophila	143
BINNEY. " " " " III. Ampullariidæ, etc.	144
CARPENTER. Mollusks of Western North America	252
CARPENTER. Chitonidæ	251
CARPENTER. Lectures on mollusca	152
Check list of shells	128
Circular for collecting shells	176
DALL. Index of names applied to brachiopoda	304
Exploring expedition, duplicate shells	193
GILL. Families of mollusks	227
LEWIS. Instructions for collecting land and fresh-water shells	363
PRIME. Corbiculadæ	145
STIMPSON. Hydrobiinæ	201
TRYON. Land and fresh-water shells, part IV. Strepomatidæ	253

ZOOLOGY—Continued.

No. in Catalogue.

Radiates.

BAIRD. Circular for collecting cray-fish 319
CLARK. Lucernariæ (s. c.) 242
RATHBUN. List of marine invertebrates distributed, series II 465
RATHBUN. " " " " " III 471
STIMPSON. Marine invertebrata of Grand Manan (s. c.) 50

Reptiles.

BAIRD and GIRARD. Catalogue of serpents 49
BAIRD. Circular on collecting reptiles 320
COPE. North American batrachia and reptilia 292
MITCHELL and MOREHOUSE. Chelonia (s. c.) 159

Shells. (See Mollusks.)

SMITHSONIAN CONTRIBUTIONS TO KNOWLEDGE. (*Quarto.*)

Vol.	Date.	Pages.	Wood-cuts.	Plates.	Maps.	No. in Series.	Contains Nos. of Catalogue.
I	1848	360	207	48	------	2	1.
II	1851	572	89	24	------	26	3, 12, 20, 13, 14, 16, 17, 23, 15, 4, 5, 6, 7, 11.
III	1852	562	------	35	------	38	35, 36, 30, 32, 22, 33, 37, 24, 29.
IV	1852	426	------	------	------	39	40.
V	1853	538	4	45	------	55	44, 41, 45, 43, 42.
VI	1854	484	9	53	------	56	46, 60, 61, 50, 52, 58, 54.
VII	1855	260	74	72	2	76	59, 63, 70, 72, 73.
VIII	1856	564	52	9	------	78	71, 81, 80, 82, 84, 85.
IX	1857	480	45	22	------	92	83, 90, 86, 88, 79, 94.
X	1858	462	1	16	1	99	95, 97, 98.
XI	1859	502	20	23	------	111	89, 100, 113, 104, 126, 114, 127.
XII	1860	538	15	8	------	112	129, 119, 103, 131, 135.
XIII	1863	558	80	4	3	151	130, 146, 155, 121, 132, 162, 166, 159.
XIV	1865	490	158	25	------	184	175, 186, 180, 172, 192.
XV	1867	620	47	13	4	206	199, 197, 202, 196.
XVI	1870	498	76	18	------	211	178, 204, 120, 208, 221, 223, 220.
XVII	1871	616	6	14	------	229	218.
XVIII	1872	646	10	5	3	246	222, 232, 239, 233.
XIX	1874	640	6	21	------	272	240, 241, 262.
XX	1876	794	4	26	------	284	268.
XXI	1876	543	30	9	3	285	280, 281, 267, 277.
XXII	1880	537	474	20	------	340	259, 269, 287, 331, 318.
XXIII	1881	766	160	18	------	346	242, 248, 310, 317, 357.

SMITHSONIAN MISCELLANEOUS COLLECTIONS. (*Octavo.*)

Vol.	Date.	Pages.	Cuts.	Plates.	No. in Series.	Contains Nos. of Catalogue.
I	1862	738	23	------	122	148, 87, 153.
II	1862	714	33	------	123	27, 115, 53, 108, 49, 128, 34, 137, 139, 163, 176, 138.
III	1862	776	49	------	124	102, 118, 136, 117.
IV	1862	762	30	------	125	134, 133.
V	1864	774	------	------	158	142, 74, 154.
VI	1867	888	15	7	169	141, 171, 140, 167.
VII	1867	878	813	------	191	165, 143, 144, 201, 145, 200, 183, 177, 156, 161, 160, 203.
VIII	1869	921	730	4	212	219, 189, 194, 210, 137, 207, 205, 178, 168, 164.
IX	1869	914	------	------	213	174, 179.
X	1873	913	5	------	250	252, 227, 235, 236, 237, 190, 234, 238, 243, 245.
XI	1874	790	55	4	273	230, 247, 256, 261, 264, 265.
XII	1874	767	86	------	274	181, 255, 263.
XIII	1878	982	45	------	312	292, 293, 294, 295, 296, 297, 303, 304, 305, 306.
XIV	1878	911	------	4	314	254, 283, 288, 276, 289, 216, 301, 311.
XV	1878	880	53	------	315	258, 266, 291, 279, 282, 300, 302, 309, 316, 319, 320.
XVI	1880	950	871	7	322	253, 270, 321, 324, 325, 334, 335, 344.
XVII	1880	1034	------	------	336	328.
XVIII	1880	851	------	------	337	329.
XIX	1880	1034	------	------	416	332, 333.
XX	1881	846	------	------	423	
XXI	1881	773	42	13	424	330, 327, 356.
XXII	1882	1200	18	4	468	425, 467.
XXIII	1882	1003	------	------	475	463, 308, 313, 326, 342.

ANNUAL REPORTS OF THE SMITHSONIAN INSTITUTION. (*Octavo.*)

	Pages.	Woodcuts.	No. in Smithsonian Catalogue.	When Published.
1st, for 1846	38		G	1847
2d, for 1847	208		H	1848
3d, for 1848	64		I	1849
4th, for 1849	272		21	1850
5th, for 1850	326		28	1851
6th, for 1851	104		51	1852
7th, for 1852	96		57	1853
8th, for 1853	310		67	1854
9th, for 1854	464	4	75	1855
10th, for 1855	440	79	77	1856
11th, for 1856	468	69	91	1857
12th, for 1857	438	100	107	1858
13th, for 1858	448	48	109	1859
14th, for 1859	450	57	110	1860
15th, for 1860	448	78	147	1861
16th, for 1861	464	25	149	1862
17th, for 1862	446	94	150	1863
18th, for 1863	420	56	187	1864
19th, for 1864	450	50	188	1865
20th, for 1865	496	189	209	1866
21st, for 1866	470	70	214	1867
22d, for 1867	506	10	215	1868
23d, for 1868	474	40	224	1869
24th, for 1869	430	38	228	1871
25th, for 1870	494	28	244	1871
26th, for 1871	478	3	249	1873
27th, for 1872	456	119	271	1873
28th, for 1873	452	33	275	1874
29th, for 1874	416	46	286	1875
30th, for 1875	422	354	298	1876
31st, for 1876	488	78	299	1877
32d, for 1877	500	49	323	1878
33d, for 1878	575	12	341	1879
34th, for 1879	631	216	345	1880
35th, for 1880	782	18	442	1881

PUBLICATIONS OF THE U. S. NATIONAL MUSEUM. (*Octavo.*)

No. of Museum Series.	TITLE.	In Vol. of Miscellaneous Collections.	No. in Smithsonian Catalogue.
1	Bulletin of the U. S. National Museum, No. 1	XIII	292
2	" " " No. 2	XIII	293
3	" " " No. 3	XIII	294
4	" " " No. 4	XIII	295
5	" " " No. 5	XIII	296
6	" " " No. 6	XIII	297
7	" " " No. 7	XIII	303
8	" " " No. 8	XIII	304
9	" " " No. 9	XIII	305
10	" " " No. 10	XIII	306
11	" " " No. 11	XXIII	463
12	" " " No. 12	XXIII	308
13	" " " No. 13	XXIII	313
14	" " " No. 14	XXIII	326
15	" " " No. 15	XXIII	342
16	" " " No. 16		
17	Proceedings Nat. Mus., Vol. I	XIX	332
18	Bulletins Nat. Mus., Vol. I, Nos. 1 to 10	XIII	312
19	Proceedings Nat. Mus., Vol. II	XIX	333
20	Bulletin of the U. S. National Museum, No. 17		412
21	" " " No. 18		413
22	" " " No. 19		470
23	" " " No. 20		
24	" " " No. 21		422
25	Proceedings Nat. Mus., Vol. III	XXII	425
26	Bulletin of the U. S. National Museum, No. 22		444
27	Proceedings Nat. Mus., Vol. IV	XXII	467
28	Bulletins Nat. Mus., Vol. II, Nos. 11 to 15	XXIII	475

PUBLICATIONS OF THE U. S. NATIONAL MUSEUM—Continued.

SEPARATE LIST OF BULLETINS.

No.	When Published.	Pages.	Cuts.	Plates.	Maps.	In Vol. of Miscellaneous Collections.	No. in Museum Series.	No. in Smithsonian Catalogue.
1	1875	108				XIII	1	292
2	1875	61				XIII	2	293
3	1876	124				XIII	3	294
4	1875	56				XIII	4	295
5	1876	84				XIII	5	296
6	1876	140				XIII	6	297
7	1877	172				XIII	7	303
8	1877	88				XIII	8	304
9	1877	56				XIII	9	305
10	1877	124		45		XIII	10	306
11	1882	77				XXIII	11	463
12	1878	237				XXIII	12	308
13	1879	189				XXIII	13	313
14	1879	367				XXIII	14	326
15	1879	179				XXIII	15	342
16							16	
17	1880	55					20	412
18	1880	279					21	413
19	1882	398					22	470
20							23	
21	1881	94					24	422
22	1881	265			1		26	444

THE BULLETINS COLLECTED IN VOLUMES.

Vol.	Contents.	Published.	Pages.	Cuts.	Plates.	In Vol. of Miscellaneous Collections.	No. in Museum Series.	No. in Smithsonian Catalogue.
I	Nos. 1–10	1878	982	------	45	XIII	18	312
II	Nos. 11–15	1882	1008	------	------	XXIII	28	475

PUBLICATIONS OF THE U. S. NATIONAL MUSEUM—Continued.

SEPARATE LIST OF PROCEEDINGS.

Vol.	For Year.	Pages.	Cuts.	Plates.	When Published.	In Vol. of Miscellaneous Collections.	No. in Museum Series.	No. in Smithsonian Catalogue.
I	1878	524	8	8	1879	XIX	17	332
II	1879	503	2	7	1880	XIX	19	333
III	1880	594	5	2	1881	XXII	25	425
IV	1881	600	13	2	1882	XXII	27	467

PUBLICATIONS OF THE BUREAU OF ETHNOLOGY OF THE SMITHSONIAN INSTITUTION. *(Imperial Octavo.)*

Title.	Published.	Pages.	Cuts.	Plates.	Maps.	No. in Smithsonian Catalogue.
First Annual Report, for 1879-80	1881	638	343	54	1	476

PUBLICATIONS HAVING SEPARATE NUMBERS IN THE SMITHSONIAN SERIES, BUT INCLUDED IN THE ANNUAL REPORTS OF THE INSTITUTION.

		Vol. of Report.
A	Journal of Regents	1847
B	Report of Organization Committee	1847
D	Address at laying corner-stone. DALLAS	1847
E	Exposition of Bequest. HENRY	1847
F	First Report of Secretary. HENRY	1848
J	Programme of Organization. HENRY	1848
K	Correspondence, Squier and Davis	1848
L	First Report of Organization Committee	1847
M	Reports of Institution to 1849	1849
N	Officers and Regents	1847
25	Public Libraries. JEWETT	1850
152	Lectures on Mollusca. CARPENTER	1860
251	Memoir of Von Martius. RAU	1869
307	Report on Centennial. BAIRD	1876
343	Annual Reports. HENRY	1865–77
348	Fishes of New Jersey. BAIRD	1854
351	Forests of North America. COOPER	1858
352	Lectures on Linguistics. WHITNEY	1863
354	Essay on Velocity of Light. DELAUNAY	1864
355	Ozone and antozone. WETHERILL	1864
360	Palafittes. DESOR	1865
361	Aborigines of California. BAEGERT	1863–4
362	Artificial Shell Deposits in New Jersey. RAU	1864
364	Classification of Birds. LILLJEBORG	1865
365	Tinneh Indians. Ross and others	1866
367	Flora of Alaska. ROTHROCK	1867
368	Indian Pottery. RAU	1866
369	Dorpat and Poulkova. ABBE	1867
370	Flint Implements in Illinois. RAU	1868
371	Metric Tables. NEWTON	1865
372	Drilling in Stone without Metal. RAU	1868
373	Meteorological Stations and Observers	1868
375	Origin and Nature of Force. TAYLOR	1870
376	Chemistry of the Earth. HUNT	1869
377	Diamond and Precious Stones. BABINET	1870
378	Dakota Language. RŒHRIG	1871
379	Eulogy on A. D. Bache. HENRY	1870

PUBLICATIONS HAVING SEPARATE NUMBERS—Continued.

		Vol. of Report.
380	Scientific Education of Mechanics. PEABODY	1872
382	North American Stone Implements. RAU	1872
385	Ancient Aboriginal Trade. RAU	1872
386	Crystallography. BREZINA	1872
389	Investigation of Illuminants. HENRY	1880
390	Tides. HILGARD	1874
392	Prehistoric Antiquities of Hungary. ROMER	1876
393	Mound Builders and Ancient Man in Michigan. GILLMAN	1873 and 1875
394	Stone Age in New Jersey. ABBOTT	1875
395	Kinetic Theories of Gravitation. TAYLOR	1876
396	History and Climate of New Mexico. MCPARLIN	1877
397	Latimer Antiquities. MASON	1876
398	Meteorological Memoirs. ABBE	1877
399	Color-blindness. HOLMGREN	1877
400	Aboriginal Structures in Georgia. JONES	1877
401	Mexican Axolotl. WEISMANN	1877
402	Stock-in-trade of Aboriginal Lapidary. RAU	1877
403	Gold Ornament from Florida. RAU	1877
404	Polychrome Bead from Florida. HALDEMAN	1877
405	Henry and the Telegraph. TAYLOR	1878
406	Researches in Sound. HENRY	1878
407	Memoir of Joseph Henry. GRAY	1878
408	Report of Secretary for 1878. BAIRD	1878
409	Report of Museum Building Commission and Architects	1879
410	Reports of Observatories. HOLDEN	1879
411	Irritation of Polarized Nerve. LAUTENBACH	1878
415	Savage Weapons. KNIGHT	1879
418	Report of Secretary for 1879. BAIRD	1879
419	Report of Secretary for 1880. BAIRD	1880
420	Anthropological Investigations. MASON	1879
421	Index to Anthropological Articles. BŒHMER	1879
426	Synopsis of Herschel's Writings. HOLDEN and HASTINGS	1880
427	Recent Progress in Astronomy. HOLDEN	1880
428	" " Geology and Mineralogy. HAWES	1880
429	" " Physics and Chemistry. BARKER	1880
430	" " Botany. FARLOW	1880
431	" " Zoology. GILL	1880
432	" " Anthropology. MASON	1880
433	Report of Visit to Luray Cave. MASON	1880
434	Report of Museum Building Commission and Architects	1880

PUBLICATIONS HAVING SEPARATE NUMBERS—Continued.

		Vol. of Report.
435	Snell's Barometric Observations. LOUD	1880
436	List of Periodicals received by Smithsonian Institution	1880
438	Reports of Observatories. HOLDEN and BŒHMER	1880
439	Warming and Ventilating Buildings. MORIN	1873–4
440	Anthropological Articles. RAU	1863–77

PUBLICATIONS NOT IN REGULAR SERIES OF "CONTRIBUTIONS," "COLLECTIONS," OR "REPORTS.

C Digest of Act of Congress.
P Hints on Public Architecture. OWEN.
Q Check-list of Periodicals.
18 Report on the Discovery of the Planet Neptune. GOULD.
47 On Construction of Catalogues of Libraries. JEWETT.
48 Bibliography of American Natural History for 1851. GIRARD.
62 Catalogue of Described Coleoptera of the United States. MELSHEIMER.
64 List of Foreign Institutions.
65 Registry of Periodical Phenomena.
66 The Annular Eclipse of May 26, 1854.
68 Vocabulary of the Jargon. MITCHELL and TURNER.
69 List of Domestic Institutions.
93 Meteorological Observations for 1855.
101 Map of the Solar Eclipse.
105 Catalogue of North American Mammals. BAIRD.
106 Catalogue of North American Birds. BAIRD.
116 List of Public Libraries. RHEES.
157 Results of Meteorological Observations, 1854–1859. Vol. I.
170 Comparative Vocabulary.
182 Results of Meteorological Observations, 1854–1859. Vol. II.
185 List of Birds of Mexico, &c. BAIRD.
193 List of Duplicate Shells collected by Wilkes.
217 Letter of M. Hoek on Meteoric Shower.
225 List of Foreign Correspondents.
226 List of Smithsonian Publications.
260 Regulations of the Smithsonian Institution.
278 Check-list of Publications of Smithsonian Institution.
290 Circular for distribution at Centennial.
347 Nomenclature of Clouds.
350 Map of Stars near the North Pole.
359 Planisphere of the Visible Heavens.
366 Directions for collecting Diatomacea, &c. EDWARDS.
414 Base Chart.
437 Check-list of Smithsonian Publications.
466 Directory of Officers and Employés.

LIST OF PAPERS PUBLISHED IN THE "SMITHSONIAN CONTRIBUTIONS TO KNOWLEDGE."

Serial Number.	Author.	Title of Work.	Commissions of Reference.
1	Squier, E. G., and Davis, E. H.	Ancient Monuments of Mississippi Valley.	E. Robinson, D. D., J. R. Bartlett, Prof. W. W. Turner, S. G. Morton, M. D., G. P. Marsh.
3	Walker, S. C.	Researches, Planet Neptune.	
4	Walker, S. C.	Ephemeris of Neptune for 1848.	
5	Walker, S. C.	Ephemeris of Neptune for 1849.	
6	Walker, S. C.	Ephemeris of Neptune for 1850.	
7	Walker, S. C.	Ephemeris of Neptune for 1851.	
8	Downes, John	Occultations in 1848.	
9	Downes, John	Occultations in 1849.	
10	Downes, John	Occultations in 1850.	
11	Downes, John	Occultations in 1851.	
12	Lieber, Francis	Vocal Sounds of L. Bridgman	Col. W. W. S. Bliss, Miss D. L. Dix.
13	Ellet, Charles	Physical Geography of U. S.	Maj. A. Mordecai, Capt. F. A. Smith, Lieut. M. L. Smith.
14	Gibbes, R. W.	Memoir on Mosasaurus	Prof. Louis Agassiz, Prof. Henry D. Rogers.
15	Squier, E. G.	Aboriginal Monuments of New York	Brantz Mayer, Wm. W. Turner.
16	Agassiz, Louis	Classification of Insects	Prof. C. D. Meigs, Thaddeus W. Harris, M. D.
17	Hare, Robert	Explosiveness of Nitre	John Torrey, M. D., Col. J. J. Abert.
20	Bailey, J. W.	Microscopic Examination of Soundings	Prof. Lewis R. Gibbes, Prof. Wm. B. Rogers.
22	Gray, Asa	Plantæ Wrightianæ. Part I	Prof. John Torrey, John Carey.
23	Bailey, J. W.	Microscopic Observations in South Carolina, Georgia, and Florida.	Prof. Wm. B. Rogers, Prof. Lewis R. Gibbes.
24	Walker, S. C.	Ephemeris of Neptune, 1852. Appendix I.	
29	Downes, John	Occultations in 1852.	
30	Girard, Charles	Fresh-water Fishes of North America	Dr. Jared P. Kirtland, Dr. J. E. Holbrook.
32	Harvey, Wm. H.	Marine Algæ of North America. Part I	Prof. J. W. Bailey, Dr. Asa Gray.
33	Davis, Chas. H.	Law of Deposit of Flood Tide	Prof L. Agassiz, Prof. A. Guyot.
35	Locke, John	Observations on Terrestrial Magnetism	Prof. Elias Loomis, Prof. Julius E. Hilgard.
36	Secchi, A.	Researches on Electrical Rheometry	J. H. Lane, Prof. Jas. Curley.
37	Whittlesey, Ch.	Ancient Works in Ohio	Brantz Mayer, E. G. Squier.
40	Riggs, S. R.	Dakota Grammar and Dictionary	Minnesota Historical Society, Prof. W. W. Turner, Prof. C. C. Felton.
41	Leidy, Joseph	Extinct American Ox	Paul B. Goddard, M. D., Joseph Pancoast, M. D.
42	Gray, Asa	Plantæ Wrightianæ. Part II	Prof. John Torrey, John Carey.
43	Harvey, Wm. H.	Marine Algæ of North America. Part II	Prof. J. W. Bailey, Dr. Asa Gray.
44	Leidy, Joseph	Flora and Fauna within Living Animals	Prof. J. W. Bailey, Charles F. Beck, M. D.
45	Wyman, Jeffries	Anatomy of Rana Pipiens	J. B. S. Jackson, M. D., Joseph Leidy, M. D.
46	Torrey, John	Plantæ Fremontianæ	Dr. W. Darlington, Dr. Asa Gray.

PAPERS PUBLISHED IN SMITHSONIAN CONTRIBUTIONS TO KNOWLEDGE—Continued.

Serial Number.	Author.	Title to Work.	Commissions of Reference.
50	Stimpson, Wm.	Marine Invertebrata of Grand Manan	A. A. Gould, M. D., Prof. J. D. Dana.
52	Coffin, Jas. H.	Winds of the Northern Hemisphere	Prof. W. B. Rogers, Prof. E. Loomis.
54	Downes, John	Occultations in 1853.	
58	Leidy, Joseph	Ancient Fauna of Nebraska	Prof. J. Hall, J. L. Leconte, M. D.
59	Chappelsmith, J.	Tornado in Indiana	Prof. J. H. Coffin, Prof. A. Caswell.
60	Torrey, John	Batis Maritima	Prof. A. Gray, John Carey.
61	Torrey, John	Darlingtonia Californica	Prof. A. Gray, John Carey.
63	Bailey, J. W.	New Species of Microscopic Organisms	Prof. C. R. Gilman, M. D., Waldo I. Burnett, M. D.
70	Lapham, I. A.	Antiquities of Wisconsin	American Antiquarian Society.
71	Haven, S. F.	Archæology of the United States	Peter Force, Brantz Mayer.
72	Leidy, Joseph	Extinct Sloth Tribe of North America	Isaac Hays, M. D., Prof. W. E. Horner.
73	....	Publications of Societies in Smithsonian Library.	
79	Runkle, John D.	Tables for Planetary Motion	Prof. Benj. Peirce, Com. Chas. H. Davis.
80	Alvord, Benj.	Tangencies of Circles and Spheres	Prof. A. E. Church, Prof. L. R. Gibbes.
81	Olmsted, D.	Secular Period of Aurora Borealis	Prof. J. B. Cherriman, Prof. J. H. Coffin.
82	Jones, Joseph	Investigation on Amer. Vertebrata	S. Jackson, M. D., J. Leidy, M. D., J. Wyman, M. D.
83	Meech, L. W.	Relative Intensity of Heat and Light of the Sun.	Prof. B. Peirce, Dr. B. A. Gould, Jr.
84	Force, Peter	Auroral Phenomena in North Latitudes.	
85	....	Publications of Societies in Smithsonian Library. Part II.	
86	Mayer, Brantz	Mexican History and Archæology	S. F. Haven, E. H. Davis, M. D.
88	Gibbs, W., and Genth, F. A.	Ammonia Cobalt Bases	Prof. John F. Frazer, Prof. John Torrey.
89	Brewer, Th. M.	North American Oology. Part I	John Gould, John Cassin.
90	Hitchcock, E.	Illustrations of Surface Geology.	
94	Runkle, John D.	Asteroid Supplement to New Tables for $b\frac{(t)}{s}$.	Prof. Benj. Peirce, Com. Chas. H. Davis.
95	Harvey, Wm. H.	Marine Algæ of North America. Part III.	Dr. John Torrey, Dr. Asa Gray.
96	Harvey, Wm. H.	Marine Algæ of North America. 3 parts complete.	Prof. J. W. Bailey, Dr. Asa Gray.
97	Kane, E. K.	Magnetic Observations in the Arctic Seas	Prof. A. D. Bache.
98	Bowen, T. J.	Yoruba Grammar and Dictionary	Prof. J. W. Gibbs, Prof. W. D. Whitney, R. Anderson.
100	Gilliss, J. M.	Eclipse of the Sun, Sept. 7, 1858	Prof. J. S. Hubbard, J. H. Lane.
103	Caswell, A.	Meteorological Observations, Providence, R. I.	
104	Kane, E. K.	Meteorological Observations in Arctic Seas.	Prof. A. D. Bache.
113	Bache, A. D.	Magnetic and Meteorological Observations at Girard College. Part I.	Prof. Benjamin Peirce, Prof. W. Chauvenet.

PAPERS PUBLISHED IN SMITHSONIAN CONTRIBUTIONS TO KNOWLEDGE—Continued.

Serial Number.	Author.	Title of Work.	Commissions of Reference.
114	Sonntag, A.	Terrestrial Magnetism in Mexico	Prof. Stephen Alexander, Prof. Arnold Guyot.
119	Whittlesey, Ch.	Fluctuations of Level in N. A. Lakes	Capt. A. A. Humphreys, Capt. A. W. Whipple.
120	Hildreth, S. P., and Wood, J.	Meteorological Observations, Marietta, Ohio.	
121	Bache, A. D.	Magnetic and Meteorological Observations at Girard College. Part II.	
126	Le Conte, John L.	Coleoptera of Kansas and New Mexico	C. Zimmerman, F.E. Melsheimer.
127	Loomis, E.	Storms in Europe and America, Dec. 1836.	Dr. S. P. Hildreth, Prof. A. Caswell.
129	Kane, E. K.	Astronomical Observations in the Arctic Seas.	Prof. A. D. Bache.
130	Kane, E. K.	Tidal Observations in the Arctic Seas	Prof. A. D. Bache.
131	Smith, N. D.	Meteorological Observations in Arkansas from 1840 to 1859.	
132	Bache, A. D.	Magnetic and Meteorological Observations at Girard College. Part III.	
135	Mitchell, S. W.	Venom of the Rattlesnake	Franklin Bache, M. D., Robley Dunglison, M. D.
146	M'Clintock, Sir F. L.	Meteorological Observations in the Arctic Seas.	
155	Whittlesey, Ch.	Ancient Mining on Lake Superior	D. Wilson, LL. D., E. H. Davis, M. D.
159	Mitchell, S. W., & Morehouse, G. R.	Anatomy and Physiology of Respiration in Chelonia.	Prof. J. Wyman, Prof. J. Leidy.
162	Bache, A. D.	Magnetic and Meteorological Observations at Girard Coll. Pt. IV, V, & VI.	
166	Bache, A. D.	Magnetic Survey of Pennsylvania.	
172	Meek, F. B., and Hayden, F. V.	Palæontology of the Upper Missouri. Part I.	Isaac Lea, Prof. Jas. D. Dana.
173	Dean, John	Gray Substance of the Medulla Oblongata.	Dr. W. A. Hammond, Prof. Jeffries Wyman.
175	Bache, A. D.	Mag. and Met. Observ. at Girard College. Parts VII, VIII, and IX.	
180	Draper, H.	Construction of a Silvered Glass Telescope.	Prof. Wolcott Gibbs, Com. J. M. Gilliss.
186	Bache, A. D.	Mag. and Met. Observ. at Girard College. Parts X, XI, and XII.	
192	Leidy, Joseph	Cretaceous Reptiles of the U. S.	Prof. L. Agassiz, Prof. E. D. Cope.
195	Bache, A. D.	Girard College Observations. Complete. Parts I to XII.	Prof. Benj. Peirce, Prof. W. Chauvenet.
196	Hayes, I. I.	Physical Observations in the Arctic Seas.	
197	Whittlesey, Ch.	Glacial Drift of Northwestern States	Prof. L. Agassiz, Prof. J. P. Lesley.
198	Kane, E. K.	Physical Observations in the Arctic Seas. Complete.	Prof. A. D. Bache.
199	Newcomb, S.	Orbit of Neptune	Adm'l C. H. Davis, Prof. Stephen Alexander.
202	Pumpelly, R.	Geological Researches in China, Mongolia, &c.	National Academy of Sciences.
204	Cleaveland, P.	Meteorological Observations, Brunswick, Me., 1807-1859.	

PAPERS PUBLISHED IN SMITHSONIAN CONTRIBUTIONS TO KNOWLEDGE—Continued.

Serial Number.	Author.	Title of Work.	Commissions of Reference.
208	Pickering, Chas...	Gliddon Mummy Case in Smithsonian Institution.	
218	Morgan, L. H........	Systems of Consanguinity and Affinity....	Prof. J. A. Hadley, J. H. Trumbull, Prof. W. D. Whitney.
220	Swan, Jas. G.........	Indians of Cape Flattery..........................	George Gibbs, Jeffries Wyman.
221	Coffin, James H...	Orbit, &c., of Meteoric Fire Ball, July 20, 1860.	Prof. H. A. Newton, C. A. Schott.
222	Schott, Chas. A.....	Tables of Rain and Snow in United States.	
223	Gould, B. A...........	Transatlantic Longitude.	
232	Stockwell, J. N....	Secular Variations of Orbits of Planets...	Prof. J. H. C. Coffin, Prof. S. Newcomb.
233	Ferrel, Wm.........	Converging Series, Ratio of Diameter, and Circumference of Circles.	
239	Harkness, Wm.......	Magnetic Observations on the Monadnock.	Pres. Acad. Sciences. Prof. J. H. C. Coffin, Prof. F. Rogers.
240	Barnard, J. G......	Problems of Rotary Motion.	
241	Wood, H. C............	Fresh-Water Algæ of North America	Dr. J. Torrey, Dr. F. A. P. Barnard.
242	Clark, H. J...........	Lucernariæ.	
248	Hilgard, E. W......	Geology of Lower Louisiana.	
259	Jones, Jos..............	Antiquities of Tennessee	Dr. G. A. Otis, Prof. O. T. Mason.
262	Newcomb, S...........	Orbit of Uranus..	Prof. J. H. C. Coffin, Prof. Asaph Hall.
267	Swan, J. G............	Haidah Indians...	J. C. Welling, LL. D., Dr. G. A. Otis.
268	Coffin, J. H..........	Winds of the Globe.	
269	Habel, Simeon......	Sculptures of Santa Lucia Cosumalwhuapa in Guatemala.	Prof. W. D. Whitney, J. H. Trumbull.
277	Schott, C. A..........	Temperature Tables.	
280	Alexander, S........	Harmonies of Solar System.	
281	Newcomb, S...........	Planetary Motion......................................	Prof. H. A. Newton, G. W. Hill.
287	Rau, Charles........	Archæological Collection, Nat. Museum.	
310	Barnard, J. G......	Internal Structure of the Earth.	
317	Elliot, D. G.........	Classification and Synopsis of Trochilidæ.	
318	Dall, Wm. H.........	Remains of Man from Caves in Aleutian Islands.	
331	Rau, Charles........	The Palenque Tablet.................................	S. F. Haven, H. H. Bancroft.
353	Schott, C. A..........	Tables of Rain Fall, (2d edition.)	
357	Wood, H. C............	Researches on Fever.................................	S. Weir Mitchell, M. D., J. J. Woodward, M. D.
383	Bransford, J. F....	Archæological Researches in Nicaragua...	Garrick Mallery, H. C. Yarrow, M. D
443	Caswell, A...........	Meteorological Observations, Providence, R. I., 1831 to 1876.	

ALPHABETICAL INDEX OF ARTICLES

IN THE

SMITHSONIAN CONTRIBUTIONS TO KNOWLEDGE,
VOLS. 1–23. 1848–1881.

SMITHSONIAN MISCELLANEOUS COLLECTIONS,
VOLS. 1–23. 1862–1882.

SMITHSONIAN ANNUAL REPORTS,
VOLS. 1–35. 1846–1880.

BULLETINS OF THE U. S. NATIONAL MUSEUM,
NOS. 1–22, (except 16 and 20,) 1875–1881,

PROCEEDINGS OF THE U. S. NATIONAL MUSEUM,
VOLS. 1–4. 1878–1881.

AND IN THE

FIRST ANNUAL REPORT OF THE BUREAU OF ETHNOLOGY OF THE SMITHSONIAN INSTITUTION,
VOL. 1. 1879–1880.

[illegible]

ALPHABETICAL INDEX.

NOTE.—The heavy-faced figures indicate the specific number in the Catalogue of a separate publication; the ordinary, or light-faced figures indicating the number of a publication of which the paper is only a constituent part.

"R." represents the annual Smithsonian Report, immediately followed by the year of the report, and the number given to it in the Catalogue.

"P." represents the Proceedings of the National Museum, followed by the year of publication and the number given to the volume in the Catalogue.

"E." represents Report of the Bureau of Ethnology.

A.

ABBE, C. Description of Observatories at Dorpat and Poulkova. (R. 1867) 215, **369**

ABBE, C. Meteorological memoirs, translated by. (R. 1877) 323, **398**

ABBOTT, C. C. Stone age in New Jersey. (R. 1875) 298, **394**

Abbreviations of names of States, etc., for labelling collections **164**

Abbreviations used in England in 1867—W. DE LA RUE. (R. 1867) 215

Abeona aurora—JORDAN and GILBERT. (P. 1880) 425

ABICH, S. Remarkable forms of hail-stones. (R. 1869) 228

Aboriginal indians of America, language of—G. GIBBS. (R. 1870) 244

Aboriginal inhabitants of Cal.—J. BAEGERT. (R. 1863; R. 1864). 187, 188, 440, **361**

Aboriginal lapidary, Stock-in-trade of—C. RAU. (R. 1877) 323, 440, **402**

Aboriginal monuments of State of New York—E. G. SQUIER **15**

Aboriginal remains of Tennessee—J. JONES **259**

Aboriginal ruins at Savannah, Tenn.—J. P. STELLE. (R. 1870) 244

Aboriginal ruins in Hardin Co., Tenn.—J. P. STELLE. (R. 1870) 244

Aboriginal shell-mounds, New Brunswick & New Eng.—S. F. BAIRD. (P. 1881). 467

Aboriginal structures in Georgia—C. C. JONES, Jr. (R. 1877) 323, **400**

Abstracts of anthropological correspondence—O. T. MASON. (R. 1879; R. 1880) 345, 442

Academy, Pontifical, Rome—*See* Prize questions.

Academy of Sciences—*See* National.

Academy of Sciences, Bordeaux—*See* Prize questions.

Academy of Sciences, Chicago, acknowledging specimens. (R. 1867) 215

Academy of Sciences, St. Petersburg, exchange system. (R. 1867) 215

Academy of Sciences, Vienna—*See* Prize questions.

Acalephæ, anatomy and physiology of—H. J. CLARK ---- **242**
Accidental or subjective colors—ABBE MOIGNO. (R. 1866) ---- 214
Account of—
aboriginal ruins at Savannah, Tenn.—J. P. STELLE. (R. 1870) ---- 244
aboriginal ruins in Hardin Co., Tenn.—J. P. STELLE. (R. 1870) ---- 244
aborigines of California—J. BAEGERT. (R. 1863; R. 1864) - 187, 188, 440, **361**
ancient mounds, Georgia—M. F. STEPHENSON. (R. 1870) ---- 244
antiquities, Tennessee—E. O. DUNNING. (R. 1870) ---- 244
antiquities, Vera Cruz, Mexico—H. FINCK. (R. 1870) ---- 244
astronomical observatory at Cordoba—B. A. GOULD. (R. 1878) ---- 275
balloon ascensions—J. GLAISHER. (R. 1863) ---- 187
barometer, new—J. GREEN. (R. 1855) ---- 77
burial of Indian squaw, California—W. M. KING. (R. 1874) ---- 286
Carib or Karif language and people. (R. 1878) ---- 275
discovery of stone image in Tennessee—E. M. GRANT. (R. 1870) ---- 244
Draper's telescope—T. W. WEBB. (R. 1864) ---- 188
eclipse of sun in Peru, 1858—J. M. GILLISS ---- **100**
hail storm in Texas—G. M. BACHE. (R. 1870) ---- 244
hail storm on Bosphorus—Com. PORTER. (R. 1870) ---- 244
Indians of British America—E. PETITOT. (R. 1865) ---- 209
lightning discharges. (R. 1867) ---- 215
Lindheimer's botanical explorations—A. GRAY. (R. 1849) ---- 21
marble used in extension of U. S. Capitol—J. HENRY. (R. 1856) ---- 91
"occultator" for indicating moon's position—T. HILL ---- **101**
old Indian village, Kushkushkee, Pa.—E. M. MCCONNELL. (R. 1871) - 249
Portland Society of Natural History—E. C. BOLLES. (R. 1867) ---- 215
Priestley's lens—J. HENRY. (R. 1859) ---- 110
remarkable accumulation of bats—M. FIGANIERRE. (R. 1863) ---- 187
sarcophagus in National Museum—A. A. HARWOOD. (R. 1870) ---- 244
storm in Butler Co., Kans., June 23, 1871—W. HARRISON. (R. 1871) ---- 249
tornado in Spruce Creek Valley, Pa.—J. B. MEEK. (R. 1871) ---- 249
tornado near New Harmony, Indiana—J. CHAPPELSMITH ---- **59**
travels in Central and South America—S. HABEL ---- **269**
Acid, sulphurous, action of, upon putrefactive bacteria. (P. 1881) ---- 467
Acknowledgment of birds—Academy of Sciences, Stockholm. (R. 1867) ---- 215
Acknowledgment of birds—J. GOULD. (R. 1867) ---- 215
Acknowledgment of contributions to National Museum. (P. 1881) ---- 467, **473**
Acknowledgment of ferns—G. METTENIUS. (R. 1862) ---- 150
Acknowledgment of perennibranchiates—J. G. FISHER. (R. 1863) ---- 187
Acknowledgment of shells, &c.—W. H. PEASE. (R. 1861) ---- 149
Acknowledgment of specimens—British Museum. (R. 1865) ---- 209
Acknowledgment of specimens—Chicago Academy of Sciences. (R. 1867) ---- 215

Acknowledgment of specimens—Regents of Univ. of State of N. Y. (R. 1865) 209
Acmæidæ, from Panama, new species of—P. P. CARPENTER 252
Acoustics applied to public buildings—J. HENRY. (R. 1856) 91
Acoustics, different kinds of refraction—W. B. TAYLOR. (R. 1875) 298
Acoustics, lectures on architecture in relation to—D. B. REID. (R. 1856) 91
Acrothele, note on—C. A. WHITE. (P. 1880) 425
Acts of Congress—*See* Congress.
ADAMS, C. B. Catalogue of shells of Panama, review of—P. P. CARPENTER 252
ADAMS, C. B. Shells collected by, description of 252
ADAMS, W. Subcutaneous surgery. Toner lecture No. VI **302**
ADAMS, W. H. Mounds in Spoon River Valley, Illinois. (R. 1879) 345
Additions to Museum by Berlin Fisheries Exhibition. (R. 1880) 442
Address at laying of corner-stone of Smithsonian building—G. M. DALLAS. **D**, 329
Address on the Smithsonian Institution—J. HENRY. (R. 1853) **E** 67
Address, Pres. Royal Society of Victoria—R. L. J. ELLERY. (R. 1868) 224
Addresses at memorial services of J. Henry—*See* Henry.
Addresses, list of, foreign institutions, since 1862. (R. 1865) 209
Administration of drugs and medicines—J. M. FLINT. (P. 1881) 467, **451**
Aerial navigation—J. HENRY. (R. 1860) 147
Aerial navigation, currents of the atmosphere and—J. HENRY. (R. 1860) 147
Aeronautic voyage across the Atlantic, Memorial relative to Lowe's. (R. 1860) 147
Aeronautic voyage, reply to memorial on Lowe's—J. HENRY. (R. 1860) 147
Aeronautic voyages—F. ARAGO. (R. 1863) 187
Aeronautic voyages—J. GLAISHER. (R. 1863) 187
Aeronautics, modes of flight in relation to—J. B. PETTIGREW. (R. 1867) 215
Affinity, systems of—L. H. MORGAN 218
Africa, stone celts in—G. J. GIBBS. (R. 1877) 323
Africa, Yoruba, account of, and grammar and dictionary **98**
AGASSIZ, L., biographical notice of—J. A. GARFIELD. (R. 1873) 275, 329
AGASSIZ, L., biographical notice of—P. PARKER. (R. 1873) 275, 329
AGASSIZ, L., biography of—E. FAVRE. (R. 1878) 341
AGASSIZ, L., memoir of—R. P. STEBBINS. (R. 1873) 275
AGASSIZ, L., supplemental list of generic names employed by—S. H. SCUDDER. **470**
AGASSIZ, L., papers by—
    Classification of insects from embryological data **16**
    Narrative of the Hassler expedition. (R. 1872) 271, 329
    On the formation of a museum. (R. 1849) 21, 329
    Report on use of new hall in Smithsonian building. (R. 1867) 215, 329
    Scientific instructions to Captain Hall. (R. 1871) 249
Age of stone—R. S. ROBERTSON. (R. 1874) 286
AGNEW, S. A. Mounds in Mississippi. (R. 1867) 215
Agonidæ, new species of, from California—W. N. LOCKINGTON. (P. 1880) 425

Agonus vulsus—JORDAN and GILBERT. (P. 1880) ---- 425
Agricultural Association of Milan, on exchanges. (R. 1863) ---- 187
Agricultural chemistry, lectures on—S. W. JOHNSON. (R. 1859) ---- 110
Agricultural flint implements in Illinois—C. RAU. (R. 1868) ---- 224, 440, **370**
Agricultural flint implements, Southern Illinois—C. RAU. (R. 1868) ---- 224, **370**
Agricultural implements of N. American stone period—C. RAU. (R. 1863) ---- 187, 440
AINSA, SANTIAGO. Tucson meteorite. (R. 1863) ---- 187
Air, temperature in ascending currents of—J. HANN. (R. 1877) ---- 323, 398
Air, temperature in ascending moist currents of—L. SOHNCKE. (R. 1877) ---- 323, 398
Air-currents, nature of—A. COLDING. (R. 1877) ---- 323, 398
AIRY, G. B. Correcting measures of the sun's distance. (R. 1859) ---- 110
Alabama, mica beds in—W. GESNER. (R. 1879) ---- 345
Alabama, shell-heaps—A. S. GAINES and K. M. CUNNINGHAM. (R. 1877) ---- 323
Alaska, bibliography of fishes of, for 1880—T. H. BEAN. (P. 1881) ---- 467
Alaska, climate of—H. M. BANNISTER. (R. 1866) ---- 214
Alaska, description of *Lycodes Turneri* from—T. H. BEAN. (P. 1878) ---- 332
Alaska, descriptions of new fishes from—T. H. BEAN. (P. 1881) ---- 467
Alaska, flora of—J. T. ROTHROCK. (R. 1867) ---- 215, **367**
Alaska, limpets and chitons of, report on—W. H. DALL. (P. 1878) ---- 332
Alaska, new fish from—T. H. BEAN. (P. 1879) ---- 333
Alaska, new fish from—W. N. LOCKINGTON. (P. 1880) ---- 425
Alaska, new forms of mollusks from—W. H. DALL. (P. 1878) ---- 332
Alaska, notes on Nichols' collection of fishes of—T. H. BEAN. (P. 1881) ---- 467
Alaska, occurrence of *Hippoglossus vulgaris* at—T. H. BEAN. (P. 1879) ---- 333
Alaska, occurrence of *Stichæus punctatus* at—T. H. BEAN. (P. 1878) ---- 332
Alaska, preliminary catalogue of fishes of—T. H. BEAN. (P. 1881) ---- 467
Alaska, remains of prehistoric man from caves in—W. H. DALL ---- **318**
Alaska, some genera and species of fishes from—T. H. BEAN. (P. 1879) ---- 333
Albany, Illinois, mound skull and bones—R. J. FARQUHARSON. (R. 1874) ---- 286
Albany Institute, memorial proceedings relative to Joseph Henry ---- 356
Album from Greece, presented by Miss E. B. Contaxaki. (R. 1857) ---- 107, 329
Alepocephalus Bairdii, from deep sea Atlantic—G. B. GOODE; T. H. BEAN. (P. 1879) ---- 333
Aleutian Islands, remains of prehistoric man from—W. H. DALL ---- **318**
ALEXANDER, B. S. Report of architect. (R. 1854) ---- 75, 329
ALEXANDER, C. A. Origin and history of Royal Society of London. (R. 1863) 187
ALEXANDER, C. A., (translations by)—
Accidental or subjective colors—ABBE MOIGNO. (R. 1866) ---- 214
American migration—F. VON HELLWALD. (R. 1866) ---- 214
Biography of Peltier by his Son. (R. 1867) ---- 215
Carlsruhe Scientific Congress—M. J. NICKLES. (R. 1860) ---- 147
Catalytic force—T. L. PHIPSON. (R. 1862) ---- 150

ALEXANDER, C. A., (translations by)—Continued.
Earthquake in Mexico—C. SARTORIUS. (R. 1866) 214
Electrical currents of the earth—C. MATTEUCCI. (R. 1867) 215
Electricity. (R. 1867) 215
Electro-physiology—C. MATTEUCCI. (R. 1865) 209
External appearance of sun's disk. (R. 1866) 214
Figures of equilibrium of a liquid mass—J. PLATEAU. (R. 1865; R. 1866) 209, 214
Formation of ice at bottom of water—M. ENGLEHARDT. (R. 1866) 214
History of Academy of Sciences of Paris—M. FLOURENS. (R. 1862) 150
History of Royal Institution of Great Britain—E. MAILLY. (R. 1867) 215
Horary variations of barometer—M. VAILLANT. (R. 1866) 214
International Archæological Congress. (R. 1866) 214
Jussieus, the, and the natural method—M. FLOURENS. (R. 1867) 215
Life of Faraday—DE LA RIVE. (R. 1867) 215
Life of Kepler—M. BERTHRAND. (R. 1869) 228
Man the contemporary of the mammoth. (R. 1867) 215
Memoir of A. Bravais—E. DE BEAUMONT. (R. 1869) 228
Memoir of D. de Blainville—M. FLOURENS. (R. 1865) 209
Memoir of von Buch—M. FLOURENS. (R. 1862) 150
Memoir of A. de Candolle—M. FLOURENS. (R. 1859) 110
Memoir of Delambre—J. FOURIER. (R. 1864) 188
Memoir of R. J. Häuy—M. CUVIER. (R. 1860) 147
Memoir of Legendre—E. DE BEAUMONT. (R. 1867) 215
Memoir of L. J. Thenard—M. FLOURENS. (R. 1862) 150
Memoir of Magendie—M. FLOURENS. (R. 1866) 214
Memoir of Priestley—M. CUVIER. (R. 1858) 109
Memoir of Geoffroy St. Hilaire—M. FLOURENS. (R. 1861) 149
Microscope. (R. 1860) 147
Movement of the stars—M. MAEDLER. (R. 1859) 110
Natural History of organized beings—M. MAREY. (R. 1867) 215
Palafittes or lacustrian constructions—E. DESOR. (R. 1865) 209
Photo-chemistry—M. JAMIN. (R. 1867) 215
Pile-work antiquities of Olmutz. (R. 1866) 214
Preservation of wood. (R. 1864) 188
Scientific Congress of Carlsruhe—M. J. NICKLES. (R. 1860) 147
Scintillation of the stars—C. D. KÄMTZ. (R. 1861) 149
Sense of feeling: sense of smell. (R. 1865) 209
Sense of hearing. (R. 1866) 214
Sense of sight. (R. 1866) 214
Sense of taste. (R. 1866) 214
Small planets between Mars and Jupiter—LESPIAULT. (R. 1861) 149

ALEXANDER, C. A., (translations by)—Continued.

State of ethnology in relation to form of human skull—A. PELZIUS. (R. 1859) ---- 110

Transactions of Geneva Society of Physics, &c. (R. 1859; R. 1864; R. 1865; R. 1866) ---- 110, 188, 209, 214

ALEXANDER, S. Harmonies of the solar system ---- **280**

ALEXANDER, S. Lecture on relations of time and space. (R. 1861) ---- 149

ALEXANDER, S. Lecture on vastness of visible creation. (R. 1857) ---- 107

Algæ—J. W. BAILEY ---- 23

Algæ, Arctic, list of—W. H. HARVEY ---- 95

Algæ, Arctic America—W. G. FARLOW ---- 342

Algæ, bibliography of—H. C. WOOD ---- 241

Algæ, Kerguelen Island—W. G. FARLOW ---- 294

Algæ, lecture on marine—W. H. HARVEY. (R. 1855) ---- 77

Algæ, marine. Part 1, Melanospermeæ—W. H. HARVEY ---- **32**

Algæ, marine. Part 2, Rhodospermeæ—W. H. HARVEY ---- **43**

Algæ, marine. Part 3, Chlorospermeæ—W. H. HARVEY ---- **95**

Algæ, marine. Parts 1, 2, 3, complete—W. H. HARVEY ---- **96**

Algæ, North American fresh water, history of—H. C. WOOD ---- **241**

Algæ, Rhode Island, list of—S. T. OLNEY ---- 241

ALLEN, H. Monograph of bats of North America ---- **165**

ALLEN, Z. Explosibility of coal oils. (R. 1861) ---- 149

Alphabetical index of genera of birds—S. F. BAIRD ---- 108

Alphabetical index to Smithsonian publications ---- **478**

Alternate generation and parthenogenesis—G. A. KORNHUBER. (R. 1871) ---- 249

Altitude, diminution of vapor with increasing—J. HANN. (R. 1877) ---- 323, 398

Altitudes, circular relative to—J. HENRY ---- **236**

ALVORD, B. Tangencies of circles and of spheres ---- **80**

Amazilia cerviniventris—R. RIDGWAY. (P. 1881) ---- 467

Amazilia yucatanensis—R. RIDGWAY. (P. 1881) ---- 467

Amblystoma, change of axolotl to—A. WEISMANN. (R. 1877) ---- 323, **401**

Amblystoma, luridum—P. R. HOY. (R. 1854) ---- 75

America—*See* Arctic, British, Central, Middle, North, Russian, South.

America, ancient history of—M. MUCH. (R. 1871) ---- 249

America, collection of charts and maps of—J. G. KOHL. (R. 1856) ---- 91

America, grasshoppers and locusts of—A. S. TAYLOR. (R. 1858) ---- 109

America, language of aboriginal Indians of—G. GIBBS. (R. 1870) ---- 244

America, storms in, December, 1836—E. LOOMIS ---- **127**

American Academy of Arts and Sciences—

On Smithsonian exchange system. (R. 1867) ---- 215

Report on organization of Smithsonian. (R. 1858) ---- 67

Thanks for exchanges. (R. 1855) ---- 77

American Antiquarian Society. Antiquities of Wisconsin **70**
American archæology circular **316**
American Association for Advancement of Science—
Combined meteorological observations proposed. (R. 1851) 51
Memorial address on Joseph Henry. A. M. MAYER **417**
American authors, North American conchology—W. G. BINNEY **142**
American Board of Commissioners for Foreign Missions. Grammar and dictionary of Dakota language **40**
American corbiculadæ, monograph of—T. PRIME **145**
American correspondents, list of **69, 238**
American Ethnological Society, report on Squier and Davis' work. (R. 1847) .. **H, K**
American migration—F. VON HELLWALD; JOS. HENRY. (R. 1866) 214
American natural history, bibliography for 1851. C. GIRARD **48**
Amiurus ponderosus, from Mississippi river—T. H. BEAN. (P. 1879) 338
Ammonia-cobalt bases—W. GIBBS; F. A. GENTH **88**
AMPÈRE, eulogy on—F. ARAGO. (R. 1872) 271
Amphorosteus, memoir on—R. W. GIBBES 14
Ampullariidæ—W. G. BINNEY 144
Analyses of Chinese and Japanese coals—J. A. MACDONALD 202
Analysis, chemical, of the sun—A. LAUGEL. (R. 1861) 149
Analysis of blood—J. JONES 82
Analysis of water destructive to fish in Gulf of Mexico—F. M. ENDLICH. (P. 1881) 467
Analysis, spectrum—W. HUGGINS. (R. 1866) 214
Anarrhichas lepturus, from Alaska, and other species—T. H. BEAN. (P. 1878) 333
Anatomical preparations, arsenic acid for protecting, from insects—J. B. S. JACKSON. (P. 1878) 332
Anatomy and physiology of chelonia—S. W. MITCHELL; G. R. MOREHOUSE .. **159**
Anatomy and physiology of lucernarians—H. J. CLARK **242**
Anatomy and physiology of the rattlesnake—S. W. MITCHELL **135**
Anatomy of the nervous system of *Rana pipiens*—J. WYMAN **45**
Ancient aboriginal trade in North America—C. RAU. (R. 1872) 271, 440, **385**
Ancient and modern purple dyeing. (R. 1863) 187
Ancient burial mound in Indiana—W. PIDGEON. (R. 1867) 215
Ancient earthworks of Ashland county, Ohio—G. W. HILL. (R. 1877) 323
Ancient earthworks of Ohio, sketch of—I. DILLE. (R. 1866) 214
Ancient earthworks on Upper Missouri—A. BARRANDT. (R. 1870) 244
Ancient fauna of Nebraska—J. LEIDY **58**
Ancient fort and burial ground, Tomp. Co., N. Y.—D. TROWBRIDGE. (R. 1863) 187
Ancient graves and shell-heaps of California—P. SCHUMACHER. (R. 1874) ... 286
Ancient history of North America—M. MUCH. (R. 1871) 249
Ancient implement of wood found in Conn.—E. W. ELLSWORTH. (R. 1876) .. 299

Ancient man in Michigan, characteristics of—H. GILLMAN. (R. 1875) --- 298, **393**
Ancient mica mines North Carolina—C. D. SMITH. (R. 1876) --- 299
Ancient mining on Lake Superior—C. WHITTLESEY --- **155**
Ancient mining on Lake Superior, circular on—J. HENRY. (R. 1861) --- 149
Ancient monuments in the Miss. val., correspondence relative to. (R. 1847) -- **H, K**
Ancient monuments in the Mississippi valley—E. G. SQUIER; E. H. DAVIS --- **1**
Ancient mound in western Pennsylvania—W. M. TAYLOR. (R. 1877) --- 323
Ancient mound near Chattanooga, Tennessee—M. C. READ. (R. 1867) --- 215
Ancient mound, near Lexington, Ky.—R. PETER. (R. 1871) --- 249
Ancient mound, St. Louis, Mo.—T. R. PEALE. (R. 1861) --- 149
Ancient mounds in Georgia—M. F. STEPHENSON. (R. 1870) --- 244
Ancient mounds in Kentucky—R. PETER. (R. 1872) --- 271
Ancient mounds of Mercer county, Illinois—T. McWHORTER. (R. 1874) --- 286
Ancient mounds of Union county, Kentucky—S. S. LYON. (R. 1870) --- 244
Ancient pottery from Phillips county, Arkansas—J. H. DEVEREUX. (R. 1872) 271
Ancient pottery on Des Moines river—R. N. and C. DAHLBERG. (R. 1879) -- 345
Ancient relic of Maya sculpture—A. SCHOTT. (R. 1871) --- 249
Ancient relics in Missouri—J. W. FOSTER. (R. 1863) --- 187
Ancient relics in northwestern Iowa—J. B. CUTTS. (R. 1872) --- 271
Ancient remains in Canada West, near Prescott—W. E. GUEST. (R. 1856) --- 91
Ancient remains in Colorado—E. L. BERTHOUD. (R. 1867) --- 215
Ancient ruin in Arizona—J. C. Y. LEE. (R. 1872) --- 271
Ancient town in Minnesota—O. H. KELLEY. (R. 1863) --- 187
Ancient works in Ohio, description of—C. WHITTLESEY --- **37**
ANDERSON, M. B. Life of Professor Chester Dewey. (R. 1870) --- 244
ANDERSON, W. Antiquities of Perry county, Ohio. (R. 1874) --- 286
ANDERSON, W. G. Mounds in Illinois and Wisconsin. (R. 1879) --- 345
ANDREWS, F. D. Indian relics from Schoharie, New York. (R. 1879) --- 345
ANDREWS, S. L. Meteors. (R. 1866) --- 214
Anemometer, description of Smithsonian—J. HENRY. (R. 1860) --- 147
Aneroid barometers, experiments—B. STEWART. (R. 1868) --- 224
Animal kingdom, list of substances derived from—G. B. GOODE --- 297
Animal kingdom, parthenogenesis in—G. A. KORNHUBER. (R. 1871) --- 249
Animal resources of United States, classification of collection—G. B. GOODE -- **297**
Animal resources of United States, collection at Centennial—G. B. GOODE --- **326**
Animals, circular for shipping—S. F. BAIRD --- **384**
Animals, flora and fauna within living—J. LEIDY --- **44**
Animals, list of all generic names of—S. H. SCUDDER --- **470**
Animals, synopsis of useful and injurious—G. B. GOODE --- 297
Anna, Illinois, mounds near—T. M. PERRIN. (R. 1872) --- 271
Annals of Philosophy, list of Smithson's papers in. (R. 1853) --- 67, 330
Annelids of Arctic America—A. E. VERRILL --- 342

Annelids of Kerguelen Island—A. E. VERRILL ---- 294
Annelids of northeastern coast of America—A. E. VERRILL. (P. 1879; P. 1880) ---- 333, 425
Annular eclipse of May 26, 1854 ---- **66**
Antennariidæ, note on—T. GILL. (P. 1878) ---- 332
Anthozoa of Kerguelen Island—A. E. VERRILL ---- 294
Anthozoa of northeast coast of America—A. E. VERRILL. (P. 1879) ---- 333
Anthropological articles, Smithsonian, index to—G. H. BOEHMER. (R. 1879) 345, **421**
Anthropological Congress, address before—F. F. ROMER. (R. 1876) ---- 299, **392**
Anthropological correspondence, abstracts of—O. T. MASON. (R. 1880) ---- 442
Anthropological correspondence, summary of—O. T. MASON. (R. 1879) ---- 345
Anthropological data, limitations to use of—J. W. POWELL. (E. 1880) ---- 476
Anthropological inquiry, queries for—C. DARWIN. (R. 1867) ---- 215
Anthropological investigations in 1879—O. T. MASON. (R. 1879) ---- 345, **420**
Anthropological measurements, table of—SCHERZER; SCHWARZ. (R. 1866) -- 214
Anthropological publications, list of C. RAU's. (P. 1881) ---- 467
Anthropological Society of Paris, transactions of—P. BROCA. (R. 1868) ---- 224
Anthropological Society of Vienna, address on ancient history of North America—M. MUCH. (R. 1871) ---- 249
Anthropology, articles on. (R. 1879) ---- 345
Anthropology, bibliography of—O. T. MASON. (R. 1880) ---- 442, **432**
Anthropology, index to Smithsonian papers on—G. H. BOEHMER. (R. 1879) -- 345
Anthropology, progress of, in 1880—O. T. MASON. (R. 1880) ---- 442, **432**
Anthropology, recent progress in—O. T. MASON. (R. 1880) ---- 442, **432**
Antigua, catalogue of Ober's collection of birds of—G. N. LAWRENCE. (P. 1878) 332
Antilles, maritime disasters of the. (R. 1867) ---- 215
Antilles—*See* Lesser Antilles.
Antiquarian Society, American. Antiquities of Wisconsin ---- **70**
Antiquities, California, Santa Rosa Island—S. BOWERS. (R. 1877) ---- 323
Antiquities, Col., Jefferson and Clear Creek Cos.—G. L. CANNON. (R. 1877) -- 323
Antiquities, Colorado, Weld county—E. L. BERTHOUD. (R. 1871) ---- 249
Antiquities, Denmark, preservation of—J. J. A. WORSAAE. (R. 1879) ---- 345
Antiquities, Florida—J. BARTRAM. (R. 1874) ---- 286
Antiquities, Florida—A. MITCHELL. (R. 1874) ---- 286
Antiquities, Georgia, Spalding county—W. B. F. BAILEY. (R. 1877) ---- 323
Antiquities, Guatemala—G. WILLIAMSON. (R. 1876) ---- 299
Antiquities, Hungary, prehistoric—F. F. ROMER. (R. 1876) ---- 299, 440, **392**
Antiquities, Illinois, Lawrence county—A. PATTON. (R. 1873) ---- 275
Antiquities, Illinois, Mason county—J. COCHRANE. (R. 1877) ---- 323
Antiquities, Illinois, Rock Island county—A. TOELLNER. (R. 1879) ---- 345
Antiquities, Illinois, Union county—T. M. PERRINE. (R. 1873) ---- 275
Antiquities, Illinois, Whitesides county—W. H. PRATT. (R. 1874) ---- 286

Antiquities, Indiana, Allen and DeKalb counties—R. S. ROBERTSON. (R. 1874) 286
Antiquities, Indiana, Knox county—A. PATTON. (R. 1873) 275
Antiquities, Indiana, Laporte county—R. S. ROBERTSON. (R. 1874) 286
Antiquities, Kentucky—S. S. LYON. (R. 1858) 109
Antiquities, Kentucky, Hancock county—J. FRIEL. (R. 1877) 323
Antiquities, Maryland, Charles county—O. N. BRYAN. (R. 1874) 286
Antiquities, Mexico, Vera Cruz—H. FINCK. (R. 1870) 244
Antiquities, Michigan, Isle Royale—A. C. DAVIS. (R. 1874) 286
Antiquities, Mississippi river and Lake Pepin—L. C. ESTES. (R. 1866) 214
Antiquities, Mississippi, Yazoo county—J. W. C. SMITH. (R. 1874) 286
Antiquities, Missouri and Tennessee—I. DILLE. (R. 1862) 150
Antiquities, Missouri, Kansas City—W. H. R. LYKINS. (R. 1877) 328
Antiquities, New Mexico—W. B. LYON. (R. 1871) 249
Antiquities, New York, Orleans county—F. H. CUSHING. (R. 1874) 286
Antiquities, Nicaragua—E. G. SQUIER. (R. 1850) 28
Antiquities, North Carolina, Lenoir county—J. M. SPAINHOUR. (R. 1871) 249
Antiquities, N. C., Stanley and Montgomery counties—F. J. KRON. (R. 1874) 286
Antiquities, Ohio—G. W. HILL. (R. 1874) 286
Antiquities, Ohio, Perry county—W. ANDERSON. (R. 1874) 286
Antiquities, Olmutz pile-work. (R. 1866) 214
Antiquities, Porto Rico, Latimer collection—O. T. MASON. (R. 1876) 299, **397**
Antiquities, Southern States—H. C. WILLIAMS. (R. 1870) 244
Antiquities, Tennessee—W. M. CLARK. (R. 1877) 323
Antiquities, Tennessee—E. O. DUNNING. (R. 1870) 244
Antiquities, Tennessee—J. JONES **259**
Antiquities, Tennessee—R. S. ROBERTSON. (R. 1877) 323
Antiquities, Tennessee—D. F. WRIGHT. (R. 1874) 286
Antiquities, Tennessee, Blount county—Miss A. E. LAW. (R. 1874) 286
Antiquities, Tennessee, Jackson county—J. HAILE; J. W. MCHENRY. (R. 1874) 286
Antiquities, United States, proposed map of—A. J. HILL. (R. 1861) 149
Antiquities, Wisconsin—I. A. LAPHAM **70**
Antiquities, Wisconsin—M. STRONG. (R. 1877) 323
Antiquity in Europe, the study of high—A. MORLOT. (R. 1862; R. 1864) 150, 188
Antiquity in United States, vestiges of—S. F. HAVEN 71
Antozone and ozone—C. M. WETHERILL. (R. 1864) 188, **355**
Apaches, Tonto, notes on the—C. SMART. (R. 1867) 215
Aphododeridæ, notes on—D. S. JORDAN 306
Apodichthys—JORDAN and GILBERT. (P. 1880) 425
Apogon pandionis, description of—G. B. GOODE; T. H. BEAN. (P. 1881) 467
Apparatus available for research, list of. (R. 1878) 341
Apparatus, blow-pipe—HAWKINS and WALE. (R. 1872) 271
Apparatus for testing perspiration and respiration—PETTENKOFER. (R. 1864) 188

Apparatus, letter relative to gift of—R. HARE. (R. 1848) ---- I
Appropriations for Museum, memorial of regents asking for. (R. 1867) --- 215, 329
Aqueous vapor, diminution of, with altitude—J. HANN. (R. 1877) ---- 323, 398
Arachnida of Arctic America—S. H. SCUDDER ---- 342
ARAGO, F. Aeronautic voyages. (R. 1863) ---- 187
Autobiography. (R. 1870) ---- 244
Biography of Condorcet. (R. 1878) ---- 341
Eulogy on Ampère. (R. 1872) ---- 271
Eulogy on Joseph Fourier. (R. 1871) ---- 249
Eulogy on Gay-Lussac. (R. 1876) ---- 299
Eulogy on Herschel. (R. 1870) ---- 244
Eulogy on La Place. (R. 1874) ---- 286
Eulogy on Alex. Volta. (R. 1875) ---- 298
Eulogy on Thomas Young. (R. 1869) ---- 228
Archæological Academy of Belgium, Archæological Congress organized by. (R. 1866) ---- 214
Archæological collection of the U. S. National Museum—C. RAU ---- **287**
Archæological Congress, International, Antwerp. (R. 1866) ---- 214
Archæological investigations, instructions for—G. GIBBS. (R. 1861) ---- 149, **160**
Archæological researches at Concise—F. TROYON. (R. 1861) ---- 149
Archæological researches in Nicaragua—J. F. BRANSFORD ---- **383**
Archæological study of jade—S. BLONDEL. (R. 1876) ---- 299
Archæology, circular relative to American ---- **316**
Archæology, French Society of. (R. 1866) ---- 214
Archæology, general views on—A. MORLOT. (R. 1860; R. 1861) ---- 147, 149
Archæology, Mexican—B. MAYER ---- **86**
Archæology, North American—J. LUBBOCK. (R. 1862) ---- 150
Archæology of the United States—S. F. HAVEN ---- **71**
Archæology, prehistoric, international code of symbols for charts of. (R. 1875) 298
Archæology and ethnology, circular for collecting specimens of ---- **205**
Architect's report—B. S. ALEXANDER. (R. 1854) ---- 75, 329
Architect's report—A. CLUSS. (R. 1867) ---- 215, 329
Architects' report for 1879—CLUSS & SCHULZE. (R. 1879) ---- 345, 409
Architects' report for 1880—CLUSS & SCHULZE. (R. 1880) ---- 442, 434
Architecture, hints on public—R. D. OWEN ---- **P**
Architecture in relation to ventilation, warming, lighting, fire-proofing, acoustics, and the general preservation of health—D. B. REID. (R. 1856) ---- 91
Arctic algæ, list of—W. H. HARVEY ---- 95
Arctic America, natural history of—L. KUMLIEN ---- **342**
Arctic atmospheric pressure—I. I. HAYES ---- 196
Arctic auroras—P. FORCE ---- **84**
Arctic expedition, Howgate—L. KUMLIEN ---- **342**

Arctic explorations, lecture on—I. I. HAYES. (R. 1861) 149
Arctic latitudes and longitudes—E. K. KANE 129
Arctic observations—*See* Force, Hall, Hayes, Kane, Kumlien, McClintock, Schott.
Arctic regions, limpets and chitons of, report on—W. H. DALL. (P. 1878) 382
Arctic regions, record of voyage of yacht "Fox" 146
Arctic seas, astronomical observations—E. K. KANE **129**
Arctic seas, magnetical observations—E. K. KANE **97**
Arctic seas, meteorological observations—E. K. KANE **104**
Arctic seas, meteorological observations—F. L. McCLINTOCK **146**
Arctic seas, physical observations in—I. I. HAYES **196**
Arctic seas, physical observations in—E. K. KANE **198**
Arctic seas, tidal observations—E. K. KANE **130**
Arctic temperature—I. I. HAYES 196
Arctic winds—I. I. HAYES 196
Argentina syrtensium, new deep-sea fish—GOODE and BEAN. (P. 1878) 332
Argentine Republic, astronomical observatory—B. A. GOULD. (R. 1873) 275
Ariopsis Milberti, breeding habits of—N. T. LUPTON. (P. 1878) 332
Arizona, ancient ruin in—J. C. Y. LEE. (R. 1872) 271
Arizona, explorations in—J. STEVENSON. (R. 1880) 442
Arizona, Pima county, ruins in—R. T. BURR. (R. 1879) 345
Arizona, Pima Indians of—F. E. GROSSMAN. (R. 1871) 249
Arizona, Tonto Apaches of—C. SMART. (R. 1867) 215
Arkansas, cretaceous fossils from—C. A. WHITE. (P. 1881) 467
Arkansas, earthworks in—Mrs. G. KNAPP. (R. 1877) 323
Arkansas, invertebrate fossils from—C. A. WHITE. (P. 1880) 425
Arkansas, meteorological observations near Washington—N. D. SMITH **131**
Arkansas, Phillips county, ancient pottery—J. H. DEVEREUX. (R. 1872) 271
ARMSTRONG, T. Mounds in Winnebago county, Wisconsin. (R. 1879) 345
Arrangement of families of birds—S. F. BAIRD **210**
Arrangement of families of fishes—T. GILL **247**
Arrangement of families of mammals—T. GILL **230**
Arrangement of families of mollusks—T. GILL **227**
Arrangement of mineralogical collection—C. U. SHEPARD. (R. 1861) 149
Arrangement of the materia medica collection—J. M. FLINT. (P. 1881) 467, **450**
Arrangements, business, of the Smithsonian Institution **325**
Arrow-heads, deposit of, near Fishkill, New York—E. M. SHEPARD. (R. 1877) 323
Arrow-heads, Indian mode of making and obtaining fire—G. CROOK. (R. 1871) 249
Arrows, lectures on wounds of poisoned—D. BRAINARD. (R. 1854) 75
Arsenic acid for protecting anatomical preparations—J. B. S. JACKSON. (P. 1878) 332
Art, on tables of constants of nature and—C. BABBAGE. (R. 1856) 91
Art Gallery, Corcoran, deed of gift of. (R. 1872) 271, 329
Art Gallery, Corcoran, deposits in, by Smithsonian Institution. (R. 1874) 286

Art Gallery, Corcoran, report of Committee of Regents on. (R. 1872) 271, 329
Artories, reparatory inflammation in. Toner lecture No. VII—E. O. SHAKESPEARE **321**
Artificial shell deposits in New Jersey—C. RAU. (R. 1864) 188, 440, **362**
Artificial shell deposits of the United States—D. G. BRINTON. (R. 1866) 214
Artisan and artist, identification of the—N. WISEMAN. (R. 1870) 244
Artisans, scientific education of mechanics and—A. P. PEABODY. (R. 1872) 271, **380**
Arts, chemical, recent improvements in—J. C. BOOTH; C. MORFIT **27**
Ascelicthys rhodorus—JORDAN and GILBERT. (P. 1880) 425
Ascensions—*See* Balloons.
Assay of coins at mint of the United States—J. POLLOCK. (R. 1868) 224
Asteroid supplement to new tables—J. D. RUNKLE **94**
Asteroids between Mars and Jupiter—D. KIRKWOOD. (R. 1876) 299
Astronomical discoveries, telegraphic announcements of—J. HENRY **263**
Astronomical observations—W. HARKNESS 239
Astronomical observations, Arctic—I. I. HAYES **196**
Astronomical observations, discussion of Piazzi's—B. A. GOULD. (R. 1863) 187
Astronomical observations in the Arctic Seas—E. K. KANE **129**
Astronomical observatories, reports of—E. S. HOLDEN; G. H. BOEHMER. (R. 1880) 442, **438**
Astronomical observatories, reports of, 1879—E. S. HOLDEN. (R. 1879) 345, **410**
Astronomical observatories, reports of, 1880—E. S. HOLDEN; G. H. BOEHMER. (R. 1880) 442, **438**
Astronomical observatory at Cordoba, Argentine Republic, account of—B. A. GOULD. (R. 1873) 275
Astronomical photography, progress of—Dr. LEE. (R. 1861) 149
Astronomical tables—J. D. RUNKLE **79, 94**
Astronomical telegram circular—J. HENRY **263**
Astronomy, lecture on—A. CASWELL. (R. 1858) 109
Astronomy, progress of, in 1879 and 1880—E. S. HOLDEN. (R. 1880) 442, **427**
Astronomy, recent progress in—E. S. HOLDEN. (R. 1880) 442, **427**
Astroscopus, species of, in Eastern United States—T. H. BEAN. (P. 1879) 333
Atlantic coast, microscopic examination of soundings—J. W. BAILEY **20**
Atlantic, Lowe's aeronautic voyage across. (R. 1860) 147
Atlas, physical, of North America, proposed—G. GIBBS. (R. 1866) 214
Atmosphere, currents of the, and aerial navigation—J. HENRY. (R. 1860) 147
Atmosphere, diminution of aqueous vapor with altitude—J. HANN. (R. 1877) 323, 398
Atmosphere, plan of research upon—C. M. WETHERILL. (R. 1866) 214
Atmosphere, vegetation and the—J. JAMIN. (R. 1864) 188
Atmospheric circulation over the earth, laws of—J. H. COFFIN 268
Atmospheric currents, relation between barometric variations and—M. PESLIN. (R. 1877) 323, 398

Atmospheric electricity—M. F. DUPREZ. (R. 1858) ---- 109
Atmospheric pressure and rain fall—J. HANN. (R. 1877) ---- 323, 398
Atmospheric pressure, Arctic—I. I. HAYES ---- 196
Atmospheric pressure, Arctic—E. K. KANE ---- 104
Atmospheric pressure, Arctic—F. L. MCCLINTOCK ---- 146
Atomic volume, bibliography of—F. W. CLARKE ---- 255
Atomic weight determinations—G. F. BECKER ---- **358**
Atomic weights, recalculation of—F. W. CLARKE ---- **441**
Atoms—J. HERSCHEL. (R. 1862) ---- 150
Atthis Ellioti, a humming bird from Guatemala—R. RIDGWAY. (P. 1878) ---- 332
Aurora and electricity—S. LEMSTRÖM; A. A. DE LA RIVE. (R. 1874) ---- 286
Auröra, connection of gales of wind and—R. T. KNIGHT. (R. 1871) ---- 249
Aurora, directions for observing—J. HENRY. (R. 1855) ---- 77
Aurora, effect of, on magnetic declination—A. D. BACHE ---- 175
Aurora, influence of, on the telegraph—W. D. SARGENT. (R. 1870) ---- 244
Aurora, instructions for observations of—Toronto Observatory ---- 148
Aurora, magnetic effect of—A. D. BACHE ---- 175
Aurora, map of stars for observations on ---- **350**
Aurora, observations on—S. MASTERMAN. (R. 1857) ---- 107
Aurora, or Polar light, its phenomena and laws—E. LOOMIS. (R. 1865) ---- 209
Aurora, phenomena in telegraphic lines during—G. B. DONATI. (R. 1872) ---- 271
Aurora, recent secular period of—D. OLMSTED ---- **81**
Auroras, articles on, received by the Institution. (R. 1871; R. 1874) ---- 249, 286
Auroras, records of, in high northern latitudes—P. FORCE ---- **84**
Autobiography, the history of my youth—F. ARAGO. (R. 1870) ---- 244
Auxis Rochei, frigate mackerel, on New England coast—G. B. GOODE. (P. 1880) 425
Awards to Smithsonian Institution at the Centennial Exhibition. (R. 1876; R. 1878) ---- 299, 341
Axolotl changed to amblystoma—A. WEISMANN. (R. 1877) ---- 323, **401**
AYRES, Dr. Notes on fishes. (P. 1880) ---- 425

B.

BABBAGE, C., extracts from writings of. (R. 1873) 275
BABBAGE, C., memoir of, by N. S. DODGE. (R. 1873) 275
BABBAGE, C. On constants of nature and art. (R. 1856) 91
BABINET, J. The diamond and other precious stones. (R. 1870) 244, **377**
BABINET, J. The northern seas. (R. 1869) 228
BACHE, A. D.—
  Bequest to National Academy of Sciences. (R. 1872) 271, 329
  Discussion of magnetic and meteorological observations. Part I **113**
  Discussion of magnetic and meteorological observations. Part II **121**
  Discussion of magnetic and meteorological observations. Part III **132**
  Discussion of magnetic and meteorological observations. Pts. IV, V, VI **162**
  Discussion of magnetic and meteorological observations. Pts. VII, VIII, IX. **175**
  Discussion of magnetic and meteorological observations. Pts. X, XI, XII **186**
  Discussion of magnetic and meteorological observations. Parts I-XII **195**
  Eulogy on James A. Pearce. (R. 1862) 150
  Lecture on Switzerland. (R. 1870) 244
  Magnetic survey of Pennsylvania **166**
  Notice of James P. Espy. (R. 1859) 110
  Notice of G. Würdemann. (R. 1859) 110
BACHE, A. D., eulogy on, by J. HENRY. (R. 1870) 244, **379**
BACHE, A. D., list of scientific papers of—B. A. GOULD. (R. 1870) 244, 329, 376
BACHE, G. M. Hail storm in Texas. (R. 1870) 244
Bacteria, putrefactive, action of dry heat and sulphurous acid upon. (P. 1881) 467
BAEGERT, J. Aboriginal inhabitants of California peninsula. (R. 1863; R. 1864) 187, 188, 440, **361**
Baffin's Bay, meteorological observations in—F. L. McCLINTOCK 146
BAILEY, J. W.—
  Algæ 23
  Diatomacea 23, 63
  Infusoria 23
  Microscopical examination of soundings, Atlantic coast **20**
  Microscopical observations in South Carolina, Georgia, Florida **23**
  New species and localities of microscopical organisms **63**
BAILEY, W. B. F. Antiquities of Spalding county, Georgia. (R. 1877) 323
BAIRD, S. F.—
  Alphabetical index of genera of birds 108
  Arrangement of families of birds **210**
  Catalogue of North American birds octavo, **108**; quarto, **106**
  Catalogue of North American mammals **105**

BAIRD, S. F.—Continued.

Circular concerning department of insects. (P. 1881) ---- 467, **448**

Circular in reference to building-stone collection. (P. 1881) ---- 467, **453**

Circular in reference to petroleum collections. (P. 1881) ---- 467, **447**

Circular in reference to shipping fresh fish and other animals ---- **384**

Circular relative to scientific and literary exchanges ---- **324**

Circular requesting material for the library of the National Museum. (P. 1881) ---- 467, **458**

Circular to friends of the Museum. (P. 1881) ---- 467, **446**

Directions for collecting, preserving, and transporting specimens of natural history. (R. 1856) ---- 91, **34**

Fishes on the coasts of New Jersey and Long Island. (R. 1854) ---- 75, **348**

Instructions for collecting insects. (R. 1858) ---- 109

Instructions for collecting nests and eggs of North American birds. (R. 1858) ---- 109, **139**

List of explorations furnishing collections to National Museum, 1838 to 1877. (R. 1877) ---- 323

List of sources from which specimens have been derived, 1838 to 1867. (R. 1867) ---- 215

Memoranda of inquiry relative to food fishes ---- **231**

Museum miscellanea ---- **164**

Notes on aboriginal shell-mounds on coast of New Brunswick and of New England. (P. 1881) ---- 467

Notes on Henry's researches on sound. (R. 1878) ---- 341, **406**

On reports of recent scientific progress. (R. 1880) ---- 442

Questions relative to food fishes ---- **234**

Register of periodical phenomena ---- **65**, **148**

Report of Secretary for 1878. (R. 1878) ---- 341, **408**

Report of Secretary for 1879. (R. 1879) ---- 345, **418**

Report of Secretary for 1880. (R. 1880) ---- 442, **419**

Report on Centennial Exhibition. (R. 1876) ---- 299, **307**

Report on and statistics of British Museum. (R. 1850) ---- 28

Report on plan of exhibit at the International Exhibition at Philadelphia. (R. 1875) ---- 298

Reports on publications, exchanges, explorations, and Museum, 1851–1877. (R. 1851–1877) -- 51, 57, 67, 75, 77, 91, 107, 109, 110, 147, 149, 150, 187, 188, 209, 214, 215, 224, 228, 244, 249, 271, 275, 286, 298, 299, 323

Review of American birds. Part I. North and Middle America ---- **181**

Scientific instructions to Captain Hall. (R. 1871) ---- 249

Scientific investigations in Russian America. Natural history ---- 207

BAIRD, S. F.; GIRARD, C. Catalogue of North American reptiles. Part I. -- **49**

BALFOUR, J. The wind and fog. (R. 1866) ---- 214

Balloon ascensions, account of—J. GLAISHER. (R. 1863) ---- 187

Balloon ascensions—*See* Aeronautics.
BALTZELL, J. Winds in Florida. (R. 1866) 214
BANCROFT, G. Memorial to Congress for new Museum building. (R. 1876) 299
BANCROFT, G. On publication of Spanish works on New Mexico. (R. 1855) 77
BANNISTER, H. M. Climate of Alaska. (R. 1866) 214
BANNISTER, H. M. Formation of clouds over Gulf stream. (R. 1866) 214
Baptist Missionary Society. Yoruba grammar and dictionary **98**
Barbuda, catalogue of Ober's collection of birds of—G. N. LAWRENCE. (P. 1878) 332
BARKER, G. F. Recent progress in chemistry. (R. 1880) 442, **429**
BARKER, G. F. Recent progress in physics. (R. 1880) 442, **429**
BARNARD, F. A. P. Lectures on the undulatory theory of light. (R. 1862) 150
BARNARD, J. G. Eulogy on Gen. Joseph G. Totten. (R. 1865) 209
BARNARD, J. G. Internal structure of the earth **310**
BARNARD, J. G. Problems of rotary motion **240**
BARNARD, V. Birds of Chester county, Pennsylvania. (R. 1860) 147
Barometer, account of Green's. (R. 1855) 77, 148
Barometer, Green's standard 148
Barometer, horary variations of the—F. VAILLANT; J. HENRY. (R. 1866) 214
Barometer, influence of rain upon the—J. HANN. (R. 1877) 323, 398
Barometer, rain and snow gauges—R. H. GARDINER. (R. 1858) 109
Barometer tables, on construction of—F. F. TUCKETT. (R. 1867) 215
Barometer tube breaking suddenly—L. F. WARD. (R. 1866) 214
Barometer tubes, on filling—J. GREEN; W. WÜRDEMANN. (R. 1859) 110
Barometers at the Kew Observatory, verification of—J. WELSH. (R. 1859) 110
Barometers, experiments on aneroid—B. STEWART. (R. 1868) 224
Barometric minima and rainfall—J. T. REYE. (R. 1877) 323, 398
Barometric observations, discussion of Snell's—F. H. LOUD. (R. 1880) 442, **435**
Barometric observations, results of 157
Barometric variations and atmospheric currents, relation between—M. PESLIN. (R. 1877) 323, 398
Barometrical tables—A. GUYOT 153
BARRANDT, A. Ancient earthworks on the upper Missouri. (R. 1870) 244
BARRANDT, A. Haystack mound, Dakota. (R. 1872) 271
BARTLETT, J. R. On publication of Squier and Davis' Ancient Monuments. (R. 1847) **H, K**
BARTRAM, J. Antiquities of Florida. (R. 1874) 286
Base chart of the United States—C. A. SCHOTT **414**
Bases, ammonia-cobalt, researches on—W. GIBBS; F. A. GENTH **88**
Bases, organic—A. BAUER. (R. 1872) 271
Batavian Society of Experimental Philosophy, Rotterdam. Prize questions. (R. 1861) 149

Bath and West of England Society for encouragement of Agriculture, Arts, etc. Exchanges. (R. 1867) ---- 215
Batis maritima—J. TORREY ---- **60**
Batrachia, North American—E. D. COPE ---- **292**
Bats, account of remarkable accumulation of—M. FIGANIERRE. (R. 1863) ---- 187
Bats of North America, monograph of—H. ALLEN ---- **165**
BAUER, A. Organic bases. (R. 1872) ---- 271
Bay of Fundy, marine invertebrata of—W. STIMPSON ---- 50
Bead, colored, from a mound at Black Hammock, Florida—A. M. HARRISON. (R. 1877) ---- 323
Bead, polychrome, from Florida—S. S. HALDEMAN. (R. 1877) ---- 323, **404**
BEAN, T. H.—
Check-list of fishes distributed by Smithsonian Institution. (P. 1880) ---- 425
Description of a new hake (*Phycis Earlii*) and note on *Phycis regius*. (P. 1880) ---- 425
Description of new fish from Alaska, *Anarrhichas lepturus*, and notes on genus. (P. 1879) ---- 333
Description of new sparoid fish, *Sargus Holbrookii*, from Savannah bank. (P. 1878) ---- 332
Description of new species of *Amiurus* from the Mississippi. (P. 1879) ---- 333
Description of new species of *Gasterosteus* from Schoodic Lakes, Maine. (P. 1879) ---- 333
Description of species of *Lycodes* (*L. Turneri*) from Alaska. (P. 1878) ---- 332
Descriptions of genera and species of Alaskan fishes. (P. 1879) ---- 333
Descriptions of new fishes from Alaska and Siberia. (P. 1881) ---- 467
Descriptions of new species of fishes (*Uranidea marginata* and *Potamocottus Bendirei*,) and of *Myctophum crenulare*. (P. 1881) ---- 467
Descriptions of species of fishes collected by Dugès in Mexico. (P. 1879) 333
Directions for collecting and preserving fish. (P. 1881) ---- 467, **464**
Fishes of Arctic America. (Bull. 15, U. S. National Museum) ---- 342
Identity of *Euchalarodus Putnami* with *Pleuronectes glaber* and notes on habits. (P. 1878) ---- 332
List of European fishes in National Museum. (P. 1879) ---- 333
Notes on collection of fishes from eastern Georgia. (P. 1879) ---- 333
Notes on fishes collected by H. E. Nichols in British Columbia and Alaska, with descriptions of new species and new genus (*Delolepis*.) (P. 1881) ---- 467
Notes on fishes from Hudson's Bay. (P. 1881) ---- 467
Occurrence of *Hippoglossus vulgaris* in Alaska. (P. 1879) ---- 333
Occurrence of *Stichæus punctatus* at St. Michael's, Alaska. (P. 1878) ---- 332
Partial bibliography of fishes of Pacific coast of United States and Alaska for 1880. (P. 1881) ---- 467
Preliminary catalogue of fishes of Alaskan waters. (P. 1881) ---- 467
Species of *Astroscopus* of Eastern United States. (P. 1879) ---- 333

BEAN, T. H.; GOODE, G. B.—
Catalogue of Stearns's fishes of Florida and descriptions of new species. (P. 1879) ---- 333
Catalogue of Velie's fishes in Gulf of Mexico and description of new species. (P. 1879) ---- 333
Craig flounder of Europe (*Glyptocephalus cynoglossus*) on coast of North America. (P. 1878) ---- 332
Description of *Alepocephalus Bairdii*, new deep-sea fish, western Atlantic. (P. 1879) ---- 333
Description of *Argentina syrtensium*, new deep-sea fish, Sable Island bank. (P. 1878) ---- 332
Description of *Caulolatilus microps* from Gulf coast of Florida. (P. 1878) ---- 332
Description of *Lycodes paxillus*. (P. 1879) ---- 333
Description of new genus and species of fish, *Lopholatilus chamæleonticeps*, from New England. (P. 1879) ---- 333
Description of new species of fish, *Apogon pandionis*, from mouth of Chesapeake Bay. (P. 1881) ---- 467
Description of new species of fish (*Lutjanus Blackfordii* and *Lutjanus Stearnsii*) from coast of Florida. (P. 1878) ---- 332
Descriptions of gadoid fishes, *Phycis chesteri* and *Haloporphyrus viola*, from northwestern Atlantic. (P. 1878) ---- 332
Identity of *Brosmius brosme Americanus*, Gill, with *Brosmius brosme* (Muller) White. (P. 1878) ---- 332
Identity of *Rhinonemus caudacuta* with *Gadus cimbrius*. (P. 1878) ---- 332
New genus of fishes, *Benthodesmus*. (P. 1881) ---- 467
New serranoid fish, *Epinephelus Drummond-Hayi*, from Bermudas and Florida. (P. 1878) ---- 332
New species of *Liparis* (*L. ranula*) from Halifax. (P. 1879) ---- 333
Note on *Platessa ferruginea* and *Platessa rostrata*. (P. 1878) ---- 332
Note upon black grouper (*Epinephelus nigritus*) of the Southern coast. (P. 1878) ---- 332
Occurrence of *Lycodes Vahlii* on La Have and Grand Banks. (P. 1879.) 333
Oceanic bonito on coast of United States. (P. 1878) ---- 332
BEAUCHAMP, W. M. Wampum belts of the Six Nations. (R. 1879) ---- 345
Beaufort, (N. C.,) library, deposit of, by E. M. Stanton. (R. 1862) ---- 150
Beaufort, N. C., notes on fishes of—D. S. JORDAN. (P. 1880) ---- 425
Beaufort harbor, notes on fishes of—D. S. JORDAN; C. H. GILBERT. (P. 1878) 332
BEAUMONT—*See* De Beaumont.
BEAUTEMPS-BEAUPRÉ, C. F., memoir of, by ELIE DE BEAUMONT. (R. 1863) -- 187
Beaver, on the habits of the—FELIX R. BRUNOT. (R. 1873) ---- 275
Beaver Island, Mich., natural history of—J. J. STRANG. (R. 1854) ---- 75
BECKER, G. F. Atomic weight determinations ---- **358**

BECQUEREL, A. E. Forests and their climatic influence. (R. 1869) 228
BECQUEREL, A. E. Preservation of copper and iron in salt water. (R. 1864.) 188
Beirut, Syria, account of sarcophagus from—A. A. HARWOOD. (R. 1870) 244
BELDING, L. Additions to North American bird fauna by—R. RIDGWAY. (P. 1881) 467
BELDING, L. Partial list of birds of central California. (P. 1878) 332
Belgium, Archæological Academy of. Archæological congress organized by. (R. 1866) 214
Belgium—*See* Prize questions.
Belgium, Society of Science, etc.—*See* Prize questions.
Belone exilis, generic relations of—D. S. JORDAN; C. H. GILBERT. (P. 1880) 425
Belone latimanus, occurrence of, in Buzzard's bay—G. B. GOODE. (P. 1878) 332
BENDIRE, C. Notes on *Salmonidæ* of Columbia river. (P. 1881) 467
Benthodesmus, a new genus of deep-sea fishes—G. B. GOODE; T. H. BEAN. (P. 1881) 467
Bequest of A. D. Bache to National Academy of Sciences. (R. 1872) 271, 329
Bequest of S. Habel. (R. 1879) 345
Bequest of J. Hamilton to Smithsonian Institution. (R. 1872; R. 1873) 271, 275
Bequest of Smithson, act of Congress, July 1, 1836, accepting. (R. 1853) 67, **N**
Bequest of Smithson, exposition of—J. HENRY **E**
Bequest of Smithson, history of 328, 330
Bequest, Smithson and his—W. J. RHEES. (R. 1879) 345, **330**
BERENDT, C. H.—
Collection of historical documents in Guatemala. (R. 1876) 299
Explorations in Central America. (R. 1867) 215
On the Carib language and people. (R. 1873) 275
recommendation of, by British Minister. (R. 1865) 209
recommendation of, by Guatemalan Minister. (R. 1865) 209
recommendation of, by L. Molina, Costa Rican Minister. (R. 1865) 209
BERLANDIER, L. Catalogue of collection of historical and geographical manuscripts, maps, &c., of Mexico. (R. 1854) 75
Berlin Fisheries Exhibition, additions to museum from. (R. 1880) 442
Berlin Fisheries Exhibition, catalogue of United States' exhibit at—G. B. GOODE **413**
Bermuda, birds of—T. BLAND; J. R. WILLIS. (R. 1858) 109
Bermudas, catalogue of fishes of—G. B. GOODE **296**
Bermudas, fishes from, mistakenly described as new by Günther—G. B. GOODE. (P. 1878) 332
Bermudas, new serranoid fish from—G. B. GOODE; T. H. BEAN. (P. 1878) 332
Bern Museum, request for bison. (R. 1865) 209
Beroids, relation of lucernarians to—H. J. CLARK 242

BERRIEN, J. McPHERSON. Construction of act establishing Smithsonian. (R. 1853) ---- 67
BERTHOUD, E. L. Ancient remains in Colorado. (R. 1867) ---- 215
BERTHOUD, E. L. Antiquities of Colorado. (R. 1871) ---- 249
BERTHRAND, M. Life and works of Kepler. (R. 1869) ---- 228
Best hours for temperature observations—C. DEWEY. (R. 1860) ---- 147
BETHUNE, C. J. Acknowledgment of books. (R. 1861) ---- 149
Bibliographia Americana Historico-Naturalis for 1851—C. GIRARD ---- **48**
Bibliographia Americana, prospectus of a—H. STEVENS. (R. 1848) ---- I
Bibliographical index of North American Botany—S. WATSON ---- **258**
Bibliographical sketches of vestiges of antiquity in United States—S. F. HAVEN 71
Bibliography of algæ—H. C. WOOD ---- 241
Bibliography of American natural history for 1851—C. GIRARD ---- **48**
Bibliography of anthropology—O. T. MASON. (R. 1880) ---- 442, **432**
Bibliography of atomic volume and specific gravity, expansion, and boiling and melting—F. W. CLARKE ---- 255
Bibliography of Chinook jargon—G. GIBBS ---- 161
Bibliography of Dakota language—S. R. RIGGS ---- 40
Bibliography of diptera—C. R. OSTEN SACKEN ---- 270
Bibliography of diseases of joints, bones, larynx, eye, gangrene, etc.—W. W. KEEN ---- 300
Bibliography of expansion—F. W. CLARKE ---- 289
Bibliography of fishes—T. GILL ---- 247
Bibliography of fishes of Pacific coast of United States and Alaska for 1880—T. H. BEAN. (P. 1881) ---- 467
Bibliography of fishes of Pacific coast of United States—T. GILL ---- **463**
Bibliography of mammals—T. GILL ---- 230
Bibliography of mollusks—T. GILL ---- 227
Bibliography of nebulæ, clusters, milky way, nebular hypothesis, etc.—E. S. HOLDEN ---- 311
Bibliography of North American conchology previous to 1860. Part I. American authors—W. G. BINNEY ---- **142**
Bibliography of North American conchology previous to 1860. Part II. Foreign authors—W. G. BINNEY ---- **174**
Bibliography of ornithology: faunal publications relative to British birds—E. COUES. (P. 1879) ---- 333
Bibliography of orthoptera—S. H. SCUDDER ---- 189
Bibliography of rattlesnakes, serpent venom, etc.—S. W. MITCHELL ---- 135
Bibliography of specific heat—F. W. CLARKE ---- 276
Bibliography of Yoruba language—T. J. BOWEN ---- 98
Bibliography, plan of—J. FRIEDLÄNDER. (R. 1858) ---- 109
Biela's comet, investigations of—J. S. HUBBARD. (R. 1862) ---- 150
Big elephant mound in Grant county, Wisconsin—J. WARNER. (R. 1872) ---- 271

BINNEY, W. G.—
Bibliography of North American conchology previous to 1860. Part I. American authors ---- **142**
Bibliography of North American conchology previous to 1860. Part II. Foreign authors ---- **174**
Check-list of shells of North America ---- **128**
Land and fresh-water shells of North America. Part I ---- **194**
Land and fresh-water shells of North America. Part II ---- **143**
Land and fresh-water shells of North America. Part III ---- **144**
Biographical memoir of Joseph Henry—A. GRAY. (R. 1878) ---- 341, 356, **407**
Biographical notice of L. Agassiz—E. FAVRE. (R. 1878) ---- 341
Biographical notice of L. Agassiz—J. A. GARFIELD. (R. 1873) ---- 275
Biographical notice of L. Agassiz—P. PARKER. (R. 1873) ---- 275
Biographical notice of S. P. Chase—J. A. GARFIELD. (R. 1873) ---- 275
Biographical notice of S. P. Chase—H. HAMLIN. (R. 1873) ---- 275
Biographical notice of W. H. Harvey—A. GRAY. (R. 1867) ---- 215
Biographical notice of Charles C. Jewett—R. A. GUILD. (R. 1857) ---- 215
Biographical sketch of Dom Pedro II—A. FIALHO. (R. 1876) ---- 299
Biography of Condorcet—F. ARAGO. (R. 1878) ---- 341
Biography—*See* Memoirs.
Bird, a new humming, from Guatemala—R. RIDGWAY. (P. 1878) ---- 332
Birds, acknowledgment of—Academy of Sciences, Stockholm. (R. 1867) ---- 215
Birds, acknowledgment of—J. GOULD. (R. 1867) ---- 215
Birds, acknowledgment of—Hungarian National Museum. (R. 1863) ---- 187
Birds, alphabetical index of genera of—S. F. BAIRD ---- 108
Birds, American, instructions for collecting nests and eggs of—S. F. BAIRD. (R. 1858) ---- 109, **139**
Birds and mammals of Missouri river, list of—E. HARRIS. (R. 1850) ---- 28
Birds, arrangement of families of—S. F. BAIRD ---- **210**
Birds, bibliography of British—E. COUES. (P. 1879) ---- 333
Birds, catalogue of North American—S. F. BAIRD. Octavo ---- **108**
Birds, catalogue of North American—S. F. BAIRD. Quarto ---- **106**
Birds, catalogue of Old World, in Nat. Museum—R. RIDGWAY. (P. 1881) 467, **462**
Birds, circular relative to collections of ---- **168**
Birds, dates of first appearance of—F. B. HOUGH ---- 182
Birds, description of new species of, from Costa Rica—R. RIDGWAY. (P. 1878) 332
Birds, descriptions of new—R. RIDGWAY. (P. 1881) ---- 467
Birds, descriptions of several new species and races of, in National Museum—R. RIDGWAY. (P. 1878) ---- 332
Birds, desiderata among North American—R. RIDGWAY. (P. 1881) ---- 467
Birds' eggs, suggestions for forming collections of—A. NEWTON ---- 139
Birds, humming, list of—D. G. ELLIOT ---- **334**

Birds, list of described, of Mexico, Central America, and the West Indies, not in Smithsonian collections ---- **185**
Birds' nests and eggs, instructions for collecting ---- 139
Birds, new species and races of American, and synopsis of genus *Tyrannus*—R. RIDGWAY. (P. 1878) ---- 332
Birds, new species of *Turdidæ*, from Dominica—G. N. LAWRENCE. (P. 1880) 425
Birds, nomenclature and catalogue of—R. RIDGWAY ---- **422**
Birds. North American oölogy—T. M. BREWER ---- **89**
Birds, notes on some Costa Rican—R. RIDGWAY, (P. 1881) ---- 467
Birds of Antigua, catalogue of Ober's collection of—G. N. LAWRENCE. (P. 1878) 332
Birds of Arctic America—L. KUMLIEN ---- 342
Birds of Barbuda, catalogue of Ober's collection—G. N. LAWRENCE. (P. 1878) 332
Birds of Bermuda—T. BLAND; J. R. WILLIS. (R. 1858) ---- 109
Birds of Caribbee Islands—F. A. OBER. (R. 1878) ---- 341
Birds of Central California—L. BELDING. (P. 1878) ---- 332
Birds of Chester county, Pennsylvania—V. BARNARD. (R. 1860) ---- 147
Birds of District of Columbia, list of—E. COUES; S. S. PRENTISS. (R. 1861) ---- 149
Birds of Dominica, catalogue of Ober's collection of—G. N. LAWRENCE. (P. 1878) ---- 332
Birds of Grenada, catalogue of Ober's collection—G. N. LAWRENCE. (P. 1878) 332
Birds of Guadeloupe, catalogue of Ober's collection—G. N. LAWRENCE. (P. 1878) 332
Birds of Heligoland—H. GÄRKE. (P. 1879) ---- 333
Birds of Kerguelen Island—J. H. KIDDER; E. COUES ---- 293
Birds of Lesser Antilles, catalogue of Ober's collection of—G. N. LAWRENCE, (P. 1878) ---- 332
Birds of Martinique, catalogue of Ober's collection of—G. N. LAWRENCE. (P. 1878) ---- 332
Birds of Middle and South America not in National Museum—R. RIDGWAY. (P. 1881) ---- 467
Birds of Missouri river—E. HARRIS. (R. 1850) ---- 28
Birds of North America, nomenclature and catalogue of—R. RIDGWAY. (P. 1880) 425
Birds of Nova Scotia—BLACKISTON; T. BLAND; J. R. WILLIS. (R. 1858) ---- 109
Birds of Saint Vincent, catalogue of Ober's collections of—G. N. LAWRENCE. (P. 1878) ---- 332
Birds of South America, circular relative to collections of ---- **168**
Birds of Southern Texas—J. C. MERRILL. (P. 1878) ---- 332
Birds of Southwestern Mexico, collected by F. E. Sumichrast—G. N. LAWRENCE ---- **295**
Birds of West coast, migrations and nesting habits of—J. G. COOPER. (P. 1879) 333
Birds of West Indies, catalogue of Ober's collections from—G. N. LAWRENCE. (P. 1878) ---- 332
Birds, review of American. Part I—S. F. BAIRD ---- **181**
Birds, revisions of nomenclature of—R. RIDGWAY. (P. 1880) ---- 425

Birds, suggestions for saving skeletons of—A. NEWTON. (R. 1860) ---------- 147
Birds, systematic review of classification of—W. LILLJEBORG. (R. 1865.) 209, **364**
Birds, two new North American, added by L. Belding—R. RIDGWAY. (P. 1881) ---------- 467
BISHOP, W. D. Commissioner of Patents, Meteorological observations ------ **157**
Bison, request of Bern Museum for. (R. 1865) ---------- 209
Bites of serpents, nature and cure of—D. BRAINARD. (R. 1854) ---------- 75
Black bass of the Ohio, habits of the—J. EOFF. (R. 1854) ---------- 75
Black Hammock, colored bead from—A. M. HARRISON. (R. 1877) ---------- 323
BLACKISTON, —; BLAND, T.; WILLIS, J. R. Birds of Nova Scotia. (R. 1858) 109
Blackmore Museum, Salisbury, England, notice of the. (R. 1868) ---------- 224
Black Mountain, North Carolina, topography of—T. L. CLINGMAN. (R. 1855) 77
BLAINVILLE, D. DE, memoir of—M. FLOURENS. (R. 1865) ---------- 209
BLAND, T.; BINNEY, W. G. Land and fresh-water shells of North America. Part I.—Pulmonata geophila ---------- **194**
BLAND; WILLIS, J. R. Birds of Bermuda. (R. 1858) ---------- 109
BLAND, T.; BLACKISTON, —; WILLIS, J. R. Birds of Nova Scotia. (R. 1858) 109
Blank check-lists, labels, figures, &c ---------- 164
Blind deaf mute, vocal sounds of Laura Bridgman, the—F. LIEBER ---------- **12**
BLODGET, L. List of meteorological observers. (R. 1853) ---------- 67
BLONDEL, S. Historical, archæological, and literary study of jade. (R. 1876) 299
Blood, analysis of—J. JONES ---------- 82
Blossoming of plants, dates of—F. B. HOUGH ---------- 182
Blowpipe apparatus of Hawkins and Wale. (R. 1872) ---------- 271
Blowpipe, qualitative determination by the—T. EGLESTON. (R. 1872) ---------- 271
BLYDEN, E. D. Mixed races in Liberia. (R. 1870) ---------- 244
Board of Commissioners for Foreign Missions—*See* American Board, etc.
Board of Regents, Journals of. (See each annual report) ---------- 329, **A**
Board of Regents—*See* Regents.
BOEHMER, G. H. Index to anthropological articles in Smithsonian publications. (R. 1879) ---------- 345, **421**
BOEHMER, G. H. Report on International Exchange ---------- **477**
BOEHMER, G. H. Reports of astronomical observatories, 1880. (R. 1880) 442, **438**
BOEHMER, G. H.; HOLDEN, E. S. Reports of observatories, 1880. (R. 1880) 442, **438**
BOERNER, C. G. Lightning discharges. (R. 1867) ---------- 215
Boiling point, bibliography of—F. W. CLARKE ---------- 255
Boiling points, tables of—F. W. CLARKE ---------- 255, 288
BOLLES, E. C. Account of Portland Society of Natural History. (R. 1867) 215
Bologna, Academy of Sciences of the Institute of. Prize questions. (R. 1862) 150
Bones, bibliography of diseases of the—W. W. KEEN ---------- 300
Bonito, oceanic, description of—V. N. EDWARDS. (P. 1878) ---------- 332
Bonito, oceanic, on coast of United States—G. B. GOODE; T. H. BEAN. (P. 1878) 332

Books, acknowledgment of—C. J. BETHUNE. (R. 1861) 149
Books, acknowledgment of—J. A. CODD. (R. 1861) 149
Books, acknowledgment of—M. LABOULAYE. (R. 1867) 215
Books, copyright, from 1846 to 1849—C. C. JEWETT. (R. 1850) 28
Books on Brazil, presented—M. M. LISBOA. (R. 1865) 209
Books on Egypt, presentation of—R. LEPSIUS. (R. 1860) 147
Books, on the classification of—J. P. LESLEY. (R. 1862) 150
Books, presentation of—Duke of Northumberland. (R. 1859) 110
Books, presented—Imperial Library of Vienna. (R. 1865) 209
BOOTH, J. C.; MORFIT, C. Recent improvements in the chemical arts **27**
Bordeaux, Chamber of Commerce of. Exchange of publications. (R. 1863) 187
Bordeaux, Imperial Academy of Sciences. Prize questions. (R. 1868) 224
Bosphorus, account of a hailstorm on the—Com. PORTER. (R. 1870) 244
Boston, Mass., American Academy—*See* American Academy.
Botanical explorations in New Mexico and California—A. GRAY. (R. 1849) 21
Botany, index to North American—S. WATSON **258**
Botany of Hawaiian and Fanning Islands and California—T. H. STREETS 303
Botany of Kerguelen Island—A. GRAY; T. P. JAMES; E. TUCKERMAN; W. G. FARLOW 294
Botany, progress in, in 1879 and 1880—W. G. FARLOW. (R. 1880) 442, **430**
Botany—*See* Plants.
Boundary line between geology and history—E. SUESS. (R. 1872) 271
BOWEN, T. J. Yoruba grammar and dictionary **98**
BOWERS, S. Explorations in Santa Rosa Island, California. (R. 1877) 323
BOYD, C. H. Remains of walrus (?) in Maine. (P. 1881) 467
Brachiopoda, index of—W. H. DALL **304**
Brachyopsis verrucosus, from California—W. N. LOCKINGTON. (P. 1880) 425
Brachyopsis xyosternus—D. S. JORDAN; C. H. GILBERT. (P. 1880) 425
BRACKETT, A. G. Shoshone or Snake Indians, religion, superstitions, manners, etc. (R. 1879) 345
BRACKETT, A. G. Sioux or Dakota Indians. (R. 1876) 299
Brain and marrow of animals, uses of, among Indians—T. R. PEALE. (R. 1870) 244
Brain, dual character of the—C. E. BROWN-SÉQUARD. Toner lecture No. II **291**
BRAINARD, D. Lecture on bites of serpents and wounds of poisoned arrows. (R. 1854) 75
BRANSFORD, J. F. Archæological researches in Nicaragua **383**
BRANSFORD, J. F., note on shells from Costa Rica kitchen-midden, collected by—W. H. DALL. (P. 1878) 332
BRAVAIS, AUGUSTE, memoir of, by E. DE BEAUMONT. (R. 1869) 228
BRAYTON, A. W. Distribution of the fishes of South Carolina, Georgia, and Tennessee 308
BRAYTON, A. W. North American ichthyology 308

Brazil, books on, presented—M. M. LISBOA. (R. 1865) ---------- 209
Brazil, specimens from, presented. Brazilian Nat. Hist. Museum. (R. 1865) 209
Brazilian Nat. Hist. Museum, specimens from Brazil presented. (R. 1865)---- 209
BREED, E. E. Earthworks in Wisconsin. (R. 1872)---------- 271
BREED, E. E. Pits at Embarrass, Wisconsin. (R. 1877) ---------- 323
Breeding habits of sea-catfish—N. T. LUPTON. (P. 1878) ---------- 332
Bremen, government of, exchange system. (R. 1865) ---------- 209
BRENNDECKE, F. Meteorites. (R. 1869)---------- 228
Brevoortia patronus, note on—S. STEARNS. (P. 1878)---------- 332
Brevoortia, revision of American species of—G. B. GOODE. (P. 1878)---------- 332
BREWER, T. M. Instructions for collecting and preserving nests and eggs ---- **139**
BREWER, T. M. Nests and eggs of North American species of *empidonaces*. (P. 1879) ---------- 333
BREWER, T. M. North American oölogy. Part I. Raptores and Fissirostres. **89**
BREZINA, A. Explanation of principles of crystallography and crystallo-physics. (R. 1872)---------- 271, **386**
Bridges, lectures on roads and—F. ROGERS. (R. 1860; R. 1861)---------- 147, 149
BRIDGMAN, L., vocal sounds of—F. LIEBER ---------- **12**
BRINTON, D. G. Artificial shell deposits in the United States. (R. 1866) ---- 214
British America, account of the Indians of—E. PETITOT. (R. 1865) ---------- 209
British America, Tinneh or Chepewyan Indians of—G. GIBBS. (R. 1866.) 214, **365**
British Association, report to, on radiant heat—B. POWELL. (R. 1859)---------- 110
British birds, list of faunal publications relative to—E. COUES. (P. 1879) ---- 333
British Columbia, Haidah Indians of—J. G. SWAN---------- **267**
British Columbia, notes on fishes of—T. H. BEAN. (P. 1881) ---------- 467
British Minister, F. W. A. Bruce, recommending Dr. Berendt. (R. 1865) --- 209
British Museum, acknowledgment of specimens. (R. 1865)---------- 209
British Museum, electrotypes of shells granted by. (R. 1863)---------- 187
British Museum, notes on typical American fishes in—D. S. JORDAN. (P. 1879) 333
British Museum, statistics of—S. F. BAIRD. (R. 1850) ---------- 28
British Provinces of North America, list of libraries, institutions, and societies in—W. J. RHEES ---------- 116
BROADHEAD, G. C. Prehistoric evidences in Missouri. (R. 1879) ---------- 345
BROCA, P. History of Anthropological Society of Paris, 1865 to 1867. (R. 1868) ---------- 224
BROCA, P. Troglodytes, or cave dwellers, of the valley of the Vézère. (R. 1872)---------- 271
BRODNAX, B. H. Mounds in Moorehouse parish, Louisiana. (R. 1879)---------- 345
Brosmius brosme Americanus, Gill, identity of, with *Brosmius brosme* (Müller) White—G. B. GOODE; T. H. BEAN. (P. 1878) ---------- 332
BROWN, D. Shell heap in Georgia. (R. 1871)---------- 249
BROWN-SÉQUARD, C. E. Dual character of the brain. Toner lecture No. II - **291**
BRUFF, J. G. Indian engravings along Green river valley. (R. 1872)---------- 271

Brunot, F. R. Habits of the beaver. (R. 1873) 275
Brunswick, Maine, meteorological observations—P. Cleaveland **204**
Brush, G. J. Catalogue of meteorites in Yale College. (R. 1868) 224
Brussels, Belgium, Royal Academy of Sciences, Literature, and the Fine Arts. *See* Prize questions.
Bryan, O. N. Antiquities of Charles county, Maryland. (R. 1874) 286
Buch, L. von, memoir of, by M. Flourens. (R. 1862) 150
Budapest, address before Anthropological Congress at—F. F. Romer. (R. 1876) 299, **392**
Building Commission, National Museum, report of, for 1879. (R. 1879) 345, **409**
Building Commission, National Museum, report of, for 1880. (R. 1880) 442, **434**
Building Committee of Regents of S. I., journal and reports of, 1847-1867 329
Building Committee of Smithsonian, report of, on architecture **P**
Building materials—R. D. Owen **P**
Building materials, mode of testing—J. Henry. (R. 1856) 91
Building materials, report on. (R. 1847) **H, 329**
Building, new, for museum, memorial to Congress for. (R. 1876) 299
Building, report on use of new hall in—L. Agassiz. (R. 1867) 215
Building-stone collection, circular in reference to—S. F. Baird. (P. 1881) 467, **453**
Building stones, report on—D. D. Owen. (R. 1847) 329, **H**
Buildings, public, acoustics applied to—J. Henry. (R. 1856) 91
Buildings, warming and ventilating—A. Morin. Part I. (R. 1873) 275, **439**
Buildings, warming and ventilating—A. Morin. Part II. (R. 1874) 286, **439**
Bulletin National Museum—
No. 1. Batrachia and reptilia—E. D. Cope **292**
No. 2. Birds of Kerguelen Island—J. H. Kidder; E. Coues **293**
No. 3. Oölogy, plants, mammals, etc., Kerguelen Island—J. H. Kidder and others **294**
No. 4. Birds of Mexico—G. N. Lawrence **295**
No. 5. Catalogue of fishes of Bermudas—G. B. Goode **296**
No. 6. Classification of animal resources of United States—G. B. Goode. **297**
No. 7. Natural history, Hawaiian Islands, etc.—T. H. Streets **303**
No. 8. Index of brachiopoda—W. H. Dall **304**
No. 9. Review of Rafinesque's fishes—D. S. Jordan **305**
No. 10. Notes on cottidæ, etc.; synopsis of siluridæ—D. S. Jordan **306**
No. 11. Bibliography of Pacific fishes—T. Gill **463**
No. 12. Fishes of South Carolina, Georgia, Tennessee; synopsis of catostomidæ—D. S. Jordan; A. N. Brayton **308**
No. 13. Flora of St. Croix and Virgin Islands—H. F. A. Eggers **313**
No. 14. Catalogue Centennial exhibit, animal resources and fisheries—G. B. Goode **326**
No. 15. Natural history and ethnology, Arctic America—L. Kumlien **342**
No. 16. (Not published.)

Bulletin National Museum—Continued.
No. 17. Zoölogical position of Texas—E. D. COPE ---------- 412
No. 18. Fishery exhibit of United States at Berlin—G. B. GOODE ---------- 413
No. 19. List of genera in zoölogy and paleontology—S. H. SCUDDER ---------- 470
No. 20. (Not published.)
No. 21. Nomenclature of North American birds—R. RIDGWAY ---------- 422
No. 22. Guide to flora of Washington, D. C.—L. F. WARD ---------- 444
Bulletin of Philosophical Society of Washington, Vols. I, II, III ---------- 423
Bulletin, Smithsonian, No. 1. Vocabulary of the jargon ---------- 68
Bulletins of the U. S. National Museum, catalogue and index of ---------- 478
Bureau of Ethnology, directory of officers and employés of ---------- 466
Burial caves—J. JONES ---------- 259
Burial ground, ancient, in Tompkins Co., N. Y.—D. TROWBRIDGE. (R. 1863) 187
Burial, modes of—J. JONES ---------- 259
Burial of an Indian squaw, California—W. M. KING. (R. 1874) ---------- 286
BURR, R. T. Ruins in Pima county, Arizona. (R. 1879) ---------- 345
Business arrangements of the Smithsonian Institution ---------- 325
BUTLER, A. P. Report of Senate Judiciary Committee on management of Smithsonian. (R. 1855) ---------- 77
Buzzard's bay, Mass., occurrence of *Belone latimanus* in—G. B. GOODE. (P. 1878) ---------- 332
By-laws of the Smithsonian Institution. (R. 1853) ---------- 67, 329

C.

Cache la Poudre river, Colorado, antiquities on—E. L. BERTHOUD. (R. 1871) 249
California—
account of botanical explorations in—A. GRAY. (R. 1849) ---------- 21
ancient graves and shell heaps of—P. SCHUMACHER. (R. 1874) ---------- 286
burial of Indian squaw in—W. M. KING. (R. 1874) ---------- 286
cave in Calaveras county—J. D. WHITNEY. (R. 1867) ---------- 215
climate of—A. GIBBONS. (R. 1854) ---------- 75
climate of—T. M. LOGAN. (R. 1855) ---------- 77
description of *Gobiesox rhessodon* from San Diego—R. SMITH. (P. 1881) 467
description of new gobioid fish from San Diego—R. SMITH. (P. 1881) ---------- 467
descriptions of new species of shells from—W. H. DALL. (P. 1878) ---------- 332
distribution of tertiary fossils of—W. H. DALL. (P. 1878) ---------- 332
fishes of—*See* D. S. JORDAN; C. H. GILBERT.
fishes of—T. H. STREETS ---------- 308

California—Continued.
fossil mollusks from later tertiaries of—W. H. DALL. (P. 1878) 332
history and antiquities of Santa Rosa Island—S. BOWERS. (R. 1877) 323
Indians of—S. POWERS. (R. 1876) 299
list of fishes of, collected by Lt. H. E. Nichols—D. S. JORDAN; C. H. GILBERT. (P. 1881) 467
meteorological observations at Sacramento—F. W. HATCH. (R. 1854) 75
meteorological observations at Sacramento—T. M. LOGAN. (R. 1854) 75
meteorology of Sacramento—T. M. LOGAN. (R. 1857) 107
natural history of—T. H. STREETS **303**
new genera and species of fishes from coast of—W. N. LOCKINGTON. (P. 1879) 333
new pitcher plant from—J. TORREY 61
notes on a collection of fishes from San Diego—D. S. JORDAN; C. H. GILBERT. (P. 1880) 425
occurrence of *Cremnobates* at San Diego—R. SMITH. (P. 1880) 425
occurrence of *Productus giganteus* in—C. A. WHITE. (P. 1880) 425
plants collected by J. C. Frémont in—J. TORREY 46
pleistocene fossils from—P. P. CARPENTER 252
postpliocene fossils in coast range of—W. H. DALL. (P. 1878) 332
wingless grasshopper of—E. P. VOLLUM. (R. 1860) 147
California, central, partial list of birds of—L. BELDING. (P. 1878) 332
California, Gulf of, lectures on shells of—P. P. CARPENTER. (R. 1859) 110
California peninsula, aboriginal inhabitants of—J. BAEGERT. (R. 1863; R. 1864) 187, 188, 440, **361**
California, upper, explorations in, 1860—J. FEILNER. (R. 1864) 188
Camaraphysema, a new type of sponge—J. A. RYDER. (P. 1880) 425
Camel, lecture on the—G. P. MARSH. (R. 1854) 75
CAMERON, H. C. Reminiscences of Joseph Henry 356
CAMPBELL, J. V. Earthquake in Peru, August 13, 1868. (R. 1870) 244
Canada, meteorological system of—J. G. HODGINS. (R. 1865) 209
Canada East, description of observatory at St. Martin, Isle Jesus—C. SMALLWOOD. (R. 1856) 91
Canada porcupine, occurrence of, in Maryland—O. LUGGER. (P. 1881) 467
Canada porcupine, occurrence of, in West Virginia—G. B. GOODE. (P. 1878) 332
Canada West, ancient Indian remains near Prescott—W. E. GUEST. (R. 1856) 91
Canada West, meteorological stations of—J. G. HODGINS. (R. 1858) 109
Canal, Washington, report of committee of Regents on. (R. 1868) 224
CANBY, S. Deposit of Bishop John's library. (R. 1862) 150
Cancerous tumors, structure of—J. J. WOODWARD **266**
Candle fish of northwest coast—J. G. SWAN. (P. 1880) 425
CANDOLLE, P. DE, memoir of, by M. FLOURENS. (R. 1859) 110
CANNON, G. L. Antiquities of Colorado. (R. 1877) 323

CANUDAS, A. Earthquakes in Guatemala. (R. 1858) ---- 109
Caoutchouc and gutta percha. (R. 1864) ---- 188
Cape Cod, littoral marine fauna of—R. RATHBUN. (P. 1880) ---- 425
Cape Flattery, Indians of—J. G. SWAN ---- **220**
CAPEN, F. L. Meteorological discovery. (R. 1866) ---- 214
Capitol, U. S., memorial exercises at ---- 356
Capitol, U. S., account of marble used in extension of—J. HENRY. (R. 1856) 91
Cara gigantesca of Yzamal, in Yucatan—A. SCHOTT. (R. 1869) ---- 228
Caracas, South America, meteorology of—G. A. ERNST. (R. 1867) ---- 215
Caranx Beani, from Beaufort, N. C., description of—D. S. JORDAN. (P. 1880) 425
Carib language and people—C. H. BERENDT. (R. 1873) ---- 275
Caribbee Islands, ornithology of—F. A. OBER (R. 1878) ---- 341
CARLETON, J. H. Excursion to Abó, Quarra, and Gran Quivira, New Mexico. (R. 1854) ---- 75
CARLETON, J. H. Meteorites in Mexico. (R. 1865) ---- 209
CARLIN, W. E. Observations of *Siredon lichenoides*. (P. 1881) ---- 467
Carlsruhe, Scientific Congress of, 1858—F. J. NICKLÉS. (R. 1860) ---- 147
CARPENTER, P. P.—
Check-list of the shells of North America ---- **128**
Lectures on mollusca, or shell-fish, and their allies. (R. 1860) ---- 147, **152**
Lectures on shells of Gulf of California. (R. 1859) ---- 110
Mollusks of western North America ---- **252**
CASE, H. B. Flint implements in Holmes county, Ohio. (R. 1877) ---- 323
CASELLA, L. Description of meteorological instruments. (R. 1859) ---- 110
CASS, L., Secretary of State. Circular to diplomatic agents relative to L. H. Morgan's research ---- 138
Castings, metallic, of delicate natural objects. (P. 1881) ---- 467
Casts, catalogue of, of Indian boys and girls at Hampton Normal Institute, Virginia—R. H. PRATT. (P. 1879) ---- 333
Casts, catalogue of, of Indian prisoners at St. Augustine, Florida—R. H. PRATT. (P. 1878) ---- 332
Casts of statues, etc., proposed by W. J. Stone. (R. 1855) ---- 77
Casts, plaster, methods of making and preserving—A. PIRZ. (P. 1881) ---- 467
CASWELL, A.—
Lecture on astronomy. (R. 1858) ---- 109
Meteorological observations at Providence, R. I., 1831-1860 ---- **103**
Meteorological observations at Providence, R. I., 1831-1876 ---- **443**
Catalogue, general stereotype, of public libraries, report of commission on. (R. 1850) ---- 28
Catalogue of—
birds of Antigua and Barbuda, collected by F. A. Ober—G. N. LAWRENCE. (P. 1878) ---- 332
birds of Dominica, collected by F. A. Ober—G. N. LAWRENCE. (P. 1878) 332

Catalogue of—Continued.
birds of Grenada, collected by F. A. Ober—G. N. LAWRENCE. (P. 1878) 332
birds of Guadeloupe, collected by F. A. Ober—G. N. LAWRENCE. (P. 1878) 332
birds of Lesser Antilles, collected by F. A. Ober—G. N. LAWRENCE. (P. 1878) 332
birds of Martinique, collected by F. A. Ober—G. N. LAWRENCE. (P. 1878) 332
birds of North America—R. RIDGWAY. (P. 1880) 425, **422**
birds of St. Vincent, collected by F. A. Ober—G. N. LAWRENCE. (P. 1878) 332
books and memoirs relating to nebulæ and clusters—E. S. HOLDEN **311**
casts taken by Clark Mills of Indian boys and girls at Hampton, Virginia—R. H. PRATT. (P. 1879) 333
casts taken by Clark Mills of Indian prisoners at St. Augustine, Florida—R. H. PRATT. (P. 1878) 332
collection at International Exhibition, 1876. (R. 1876) 299, **326**
collection of Japanese cotton fibre presented by Government of Japan. (P. 1881) 467
collection of Japanese woods presented by University of Tokio—L. F. WARD. (P. 1881) 467
collection to illustrate animal resources and fisheries of United States exhibited at Philadelphia, 1876—G. B. GOODE **326**
described coleoptera of the United States—F. E. MELSHEIMER **62**
described diptera of North America—C. R. OSTEN SACKEN **102**, **270**
described lepidoptera of North America—J. G. MORRIS **118**
engravings presented to Smithsonian—C. B. KING. (R. 1861) 149
fishes from Pensacola, Florida, collected by S. Stearns—G. B. GOODE; T. H. BEAN. (P. 1879) 333
fishes obtained in the Gulf of Mexico by J. W. Velie—G. B. GOODE; T. H. BEAN. (P. 1879) 333
fishes of Alaskan and adjacent waters—T. H. BEAN. (P. 1881) 467
fishes of the Bermudas—G. B. GOODE **296**
fishes of the east coast of North America—T. GILL **283**
fishes of St. John's river and east coast of Fla.—G. B. GOODE. (P. 1879) 333
geological specimens—D. D. OWEN. (R. 1854) 75
historical and geographical manuscripts, maps, etc.—L. BERLANDIER. (R. 1854) 75
Indian relics presented to Smithsonian—J. H. DEVEREUX. (R. 1872) 271
library of James Smithson 330
linguistic manuscripts in library of Bureau of Ethnology—J. C. PILLING. (E. 1879-80) 476
meteorites in Yale College—G. J. BRUSH. (R. 1868) 224
minerals, with their formulas—T. EGLESTON **156**

Catalogue of—Continued.
mollusca added to fauna of southern New England—A. E. VERRILL. (P. 1880) ---- 425
North American birds—S. F. BAIRD ---- octavo, **108**
North American birds—S. F. BAIRD ---- quarto, **106**
North American mammals—S. F. BAIRD ---- **105**
North American reptiles. Part I—Serpents—S. F. BAIRD; C. GIRARD. **49**
Old World birds in United States National Museum—R. RIDGWAY. (P. 1881) ---- 467, **462**
orthoptera of North America—S. H. SCUDDER ---- **189**
photographic portraits of Indians in gallery of Smithsonian Institution ---- **216**
portraits of North American Indians, painted by J. M. Stanley ---- **53**
publications of Smithsonian Institution ---- **74, 203, 226, 245, 278, 478**
publications of societies in Smithsonian library ---- **73, 85, 117, 179**
rocks, minerals, and ores in Michigan—C. T. JACKSON. (R. 1854) ---- 75
rocks, minerals, etc.—J. W. FOSTER. (R. 1854) ---- 75
rocks, minerals, etc.—J. D. WHITNEY. (R. 1854) ---- 75
rocks, minerals, ores, and fossils—J. LOCKE. (R. 1854) ---- 75
serpents—S. F. BAIRD; C. GIRARD ---- **49**
trees of the United States—J. G. COOPER. (R. 1858) ---- 109, **351**
trochilidæ in collection of National Museum—R. RIDGWAY. (P. 1880) 425
Catalogue system for libraries—C. C. JEWETT. (R. 1849; R. 1850) ---- 21, 28, **47**
Catalogues of libraries, construction of—C. C. JEWETT ---- **47**
Catalytic force, or phenomena of contact—T. L. PHIPSON. (R. 1862) ---- 150
Catfish, sea, breeding habits of—N. T. LUPTON. (P. 1878) ---- 332
Catherina Archipelago, Alaska, remains of prehistoric man from—W. H. DALL. 318
CATLIN, G., notes relative to life and paintings of—J. HENRY. (R. 1872) ---- 271
CATLIN, G., account of Mandan ceremonies by, accuracy of—J. KIPP. (R. 1872) 271
Catostomidæ, synopsis of—D. S. JORDAN ---- 308
CATTIE, S. T. Genitalia of male eels and their sexual characters. (P. 1880) ---- 425
Caulolatilus microps, from Gulf coast of Florida—G. B. GOODE; T. H. BEAN. (P. 1878) ---- 332
Causes which limit vegetable species—A. DE CANDOLLE. (R. 1858) ---- 109
Cave dwellers of the valley of the Vézère—P. BROCA. (R. 1872) ---- 271
Cave in Calaveras county, California—J. D. WHITNEY. (R. 1867) ---- 215
Cavern, Luray, in Virginia, report of visit to—O. T. MASON and others. (R. 1880) ---- 442, **433**
Caves in Alaska, remains of prehistoric man from—W. H. DALL ---- **318**
CAZIN, A. Recent progress in relation to the theory of heat. (R. 1868) ---- 224
Celts, stone, in West Indies and Africa—G. J. GIBBS. (R. 1877) ---- 323
Cenozoic rocks, fossils from—C. A. WHITE. (P. 1880) ---- 425
Centennial awards to Smithsonian Institution. (R. 1876; R. 1878) ---- 299, 341

Centennial Exhibition, catalogue of collection of animal resources and fisheries at—G. B. GOODE ---------- **326**
Centennial Exhibition, circular for distribution at---------- **290**
Centennial Exhibition, plan of proposed Smithsonian exhibit at—S. F. BAIRD. (R. 1875) ---------- 298
Centennial Exhibition, report on—S. F. BAIRD. (R. 1876)---------- 299, **307**
Centennial Exhibition, savage weapons at—E. H. KNIGHT. (R. 1879)---- 345, **415**
Centennial mission to Indians of Western Nevada and California—S. POWERS. (R. 1876) ---------- 299
Centigrade degrees, tables for conversion of, to Fahrenheit. (R. 1863)-------- 187
Central America—
circular relative to collections of birds of---------- **168**
description of new fishes from—D. S. JORDAN; C. H. GILBERT. (P. 1881)---------- 467
explorations in—C. H. BERENDT. (R. 1867) ---------- 215
list of birds of, not in Smithsonian collection---------- **185**
rain-fall in—C. A. SCHOTT ---------- 222, **353**
review of birds of—S. F. BAIRD---------- 181
studies in picture writing of—E. S. HOLDEN. (E. 1879-80)---------- 476
travels in—S. HABEL---------- **269**
Centrarchidæ, notes on—D. S. JORDAN ---------- 306
Centrarchidæ, review of family—C. L. MCKAY. (P. 1881) ---------- 467
Centurus, review of genus—R. RIDGWAY. (P. 1881) ---------- 467
Cephaloscyllium laticeps—D. S. JORDAN; C. H. GILBERT. (P. 1880)-------- 425
Ceratiidæ, note on—T. GILL. (P. 1878) ---------- 332
Ceremonies at laying of corner-stone of Smithsonian Institution. (R. 1847)- **H**, 329
Ceremonies, Mandan, accuracy of Catlin's account of—J. KIPP. (R. 1872)--- 271
Cessions of land by Indian tribes to United States—C. C. ROYCE. (E. 1879-80) 476
CHACE, G. I. Lecture on oxygen and its combinations. (R. 1855) ---------- 77
Chalk found in United States—T. A. CONRAD. (R. 1865)---------- 209
Chamber of Commerce of Bordeaux. Exchange of publications. (R. 1863)-- 187
Change of Mexican axolotl to amblystoma—A. WEISMANN. (R. 1877) -- 323, **401**
CHANNING, W. F. Lecture on the American fire-alarm telegraph. (R. 1854) 75
CHANTRE, E. Code of symbols for prehistoric archæology. (R. 1875) ------- 298
Chapala Lake, notes on Dugès' fishes from—D. S. JORDAN. (P. 1879) ------- 333
CHAPPELSMITH, J. Tornado near New Harmony, Indiana, April 30, 1852 --- **59**
Characteristics of ancient man in Michigan—H. GILLMAN. (R. 1875) --- 298, **393**
Chart, base, of the United States—C. A. SCHOTT ---------- **414**
Chart, temperature, of the United States, year—C. A. SCHOTT ---------- **381**, **388**
Charts and maps of America, on a collection of—J. G. KOHL. (R. 1856)----- 91
Charts of prehistoric archæology, international code of symbols for—G. DE MORTILLET; E. CHANTRE. (R. 1875)---------- 298
Charts, rain, of the United States, summer, winter, year—C. A. SCHOTT ------ **374**

Charts, temperature, of United States, summer, winter, year—C. A. SCHOTT -- **387**
Charts, wind—J. H. COFFIN; S. J. COFFIN -------- 268
CHASE, S. P., biographical notice of, by J. A. GARFIELD. (R. 1873) -------- 275
CHASE, S. P., biographical notice of, by H. HAMLIN. (R. 1873) -------- 275
CHASE, S. P., statement of, relative to the telegraph. (R. 1857) -------- 107, 115
Chattanooga, Tenn., ancient mound near—M. C. READ. (R. 1867) -------- 215
Check-list of—
duplicates of fishes from Pacific coast, distributed by Smithsonian Institution in 1881—D. S. JORDAN; P. L. JOUY. (P. 1881) -------- 467
fishes, distributed by Smithsonian Institution for National Museum—T. H. BEAN. (P. 1880) -------- 425
fossils of North America, miocene—F. B. MEEK -------- **183**
invertebrate fossils of North America, cretaceous and jurassic—F. B. MEEK -------- **177**
invertebrate fossils of North America, eocene and oligocene—T. A. CONRAD -------- **200**
North American batrachia and reptilia—E. D. COPE -------- **292**
periodicals received by Smithsonian Institution, 1858 -------- **Q**
plants of Washington and vicinity—L. F. WARD -------- **460**
publications of Smithsonian Institution to July, 1872 -------- **245**
publications of Smithsonian Institution to July, 1874 -------- **278**
publications of Smithsonian Institution to July, 1877 -------- **301**
publications of Smithsonian Institution to July, 1879 -------- **344**
publications of Smithsonian Institution to December, 1881 -------- **437**
shells—LEA, CARPENTER, and others -------- **128**
Smithsonian publications -------- 74, 203, 226, 290
Check-lists, blank -------- **164**
Chelonia, anatomy and physiology of—S. W. MITCHELL; G. R. MOREHOUSE -- **159**
Chelonia, extinct, of Nebraska—J. LEIDY -------- 58
Chelura terebrans, occurrence of, on coast of U. S.—S. I. SMITH. (P. 1879) -- 333
Chemical analysis of the sun—A. LAUGEL. (R. 1861) -------- 149
Chemical and physiological investigations of vertebrata—J. JONES -------- **82**
Chemical arts, recent improvements in—J. C. BOOTH; C. MORFIT -------- **27**
Chemical equivalents of sixty-three elements, table of. (R. 1864) -------- 188
Chemical formulæ, tables of—F. W. CLARKE -------- 255
Chemical types, modern theory of—C. M. WETHERILL. (R. 1863) -------- 187
Chemist, report of—F. W. TAYLOR. (R. 1880) -------- 442
Chemistry, lectures on agricultural—S. W. JOHNSON. (R. 1859) -------- 110
Chemistry of the earth—T. S. HUNT. (R. 1869) -------- 228, **376**
Chemistry, photographic—M. JAMIN. (R. 1867) -------- 215
Chemistry, recent progress in, 1879 and 1880—G. F. BARKER. (R. 1880) -- 442, **429**
Chepewyan Indians, notes on the—G. GIBBS and others. (R. 1866) -------- 214, **365**

Cherbourg, Imperial Society of Natural Sciences of. Prize questions. (R. 1864) 188
Chesapeake Bay, new fish from mouth of—G. B. Goode; T. H. Bean. (P. 1881) ---- 467
Chester county, Pennsylvania, birds of—V. Barnard. (R. 1860) ---- 147
Chester county, Pennsylvania, history of—W. Darlington. (R. 1862) ---- 150
Chicago Academy of Sciences. Acknowledging specimens. (R. 1867) ---- 215
China, geological researches in—R. Pumpelly ---- **202**
Chinese coal-bearing rocks, fossil plants from—J. S. Newberry ---- 202
Chinese coals, analyses of—J. A. MacDonald ---- 202
Chinese mineral called yu, study of—S. Blondel. (R. 1876) ---- 299
Chinook jargon—H. Hale ---- 161
Chinook jargon—M. Lionnet; B. R. Mitchell ---- **68**
Chinook jargon, bibliography of—G. Gibbs ---- 161
Chinook jargon, dictionary of—G. Gibbs ---- 161
Chinook names of salmon in Columbia river—S. B. Smith. (P. 1881) ---- 467
Chionis minor, study of—J. H. Kidder; E. Coues ---- 294
Chiroid fish (*Myriolepis zonifer*) from California, new—W. N. Lockington. (P. 1880) ---- 425
Chirus, remarks on genus—W. N. Lockington. (P. 1880) ---- 425
Chitonidæ, new species of, from Panama—P. P. Carpenter ---- **252**
Chitons of Alaskan and Arctic regions, report on—W. H. Dall. (P. 1878) ---- 332
Chitons from deep waters off eastern coast of U. S.—W. H. Dall. (P. 1881.) 467
Chitons, on genera of—W. H. Dall. (P. 1881) ---- 467
Chlorospermeæ, marine algæ of North America—W. H. Harvey ---- **95**
Chorea, inquiries relative to disease known as—S. W. Mitchell. (R. 1874) ---- 286
Chossat, Dr. Transactions of Geneva Society of Physics and Natural History, 1863 to 1864. (R. 1865) ---- 209
Christiania, Norway, University of, ethnological specimens presented. (R. 1863) 187
Chrysotis, new species of, from Dominica—G. N. Lawrence. (P. 1880) ---- 425
Cibola, Coronado's march in search of cities of—J. H. Simpson. (R. 1869) ---- 228
Circle, ratio between diameter and circumference of—W. Ferrel ---- **233**
Circles and spheres, tangencies of—B. Alvord ---- **80**
Circular—
ancient mining in Lake Superior copper region. (R. 1861) ---- 149
for distribution at the Centennial Exhibition ---- **290**
giving directions for constructing lightning-rods—J. Henry ---- **237**
in reference to collecting North American shells ---- **176**
in reference to history of North American grasshoppers—P. R. Uhler ---- **163**
of inquiries relative to crawfish and other fresh water crustacea ---- **319**
of Institute of Rupert's Land. (R. 1861) ---- 149
of instructions for observations of thunder storms—J. Henry ---- **235**
of instructions to observatories, relative to telegraph announcements of astronomical discoveries ---- **263**

Circular—Continued.
philological—G. GIBBS. (R. 1862) 150
relating to collections in archæology and ethnology **205**
relating to collections of living reptiles **320**
relative to American archæology—O. T. MASON. (R. 1879) 345, **316**
relative to collections of birds from Middle and South America **168**
relative to food fishes **234**
relative to heights **236**
relative to observations in Russian America **207**
relative to scientific and literary exchanges **324**
relative to shipping fresh fish and other animals **384**
respecting copyright. (R. 1854) 57
respecting new report on libraries. (R. 1854) 75
respecting system of relationship—L. H. MORGAN **138**
sent with specimens presented. (R. 1872) 271
to entomologists **178**
to officers of Hudson's Bay Company **137**

Circulars of United States National Museum:
No. 1. Plan of organization and regulations of the Museum—G. B. GOODE. (P. 1881) 467, **445**
No. 2. To friends of the Museum—S. F. BAIRD. (P. 1881) 467, **446**
No. 3. Petroleum collections—S. F. BAIRD. (P. 1881) 467, **447**
No. 4. Department of insects—S. F. BAIRD. (P. 1881) 467, **448**
No. 5. Establishment and officers of S. I. and Nat. Mus. (P. 1881) 467, **449**
No. 6. Materia-medica collection—J. M. FLINT. (P. 1881) 467, **450**
No. 7. Forms of drugs and medicines—J. M. FLINT. (P. 1881) 467, **451**
No. 8. Collections of drugs for materia-medica section—J. M. FLINT. (P. 1881) 467, **452**
No. 9. Building-stone collection—S. F. BAIRD. (P. 1881) 467, **453**
No. 10. Letters on the National Museum—B. PHILLIPS. (P. 1881) 467, **454**
No. 11. Provisional classification of the food collections—G. B. GOODE. (P. 1881) 467, **455**
No. 12. Classification of the collections to illustrate taxidermy—W. T. HORNADAY. (P. 1881) 467, **456**
No. 13. Scheme of classification for the collections in the Museum—G. B. GOODE. (P. 1881) 467, **457**
No. 14. Asking for contributions to library of Museum—S. F. BAIRD. (P. 1881) 467, **458**
No. 15. Organization and objects of the Museum—G. B. GOODE. (P. 1881) 467, **459**
No. 16. Plans for installation of collections—G. B. GOODE. (P. 1881) 467, **472**
No. 17. Contributions to the Museum and their acknowledgment. (P. 1881) 467, **473**
No. 18. List of publications of the Museum. (P. 1881) 467, **474**

Cists, stone, Madison county, Illinois—A. OEHLER. (R. 1879) ... 345
Citizens of Philadelphia, memorial of, relative to aeronautic voyage of Lowe. (R. 1860) ... 147
Civil Engineers, London Institution of. Prize questions. (R. 1862) ... 150
Clackamas river, Oregon, notes on fishes from—D. S. JORDAN. (P. 1878) ... 332
CLARK, H. J. Lucernariæ and their allies, anatomy, physiology, and relations of **242**
CLARK, H. J., memoir of, by A. S. PACKARD ... 242
CLARK, W. M. Antiquities of Tennessee. (R. 1877) ... 323
CLARKE, FLADGATE, and FINCH. Residuary legacy of Smithson. (R. 1861) 149, 328
CLARKE, F. W.—
Bibliography of atomic volume, specific gravity, &c. ... 255
Recalculation of atomic weights ... **441**
Specific gravities, boiling and melting points, chemical formulæ, tables ... **255**
Specific gravities, &c. Supplementary tables ... **288**
Specific heat tables for solids and liquids ... **276**
Tables of expansion by heat, for solids and liquids ... **289**
Classification and arrangement of materia medica collection—J. M. FLINT. (P. 1881) ... 467, **450**
Classification and synopsis of *trochilidæ*—D. G. ELLIOT ... **317**
Classification of—
birds, review of the—W. LILLJEBORG. (R. 1865) ... 209, **364**
books, on the—J. P. LESLEY. (R. 1862) ... 150
clouds—A. POEY. (R. 1870) ... 244
coleoptera. Part I—J. L. LE CONTE ... **136**
coleoptera. Part II—J. L. LE CONTE ... **265**
collection to illustrate animal resources of United States—G. B. GOODE ... **297**
collections of U. S. National Museum—G. B. GOODE. (P. 1881) ... 467, **457**
collections of United States National Museum to illustrate taxidermy—W. T. HORNADAY. (P. 1881) ... 467, **456**
food collections—G. B. GOODE. (P. 1881) ... 467, **455**
forms in which drugs and medicines appear and are administered—J. M. FLINT. (P. 1881) ... 467, **451**
insects from embryological data—L. AGASSIZ ... **16**
methods of capture and utilization of animals—G. B. GOODE ... 297
Classified list of meteorological publications and articles in periodicals received by Smithsonian Institution. (R. 1873) ... 275
Classified record of meteorological material preserved in Smithsonian. (R. 1874) ... 286
Classified record of monthly meteorological reports. (R. 1873) ... 275
CLEAVELAND, P. Meteorological observations at Brunswick, Maine ... **204**
CLEAVELAND, P., notice of, by J. HENRY. (R. 1859) ... 110
CLEMENS, B. Instructions for collecting hymenoptera. (R. 1858) ... 109

CLEMENS, B. Instructions for collecting lepidoptera. (R. 1858) 109
CLEMENS, B. On lepidoptera 133
Climate and history of New Mexico—T. A. McPARLIN. (R. 1877) 323, **396**
Climate of Alaska—H. M. BANNISTER. (R. 1866) 214
Climate of California—T. M. LOGAN. (R. 1855) 77
Climate of Colorado—J. EVANS. (R. 1865) 209
Climate of Kansas—R. S. ELLIOTT. (R. 1870) 244
Climate of Kelley's Island, Ohio—G. C. HUNTINGTON. (R. 1866) 214
Climate of San Francisco—H. GIBBONS. (R. 1854) 75
Climate—*See* Meteorology.
Climatic influence of forests—M. BECQUEREL. (R. 1869) 228
CLINGMAN, T. L. Topography of Black Mountain, N. C. (R. 1855) 77
Clinton, N. Y.—*See* Hamilton College.
Closing of Kennebec river, Maine—R. H. GARDINER. (R. 1858) 109
Cloud-bursts—W. J. YOUNG. (R. 1867) 215
Cloud, dispersion of, by an electrical discharge—D. W. NAILL. (R. 1858) 109
Clouds, electricity of induction in—F. ZANTEDESCHI. (R. 1870) 244
Clouds, formation of, over Gulf Stream—H. M. BANNISTER. (R. 1866) 214
Clouds, new classification of—A. POEY. (R. 1870) 244
Clouds, nomenclature of **347**
Clupea tyrannus of Latrobe—G. B. GOODE. (P. 1878) 332
CLUSS, A. Report of architect. (R. 1867) 215
CLUSS & SCHULZE, report of, for 1879. (R. 1879) 345, **409**
CLUSS & SCHULZE, report of, for 1880. (R. 1880) 442, **434**
CLYMER, H. Memorial of J. Henry 356
CLYMER, H., and others. Report on Museum. (R. 1876) 299
Coal, Chinese and Japanese, analyses of—J. A. MACDONALD 202
Coal, Chinese, fossil plants in—J. S. NEWBERRY 202
Coal, lecture on—J. LE CONTE. (R. 1857) 107
Coal oils, explosibility of—Z. ALLEN. (R. 1861) 149
Coast Survey expedition of 1866, to determine transatlantic longitude—B. A. GOULD 223
Coast Survey soundings on Atlantic coast, examination of—J. W. BAILEY 20
Cobalt (ammonia-) bases—W. GIBBS; F. A. GENTH 88
COCHRANE, J. Antiquities of Mason county, Illinois. (R. 1877) 323
CODD, J. A. Acknowledgment for books. (R. 1861) 149
Code of symbols for charts of archæology—G. DE MORTILLET; E. CHANTRE. (R. 1875) 298
COFFIN, J. H.—
Orbit and phenomena of meteoric fire ball **221**
Psychrometrical tables **87**
Storms of 1859 182

COFFIN, J. H.—Continued.
Winds of the globe ---- **268**
Winds of the Northern Hemisphere ---- **52**
COFFIN, S. J. Tables and maps of winds of the globe ---- 268
COGSWELL, J. G. Report on Jewett's general stereotype catalogue of public libraries ---- 47
Coins, assay of gold and silver, at United States mint—J. POLLOCK. (R. 1868) 224
Coins, table of foreign, gold and silver. (R. 1868) ---- 224
COLDING, A. Meteorology. (R. 1877) ---- 323, 398
COLDING, A. Nature of currents of air. (R. 1877) ---- 323, 398
COLDING, A. Theory of relation between pressure and the velocity of the wind. (R. 1877) ---- 323' 398
COLDING, A. Whirlwind at St. Thomas in August, 1871. (R. 1877) ---- 323, 398
Coleoptera—
catalogue of the described, of the United States—F. E. MELSHEIMER ---- **62**
classification of. Part I—J. L. LE CONTE ---- **136**
classification of. Part II—J. L. LE CONTE ---- **265**
instructions for collecting—J. L. LE CONTE. (R. 1858) ---- 109
new species of North American. Part I—J. L. LE CONTE ---- **167**
new species of North American. Part II—J. L. LE CONTE ---- **264**
of Arctic America—S. H. SCUDDER ---- 342
of Kansas and eastern New Mexico—J. L. LE CONTE ---- **126**
of North America, list of—J. L. LE CONTE ---- **140**
Colima, eruption of the volcano of—C. SARTORIUS. (R. 1869) ---- 228
Collaborators of Smithsonian Institution, directory of ---- 466
Collecting—
and preserving diptera, directions for—C. R. OSTEN SACKEN ---- 102
and preserving fish, directions for—T. H. BEAN. (P. 1881) ---- 467, **464**
and preserving plants, directions for—L. F. WARD ---- **460**
insects, directions for—A. S. PACKARD ---- **261**
insects, instructions for—S. F. BAIRD. (R. 1858) ---- 109
land and fresh-water shells, instructions for—J. LEWIS. (R. 1866) 214, **363**
microscopic organisms, directions for ---- 63
myriapods, phalangidæ, etc.—H. C. WOOD. (R. 1866) ---- 214
nests and eggs, instructions for—T. M. BREWER ---- **139**
nests and eggs of birds—S. F. BAIRD. (R. 1858) ---- 109
North American shells, circular in reference to ---- **176**
specimens, directions for—S. F. BAIRD. (R. 1856) ---- 91, **34**
specimens of diatomacea, directions for—A. M. EDWARDS ---- **366**
specimens of natural history—S. F. BAIRD ---- **34**
Collection—
and preservation of marine invertebrates—W. STIMPSON ---- 34
archæological, of United States National Museum—C. RAU ---- **287**

Collection—
of historical documents in Guatemala—C. H. BERENDT. (R. 1876) 299
of meteorological tables—A. GUYOT 31, **153**
to illustrate animal resources and fisheries of United States, exhibited at Philadelphia, in 1876, catalogue of—G. B. GOODE **326**
to illustrate animal resources of United States, classification of—G. B. GOODE **297**
Collections—
additions to. (See each annual report.)
furnished by explorations from 1838 to 1877—S. F. BAIRD. (R. 1877) 323
in archæology and ethnology, circular relative to—J. HENRY **205**
made by Lt. G. K. Warren, report on—F. B. MEEK; F. V. HAYDEN 172
of living reptiles, circular relating to **320**
presented to United States by foreign commissioners at Centennial Exhibition, list of. (R. 1876) 299
to illustrate art of taxidermy—W. T. HORNADAY. (P. 1881) 467, **456**
Collections—*See* Ethnographical.
Collectors of customs to receive and transmit specimens to the Smithsonian 34
Collectors of drugs, memoranda for—J. M. FLINT. (P. 1881) 467, **452**
College—*See* Girard, Hamilton, Liberia.
Colleges in United States in correspondence with Smithsonian Inst., list of 288
COLLINS, Colonel. Meteorology of the Green river country. (R. 1871) 249
Colonia Tovar, Venezuela, meteorology and ethnology of—A. FENDLER. (R. 1857) 107
Colonia Tovar, Venezuela, meteorology of—A. FENDLER. (R. 1866) 214
Colorado—
ancient remains in—E. L. BERTHOUD. (R. 1867) 215
climate of—J. EVANS. (R. 1865) 209
cretaceous fossils from—C. A. WHITE. (P. 1881) 467
descriptions of new invertebrate fossils from—C. A. WHITE. (P. 1880) 425
heights of mountains in—G. ENGELMANN. (R. 1862) 150
Jefferson and Clear Creek Cos., antiquities—G. L. CANNON. (R. 1877) 323
Weld county, antiquities of—E. L. BERTHOUD. (R. 1871) 249
Color-blindness—J. HENRY. (R. 1877) 323
Color-blindness—A. MOIGNO. (R. 1866) 214
Color-blindness in its relations to accidents by rail and sea—F. HOLMGREN. (R. 1877) 323, **399**
Colored bead from mound in Florida—A. M. HARRISON. (R. 1877) 323
Colors, accidental or subjective—A. MOIGNO. (R. 1866) 214
Columbia river, Chinook names of salmon in—S. B. SMITH. (P. 1881) 467
Columbia river, *Salmonidæ* of—C. BENDIRE. (P. 1881) 467
Combustion of gun-cotton and gunpowder, products of—Lieut. VON KAROLYI; B. F. CRAIG. (R. 1864) 188

Comet, investigations of Biela's—J. S. HUBBARD. (R. 1862) 150
Comets, directions for telegrams of discovery of 263
COMFORT, A. J. Indian mounds near Fort Wadsworth, Dakota. (R. 1871) 249
Commemoration of J. Henry 356
Commission, National Museum—*See* Museum.
Commissioner of Patents. Meteorological observations, Vol. I 157
Commissioner of Patents. Meteorological observations, Vol. II 182
Commissioners for Foreign Missions—*See* American Board.
Commissioners, report of, on plan of forming general stereotype catalogue for public libraries in United States. (R. 1850) 28, 47
Committee of American Association for Advancement of Science. Report on meteorology. (R. 1851) 51
Committee of Regents—
report on architecture P
report on fire at Smithsonian—R. WALLACH; J. HENRY. (R. 1864) 188, 329
report on income—J. A. PEARCE. (R. 1853) 67, 329
report on income—J. MEACHAM. (R. 1853) 67, 329
report on Museum—A. GRAY; A. A. SARGENT; H. CLYMER. (R. 1876) 299, 329
report on organization B, 328
report on organization, (first) L, 328
Committee—*See* Report.
Comparative action of dry heat and sulphurous acid upon putrefactive bacteria. (P. 1881) 467
Comparative vocabulary—A. GALLATIN 160
Comparative vocabulary, English, Spanish, French, Latin—G. GIBBS 170
Compasses, deviations of, on iron-clad—W. HARKNESS 289
Conchology, North American, bibliography of. Part I. American authors—W. G. BINNEY 142
Conchology, North American, bibliography of. Part II. Foreign authors—W. G. BINNEY 174
Conchology—*See* Mollusks, Shells.
Concise, archæological researches at—F. TROYON. (R. 1861) 149
CONDORCET, biography of, by F. ARAGO. (R. 1878) 341
Cone-in-cone—H. POOLE. (R. 1863) 187
Congress, International Anthropological, address at—F. F. ROMER. (R. 1876) 299, **392**
Congress, International Archæological, Antwerp, 1866. (R. 1866) 214
Congress of Carlsruhe, 1858, scientific—F. J. NICKLÉS. (R. 1860) 147
Congress, United States—
act of, accepting bequest, July 1, 1836. (R. 1853) 67, 328, N
act of, to establish Smithsonian Institution. (R. 1853) 67' 329, **391**, B, N, O
act of, to establish Smithsonian Institution, construction of—J. McP. BERRIEN. (R. 1853) 67
act of, to establish Smithsonian, digest of—J. HENRY 328, C

Congress, United States—Continued.
act of, to receive residuary legacy and increase fund. (R. 1866) 214, 329
act of, to transfer Smithsonian library to Library of Congress. (R. 1865) 209, 328
acts of, (45th Congress,) relative to Smithsonian. (R. 1878) 341
acts of, (45th and 46th Congresses,) relative to Smithsonian, 1878-1880. (R. 1879) 345
memorial of J. Henry, published by order of **356**
memorial of Regents to, asking appropriations for Museum. (R. 1866; R. 1867) 214, 215, 328
memorial of Regents to, relative to new Museum building. (R. 1876) .. 299
memorial of Regents to, relative to Smithson fund. (R. 1850) 28
proceedings of, relative to appropriations for Museum 328
proceedings of, relative to monument of J. Henry 356
proceedings of, relative to new Museum building 328
proceedings of, relative to Smithson bequest 328
proceedings of, relative to Smithsonian Institution, 1835-1877 328
Connecticut Academy of Arts and Sciences, planisphere of the heavens by **359**
Connecticut, ancient implement of wood from—E. W. ELLSWORTH. (R. 1876) 299
Conosaurus, memoir on—R. W. GIBBES 14
CONRAD, C. M., Secretary of War. Authority to officers of Quartermaster's Department toreceive and transmit specimens to Smithsonian 34
CONRAD, T. A. Chalk found in the United States. (R. 1865) 209
CONRAD, T. A. Check-list of invertebrate fossils of North America. *Eocene and oligocene* **200**
Consanguinity and affinity of the human family, circular—L. H. MORGAN **138**
Consanguiniiy and affinity of the human family, systems of—L. H. MORGAN .. **218**
Considerations on electricity. (R. 1867) 215
Constantinople, account of hail storm at—Com. PORTER. (R. 1870) 244
Constants of Nature—
Part I. Specific gravities, boiling and melting points, and chemical formulæ—F. W. CLARKE **255**
Part II. Table of specific heats for solids and liquids—F. W. CLARKE. **276**
Part III. Tables of expansion by heat for solids and liquids—F. W. CLARKE **289**
Part IV. Atomic weight determinations—G. F. BECKER **358**
Part V. Recalculation of atomic weights—F. W. CLARKE **441**
First supplement to Part I. Specific gravities, boiling points and melting points—F. W. CLARKE **288**
Constants of nature—J. LE CONTE. (R. 1878) 341
Constants of nature and art, tables of—C. BABBAGE. (R. 1856) 91
Construction of act establishing Institution—J. McP. BERRIEN. (R. 1853) ... 67
Construction of catalogues of libraries—C. C. JEWETT **47**
Construction of silvored glass telescope—H. DRAPER **180**

Contact, catalytic force or phenomena of—T. L. PHIPSON. (R. 1862) 150
CONTAXAKI, Miss E. B., present of album from Greece. (R. 1857) 107, 327
Contrast of colors—A. MOIGNO. (R. 1866) 214
Contribution to history of fresh-water algæ of North America—H. C. WOOD.. **241**
Contributions to Annals of Philosophy—J. SMITHSON. (R. 1853) 67, 330
Contributions to history of marine algæ of North America—*See* W. H. Harvey.
Contributions to Knowledge, vols. I–XXIII.. **2, 26, 38, 39, 55, 56, 76, 78, 92, 99, 111, 112, 151, 184, 206, 211, 229, 246, 272, 284, 285, 340, 346**
Contributions to Knowledge, catalogue of, and index 478
Contributions to National Museum, and their acknowledgment. (P. 1881.) 467, **473**
Contributions to natural history of—
Arctic America—L. KUMLIEN **342**
Fanning Islands—T. H. STREETS 303
fresh-water fishes of North America—C. GIRARD **30**
Hawaiian Islands—T. H. STREETS 303
Kerguelen Island. I. Ornithology—E. COUES 293
Kerguelen Island. II. Oölogy, botany, etc.—J. H. KIDDER and others.. 294
Lower California—T. H. STREETS 303
Contributions to North American ichthyology—
Part I. Review *Rafinesque's* memoirs—D. S. JORDAN **305**
Part II. Notes on *Cottidæ;* sysopsis *Siluridæ*—D. S. JORDAN **306**
Part III. Fishes Alleghany region; synopsis *Catostomidæ*—D. S. JORDAN; A. W. BRAYTON **308**
Contributions to physical geography of United States—C. ELLET, Jr **13**
Contributions toward monograph of the pandoridæ—P. P. CARPENTER 252
Converging series expressing ratio between diameter and circumference of circle—W. FERREL **233**
COOK, C. Manufacture of porpoise oil. (P. 1878) 332
COOPER, J. G.—
Distribution of forests and trees of North America, and catalogue of native trees of United States. (R. 1858) 109, **351**
Forests and trees of Florida and Mexican boundary. (R. 1860) 147
Migrations and nesting habits of west coast birds. (P. 1879) 333
COPE, E. D.—
Genera and species of rattlesnakes 135
North America batrachia and reptilia **292**
Zoölogical position of Texas **412**
COPPÉE, H. Report of Committee on Smithsonian Museum. (R. 1874) 286
Copper and iron in salt water, preservation of—A. E. BECQUEREL. (R. 1864.) 188
Copper region, circular, ancient mining in Lake Superior—J. HANN. (R. 1861) 149
Coptic language, introduction to the study of the—M. KABIS. (R. 1867) 215
Copyright books from 1846–1849, list of—C. C. JEWETT. (R. 1850) 28

Copyright system and Smithsonian library—C. C. JEWETT. (R. 1851) 51
Copyrights, circular respecting—J. HENRY. (R. 1854) 75
Corbiculadæ, American, monograph of—T. PRIME **145**
Corcoran Art Gallery, list of deposits in, by Smithsonian Institution. (R. 1874) 286
Corcoran Art Gallery, report of Committee of Regents on. (R. 1872) 271
CORCORAN, W. W. Deed of gift establishing Art Gallery. (R. 1872) 271, 329
Cordoba, Argentine Republic, account of astronomical observatory at—B. A. GOULD. (R. 1873) 275
Corner-stone of Smithsonian building, address at laying—G. M. DALLAS... **D**, 329
Corner-stone of Smithsonian building, ceremonies at laying of. (R. 1847) .. **H**, 329
Coronado's march in search of the "seven cities of Cibola"—J. H. SIMPSON. (R. 1869) 228
Correspondence—
abstracts of anthropological—O. T. MASON. (R. 1880) 442
extracts from. (R. 1855, 1858-1863, 1865-1867, 1873) .. 77, 109, 110, 147, 149, 150, 187, 209, 214, 215, 275
meteorological—E. FOREMAN. (R. 1851) 51
relative to publication of memoir by Squier and Davis .... **K**
relative to Smithson and his bequest 328
summary of anthropological. (R. 1879) 345
Correspondents—
domestic, list of. (R. 1853; R. 1872) 67, 271, **69**, **238**
foreign, list of **64**, **154**, **225**, **243**, **309**
foreign, systematic index of **257**
Costa Rica—
kitchen-midden, note on shells from—W. H. DALL. (P. 1878) 332
minister, letter of, recommending Dr. Berendt. (R. 1865) 209
notes on birds of—R. RIDGWAY. (P. 1878; P. 1881) 332, 467
University of, exchange of specimens. (R. 1867) 215
Cottidæ, description of a new genus and species of—W. N. LOCKINGTON. (P. 1881) 467
Cottidæ, notes on—D. S. JORDAN 306
Cottoids, monograph of—C. GIRARD **30**
Cotton, amount of crop, and price in Japan—JAPANESE LEGATION. (P. 1881) 467
Cotton fibre, catalogue of Japanese, presented to National Museum. (P. 1881) 467
COUES, E.—
Birds of Kerguelen Island **293**
List of faunal publications relating to British birds. (P. 1879) 333
Oölogy of Kerguelen Island 294
COUES, E.; KIDDER, J. H. Study of *Chionis minor* 294
COUES, E.; PRENTISS, S. S. List of birds of District of Columbia. (R. 1861) 149
COX, S. S. Address, memorial of Joseph Henry 356
COX, S. S. Eulogy on Stephen A. Douglas. (R. 1861) 149, 329

CRAIG, B. F. Nitrification. (R. 1861) 149

CRAIG, B. F.; Lieut. VON KAROLYI. Products of combustion of gun-cotton and gunpowder. (R. 1864) 188

Craig flounder of Europe (*Glyptocephalus cynoglossus*) on coast of North America—G. B. GOODE; T. H. BEAN. (P. 1878) 332

Crania Helvetica—F. TROYON. (R. 1864) 188

Craw-fish, circular of inquiries relative to **319**

Creation, visible, lecture on vastness of—S. ALEXANDER. (R. 1857) 107

Cree Indians, system of relationship of—E. A. WATKINS. (R. 1862) 150

Cremnobates, occurrence of, at San Diego, California—R. SMITH. (P. 1880) 425

CRESSON, J. C. Lightning discharges. (R. 1867) 215

Cretaceous fossils, check-list of—F. B. MEEK **177**

Cretaceous fossils from Arkansas and Colorado—C. A. WHITE. (P. 1881) 467

Cretaceous reptiles of United States—J. LEIDY. (R. 1864) 188, **192**

Cricetodipus parvus, a rare rodent—F. W. TRUE. (P. 1881) 467

Criocardium, note on—C. A. WHITE. (P. 1879) 333

Criticisms of Dr. J. Hann, replies to the—W. FERREL. (R. 1877) 323, 398

CROOK, G. Indian mode of making arrow-heads and obtaining fire. (R. 1871.) 249

Crozet flora—J. H. KIDDER 294

CRUMMELL, A. Facts respecting Liberia College. (R. 1861) 149

Crust of the earth, revolutions of the—G. PILAR. (R. 1876) 299

Crustacea—

fresh water, circular of inquiries relative to **319**

notice of, dredged off south coast of New England by Fish Commission—S. I. SMITH. (P. 1880) 425

notice of new species of Willemæsia group of—S. I. SMITH. (P. 1879.) 333

of Hawaiian and Fanning Islands and California—T. A. STREETS 303

Crustacean destructive to submarine timber on coast of United States—S. I. SMITH. (P. 1879) 333

Crustaceans of Kerguelen Island—S. I. SMITH 294

Crustaceans, voices of—G. B. GOODE. (P. 1878) 332

Cryolite of Greenland—LEWIS; QUALE. (R. 1866) 214

Cryptogamous plants, present state of knowledge of—W. REICHARDT. (R. 1871) 249

Crystalline rocks, metamorphism and the formation of—G. A. DAUBRÉE. (R. 1861) 149

Crystallography, explanation of principles of—A. BREZINA. (R. 1872) 271, **386**

Crystallophysics, explanation of principles of—A. BREZINA. (R. 1872) 271, **386**

CULBERTSON, T. A.—

Expedition to the Mauvaises Terres and Upper Missouri. (R. 1850) 28

Indian tribes in Upper Missouri. (R. 1850) 28

Sioux of the Upper Missouri. (R. 1850) 28

Culture, fish—*See* Fish.

CUNARD, E. Free freight between United States and England. (R. 1859.) 110, 329

CUNNINGHAM, K. M.; GAINES, A. S. Shell-heaps on Mobile river. (R. 1877.) 323
Currents, electrical, of the earth—C. MATTEUCCI. (R. 1867) 215
Currents of air—
and aerial navigation—J. HENRY. (R. 1860) 147
law of variation of temperature in ascending—J. HANN. (R. 1877.) 323, 398
law of variation of temperature in ascending moist—L. SOHNCKE. (R. 1877) 323, 398
nature of—A. COLDING. (R. 1877) 323, 398
relation between barometric variations and—M. PESLIN. (R. 1877) 323, 398
Curtiss, A. H., notes on collection of fishes made by—D. S. JORDAN. (P. 1880) 425
CUSHING, F. H. Antiquities of Orleans county, New York. (R. 1874) 286
Customs, collectors of, to receive and transmit specimens to Smithsonian 34
CUTTS, J. B. Ancient relics in northwestern Iowa. (R. 1872) 271
CUVIER, Baron G.—
history of the works of, by M. FLOURENS. (R. 1868) 224
memoir of, by M. FLOURENS. (R. 1868) 224
Memoir of René Just Haüy. (R. 1860) 147
Memoir of Priestley. (R. 1858) 109
Cybium, notes on American species of—F. POEY. (P. 1878) 332
Cyclone in the Indian Ocean—N. PIKE. (R. 1867) 215
Cyclophoridæ—W. G. BINNEY 144
Cymatogaster rosaceus—D. S. JORDAN; C. H. GILBERT. (P. 1880) 425
Cyprinidæ, notes on—D. S. JORDAN 306
Cyprinoid fishes of San Francisco market—D. S. JORDAN. (P. 1880) 425

D.

DAA, L. K. Ethnological museum of Norway. (R. 1862) 150
Dacentrus, note on—D. S. JORDAN. (P. 1880) 425
DA COSTA, J. M. On strain and over-action of the heart. Toner lecture No. III. 279
DAHLBERG, R. N. and C. Ancient pottery at Pittsburg, on Des Moines river. (R. 1879) 345
Dakota—
bibliography—S. R. RIGGS 40
fable, A dog's revenge—S. R. RIGGS. (E. 1879–80) 476
grammar and dictionary—S. R. RIGGS 40
Fort Wadsworth, Indian mounds near—A. J. COMFORT. (R. 1871) 249

Dakota, Lincoln county, haystack mound in—A. BARRANDT. (R. 1872) 271
Dakota or Sioux Indians—A. G. BRACKETT. (R. 1876) 299
Dakota or Sioux Indians, language of—F. L. O. ROEHRIG. (R. 1871) 249, 378
DALL, W. H.—
Distribution of California tertiary fossils. (P. 1878) 332
Explorations on western coast of North America. (R. 1873) 275
Fossil mollusks from later tertiaries of California. (P. 1878) 332
Index of Brachiopoda **304**
Limpets and chitons of Alaskan and Arctic regions. (P. 1878) 332
Mollusks of Arctic America 342
Mollusks of Kerguelen Island 294
New mollusks from Alaska in National Museum. (P. 1878) 332
New species of shells from California in National Museum. (P. 1878) 332
Note on shells from Costa Rica kitchen-midden collected by Drs. Flint and Bransford. (P. 1878) 332
On genera of chitons. (P. 1881) 467
Postpliocene fossils in coast range of California. (P. 1878) 332
Remains of later prehistoric man from caves in Alaska **318**
DALLAS, G. M. Address at laying corner-stone of Smithsonian building **D**, 329
DALTON, J. C. Origin and propagation of disease. (R. 1873) 275
Daltonism, etc.—A. MOIGNO. (R. 1866) 214
DANILSEN, A. F. Mound in East Tennessee. (R. 1863) 187
Danish Royal Society of Arts and Sciences. Prize questions. (R. 1862, 1865, 1867) 150, 209, 215
DARLINGTON, W. History of Chester county, Pennsylvania. (R. 1862) 150
Darlingtonia Californica—J. TORREY **61**
DARWIN, C. Queries about expression for anthropological inquiry. (R. 1867) 215
DAUBRÉE, G. A. Metamorphism and formation of crystalline rocks. (R. 1861) 149
DAUBRÉE, G. A. Synthetic experiments relative to meteorites. (R. 1868) 224
DAVIS, A. C. Antiquities of Isle Royale, Lake Superior. (R. 1874) 286
DAVIS, C. H. Law of deposit of flood-tide **33**
DAVIS, C. H. Occultations in United States, 1852 29
DAVIS, E. H. On ethnological research. (R. 1866) 214
DAVIS, E. H.; SQUIER, E. G. Ancient monuments of Mississippi valley **1**
DAYTON, E. A. Explorations in Tennessee. (R. 1870) 244
Deaf mutes, sign language of—G. MALLERY. (E. 1879-80) 476
DEAN, C. K. Mound in Wisconsin. (R. 1872) 271
DEAN, C. W. Lightning discharges. (R. 1867) 215
DEAN, J. Gray substance of medulla oblongata **173**
DE BEAUMONT, E.—
Memoir of C. F. Beautemps-Beaupré. (R. 1863) 187

DE BEAUMONT, E.—Continued.
Memoir of Auguste Bravais. (R. 1869) 228
Memoir of Legendre. (R. 1867) 215
Memoir of Oersted. (R. 1868) 224
DE BLAINVILLE, D., memoir of, by M. FLOURENS. (R. 1865) 209
DE CANDOLLE, A.—
Causes which limit vegetable species towards the north. (R. 1858) 109
Probable future of the human race. (R. 1875) 298
Report on transactions of Society of Physics and Natural History of Geneva for 1862. (R. 1864) 188
Report on transactions of Society of Physics and Natural History of Geneva, 1873–1874. (R. 1875) 298
DE CANDOLLE, A.; GRAY, J. E. On a dominant language for science. (R. 1874) 286
DE CANDOLLE, P., memoir of, by M. FLOURENS. (R. 1859) 110
Deduction and induction—J. VON LIEBIG. (R. 1870) 244
Deed of foundation of Toner lectures—J. M. TONER. (R. 1872) 271, 329
Deed of foundation of Tyndall scientific fund—J. TYNDALL. (R. 1872) 271, 329
Deed of gift of Art Gallery—W. W. CORCORAN. (R. 1872) 271, 329
DE FOREST, E. L. Methods of interpolation. Part I. (R. 1871) 249
DE FOREST, E. L. Additions to memoir on methods of interpolation. Part II. (R. 1873) 275
DE HART, J. N. Mounds and osteology of mound-builders of Wisconsin. (R. 1877) 323
DE IRISARRI, Guatemalan minister, recommendation of Dr. Berendt by. (R. 1865) 209
DELAFIELD, R. Report of Committee of Regents on Washington canal. (R. 1868) 224, 329
DELAMBRE, J. B. J., memoir of, by J. FOURIER. (R. 1864) 188
DE LA RIVE, A. A.—
Eulogy on, by J. B. DUMAS. (R. 1874) 286
Michael Faraday, his life and works. (R. 1867) 215
Phenomena accompanying propagation of electricity in rarefied elastic fluids. (R. 1863) 187
Report on transactions of Society of Physics and Natural History of Geneva, 1858–1859, 1872–1873. (R. 1859; R. 1874) 110, 286
DE LA RIVE, A. A.; LEMSTRÖM, S. Electricity of the atmosphere and the aurora borealis. (R. 1874) 286
DE LA RUE, W. Abbreviations used in England in 1867. (R. 1867) 215
DELAUNAY, C. Essay on the velocity of light. (R. 1864) 188, **354**
Delolepis, new genus of fishes, description of—T. H. BEAN. (P. 1881) 467
Denmark, preservation of antiquities in—J. J. A. WORSAAE. (R. 1879) 345
DENNIS, W. C. Evaporation in Florida. (R. 1866) 214
DENNIS, W. C. Fresh water in the ocean. (R. 1866) 214

Deposit of—
arrow-heads near Fishkill, New York—E. M. SHEPARD. (R. 1877) ---- 323
articles by Smithsonian in Corcoran Art Gallery. (R. 1874) ---------- 286
Beaufort Library—E. M. STANTON. (R. 1862) ---------- 150
Bishop Johns' Library—E. CANBY. (R. 1862) ---------- 150
flint implements in Illinois—J. F. SNYDER. (R. 1876) ---------- 299
flint implements in Southern Illinois—C. RAU. (R. 1868) ---- 224, 440, **370**
flood-tide, law of—C. H. DAVIS ---------- **33**
Deposit, shell, in New Jersey—C. RAU. (R. 1864) ---------- 188, 440, **362**
Deposits—*See* Shell deposits.
DE PRADOS, Baron. Eclipse of the sun, April 25, 1865. (R. 1864) ---------- 188
DE SAUSSURE, H.—
Electric resonance of mountains. (R. 1868) ---------- 224
Hymenoptera. (R. 1862) ---------- 150
Report on transactions of Society of Physics and Natural History of Geneva, 1870-1871. (R. 1871) ---------- 249
Synopsis of *Vespidæ*, (American wasps) ---------- **254**
DE SCHLAGINTWEIT, H. Ethnographical collections. (R. 1862) ---------- 150
Description of—
a new fish, *Apogon pandionis*—G. B. GOODE; T. H. BEAN. (P. 1881) -- 467
a new fly-catcher and new petrel from Sandwich Islands—R. RIDGWAY. (P. 1881) ---------- 467
a new genus and species of *Cottidæ*—W. N. LOCKINGTON. (P. 1881) --- 467
a new gobioid fish (*Othonops eos*) from San Diego, California—R. SMITH. (P. 1881) ---------- 467
a new owl from Porto Rico—R. RIDGWAY. (P. 1881) ---------- 467
birds—*See* Proceedings National Museum.
chitonidæ and acmæidæ from Panama—P. P. CARPENTER ---------- 252
country and people of Yoruba, Africa—T. J. BOWEN ---------- 98
fishes—*See* Proceedings of National Museum.
fossil plants from China—J. S. NEWBERRY ---------- 202
Gobiesox rhessodon from San Diego, California—R. SMITH. (P. 1881) -- 467
human skull from Rock Bluff, Illinois—J. A. MEIGS, (R. 1867) ------ 215
magnetic observatory at Smithsonian. (R. 1859) ---------- 110
meteorological instruments—L. CASELLA. (R. 1859) ---------- 110
new fishes—T. H. BEAN. (P. 1881) ---------- 467
new fishes—*See* D. S. JORDAN; C. H. GILBERT.
new species of *Centrarchidæ*—C. L. MCKAY. (P. 1881) ---------- 467
new subspecies of *Loxigilla* from island of St. Christopher, West Indies—G. N. LAWRENCE. (P. 1881) ---------- 467
new thrushes—R. RIDGWAY. (P. 1881) ---------- 467
observatories at Dorpat and Poulkova—C. ABBE. (R. 1867) ------ 215, **369**

Description of—Continued.

observatory at St. Martin, Isle Jesus, Canada East—C. SMALLWOOD. (R. 1856) ---- 91

plants collected by J. C. Frémont in California—J. TORREY ---- **46**

remains of extinct mammalia and chelonia from Nebraska—J. LEIDY -- **58**

Descriptions of—

ancient works in Ohio—C. WHITTLESEY ---- **37**

several new races of American birds—R. RIDGWAY. (P. 1881) ---- 467

Smithsonian anemometer—J. HENRY. (R. 1860) ---- 147

Squalius aliciæ from Utah Lake—P. L. JOUY. (P. 1881) ---- 467

two new races of *Myadestes obscurus*—L. STEJNEGER. (P. 1881) ---- 467

Desiderata, special, among North American birds, list of—R. RIDGWAY. (P. 1881) ---- 467

Des Moines river, ancient pottery from—R. N. and C. DAHLBERG. (R. 1879.) 345

Des Moines valley, mounds in—S. B. EVANS. (R. 1879) ---- 345

DESOR, E. Palafittes or lacustrian constructions, Lake Neuchâtel. (R. 1865.) 209, **360**

Destruction of fish in Gulf of Mexico—J. Y. PORTER. (P. 1881) ---- 467

Destruction of fish—*See also* Fish.

Destructive effect of iron rust. (R. 1861) ---- 149

DEVEREUX, J. H. Ancient pottery from Arkansas. (R. 1872) ---- 271

DEVEREUX, J. H. Catalogue of Indian relics presented to Smithsonian Institution. (R. 1872) ---- 271

DEWEY, C.—

Best hours for temperature observations. (R. 1860) ---- 147

Best hours to find mean temperature. (R. 1857) ---- 107

life of, by M. B. ANDERSON. (R. 1870) ---- 244

The winds. (R. 1866) ---- 214

Diagnoses des mollusques nouveaux provenant de Californie et faisant partie du Musée de l'Institution Smithsonienne—P. P. CARPENTER ---- 252

Diagnoses of new forms of mollusks collected at Cape St. Lucas, Lower California—P. P. CARPENTER ---- 252

Diagnoses of new mollusks—

collected on west tropical shores of North America—P. P. CARPENTER- 252

from Reigen Mazatlan collection—P. P. CARPENTER ---- 252

from Vancouver district—P. P. CARPENTER ---- 252

from west coast of North America—P. P. CARPENTER ---- 252

from west tropical region of North America—P. P. CARPENTER ---- 252

Diamond and other precious stones—J. BABINET. (R. 1870) ---- 244, **377**

Diary of an excursion in New Mexice—J. H. CARLETON. (R. 1854) ---- 75

Diatomacea—J. W. BAILEY ---- 23, 63

Diatomacea, instructions for collecting, preserving, and transporting—A. M. EDWARDS ---- **366**

DICKINSON, A. B Eruption of volcano in Nicaragua. (R. 1867) ---- 215

Dictionary of—
Carib or Karif language—C. H. BERENDT. (R. 1873) 275
Chinook jargon, or trade language of Oregon—G. GIBBS **161**
Dakota language—S. R. RIGGS **40**
Yoruba language of Africa—T. J. BOWEN **98**
Yoruba language of Africa—W. W. TURNER 98
Digest of act of Congress establishing Smithsonian Institution—J. HENRY **C**, 328
DILLE, I. Antiquities in Missouri and Tennessee. (R. 1862) 150
DILLE, I. Sketch of ancient earthworks of Ohio. (R. 1866) 214
Diminution of aqueous vapor with increasing altitude—J. HANN. (R. 1877) 323, 398
Diminution of water of rivers and streams—H. G. WEX. (R. 1875) 298
Diplomatic agents, circular to, relative to Morgan's research 138
Diptera—
described, of North America, catalogue of—R. OSTEN SACKEN **102**, **270**
directions for collecting and preserving—R. OSTEN SACKEN 102
instructions for collecting—H. LOEW; R. OSTEN SACKEN. (R. 1858) 109
of Arctic America—S. H. SCUDDER 342
Diptera of North America, monographs of—
Parts I–III—H. LOEW **141**, **171**, **256**
Part IV—R. OSTEN SACKEN **219**
Directions for—
auroral observations—J. HENRY. (R. 1855) 77
collecting and preserving diptera—R. OSTEN SACKEN 102
collecting and preserving fish—T. H. BEAN. (P. 1881) 467, **464**
collecting and preserving insects—A. S. PACKARD **261**
collecting and preserving plants—L. F. WARD **460**
collecting microscopic organisms—J. W. BAILEY 63
collecting, preserving, and transporting specimens of *Diatomaceæ*—A. M. EDWARDS **366**
collecting, preserving, and transporting specimens of natural history—S. F. BAIRD. (R. 1856) 91, **34**
constructing lightning-rods—J. HENRY **237**
earthquake observations—J. HENRY. (R. 1855) 77
meteorological observations—A. GUYOT; J. HENRY. (R. 1855) 77, **19**, **148**
Directory of officers, collaborators, employés, etc., of the Smithsonian Institution, National Museum, Geological Survey, Bureau of Ethnology, and Fish Commission **466**
Discourse on J. Henry—S. B. DOD 356
Discovery, meteorological—F. L. CAPEN. (R. 1866) 214
Discovery of—
a large meteorite in Mexico—W. M. PIERSON. (R. 1873) 275
planet Neptune, report on history of the—B. A. GOULD **18**
stone image in Tennessee—E. M. GRANT. (R. 1870) 244

Discovery relative to magnetism, history of. (R. 1868) 187
Discussion of magnetic and meterological observations made at Girard College Observatory—A. D. BACHE:—
Part I. Eleven year period, solar diurnal variation **113**
Part II. Solar diurnal variation and annual inequality **121**
Part III. Influence of moon on declination **132**
Parts IV, V, VI. Horizontal component of magnetic force, etc. **162**
Parts VII, VIII, IX. Vertical force **175**
Parts X, XI, XII. Dip and total force **186**
Parts I–XII. Complete **195**
Discussion of—
meteorological observations—*See* Schott.
Piazzi's astronomical observations—B. A. GOULD. (R. 1863) 187
relations of lucernarians to other acalephæ, beroids, and polypi—H. J. CLARK 242
Snell's barometric observations—F. H. LOUD. (R. 1880) 442, **435**
tables and charts of winds—A. WOEIKOF 268
Disease known as "chorea," inquiries relative to—S. W. MITCHELL. (R. 1874) 286
Disease, origin and propagation of—J. C. DALTON. (R. 1873) 275
Diseases of joints, bones, etc., bibliography of works on—W. W. KEEN 300
Dispersion of cloud by an electrical discharge—D. W. NAILL. (R. 1858) 109
Distinction between tornadoes and tempests—J. B. LAMARCK. (R. 1871) 249
Distribution of—
duplicate fishes of Pacific coast, check-list of—D. S. JORDAN; P. L. JOUY. (P. 1881) 467
fishes of Alleghany region of South Carolina, Georgia, and Tennessee—D. S. JORDAN; A. W. BRAYTON 308
forest trees in Montana, Idaho, and Washington—W. W. JOHNSON. (R. 1870) 244
forests and trees of North America—J. G. COOPER. (R. 1858) 109, **351**
marine invertebrates from National Museum, list of—R. RATHBUN. (P. 1881) 467, **465**, **471**
Smithson income, majority and minority reports of Committee of Regents on—J. A. PEARCE; J. MEACHAM. (R. 1853) 67, 329
specimens—*See* each annual report.
District of Columbia—
flora of—L. F. WARD. (P. 1881) 467, **444**
list of birds of—E. COUES; S. S. PRENTISS. (R. 1861) 149
meteorology of—J. WISSNER. (R. 1857) 107
prehistoric remains in—T. R. PEALE. (R. 1872) 271
Ditrema atripes, new embiotocoid fish from coast of California—D. S. JORDAN; C. H. GILBERT. (P. 1880) 425
Documents, collection of historical, in Guatemala—C. H. BERENDT. (R. 1876) 299

Documents relative to origin and history of Smithsonian Institution—W. J. RHEES ---- **328**
DOD, S. B. Memorial discourse on J. Henry ---- 356
DODGE, G. W. Lightning discharges. (R. 1867) ---- 215
DODGE, N. S. Memoir of C. Babbage. (R. 1873) ---- 275
DODGE, N. S. Memoir of Sir John F. W. Herschel. (R. 1871) ---- 249
Dog's revenge, a Dakota fable—S. R. RIGGS. (E. 1879–80) ---- 476
Dolichopodidæ, monograph of—H. LOEW ---- 171
Domestic institutions in correspondence with Smithsonian Institution, list of -- **69**, **238**
Domestic institutions in correspondence with Smithsonian Institution, number of ---- 290
Dominant language for science—A. DE CANDOLLE; J. E. GRAY. (R. 1874) -- 286
Dominica, catalogue of Ober's collections of birds from—G. N. LAWRENCE. (P. 1878) ---- 332
Dominica, new species of *Turdidæ* from—G. N. LAWRENCE. (P. 1880) ---- 425
DONATI, G. B. Phenomena in telegraphic lines during aurora. (R. 1872) ---- 271
Donations to library from foreign institutions, list of. (R. 1864) ---- 188
Dorosoma cepedianum heterurum, (western gizzard shad,) notes on—S. WILMOT. (P. 1878) ---- 332
Dorpat and Poulkova, description of observatories at—C. ABBE. (R. 1867) 215, **369**
DORSEY, J. O. Illustrations of method of recording Indian languages. (E. 1879–80) ---- 476
Dorysomatidæ, notes on—D. S. JORDAN ---- 306
DOUGLAS, S. A., eulogy on, by S. S. COX. (R. 1861) ---- 149
DOUGLASS, H. M. Translation of Weismann on change of Mexican axolotl. (R. 1877) ---- 323, **401**
DOWNES, J. Occultations of planets and stars by the moon, 1853 ---- **54**
DOWNES, J. Occultations visible in the United States, 1848–1852 -- **8**, **9**, **10**, **11**, **29**
DOYLE, W. E. Indian forts and dwellings, Indian Territory. (R. 1876) ---- 299
Drainage, sanitary, of Washington city, suggestions for—G. E. WARING ---- 349
DRAPER, H., account of telescope of, by T. W. WEBB. (R. 1864) ---- 188
DRAPER, H. Construction of silvered glass telescope and its use in celestial photography ---- **180**
DREUTZER, O. E. Statistics relative to Norwegian mountains, lakes, and snow line. (R. 1866) ---- 214
Drift, fresh water glacial, of the Northwestern States—C. WHITTLESEY ---- **197**
Drilling in stone without metal—C. RAU. (R. 1868) ---- 224, 440, **372**
Drugs, classification of forms in which medicines and, appear and are administered—J. M. FLINT. (P. 1881) ---- 467, **451**
Drugs, memoranda for collectors of—J. M. FLINT. (P. 1881) ---- 467, **452**
Dual character of the brain. Toner lecture No. II—C. E. BROWN-SÉQUARD -- **291**
DUBY, P. A. Report on transactions of Society of Physics and Natural History of Geneva, 1861. (R. 1864) ---- 188

Duck, new to North American fauna—R. RIDGWAY. (P. 1881) 467
DUDLEY, T. Earthquake at New Madrid, Missouri. (R. 1858) 109
DUFOUR, C.; KÄMTZ. Scintillation of the stars. (R. 1861) 149
DUGÈS, A., notes on fishes collected by, in Mexico—T. H. BEAN. (P. 1879) 333
DUGÈS, A., notes on fishes collected by, in Mexico—D. S. JORDAN. (P. 1879) 333
Duke of Northumberland, account of 330
Duke of Northumberland, books presented by. (R. 1859) 110
DUMAS, J. B. Eulogy on A. A. De La Rive. (R. 1874) 286
DUNCAN, M. L. Translation of Holmgren on color-blindness. (R. 1877.) 323, **399**
Dunkirk Society for the Encouragement of Sciences. Prize questions. (R. 1865; R. 1873) 209, 275
DUNNING, E. O. Antiquities in Tennessee. (R. 1870) 244
Duplicate fishes distributed by Smithsonian—T. H. BEAN. (P. 1880) 425
Duplicate shells collected by the United States Exploring Expedition under C. Wilkes **193**
DUPRÉ, W.; HENRY, J. Earthquakes in North Carolina, 1874. (R. 1874) 286
DUPREZ, F. Atmospheric electricity. (R. 1858) 109
Dwellings and forts, Indian, in Indian Territory—W. E. DOYLE. (R. 1876) 299
Dyeing purple, ancient and modern. (R. 1863) 187

E.

Earth—
chemistry of the—T. S. HUNT. (R. 1869) 228, **376**
electrical currents of the—C. MATTEUCCI. (R. 1867; R. 1869) 215, 228
figure of the—ST. M. MERINO. (R. 1863) 187
internal structure of the—J. G. BARNARD **310**
laws of atmospheric circulation over the—J. H. COFFIN 268
revolutions of crust of the—G. PILAR. (R. 1876) 299
secular variation of elements of orbit of—J. N. STOCKWELL 232
Earthquake—
at New Madrid, Missouri—T. DUDLEY. (R. 1858) 109
directions—J. HENRY. (R. 1855) 77
in Eastern Mexico, January, 1866—C. SARTORIUS. (R. 1866) 214
in Peru, August 13, 1868—J. V. CAMPBELL. (R. 1870) 244
phenomena, on observations of—R. MALLET. (R. 1859) 110
Earthquakes—
articles on, received by Smithsonian Institution and deposited in Library of Congress. (R. 1871) 249
circular relative to—J. HENRY 148

Earthquakes—Continued.
in Guatemala—A. CANUDAS. (R. 1858) 109
in North Carolina, 1874—W. DU PRÉ; J. HENRY. (R. 1874) 286
in St. Thomas—G. A. LATIMER. (R. 1867) 215
Earthwork, double-walled, in Ashtabula county, Ohio—S. D. PEET. (R. 1876) 299
Earthworks—
ancient, of Ashland county, Ohio—G. W. HILL. (R. 1877) 323
ancient, of Ohio, sketch of—I. DILLE. (R. 1866) 214
ancient, on upper Missouri—A. BARRANDT. (R. 1870) 244
in Tennessee—J. JONES 259
in Wisconsin—E. E. BREED. (R. 1872) 271
on Arkansas river—Mrs. G. KNAPP. (R. 1877) 323
Earthworks—*See* Mounds.
Echinoderms of Kerguelen Island—A. E. VERRILL 294
Echinoderms of northeastern coast of America—A. E. VERRILL. (P. 1879; P. 1880) 333, 425
Eclipse—
annular, of May 26, 1854 **66**
of the sun, April 25, 1865—Baron DE PRADOS. (R. 1864) 188
of the sun, March 15, 1858, map of—T. HILL **101**
of the sun, July 18, 1860—J. LAMONT. (R. 1864) 188
of the sun, September 7, 1858, in Peru—J. M. GILLISS **100**
Ecliptic, obliquity of the—J. N. STOCKWELL 232
Economic geology of Trinidad—G. P. WALL; J. G. SAWKINS. (R. 1856) 91
Education—
acknowledgment of books on—E. LABOULAYE. (R. 1867) 215
in the United States, project of an outline history of—F. A. PACKARD. (R. 1863) 187
scientific, of mechanics and artisans—A. P. PEABODY. (R. 1872) 271, **380**
Education, Illinois State Board of. Meteorological system for every State. (R. 1855) 77
Educational series of marine invertebrates distributed by United States National Museum—R. RATHBUN. (P. 1881) 467, **465**, **471**
EDWARDS, A. M. Directions for collecting, preserving, and transporting diatomacea **366**
EDWARDS, A. M. Results of examination under microscope of Japanese infusorial earths 202
EDWARDS, V. N. Occurrence of oceanic bonito (*Orcynus pelamys*) in Vineyard Sound, Massachusetts. (P. 1878) 332
EDWARDS, W. H. Diurnal lepidoptera of Arctic America 342
EDWARDS, W. H. On lepidoptera 133
Eels, genitalia of male—S. T. CATTIE. (P. 1880) 425
Effect of irritation of polarized nerve—B. F. LAUTENBACH. (R. 1878) 341, **411**
Effect of lightning—S. L. HILLIER. (R. 1866) 214

Effect of moon on the weather—J. HENRY. (R. 1871) ---- 249
EGGERS, H. F. A. Flora of St. Croix and Virgin Islands ---- **313**
Egging expedition to Shoal Lake, Lake Winnipeg—D. GUNN. (R. 1867) ---- 215
Eggs—
instructions for collecting—S. F. BAIRD. (R. 1858) ---- 109, 139
instructions for collecting—A. NEWTON ---- 139
instructions for collecting and preserving—T. M. BREWER ---- 139
North American—T. M. BREWER ---- **89**
of the eight North American species of *Empidonaces*—T. M. BREWER. (P. 1879) ---- 338
suggestions for forming collections of—A. NEWTON ---- 139
EGLESTON, T.—
Catalogue of minerals with their formulas ---- **156**
Scheme for qualitative determinations by blowpipe. (R. 1872) ---- 271
translation by, of Brezina on crystallography ---- **386**
Egypt, presentation of books on—R. LEPSIUS. (R. 1860) ---- 147
Elastic force of aqueous vapor, table for determining—J. H. COFFIN ---- 87
Electric phenomenon—W. F. GIVEN. (R. 1865) ---- 209
Electric resonance of mountains, observations on—H. DE SAUSSURE. (R. 1868.) 224
Electrical—
currents of the earth—C. MATTEUCCI. (R. 1867; R. 1869) ---- 215, 228
discharge, dispersion of a cloud, by D. W. NAILL, (R. 1858) ---- 109
rheometry, researches on—A. SECCHI ---- **36**
Electricity—
accounts of lightning discharges. (R. 1867) ---- 215
and galvanism, report on recent progress in—J. MÜLLER. (R. 1857) ---- 107
and magnetism, later views of connection of—H. HELMHOLTZ; J. C. MAXWELL. (R. 1873) ---- 275
atmospheric—F. DUPREZ. (R. 1858) ---- 109
considerations on. (R. 1867) ---- 215
of atmosphere and the aurora borealis—S. LEMSTRÖM; A. A. DE LA RIVE. (R. 1874) ---- 286
of induction in clouds resolving into rain, snow, and hail—F. ZANTEDESCHI. (R. 1870) ---- 244
phenomena accompanying propagation of, in rarefied elastic fluids—A. A. DE LA RIVE. (R. 1868) ---- 187
presence of, during fall of rain—Prof. PALMIERI. (R. 1870) ---- 244
report of recent progress in—J. MÜLLER. (R. 1856) ---- 91
Electro-magnetic—
seismograph—Prof. PALMIERI. (R. 1870) ---- **244**
telegraph, Henry's contribution to—W. B. TAYLOR. (R. 1878) ---- 341, **405**
telegraph—*See* Henry; Telegraph.
Electro-physiology, lectures on—C. MATTEUCCI. (R. 1865) ---- **209**

Electrotypes of engravings of shells granted by British Museum. (R. 1863) -- 187

Elements, table of chemical equivalents of. (R. 1864) ---------- 188

Elephant mound in Grant county, Wisconsin—J. WARNER. (R. 1872) ------ 271

ELLERY, R. L. J. Address of the President of the Royal Society of Victoria. (R. 1868) ---------- 224

ELLET, C. Physical geography of Mississippi valley ---------- **13**

ELLIOT, D. G. Classification and synopsis of *Trochilidæ* ---------- **317**

ELLIOT, D. G. List of described species of humming birds ---------- **334**

ELLIOTT, R. S. Climate of Kansas. (R. 1870) ---------- 244

ELLSWORTH, E. W. Ancient implement of wood from Connecticut. (R. 1876) 299

Embarrass, Wisconsin, pits at—E. E. BREED. (R. 1877) ---------- 328

Embryology of insects—L. AGASSIZ ---------- 16

Empidonaces, notes on nests and eggs of the eight North American species of—T. M. BREWER. (P. 1879) ---------- 333

Employés of Smithsonian Institution, National Museum, Geological Survey, Bureau of Ethnology, and Fish Commission, directory of ---------- **466**

ENCKE, J. F., memoir of, by G. HAGEN. (R. 1868) ---------- 224

ENDLICH, F. M.—

- Analysis of water destructive to fish in Gulf of Mexico. (P. 1881) ---- 467
- Geology of Kerguelen Island ---------- 294
- List of minerals in National Museum, 1873, 1879. (R. 1873; P. 1880) 275, 425

Endothyra ornata, note on—C. A. WHITE. (P. 1879) ---------- 333

ENGELHARDT, M. Formation of ice at the bottom of water. (R. 1866) ------ 214

ENGELMANN, G. Heights of mountains in Colorado. (R. 1862) ---------- 150

Engineers, Civil, London Institution of. Prize questions. (R. 1862) -------- 150

England—

- abbreviations used in—W. DE LA RUE. (R. 1867) ---------- 215
- free freights between the United States and—E. CUNARD. (R. 1859) --- 110
- Salisbury, notice of Blackmore Museum at. (R. 1868) ---------- 224

English and French weights and measures—*See* Tables.

English vocabulary with comparative words in Spanish, French, and Latin --- 170

Engravings—

- of shells, electrotypes of, granted by British Museum. (R. 1863) ------ 187
- on the face of rocks in the Sierra Nevada—J. G. BRUFF. (R. 1872) --- 271
- presented to Smithsonian Institution, catalogue of—C. B. KING. (R. 1861.) 149

Entomologists, circular to ---------- **178**

Entomologists, instructions to ---------- **261**

Eocene and oligocene invertebrate fossils of North America, check-list of—T. A. CONRAD ---------- **200**

EOFF, J. Habits of black bass of the Ohio. (R. 1854) ---------- 75

Ephemeris of the planet Neptune, 1848-1852—S. C. WALKER ------- **4, 5, 6, 7, 24**

Epinephelus Drummond-Hayi, a new serranoid fish from the Bermudas—G. B. GOODE; T. H. BEAN. (P. 1878) ---------- 332

Epinephelus nigritus of the southern coast, note upon—G. B. GOODE; T. H. BEAN. (P. 1878) ---- 332

Equilibrium of a liquid mass withdrawn from the action of gravity—*See* J. Plateau.

Equinoxes, precession of the—J. G. BARNARD ---- 240

Equinoxes, precession of the—J. N. STOCKWELL ---- 282

Equivalents, chemical, of sixty-three elements, table of. (R. 1864) ---- 188

ERNST, G. A. Meteorology of Caracas, South America. (R. 1867) ---- 215

Erosions of the earth's surface by rivers, etc.—E. HITCHCOCK ---- 90

Eruption of volcano in Nicaragua—A. B. DICKINSON. (R. 1867) ---- 215

Eruption of volcano of Colima—C. SARTORIUS. (R. 1869) ---- 228

Eryontidæ, notice of recent—S. I. SMITH. (P. 1879) ---- 333

ESPY, J. P., notice of, by A. D. BACHE. (R. 1859) ---- 110

ESPY, J. P. On meteorology. (R. 1847) ---- **H**

Essay on geographical distribution of batrachia and reptilia—E. D. COPE ---- 292

Essay on velocity of light—C. DELAUNAY. (R. 1864) ---- 188, **354**

Establishment and officers of the Smithsonian Institution and National Museum. **449**

Establishment of the Smithsonian Institution, Journal and By-Laws of. (R. 1853) ---- 67, 329

ESTES, L. C. Antiquities of Minnesota, Mississippi river, and Lake Pepin. (R. 1866) ---- 214

Estimate of population of the world—E. MAILLY. (R. 1873) ---- 275

Etheostomatidæ, notes on—D. S. JORDAN ---- 306

Ethmocardium, note on—C. A. WHITE. (P. 1879) ---- 333

Ethnographical—
- collections—T. LYMAN. (R. 1862) ---- 150
- collections—H. DE SCHLAGINTWEIT. (R. 1862) ---- 150
- collections, the Schlagintweit—H. ZISGENBALS. (R. 1867) ---- 215

Ethnological—
- collections of museum at Lausanne, report on—F. TROYON. (R. 1861) ---- 149
- department of the French Exposition, 1867. (R. 1867) ---- 215
- map of North America, suggestions relative to—L. H. MORGAN. (R. 1861) 149
- map of the United States—G. GIBBS. (R. 1862) ---- 150
- memoir of Squier and Davis, correspondence relative to acceptance of, for publication ---- **K**
- museum of Norway—L. K. DAA. (R. 1862) ---- 150
- research—E. H. DAVIS. (R. 1866) ---- 214
- specimens presented by University of Christiania, Norway. (R. 1863) ---- 187
- suggestions for Russian America—G. GIBBS ---- 207

Ethnology and archæology, circular relative to collections in ---- **205**

Ethnology and philology, instructions for—G. GIBBS ---- **160**

Ethnology, articles on. (R. 1867–1870–1877, 1879, 1880) 215, 244, 249, 271, 275, 286, 298, 299, 328, 345, 442

Ethnology—
Leipsic Museum of—O. T. MASON. (R. 1873) 275
of Arctic America—L. KUMLIEN 342
of Colonia Tovar, Venezuela, South America—A. FENDLER. (R. 1857) 107
of Indians of Red river of the North—W. H. GARDNER. (R. 1870) 244
physical, lectures on—D. WILSON. (R. 1862) 150
present state of, in relation to form of human skull—A. RETZIUS. (R. 1859) 110
Ethnology, Bureau of—
catalogue of linguistic manuscripts in library of—J. C. PILLING. (E. 1879-80) 476
directory of officers and employés of 466
first annual report of—J. W. POWELL **476**
Euchalarodus Putnami, identity of, with *Pleuronectes glaber*—T. H. BEAN. (P. 1878) 332
Eulachon or candle fish of northwest coast—J. G. SWAN. (P. 1880) 425
Eulogy on—
Ampère, by F. ARAGO. (R. 1872) 271
A. D. Bache, by J. HENRY. (R. 1870) 244, **379**
A. A. De La Rive, by J. B. DUMAS. (R. 1874) 286
Stephen A. Douglass, by S. S. COX. (R. 1861) 149
Cornelius C. Felton, by T. D. WOOLSEY. (R. 1861) 149
Joseph Fourier, by F. ARAGO. (R. 1871) 249
Herschel, by F. ARAGO. (R. 1870) 244
Gay-Lussac, by F. ARAGO. (R. 1876) 299
La Place, by F. ARAGO. (R. 1874) 286
Quetelet, by A. MAILLY. (R. 1874) 286
James A. Pearce, by A. D. BACHE. (R. 1862) 150
Gen. J. G. Totten, by J. G. BARNARD. (R. 1865) 209
Alexander Volta, by F. ARAGO. (R. 1875) 298
Henry Wilson, by P. PARKER. (R. 1875) 298
Thomas Young, by F. ARAGO. (R. 1869) 228
Eulogy—*See* Memoir, Life, Biography.
Europe—
causes which limit vegetable species towards the north, in—A. DE CANDOLLE. (R. 1858) 109
certain storms in America and, December, 1836—E. LOOMIS **127**
man as the contemporary of the mammoth and reindeer in. (R. 1867) 215
study of high antiquity in—A. MORLOT. (R. 1862; R. 1864) 150, 188
Europe, middle, fauna of, during stone age—L. RÜTIMEYER. (R. 1861) 149
EVANS, J. Climate of Colorado. (R. 1865) 209
EVANS, S. B. Notes on mounds in Des Moines valley. (R. 1879) 345
Evaporation in Florida—W. C. DENNIS. (R. 1866) 214

Evaporation observed at Palermo in 1865 and 1866—P. TACCHINI. (R. 1870.) 244
EVERETT, E. Report on Jewett's general stereotype catalogue of public libraries. 47
EVERETT, E. Report on organization of Smithsonian Institution. (R. 1853.) 67
EVERETT, J. D. Under-ground temperature. (R. 1874) 286
Evolution of language—J. W. POWELL. (E. 1879-80) 476
Examination—
microscopical, of soundings—J. W. BAILEY 20
of J. Henry by English Scientific Commission 329
of specimens, rules for. (R. 1880) 442
of Spencer's telescope for Hamilton College. (R. 1855) 77
Excelsior, Minnesota, mounds near—F. H. NUTTER. (R. 1879) 345
Exchange of publications—
Agricultural Association of Milan. (R. 1863) 187
Chamber of Commerce of Bordeaux. (R. 1863) 187
Royal Horticultural Society, London. (R. 1861) 149
Exchange of specimens—
Hamburg Zoölogical Gardens. (R. 1867) 215
Hamilton College, Clinton, New York. (R. 1861) 149
W. A. LLOYD. (R. 1867) 215
Museum of National University of Greece. (R. 1867) 215
University of Costa Rica. (R. 1867) 215
Exchanges—
American Academy of Arts and Sciences, Boston, thanks for. (R. 1855; R. 1867) 77, 215
Bath and West of England Society for Encouragement of Agriculture, Arts, etc. (R. 1867) 215
circular relative to scientific and literary **324**
Government of Bremen. (R. 1865) 209
W. HINCKS. (R. 1860) 147
international, report on—G. H. BOEHMER **477**
list of. Parts I, II **73, 85**
list of, to 1858 **117**
Mexican Society of Geography and Statistics. (R. 1861, 1865) 149, 209
Mining Department, Melbourne. (R. 1865) 209
F. MÜLLER. (R. 1860) 147
reports on. (R. 1853-1867, 1873) 67, 75, 77, 91, 107, 109, 110, 147, 149, 150, 187, 188, 209, 214, 215, 275
J. ROSING. (R. 1865) 209
Royal Academy of Science, Madrid. (R. 1861) 149
St. Petersburg Academy of Sciences. (R. 1867) 215
statistics of, 1846-1877 329
Excursion in New Mexico, diary of—J. H. CARLETON. (R. 1854) 75
Executive Committee of Regents—*See also* each annual report.

Executive Committee of Regents, journal and reports of, 1846-1876 ---------- 329
Exhibit by the Smithsonian Institution at Centennial Exhibition, report on proposed plan of—S. F. BAIRD. (R. 1875) ---------- 298
Exhibit of fisheries of United States at Berlin Fisheries Exhibition—G. B. GOODE ---------- **413**
Exhibition, Centennial, report on—S. F. BAIRD. (R. 1876) ---------- 299, **307**
Expansion, bibliography of—F. W. CLARKE ---------- 255
Expansion by heat, tables of—F. W. CLARKE ---------- **289**
Expedition—
Coast Survey, for transatlantic longitude—B. A. GOULD ---------- 223
Hassler, narrative of the—L. AGASSIZ. (R. 1872) ---------- 271
North Pacific Surveying, contributions to natural history made in connection with the—T. H. STREETS ---------- 303
to Arctic Seas—*See* Hayes, Kane, McClintock.
to Kerguelen Island—J. H. KIDDER and others ---------- 293, 294
to Lake Winnipeg—D. GUNN. (R. 1867) ---------- 215
to Mexico, scientific. (R. 1864) ---------- 188
to the Mauvaises Terres and Upper Missouri—T. A. CULBERTSON. (R. 1850) ---------- 28
toward the North pole, scientific instructions for—J. HENRY and others. (R. 1871) ---------- 249
Expeditions, account of—*See* each annual report.
Expeditions contributing specimens, list of—S. F. BAIRD. (R. 1867) ---------- 215
Experimental and theoretical researches on figures of equilibrium—*See* J. Plateau.
Experiments—
on aneroid barometers at Kew Observatory—B. STEWART. (R. 1868) ---------- 224
relative to meteorites—G. A. DAUBRÉE. (R. 1868) ---------- 224
upon animal heat of fishes—J. H. KIDDER. (P. 1879) ---------- 333
Explanation of principles of crystallography and crystallophysics—A. BREZINA. (R. 1872) ---------- 271, **386**
Exploration of ancient mounds in Union county, Ky.—S. LYON. (R. 1870) ---------- 244
Explorations—
among Indian mounds in southern Florida—S. T. WALKER. (R. 1879.) 345
and surveys, Government, report of—S. F. BAIRD. (R. 1878) ---------- 341
Arctic, lecture on—I. I. HAYES. (R. 1861) ---------- 149
articles on—*See* each annual report.
botanical, in New Mexico and California, account of—A. GRAY. (R. 1849) ---------- 21
furnishing collections to National Museum, 1838-1877, list of—S. F. BAIRD. (R. 1877) ---------- 323
in Central America—C. H. BERENDT. (R. 1867) ---------- 215
in Greenland—L. KUMLIEN. (R. 1878) ---------- 341
in New Mexico and Arizona—J. STEVENSON. (R. 1880) ---------- 442

Explorations—Continued.
in New York—E. G. Squier 15
in Tennessee—E. A. Dayton. (R. 1870) 244
in upper California in 1860—J. Feilner. (R. 1864) 188
Kennicott's—Hudson's Bay Company. (R. 1863) 187
of aboriginal remains of Tennessee—J. Jones **259**
of the Nile—C. Hale. (R. 1865) 209
of western Missouri in 1854—P. R. Hoy. (R. 1864) 188
of John Xantus in Mexico—M. Romero. (R. 1862) 150
on western coast of North America—W. H. Dall. (R. 1873) 275
reports on—S. F. Baird. (R. 1851–1866, 1875–1877) .. 51, 57, 75, 77, 91, 107, 109, 110, 147, 149, 150, 187, 188, 209, 214, 298, 299, 328
scientific, in America, in 1852—S. F. Baird. (R. 1852) 57
scientific, in Mexico. (R. 1864) 188
Exploring expedition under Capt. C. Wilkes, duplicate shells collected by the .. **193**
Explosibility of coal oils—Z. Allen. (R. 1861) 149
Explosiveness of nitre—R. Hare **17**
Exposition of harmonies in the solar system—S. Alexander **280**
Exposition—*See* French.
Expression for anthropological inquiry, queries about—C. Darwin. (R. 1867) 215
External appearance of the sun's disk. (R. 1866) 214
Extinct—
mammalia and chelonia of Nebraska—J. Leidy **58**
reptiles—J. Leidy 192
sloth tribe of North America—J. Leidy **72**
species of American ox—J. Leidy **41**
Eye, bibliography of diseases of the—W. W. Keen 300

F.

Facts respecting Liberia College—A. CRUMMELL. (R. 1861) 149
Fahrenheit's scale, tables for conversion of centigrade degrees to. (R. 1863) .. 187
Families—
of fishes, arrangement of—T. GILL **247**
of mammals, arrangement of—T. GILL **230**
of mollusks, arrangement of—T. GILL **227**
Family, human, systems of consanguinity and affinity of—L. H. MORGAN .. 138, 218
Fanning Islands, natural history of—T. H. STREETS 303
Faraday, M., his life and works—A. A. DE LA RIVE. (R. 1867) 215
FARLOW, W. G.—
Algæ of Arctic America 342
Algæ of Kerguelen Island 294
Recent progress in botany, 1879, 1880. (R. 1880) 442, **430**
Report on water from Gulf of Mexico. (P. 1881) 467
Farming and gardening, natural history as applied to—J. G. MORRIS. (R. 1855.) 77
Faroe Isles, vegetable colonization of—C. MARTINS. (R. 1858) 109
FARQUHARSON, R. J. Study of skull and long bones from mound in Illinois. (R. 1874) 286
Fauna—
and flora within living animals—J. LEIDY **44**
littoral marine, of Provincetown, Mass.—R. RATHBUN. (P. 1880) 425
of middle Europe during the stone age—L. RÜTIMEYER. (R. 1861) 149
of Nebraska, ancient—J. LEIDY **58**
FAVRE, A. Report on transactions of Geneva Society of Physics and Natural History, July, 1876, to June, 1877. (R. 1877) 323
FAVRE, E. Biographical notice of Louis Agassiz. (R. 1878) 341
Feeling, sense of. (R. 1865) 209
FEILNER, J. Explorations in upper California in 1860. (R. 1864) 188
Feldspar, determination of, in thin sections of rocks—G. W. HAWES. (P. 1881) 467
Felton, C. C., eulogy on, by T. D. WOOLSEY. (R. 1861) 149
FELTON, C. C.—
Notice of Washington Irving. (R. 1859) 110
Notice of W. W. Turner. (R. 1859) 110
Report on Prof. Henry and the telegraph. (R. 1857) 107
Fendler, A., botanical explorations by, in New Mexico and California—A. GRAY. (R. 1849) 21
FENDLER, A.—
Meteorology and ethnology of Colonia Tovar, Venezuela. (R. 1857) 107
Meteorology of Colonia Tovar. (R. 1866) 214
Temperature of St. Louis, Missouri. (R. 1860) 147

Ferns, acknowledgment for—G. METTENIUS. (R. 1862) 150
FERREL, W. Converging series expressing ratio between diameter and circumference of a circle **233**
FERREL, W. Reply to the criticisms of Dr. J. Hann. (R. 1877) 323, 398
Ferrel, W., theories of, as to relation between difference of pressure and velocity of wind—J. HANN. (R. 1877) 323, 398
Fever—
a study in morbid and normal physiology—H. C. WOOD **357**
researches on—H. C. WOOD. (R. 1878) 341
study of the nature and mechanism of. Toner lecture No. IV—H. C. WOOD **282**
Fevers, surgical complications and sequels of. Toner lecture No. V—W. W. KEEN **300**
FIALHO, A. Biographical sketch of Dom Pedro II. (R. 1876) 299
FIGANIERRE, M. Account of remarkable accumulation of bats. (R. 1863) 187
Figure of the earth—ST. M. MERINO. (R. 1863) 187
Figures of equilibrium of a liquid mass withdrawn from the action of gravity—*See* Plateau.
Figures, series of, for labels 164
Filices of Kerguelen Island—A. GRAY 294
Finances of the Institution, 1846–1877 329
FINCH, FLADGATE, and CLARKE. Residuary legacy of Smithson. (R. 1861.) 149, 328
FINCK, H. Antiquities in the State of Vera Cruz, Mexico. (R. 1870) 244
Fire at Smithsonian, January, 1865, report of Committee of Regents relative to—R. WALLACH; J. HENRY. (R. 1864) 188
Fire, Indian mode of obtaining—G. CROOK. (R. 1871) 249
Fire-alarm telegraph, American, lecture on—W. F. CHANNING. (R. 1854) 75
Fire ball, meteoric, orbit and phenomena of—J. H. COFFIN **221**
Fire-proofing buildings, architecture in relation to—D. B. REID. (R. 1856) 91
First decade of United States Fish Commission—G. B. GOODE. (R. 1880) 442
FISCHER, F. Scientific labors of Edward Lartet. (R. 1872) 271
Fish Commission—
account of work of—S. F. BAIRD. (R. 1880) 442
catalogue of exhibit of, at Centennial, 1876—G. B. GOODE **326**
directory of officers and employés of 466
exhibit by, at Berlin Fisheries Exhibition—G. B. GOODE 413
experiments on animal heat in fishes, made in connection with—J. H. KIDDER. (P. 1879) 333
first decade of—G. B. GOODE. (R. 1880) 442
list of marine invertebrata from New England coast distributed by—A. E. VERRILL; R. RATHBUN. (P. 1879) 333
mollusca collected by—A. E. VERRILL. (P. 1880) 425
notice of crustacea dredged by, off south coast of New England—S. I. SMITH. (P. 1880) 425

Fish—
analysis of water destructive to, in Gulf of Mexico—F. M. ENDLICH. (P. 1881) 467
candle, of northwest coast—J. G. SWAN. (P. 1880) 425
dates of first appearance of—F. B. HOUGH 182
description of new species of, (*Apogon pandionis*)—G. B. GOODE; T. H. BEAN. (P. 1881) 467
destruction of, by poisonous water in Gulf of Mexico—J. Y. PORTER. (P. 1881) 467
destruction of, by polluted waters in Gulf of Mexico—W. C. W. GLAZIER. (P. 1881) 467
directions for collecting and preserving—T. H. BEAN **464**
fresh, circular on shipping—S. F. BAIRD **384**
from deep-sea fauna of western Atlantic, description of new species of, (*Alepocephalus Bairdii*)—G. B. GOODE; T. H. BEAN. (P. 1879) 333
mortality of, in Gulf of Mexico—E. INGERSOLL. (P. 1881) 467
mortality of, in Gulf of Mexico—M. A. MOORE. (P. 1881) 467
new, from Alaska, with notes on genus *Anarrhichas*—T. H. BEAN. (P. 1879) 333
new, (*Lopholatilus chamæleonticeps*,) from south of New England—G. B. GOODE; T. H. BEAN. (P. 1879) 333
new gobioid, (*Othonops eos*,) from San Diego, Cal.—R. SMITH. (P. 1881) 467
new serranoid, (*Epinephelus Drummond-Hayi*,) from Bermudas and Florida—G. B. GOODE; T. H. BEAN. (P. 1878) 332
new sparoid, (*Sargus Holbrookii*,) from Savannah Bank, description of—T. H. BEAN. (P. 1878) 332
Fish-culture of United States, exhibit of, at Berlin Fisheries Exhibition—G. B. GOODE 413
FISHER, J. G. Acknowledgment of perennibranchiates. (R. 1863) 187
Fisheries—
of United States, catalogue of collection to illustrate, at Philadelphia—G. B. GOODE **326**
of United States, exhibit of, at Berlin Fisheries Exhibition—G. B. GOODE. **413**
Fisheries Exhibition, Berlin, additions to Museum from. (R. 1880) 442
Fishes—
Alaskan, catalogue of—T. H. BEAN. (P. 1881) 467
American, in British Museum and Museum d'Histoire Naturelle, Paris, notes on typical—D. S. JORDAN. (P. 1879) 333
arrangement of families of—T. GILL **247**
bibliography of—T. GILL 247
check-list of duplicates of, distributed by Smithsonian Institution—T. H. BEAN. (P. 1880) 425
collected by H. E. Nichols in British Columbia and Alaska, notes on—T. H. BEAN. (P. 1881) 467

Fishes—Continued.

cottoids, monograph of the—C. GIRARD 30

description of new species of North American—D. S. JORDAN. (P. 1879.) 333

descriptions of and notes on—*See* D. S. JORDAN; C. H. GILBERT.

descriptions of deep-sea species from New England, diagnoses of two undescribed genera of flounders and genus related to *Merlucius*—G. B. GOODE. (P. 1880) 425

descriptions of new species of, (*Uranidea marginata*, *Potamocottus Bendirei*,) and of *Myctophum crenulare*—T. H. BEAN. (P. 1881) 467

directions for collecting and preserving—T. H. BEAN. (P. 1881) 467

European, in National Museum, list of—T. H. BEAN. (P. 1879) 333

experiments upon animal heat of—J. H. KIDDER. (P. 1879) 333

from deep waters on south coast of New England, obtained by Fish Commission in 1880—G. B. GOODE. (P. 1880) 425

from eastern Georgia, notes on—T. H. BEAN. (P. 1879) 333

from eastern Mississippi, collection of—O. P. HAY. (P. 1880) 425

from Hudson's Bay, notes on—T. H. BEAN. (P. 1881) 467

from Utah Lake, notes on a collection of—D. S. JORDAN; C. H. GILBERT. (P. 1880) 425

mortality of, in Gulf of Mexico—J. P. JEFFERSON. (P. 1878) 332

mortality of, in vicinity of Tortugas—J. P. JEFFERSON; J. Y. PORTER; T. MOORE. (P. 1878) 332

new genus of, (*Benthodesmus*)—G. B. GOODE; T. H. BEAN. (P. 1881.) 467

new genus of, (*Delolepis*)—T. H. BEAN. (P. 1881) 467

North American, check-list of duplicates distributed by Smithsonian—T. H. BEAN. (P. 1880) 425

North American, review of Rafinesque's memoirs on—D. S. JORDAN 305

notes on—D. S. JORDAN 305, 306, 308

notes on collection of, from Clackamas river, Oregon—D. S. JORDAN. (P. 1878) 332

of Alaska, some genera and species of—T. H. BEAN. (P. 1879) 333

of Alaska and Siberia, descriptions of new—T. H. BEAN. (P. 1881) 467

of Alleghany region of South Carolina, Georgia, and Tennessee, distribution of—D. S. JORDAN; A. W. BRAYTON 308

of Arctic America—T. H. BEAN 342

of Beaufort Harbor, North Carolina, notes on—D. S. JORDAN; C. H. GILBERT. (P. 1878) 332

of Bermuda, catalogue of—G. B. GOODE 296

of Bermuda mistakenly described as new by Günther—G. B. GOODE. (P. 1878) 332

of California—T. H. STREETS 303

of California, descriptions of new genera and species of—W. N. LOCKINGTON. (P. 1879) 333

of east coast of North America, catalogue of—T. GILL 283

Fishes—Continued.

of Fanning Islands—T. H. STREETS ... 303

of Florida, description of new species of, (*Seriola Stearnsii*)—G. B. GOODE. (P. 1879) ... 333

of Florida, preliminary catalogue of, with new genus and three new species—G. B. GOODE. (P. 1879) ... 333

of Gulf of Mexico, collected by J. W. Velie, catalogue of and description of seven new species—G. B. GOODE; T. H. BEAN. (P. 1879) ... 333

of Hawaiian Islands—T. H. STREETS ... 303

of Kerguelen Island—T. GILL ... 294

of Mexico, descriptions of two species of, collected by Dugès—T. H. BEAN. (P. 1879) ... 333

of Mexico, notes on Dugès collection of—D. S. JORDAN. (P. 1879) ... 333

of New York—T. GILL. (R. 1856) ... 91

of Pacific coast of United States, bibliography of—T. GILL ... 463

of Pacific coast and Alaska, bibliography of—T. H. BEAN. (P. 1881) ... 467

of Pacific coast, check-list of duplicates of, distributed by Smithsonian Institution in 1881—D. S. JORDAN; P. L. JOUY. (P. 1881) ... 467

of Pacific coast, notes on—D. S. JORDAN; C. H. GILBERT. (P. 1881) ... 467

of Pacific coast of United States, list of—D. S. JORDAN; C. H. GILBERT. (P. 1880) ... 425

of Pensacola, Florida, catalogue of Stearn's collection and description of new species—G. B. GOODE; T. H. BEAN. (P. 1879) ... 333

of St. John's river—G. B. GOODE. (P. 1879) ... 333

of Samoan Islands—T. H. STREETS ... 303

on coast of New Jersey and Long Island—S. F. BAIRD. (R. 1854) ... 75, **348**

pediculate, of eastern coast of extratropical North America, synopsis of—T. GILL. (P. 1878) ... 332

Potamocottus Bendirei, description of—T. H. BEAN. (P. 1881) ... 467

trunk, *Ostraciontidæ*, a study of, with notes on American species—G. B. GOODE. (P. 1879) ... 333

Uranidea marginata, description of—T. H. BEAN. (P. 1881) ... 467

Fishes, food—*See* G. B. Goode, T. H. Bean, D. S. Jordan, S. Stearns, F. Steindachner, S. Wilmot.

Fishes, food—

circular relative to—S. F. BAIRD ... 234

memoranda of inquiry relative to—S. F. BAIRD ... **231**

questions relative to—S. F. BAIRD ... **234**

Fishkill, New York, deposit of arrow-heads near—E. M. SHEPARD. (R. 1877.) 323

Fissirostres, oölogy of—T. M. BREWER ... 89

FLACHENECKER, G. Indian languages. (R. 1862) ... 150

FLADGATE, CLARKE, and FINCH. Smithson's residuary legacy. (R. 1861.) 149, 328

Flamingo from south Florida, specimens of—G. WURDEMAN. (R. 1860) ... 147

Flight in the animal kingdom, phenomena of—E. J. MAREY. (R. 1869) ... 228

Flight, modes of, in relation to aeronautics—J. B. Pettigrew. (R. 1867) 215
Flint, E., shells from Costa Rica kitchen-midden collected by—W. H. Dall. (P. 1878) 332
Flint, J. M.—
Classification and arrangement of the materia medica collection **450**
Classification of forms of drugs and medicines **451**
Memoranda for collectors of drugs **452**
Flint implements—
in Illinois, agricultural—C. Rau. (R. 1868) 224, 440, **370**
in Illinois, deposits of—J. F. Snyder. (R. 1876) 299
in Ohio, Holmes county—H. B. Case. (R. 1877) 323
Flood-tide, law of deposit of—C. H. Davis **33**
Flora—
and fauna within living animals—J. Leidy **44**
of Alaska, sketch of the—J. T. Rothrock. (R. 1867) 215, **367**
of Crozet and Kerguelen Islands—J. H. Kidder and others 294
of North America, index of authorities for species of—S. Watson 258
of St. Croix and the Virgin Islands—H. F. A. Eggers **313**
of Washington and vicinity—L. F. Ward **444**
Florida—
antiquities of—J. Bartram. (R. 1874) 286
antiquities of—A. Mitchell. (R. 1874) 286
catalogue of casts of Indian prisoners in—R. H. Pratt. (P. 1878) 332
colored bead from mound in—A. M. Harrison. (R. 1877) 323
Curtiss' collection of fishes from—D. S. Jordan. (P. 1880) 425
evaporation in—W. C. Dennis. (R. 1866) 214
fishes of—G. B. Goode; T. H. Bean. (P. 1878) 332
fishes of, preliminary catalogue and new genus and species of—G. B. Goode. (P. 1879) 333
forests and trees of—J. G. Cooper. (R. 1860) 147
gold ornament from mound in—C. Rau. (R. 1877) 323, 440, **403**
Henshall's collection of fishes from—D. S. Jordan. (P. 1880) 425
Indian mounds in—S. T. Walker. (R. 1879) 345
microscopical observations in—J. W. Bailey 28
new fish, *Caulolatilus microps*, from—G. B. Goode. (P. 1878) 332
polychrome bead from—S. S. Haldeman. (R. 1877) 323, **404**
shell-heaps at mouth of St. John's river—S. P. Mayberry. (R. 1877) 323
shell-heaps of Tampa Bay—S. T. Walker. (R. 1879) 345
specimens of flamingo from—G. Würdeman. (R. 1860) 147
winds in—J. Baltzell. (R. 1866) 214
Flounders, diagnoses of two undescribed genera of—G. B. Goode. (P. 1880) 425
Flourens, M. J.—
Historical sketch of the Academy of Sciences, Paris. (R. 1862) 150

FLOURENS, M. J.—Continued.

History of the works of Cuvier. (R. 1868) 224

Memoir of Ducrotay De Blainville. (R. 1865) 209

Memoir of Leopold von Buch. (R. 1862) 150

Memoir of Pyramus de Candolle. (R. 1859) 110

Memoir of Cuvier. (R. 1868) 224

Memoir of Magendie. (R. 1866) 214

Memoir of Geoffroy Saint-Hilaire. (R. 1861) 149

Memoir of Louis Jacques Thénard. (R. 1862) 150

The Jussieus and the natural method. (R. 1867) 215

Fluctuations of level in North American lakes—C. WHITTLESEY **119**

Fluids, elastic, electricity in—A. A. DE LA RIVE. (R. 1863) 187

Fly-catcher from Sandwich Islands, description of a new—R. RIDGWAY. (P. 1881) 467

Fog, the wind and—J. BALFOUR. (R. 1866) 214

FOLSOM, C. Report on Jewett's general stereotype catalogue of public libraries. 47

Food, relation of, to work, and its bearings on medical practice—S. HAUGHTON. (R. 1870) 244

Food collections, provisional classification of—G. B. GOODE **455**

Food-fishes, inquiry relative to—S. F. BAIRD **231**

Food-fishes, questions relative to—S. F. BAIRD **234**

Force, thoughts on the nature and origin of—W. B. TAYLOR. (R. 1870) 244, **375**

FORCE, P. Record of auroral phenomena in high northern latitudes **84**

Foreign—

authors. North American conchology—W. G. BINNEY **174**

Commissioners, collections presented to United States by. (R. 1876) 299

correspondents of Smithsonian Institution, list of **154**, **225**, **309**, **469**

correspondents of Smithsonian Institution, number of 290

correspondents of Smithsonian Institution, systematic index of **257**

gold and silver coins, table of. (R. 1868) 224

institutions in correspondence with Smithsonian Inst., list of **64**, **225** **243**

institutions, list of addresses of, since 1862. (R. 1865) 209

institutions making donations to Smithsonian library, list of. (R. 1864) 188

works in library of Smithsonian—*See* Library.

FOREMAN, E. Meteorological system and correspondence of Smithsonian Institution. (R. 1851) 51

FOREMAN, E. Report on meteorological system. (R. 1852) 57

Forest trees, distribution of, in Montana, Idaho, and Washington—W. W. JOHNSON. (R. 1870) 244

Forests and their climatic influence—A. E. BECQUEREL. (R. 1869) 228

Forests and trees of Florida and the Mexican boundary—J. G. COOPER. (R. 1860) 147

Forests and trees of North America, distribution of, and catalogue of native trees of the United States—J. G. COOPER. (R. 1858) ... 109, **351**

Formation—

of a museum—L. AGASSIZ. (R. 1849) ... 21

of clouds over Gulf Stream—H. M. BANNISTER. (R. 1866) ... 214

of ice at bottom of water—M. ENGELHARDT. (R. 1866) ... 214

of precipitation—J. HANN. (R. 1877) ... 323, 398

Forms in which drugs and medicines appear—J. M. FLINT. (P. 1881) ... 467, **451**

Formulas, chemical, tables of—F. W. CLARKE ... 255

Fort, ancient, and burial ground in Tompkins Co., N. Y.—D. TROWBRIDGE. (R. 1863) ... 187

Fort Brown, Texas, list of birds from—J. C. MERRILL. (P. 1878) ... 332

Fort Ellis, prehistoric remains near—P. W. NORRIS. (R. 1879) ... 345

Fort Marion, Florida, list of casts of heads of Indian prisoners in—R. H. PRATT. (P. 1878) ... 382

Fort Ripley, Minn., natural history of country about—J. E. HEAD. (R. 1854.) 75

Fort Wadsworth, Dakota, Indian mounds near—A. J. COMFORT. (R. 1871) ... 249

Forts and dwellings, Indian, in Indian Territory—W. E. DOYLE. (R. 1876) ... 299

Fossil—

corbiculadæ—T. PRIME ... 145

gasteropod, from Mexico, description of—C. A. WHITE. (P. 1880) ... 425

mollusks from later tertiaries of California—W. H. DALL. (P. 1878) ... 332

ox—J. LEIDY ... **41**

plants from China, description of—J. S. NEWBERRY ... 202

Fossils—

carboniferous invertebrate, description of new species of—C. A. WHITE. (P. 1879) ... 333

catalogue of rocks, minerals, ores, and—J. LOCKE. (R. 1854) ... 75

cretaceous, from Arkansas and Colorado—C. A. WHITE. (P. 1881) ... 467

cretaceous invertebrate, from Kansas and Texas, description of new—C. A. WHITE. (P. 1879) ... 333

from Nebraska, report on—J. LEIDY. (R. 1851) ... 51

from Santa Barbara, California—P. P. CARPENTER ... 252

invertebrate, from Arkansas, Wyoming, Colorado, Utah—C. A. WHITE. (P. 1880) ... 425

invertebrate, of North America, check-list of—T. A. CONRAD ... **200**

invertebrate, of North America, check-list of—F. B. MEEK ... **177**, **183**

invertebrate, of North America, cretaceous and jurassic—F. B. MEEK ... **177**

invertebrate, of North America, eocene and oligocene—T. A. CONRAD ... **200**

invertebrate, of North America, miocene—F. B. MEEK ... **183**

postpliocene, in coast range of California—W. H. DALL. (P. 1878) ... 332

tertiary, distribution of Californian—W. H. DALL. (P. 1878) ... 332

tertiary, presented by Imperial Geological Institute, Vienna. (R. 1863) 187

FOSTER, J. W. Ancient relics in Missouri. (R. 1863) ---------- 187
FOSTER, J. W. Catalogue of rocks, minerals, etc. (R. 1854) ---------- 75
Fourier, J., eulogy on, by F. ARAGO. (R. 1871) ---------- 249
FOURIER, J. Memoir of Delambre. (R. 1864) ---------- 188
FOWLER, J. Shell-heaps of New Brunswick. (R. 1870) ---------- 244
Fox, (yacht,) meteorological observations in Arctic Seas made on—F. L. McCLINTOCK ---------- **146**
Fox, (yacht,) record of voyage of, in Arctic regions—F. L. McCLINTOCK ---------- 146
France, Emperor of, report to, by Minister of Public Instruction, on scientific expedition to Mexico. (R. 1864) ---------- 188
France—*See* Paris, Prize questions.
Franklin, Sir John, expedition in search of—*See* Kane.
Free freight between Germany and the United States by North German Lloyd—R. SCHLEIDEN. (R. 1858) ---------- 109
Free freight between United States and England—E. CUNARD. (R. 1859) ---------- 110
Free freight between United States and Germany—KUNHARDT & Co. (R. 1861) 149
FRÉMONT, J. C., description of plants collected by—J. TORREY ---------- **46**
Frémontianæ, plantæ—J. TORREY ---------- **46**
French—
Exposition of 1867, ethnological department of the. (R. 1867) ---------- 215
half-breeds of the northwest—V. HAVARD. (R. 1879) ---------- 345
Institute, history of—M. FLOURENS. (R. 1862) ---------- 150
Society of Archæology, Archæological Congress organized by. (R. 1866) 214
vocabulary with comparative words in English, Spanish, and Latin ---------- 170
weights and measures—*See* Tables.
Fresh fish and other animals, circular relative to shipping ---------- **384**
Fresh-water—
algæ of North America—H. C. WOOD ---------- **241**
glacial drift of northwestern States—C. WHITTLESEY ---------- **197**
in the ocean—W. C. DENNIS. (R. 1866) ---------- 214
shells—*See* Shells.
FRIEDLÄNDER, J. Plan of a bibliography. (R. 1858) ---------- 109
FRIEL, J. Antiquities of Hancock county, Kentucky. (R. 1877) ---------- 323
Friends of the Museum, circular addressed to—S. F. BAIRD. (P. 1881) -- 467, **446**
Frigate mackerel (*Auxis Rochei*) on New England coast—G. B. GOODE. (P. 1880) ---------- 425
FROEBEL, J. Physical geography of North American Continent. (R. 1854.) 75
Frost, disintegrating effects of, on building stones—C. G. PAGE ---------- 329
Fruits, dates of ripening of—F. B. HOUGH ---------- 182
Fuca, Straits of, Indians of—*See* J. G. Swan.
Fund, Smithson, memorial of Regents to Congress relative to. (R. 1850) ---------- 28
Fund, Smithson, statement of, 1846-1877 ---------- 329

Fundy, Bay of, synopsis of marine invertebrata of—W. STIMPSON ---------- 50
Funeral of J. Henry ---------- 356
Future of geology—J. PRESTWICH. (R. 1875) ---------- 298
Future of the human race—A. DE CANDOLLE. (R. 1875) ---------- 298

G.

Gadus cimbrius, identity of, with *Rhinonemus caudacuta*—G. B. GOODE; T. H. BEAN. (P. 1878) ---------- 332
GAINES, A. S.; CUNNINGHAM, K. M. Shell-heaps on Mobile river, Alabama. (R. 1877) ---------- 323
GALE, L. D., statement of, on telegraph. (R. 1857) ---------- 107
Galeorhinus galeus—D. S. JORDAN; C. H. GILBERT. (P. 1880) ---------- 425
Gales of wind and appearance of aurora, connection of—R. T. KNIGHT; J. HENRY. (R. 1871) ---------- 249
GALLATIN, A. Comparative vocabulary ---------- 160
GALLATIN, A. On publication of Squier and Davis' work. (R. 1847) ---------- **H, K**
Gallery, Art—*See* Corcoran.
GALT, F. L. Indians of Peru. (R. 1877) ---------- 323
Galvanism, recent progress in. J. MÜLLER. (R. 1855) ---------- 77
Galvanometer, use of, as a measuring instrument—J. C. POGGENDORF. (R. 1859) ---------- 110
Gangrene, bibliography of—W. W. KEEN ---------- 300
Gardening, natural history as applied to farming and—J. G. MORRIS. (R. 1855) ---------- 77
GARDINER, R. H.—
  Barometer, rain, and snow gauges. (R. 1858) ---------- 109
  Disappearance of ice. (R. 1860) ---------- 147
  Opening and closing of Kennebec river, Maine. (R. 1858) ---------- 109
GARDNER, W. H. Indians of valley of Red river of the North. (R. 1870) ---------- 244
GARFIELD, J. A. Biographical notice of S. P. Chase and L. Agassiz. (R. 1873) ---------- 275, 329
GARFIELD, J. A. Memorial address on J. Henry ---------- 356
GÄRKE, H. Birds of Heligoland. (P. 1879) ---------- 333
GARMAN, S. American *Rhinobatidæ*, synopsis and description of. (P. 1880) ---------- 425
Gas, hydrogen, as metal and—J. E. REYNOLDS. (R. 1870) ---------- 244
Gasteropod, large fossil from Puebla, Mexico—C. A. WHITE. (P. 1880) ---------- 425
Gasterosteus, description of new species of, from Schoodic Lakes, Maine—T. H. BEAN. (P. 1879) ---------- 333

GATSCHET, A. S.—
Klamath lake Indian conjurer's practice. (E. 1879-80) 476
"The relapse" in Klamath lake dialect. (E. 1879-80) 476
Gauge, snow—W. E. GUEST. (R. 1858) 109
Gauges, rain and snow—R. H. GARDINER. (R. 1858) 109
GAUTIER, Prof. Researches relative to nebulæ. (R. 1863) 187
General catalogue system for libraries—C. C. JEWETT. (R. 1850) 28
Generation, alternate and parthenogenesis in the animal kingdom—G. A. KORNHUBER. (R. 1871) 249
Generic names of recent and fossil animals, list of—S. H. SCUDDER **470**
Geneva, Society of Physics and Natural History of, report on transactions of—
July, 1858, to June, 1859—A. A. DE LA RIVE. (R. 1859) 110
" 1860, " 1861—P. DUBY. (R. 1864) 188
" 1861, " 1862—A. DE CANDOLLE. (R. 1864) 188
" 1862, " 1863—Prof. MARCET. (R. 1863) 187
" 1863, " 1864—Dr. CHOSSAT. (R. 1865) 209
" 1864, " 1865—E. PLANTAMOUR. (R. 1865) 209
" 1865, " 1866—Dr. GOSSE. (R. 1866) 214
" 1867, " 1868—E. WARTMANN. (R. 1868) 224
" 1868, " 1869—H. C. LOMBARD. (R. 1869) 228
" 1870, " 1871—H. DE SAUSSURE. (R. 1871) 249
" 1872, " 1873—A. A. DE LA RIVE. (R. 1874) 286
" 1873, " 1874—A. DE CANDOLLE. (R. 1875) 298
" 1874, " 1875—E. PLANTAMOUR. (R. 1877) 323
" 1875, " 1876—J. MÜLLER. (R. 1877) 323
" 1876, " 1877—A. FAVRE. (R. 1877) 323
Genitalia of male eels—S. T. CATTIE. (P. 1880) 425
GENTH, F. A.; GIBBS, W. Ammonia-cobalt bases **88**
Geographical distribution of batrachia and reptilia—E. D. COPE 292
Geographical manuscripts, catalogue of collection of—L. BERLANDIER. (R. 1854) 75
Geography—*See* Physical Geography.
Geography of North American Continent—J. FROEBEL. (R. 1854) 75
Geological—
researches in China, Mongolia, and Japan—R. PUMPELLY **202**
specimens, catalogue of—D. D. OWEN. (R. 1854) 75
survey in Michigan, catalogue of rocks, minerals, and ores collected on—C. T. JACKSON. (R. 1854) 75
Geological Survey, directory of officers and employés of 466
Geological surveys—*See* annual reports; *also* Hayden, Powell, Wheeler.
Geology—
and history, boundary line between—E. SUESS. (R. 1872) 271
economic, of Trinidad, report on survey of—G. P. WALL; J. G. SAWKINS. (R. 1856) 91
of Kerguelen Island—F. M. ENDLICH 294

Geology—Continued.
of lower Louisiana and salt deposit on Petite Anse Island—E. W. HILGARD 248
past and future of—J. PRESTWICH. (R. 1875) 298
progress in, in 1879, 1880—G. W. HAWES. (R. 1880) 442, 428
surface, illustrations of—E. HITCHCOCK 90
Georgia—
aboriginal structures in—C. C. JONES. (R. 1877) 323, 400
ancient mounds in—M. F. STEVENSON. (R. 1870) 244
Bartow county, mound in—M. F. STEVENSON. (R. 1872) 271
description of fishes of Alleghany region of—D. S. JORDAN; A. W. BRAYTON 308
habits of pouched rat, or salamander of—W. GESNER. (R. 1860) 147
McIntosh and Early counties, mounds in—W. McKINLEY. (R. 1872) 271
microscopical observations in—J. W. BAILEY 23
notes on collection of fishes from—T. H. BEAN. (P. 1879) 333
occurrence of *Stricklandia salteri* and *Stricklandia Davidsoni* in—C. A. WHITE. (P. 1880) 425
remarkable forms of hail stones in—S. ABICH. (R. 1869) 228
shell-heaps in—D. BROWN (R. 1871) 249
Spalding county, antiquities of—W. B. F. BAILEY. (R. 1877) 323
Gephyræa of northeast coast of America—A. E. VERRILL. (P. 1879) 333
Germany and United States, free freight between, by North German Lloyd—R. SCHLEIDEN. (R. 1858) 109
Germany and United States, free freight between—KUNHARDT & Co. (R. 1861) 149
GESNER, W. Habits of pouched rat, or salamander of Georgia. (R. 1860) 147
GESNER, W. Mica beds in Alabama. (R. 1879) 345
GIBBONS, H. Climate of San Francisco. (R. 1854) 75
GIBBES, R. W. Memoir on *Mosasaurus* and allied new genera, *Holcodus*, *Conosaurus*, *Amphorosteus* 14
GIBBS, G.—
Archæology in the United States. (R. 1861) 149
Bibliography of Chinook jargon 161
Comparative vocabulary 170
Dictionary of Chinook jargon, or trade language of Oregon 161
Ethnological instructions 160
Ethnological map of the United States. (R. 1862) 150
Ethnological suggestions 207
Indian languages. (R. 1865) 209
Indian vocabularies. (R. 1862) 150
Instructions for archæological investigations. (R. 1861) 149
Instructions for ethnology and philology 160

GIBBS, G.—Continued.
Intermixture of races. (R. 1864) ---- 188
Language of aboriginal Indians of America. (R. 1870) ---- 244
Makah Indians ---- 220
Philological circular. (R. 1862) ---- 150
Physical atlas of North America. (R. 1866) ---- 214
Suggestions for scientific investigations in Russian America ---- **207**
Gibbs, G., memoir of, by J. A. STEVENS. (R. 1873) ---- 275
GIBBS, G., and others. Recommendation of Shea's Indian linguistics. (R. 1861) ---- 149
GIBBS, G., and others. Tinneh or Chepewyan Indians of British and Russian America. (R. 1866) ---- 214, **365**
GIBBS, G. J. Stone celts in the West Indies and Africa. (R. 1877) ---- 323
GIBBS, W.; GENTH, F. A. Researches in ammonia-cobalt bases ---- **88**
Gideon's Farm, Hennepin county, Minnesota, mounds on—F. H. NUTTER. (R. 1879) ---- 345
GILBERT, C. H.—*See* D. S. Jordan; C. H. Gilbert.
GILBERT, Sir D. Notice of Smithson. (R. 1853) ---- 67, 330
GILL, T.—
Arrangement of families of fishes ---- **247**
Arrangement of families of mammals ---- **230**
Arrangement of families of mollusks ---- **227**
Bibliography of fishes ---- 247
Bibliography of fishes of Pacific coast of United States ---- 463
Bibliography of mammals ---- 230
Bibliography of mollusks ---- 227
Catalogue of fishes of east coast of North America ---- **283**
Fishes of Kerguelen Island ---- 294
Fishes of New York. (R. 1856) ---- 91
Identity of the genus *Leurynnis* Lockington, with *Lycodopsis* Collett. (P. 1880) ---- 425
Note on *Antennariidæ*. (P. 1878) ---- 332
Note on *Ceratiidæ*. (P. 1878) ---- 332
Note on the Latiloid genera. (P. 1881) ---- 467
Note on *Maltheidæ*. (P. 1878) ---- 332
Recent progress in zoölogy. (R. 1880) ---- 442, **431**
Status of ichthyology ---- 247
Synopsis of pediculate fishes of the eastern coast of extratropical North America. (P. 1878) ---- 332
Synoptical tables of mammals ---- 230
GILLISS, J. M. Solar eclipse, Peru, September 7, 1858 ---- **100**
GILLMAN, H. Characteristics of ancient man in Michigan. (R. 1875) ---- 298, **393**
GILLMAN, H. Mound builders and platycnemism in Michigan. (R. 1873.) 275, **393**

GILMAN, W. S. Lightning discharges. (R. 1867) ---- 215
GIRARD, C.—
Bibliography of American natural history for 1851 ---- **48**
Monograph of Cottoids ---- **30**
GIRARD, C.; BAIRD, S. F. Catalogue of North American reptiles ---- **49**
Girard College observations—*See* A. D. Bache.
GIVEN, W. F. Remarkable electric phenomenon. (R. 1865) ---- 209
Glacial drift (fresh water) of the northwestern States—C. WHITTLESEY ---- **197**
Glaciers, traces of, in Massachusetts and Vermont—E. HITCHCOCK ---- 90
GLAISHER, J. Account of balloon ascensions. (R. 1863) ---- 187
GLAZIER, W. C. W. On destruction of fish in Gulf of Mexico. (P. 1881) ---- 467
Gliddon mummy case—C. PICKERING ---- **208**
Globe, winds of the—J. H. COFFIN ---- **268**
Glyptocephalus cynoglossus on coast of North America—G. B. GOODE; T. H. BEAN. (P. 1878) ---- 332
Goat, Rocky Mountain, habits of—J. C. MERRILL. (P. 1879) ---- 333
Gobiesox rhessodon, from San Diego, California, description of—R. SMITH. (P. 1881) ---- 467
Gobioid fish, description of a new, from San Diego, California—R. SMITH. (P. 1881) ---- 467
Gold and silver coins, assay of, at United States Mint—J. POLLOCK. (R. 1868.) 224
Gold and silver coins, foreign, table of. (R. 1868) ---- 224
Gold ornament from a mound in Florida, observations on—C. RAU. (R. 1877.) 323, 440, **403**
GOODE, G. B.—
Catalogue of collection to illustrate animal resources and fisheries of the United States, exhibited at Philadelphia, 1876 ---- **326**
Catalogue of fishes of the Bermudas ---- **296**
Catalogue of United States Fish Commission's exhibit at Berlin, 1880 ---- **413**
Classification of collection of animal resources ---- **297**
Clupea tyrannus of Latrobe. (P. 1878) ---- 332
Description of new species of amber fish, (*Seriola Stearnsii*,) obtained from Florida by S. Stearns. (P. 1879) ---- 333
Descriptions of new species of fishes from deep soundings on southern New England coast, with diagnoses of two undescribed genera of flounders and genus related to *Merlucius*. (P. 1880) ---- 425
First decade of the United States Fish Commission. (R. 1880) ---- 442
Fishes from Bermuda mistakenly described as new by Gunther. (P. 1878) 332
Fishes from deep waters on south coast of New England obtained by Fish Commission in 1880. (P. 1880) ---- 425
Frigate mackerel, (*Auxis Rochei*,) on New England coast. (P. 1880) ---- 425
List of substances derived from animal kingdom ---- 297
Methods of capture and utilization of animals ---- 297

GOODE, G. B.—Continued.

Notacanthus phasganorus, new species of *Notacanthidæ* from Grand Banks of Newfoundland. (P. 1880) 425

Occurrence of *Belone latimanus* in Buzzard's Bay, Mass. (P. 1878) 332

Occurrence of Canada porcupine in West Virginia. (P. 1878) 332

Occurrence of *Hippocampus antiquorum* on St. George's Banks. (P. 1878) 332

Organization and objects of the U. S. National Museum. (P. 1881.) 467, **459**

Plan of organization and regulations of the U. S. National Museum. (P. 1881) 467, **445**

Plans for installation of collections in the U. S. National Museum **472**

Preliminary catalogue of fishes of St. John's river and east coast of Florida, with descriptions of new genus and three new species. (P. 1879) 333

Provisional classification of the food collection. (P. 1881) 467, **455**

Revision of American species of genus *Brevoortia*, with description of new species from Gulf of Mexico. (P. 1878) 332

Scheme of classification of collections in the U. S. National Museum. (P. 1881) 467, **457**

Study of trunk fishes, (*Ostraciontidæ*,) with notes on American species. (P. 1879) 333

Synopsis of useful and injurious animals 297

Taxonomic relations and geographical distribution of swordfish family, (*Xiphiidæ*.) (P. 1881) 467

Voices of crustaceans. (P. 1878) 332

GOODE, G. B.; BEAN, T. H.—

Catalogue of Stearns's fishes of Florida and descriptions of new species. (P. 1879) 333

Catalogue of Velie's fishes in Gulf of Mexico and description of new species. (P. 1879) 333

Craig flounder of Europe (*Glyptocephalus cynoglossus*) on coast of North America. (P. 1878) 332

Description of *Alepocephalus Bairdii*, new deep-sea fish, western Atlantic, (P. 1879) 333

Description of *Argentina syrtensium*, new deep-sea fish, Sable Island bank. (P. 1878) 332

Description of *Caulolatilus microps* from Gulf coast of Florida. (P. 1878) 332

Description of gadoid fishes, *Phycis Chesteri* and *Haloporphyrus viola*, from northwestern Atlantic. (P. 1878) 332

Description of *Lycodes paxillus*. (P. 1879) 333

Description of new genus and species of fish, *Lopholatilus chamæleonticeps*, from New England. (P. 1879) 333

Description of new species of fish, *Apogon pandionis*, from mouth of Chesapeake Bay. (P. 1881) 467

GOODE, G. B.; BEAN, T. H.—Continued.
Description of new species of fish (*Lutjanus Blackfordii* and *Lutjanus Stearnsii*) from coast of Florida. (P. 1878) ---- 332
Identity of *Brosmius brosme Americanus*, Gill, with *Brosmius brosme* (Müller) White. (P. 1878) ---- 332
Identity of *Rhinonemus caudacuta* with *Gadus cimbrius*. (P. 1878) ---- 332
New genus of fishes, *Benthodesmus*. (P. 1881) ---- 467
New serranoid fish, *Epinephelus Drummond-Hayi*, from Bermudas and Florida. (P. 1878) ---- 332
New species of *Liparus* (*L. ranula*) from Halifax. (P. 1879) ---- 333
Note on *Platessa ferruginea* and *Platessa rostrata*. (P. 1878) ---- 332
Note upon black grouper (*Epinephelus nigritus*) of the Southern coast. (P. 1878) ---- 332
Occurrence of *Lycodes Vahlii* on La Have and Grand Banks. (P. 1879) 333
Oceanic bonito on coast of United States. (P. 1878) ---- 332
Gopher of Illinois, habits of the—J. B. PARVIN. (R. 1854) ---- 75
GOSSE, Dr. Report on transactions of the Society of Physics and Natural History of Geneva, 1865–1866. (R. 1866) ---- 214
GOULD, B. A.—
Account of astronomical observatory at Cordoba, Argentine Republic. (R. 1873) ---- 275
Discussion of Piazzi's astronomical observations. (R. 1863) ---- 187
List of scientific papers of A. D. Bache. (R. 1870) ---- 244, 329, **379**
Report on history of discovery of Neptune ---- **18**
Transatlantic longitude ---- **223**
GOULD, J. Acknowledgment of birds. (R. 1867) ---- 215
Government Museum—*See* Museum.
Government of Bremen, exchange system. (R. 1865) ---- 209
Graham, T., scientific work of—W. ODLING. (R. 1871) ---- 249
Grammar and dictionary of the Carib or Karif language—C. H. BERENDT. (R. 1873) ---- 275
Grammar and dictionary of the Dakota language—S. R. RIGGS ---- **40**
Grammar and dictionary of the Yoruba language—T. J. BOWEN ---- **98**
Grammar of Yoruba language—W. W. TURNER ---- 98
Grand Bank, new species of *Notacanthidæ* from—G. B. GOODE. (P. 1880) ---- 425
Grand Bank, occurrence of *Lycodes Vahlii* on—G. B. GOODE; T. H. BEAN. (P. 1879) ---- 333
Grand Manan, marine invertebrata of—W. STIMPSON ---- **50**
GRANT, E. M. Account of discovery of stone image in Tennessee. (R. 1870.) 244
Grasshopper, means of destroying—V. MOTSCHULSKY. (R. 1858) ---- 109
Grasshopper, wingless, of California—E. P. VOLLUM. (R. 1860) ---- 147
Grasshoppers and locusts of America—A. S. TAYLOR. (R. 1858) ---- 109
Grasshoppers, North American, circular in reference to history of—P. R. UHLER ---- 163

Graves, ancient, and shell-heaps of California—P. SCHUMACHER. (R. 1874) ... 286
Gravitation, figures of equilibrium of liquid mass withdrawn from action of—*See* Plateau.
Gravitation, kinetic theories of—W. B. TAYLOR. (R. 1876) ... 299, **395**
GRAY, A.—
Address at memorial of J. Henry. (R. 1878) ... 341, 356
Biographical memoir of J. Henry. (R. 1878) ... 341, **407**
Biographical notice of W. H. Harvey. (R. 1867) ... 215
Memoir of John Torrey. (R. 1873) ... 275
Plantæ Wrightianæ Texano-Neo-Mexicanæ. Part I ... **22**
Plantæ Wrightianæ Texano-Neo-Mexicanæ. Part II ... **42**
Plants of Arctic America ... **342**
Plants of Kerguelen Island ... **294**
Report on Lindheimer's, Fendler's, and Wright's botanical explorations in New Mexico and California. (R. 1849) ... 21
GRAY, A., and others. Report on organization of Smithsonian Institution. (R. 1853) ... 67
GRAY, A.; COPPÉE, H. Report of Committee of Regents on Smithsonian Museum. (R. 1874) ... 286
GRAY, A.; SARGENT, A. A.; CLYMER, H. Report of Committee on Museum. (R. 1876) ... 299
GRAY, J. E.; DE CANDOLLE, A. Dominant language for science. (R. 1874.) 286
Gray substance of medulla oblongata, and trapezium—J. DEAN ... **173**
Great Britain, history of the Royal Institution of—E. MAILLY. (R. 1867) ... 215
Greece, Museum of National University of, exchange of specimens. (R. 1867.) 215
Greece, ornamental album from—Miss E. B. CONTAXAKI. (R. 1857) ... 107
GREEN, J. Account of a new barometer. (R. 1855) ... 77, 148
GREEN, J.; WÜRDEMANN, W. On filling barometer tubes. (R. 1859) ... 110
Green's standard barometer ... 148
Greenland—
account of cryolite of—LEWIS; QUALE. (R. 1866) ... 214
observations in—*See* Kane.
report of explorations in—L. KUMLIEN. (R. 1878) ... 341
Green river country, meteorology of—Col. COLLINS. (R. 1871) ... 249
Green river valley, rock engravings on—J. G. BRUFF. (R. 1872) ... 271
Grenada, catalogue of Ober's collection of birds of—G. N. LAWRENCE. (P. 1878) ... 332
Grinnell expedition to Arctic seas—*See* Kane.
GROSSMANN, F. E. Pima Indians of Arizona. (R. 1871) ... 249
Guadeloupe, catalogue of Ober's collection of birds of—G. N. LAWRENCE. (P. 1878) ... 332
Guanajuato, notes on Dugès' fishes from—D. S. JORDAN. (P. 1879) ... 333
Guatemala—
antiquities in—G. WILLIAMSON. (R. 1876) ... 299

Guatemala—Continued.
collection of historical documents in—C. H. BERENDT. (R. 1876) 299
earthquakes in—A. CANUDAS. (R. 1858) 109
new humming bird (*Atthis Ellioti*) from—R. RIDGWAY. (P. 1878) 332
sculptures of Santa Lucia Cosumalwhuapa in—S. HABEL **269**
Guatemalan minister, A. T. De Irisarri, letter from, recommending Dr. Berendt. (R. 1865) 209
GUEST, W. E. Ancient Indian remains near Prescott, Canada West. (R. 1856) 91
GUEST, W. E. Snow gauge. (R. 1858) 109
Guide to the flora of Washington and vicinity—L. F. WARD **444**
GUILD, R. A. Biographical notice of Chas. C. Jewett. (R. 1867) 215
Gulf of California, lecture on shells of—P. P. CARPENTER. (R. 1859) 110
Gulf of California, list of fishes of—D. S. JORDAN; C. H. GILBERT. (P. 1881) 467
Gulf of Mexico—
analysis of water destructive to fish in—F. M. ENDLICH. (P. 1881) 467
destruction of fish in—W. C. W. GLAZIER. (P. 1881) 467
destruction of fish in—J. Y. PORTER. (P. 1881) 467
fish mortality in—E. INGERSOLL. (P. 1881) 467
fish mortality in—M. A. MOORE. (P. 1881) 467
notes on mortality among fishes in—S. H. JOHNSON. (P. 1881) 467
report on water from—W. G. FARLOW. (P. 1881) 467
Gulf of Mexico—*See* Mexico.
Gulf-stream, formation of clouds over—H. M. BANNISTER. (R. 1866) 214
Gun-cotton and gunpowder—Lieut. VON KAROLYI; B. F. CRAIG. (R. 1864.) 188
GUNN, D. Egging expedition to Shoal Lake, Lake Winnipeg. (R. 1867) 215
GUNN, D. Indian remains in Red River Settlement, Hudson's Bay Territory. (R. 1867) 215
Guthrie, J., authority given by, to collectors of customs, etc., to receive and transmit specimens to Smithsonian 34
Gutta-percha and caoutchouc. (R. 1864) 188
GUYOT, A.—
Directions for meteorological observations. (R. 1855) 77, **19**, **148**
Meteorological tables **31**
Meteorological and physical tables **153**
Metric system for scientific observations. (R. 1848) ..... **I**
Mountain measurements. (R. 1862) 150
GUYOT, A.; HENRY, J. Directions for meteorological observations. (R. 1855.) 77, **19**, **148**
Gyroscope, problems of rotary motion presented by—J. G. BARNARD **240**

H.

Haarlem, Holland, Society of Sciences of—*See* Harlem.
HAAS, H. Account of lightning discharges. (R. 1867) 215
HABEL, S. Sculptures of Santa Lucia Cosumalwhuapa in Guatemala **269**
Habits of—
beaver—F. R. BRUNOT. (R. 1873) 275
black bass of the Ohio—J. EOFF. (R. 1854) 75
gopher of Illinois—J. B. PARVIN. (R. 1854) 75
pouched rat or salamander of Georgia—W. GESNER. (R. 1860) 147
Rocky Mountain goat—J. C. MERRILL. (P. 1879) 333
species of salamander—C. MANN. (R. 1854) 75
Hæmatoma, bibliography of—W. KEEN 300
HAGEN, G. Memoir of Encke. (R. 1868) 224
HAGEN, H.—
Neuroptera. (R. 1861) 149
Pseudo-neuroptera of Kerguelen Island 294
Synopsis of North American neuroptera **134**
Haidah Indians of Queen Charlotte Islands—J. G. SWAN **267**
HAIDINGER, W. Honorary medal to von Martius. (R. 1863) 187
Hail, on the electricity of induction in—F. ZANTEDESCHI. (R. 1870) 244
Hail-stones in Georgia, remarkable forms of—S. ABICH. (R. 1869) 228
Hail-storm in Texas—G. M. BACHE. (R. 1870) 244
Hail-storm on Bosphorus—Com. PORTER. (R. 1870) 244
HAILE, J.; MCHENRY, J. W. Antiquities of Jackson Co., Tenn. (R. 1874.) 286
Hainault, Belgium, Society of Science, Art, and Literature. Prize questions. (R. 1873) 275
Hake, description of a new—T. H. BEAN. (P. 1880) 425
HALDEMAN, S. S. Coleoptera of the United States **62**
HALDEMAN, S. S. On a polychrome bead from Florida. (R. 1877) 323, **404**
HALE, C. Exploration of the Nile. (R. 1865) 209
HALE, E. E. Report on Jewett's general stereotype catalogue of public libraries. 47
HALE, H. Vocabulary of Chinook jargon 161
Half-breeds of the northwest—V. HARVARD. (R. 1879) 345
Haliclystus auricula, anatomy and physiology of—H. J. CLARK 242
Halifax, description of fish obtained at—*See* G. B. GOODE; T. H. BEAN.
Hall in Smithsonian building, report on use of—L. AGASSIZ. (R. 1867) 215
Hall, C. F., scientific instructions to—J. HENRY; J. E. HILGARD; S. NEWCOMB; S. F. BAIRD; F. B. MEEK; L. AGASSIZ. (R. 1871) 249
HALL, J, statement of, on telegraph. (R. 1857) 107, 115
Halliwell manuscripts, report on—C. C. JEWETT. (R. 1852) 57

Haloporphyrus viola from deep-sea fauna of northwestern Atlantic—G. B. GOODE; T. H. BEAN. (P. 1878) ---- 332
Hamburg Zoölogical Gardens, exchange of specimens. (R. 1867) ---- 215
Hamilton College, Clinton, N. Y., exchange of specimens. (R. 1861) ---- 149
Hamilton College, Clinton, N. Y., examination of Spencer's telescope. (R. 1855) ---- 77
HAMILTON, J. Bequest deposited in United States Treasury. (R. 1873) -- 275, 329
HAMILTON, J. Bequest of $1,000 to Smithsonian Institution. (R. 1872) -- 271, 329
HAMLIN, H. Address on death of Joseph Henry ---- 356
HAMLIN, H. Biographical notice of S. P. Chase. (R. 1873) ---- 275
Hampton, Virginia, Normal and Agricultural Institute, casts of heads of Indian boys and girls at—R. H. PRATT. (P. 1879) ---- 333
Hann, J., reply to criticisms of, by W. FERREL. (R. 1877) ---- 323, 398
HANN, J.—
Atmospheric pressure and rain-fall. (R. 1877) ---- 323, 398
Diminution of aqueous vapor with increasing altitude. (R. 1877) -- 323, 398
Influence of rain upon the barometer. (R. 1877) ---- 323, 398
Laws of variation of temperature in ascending currents of air. (R. 1877) 323, 398
Relation between pressure of air and velocity of wind. (R. 1877) -- 323, 398
Harbors, dates of opening and closing of—F. B. HOUGH ---- 182
Harbors, tides and tidal action in—J. E. HILGARD. (R. 1874) ---- 286, **390**
HARDISTY, W. L. The Loucheux Indians. (R. 1866) ---- 214, 365
HARE, R.—
Explosiveness of nitre ---- **17**
Letter relative to gift of apparatus. (R. 1848) ---- I
Method of forming small weights. (R. 1858) ---- 109
On John Wise's observation of a thunder storm. (R. 1854) ---- 75
HARGER, O. Notes on New England *Isopoda*. (P. 1879) ---- 333
HARKNESS, W. Observations on terrestrial magnetism and deviation of compasses on iron-clads ---- **239**
Harlem, Holland, Society of Science. Prize questions. (R. 1861, 1864, 1868, 1873) ---- 149, 188, 224, 275
Harmonies of the solar system—S. ALEXANDER ---- **280**
HARRIOTT, J. Account of the city of Washington, 1808 ---- 330
HARRIS, E. List of birds and mammalia of Missouri river. (R. 1850) ---- 28
HARRISON, A. M. Colored bead from mound in Florida. (R. 1877) ---- 323
HARRISON, W. Account of storm in Butler county, Kansas. (R. 1871) ---- 249
HART, J. N. DE. Mounds and osteology of the mound builders of Wisconsin. (R. 1877) ---- 323
Harvey, W. H., biographical notice of, by A. GRAY. (R. 1867) ---- 215
HARVEY, W. H.—
Lecture on marine algæ. (R. 1855) ---- 77
List of arctic algæ ---- 95

HARVEY, W. H.—Continued.
Marine algæ. Part I. *Melanospermeæ* ---- 32
Marine algæ. Part II. *Rhodospermeæ* ---- 43
Marine algæ. Part III. *Chlorospermeæ* ---- 95
Marine algæ. Parts I, II, III. Complete ---- 96
HARWOOD, A. A. Account of sarcophagus from Syria. (R. 1870) ---- 244
Hassler expedition, narrative of the—L. AGASSIZ. (R. 1872) ---- 271
HASTINGS, C. S.; HOLDEN, E. S. Synopsis of Herschel's writings. (R. 1880.) 442, 426
HATCH, F. W. Meteorological observations at Sacramento, Cal. (R. 1854) ---- 75
HAUGHTON, S. Relation of food to work, and its bearing on medical practice. (R. 1870) ---- 244
HAÜY, René Just, memoir of, by G. CUVIER. (R. 1860) ---- 147
HAVARD, V. French half-breeds of the northwest. (R. 1879) ---- 345
HAVEN, S. F. Archæology of the United States ---- 71
HAVEN, S. F. Report on Jewett's general stereotype catalogue of public libraries ---- 47
Hawaiian Islands, fishes of—T. H. STREETS ---- 303
Hawaiian Islands, natural history of—T. H. STREETS ---- 303
HAWES, G. W.—
Determination of feldspar in thin sections of rocks. (P. 1881) ---- 467
On mineralogical composition of normal mesozoic diabase upon Atlantic border. (P. 1881) ---- 467
Progress in geology and mineralogy, 1879–80. (R. 1880) ---- 442, 428
HAWKES, F. L., and others. On publication of Spanish works on New Mexico. (R. 1855) ---- 77
Hawkins and Wale, blow-pipe apparatus of. (R. 1872) ---- 271
HAY, O. P. On a collection of fishes from eastern Mississippi. (P. 1880) ---- 425
HAYDEN, F. V. Notes on Indian history. (R. 1867) ---- 215
HAYDEN, F. V.; MEEK, F. B. Palæontology of the upper Missouri ---- 172
HAYES, I. I.—
Astronomical observations in Arctic Seas ---- 196
Atmospheric pressure, wind, temperature, tides, in Arctic Seas ---- 196
Lecture on Arctic explorations. (R. 1861) ---- 149
Magnetic observations in Arctic Seas ---- 196
Physical observations in the Arctic Seas ---- 196
Haystack mound, Lincoln county, Dakota—A. BARRANDT. (R. 1872) ---- 271
HEAD, J. E. Natural history of country about Fort Ripley, Minn. (R. 1854) 75
Health, architecture in relation to—D. B. REID. (R. 1856) ---- 91
Hearing, sense of. (R. 1866) ---- 214
Heart, strain and over-action of the. Toner lecture No. III—J. M. DA COSTA. 279
Heat—
and light of the sun, relative intensity of—L. W. MEECH. (R. 1856.) 91, 83
animal, of fishes, experiments upon—J. H. KIDDER. (P. 1879) ---- 333

Heat—Continued.
dry, comparative action of sulphurous acid and, upon putrefactive bacteria. (P. 1881) 467
principles of the mechanical theory of—J. MÜLLER. (R. 1868) 224
radiant, report on state of knowledge of—B. POWELL. (R. 1859) 110
recent progress in relation to the theory of—A. CAZIN. (R. 1868) 224
specific, table of—F. W. CLARKE 276
tables of expansion by—F. W. CLARKE **289**
Heavenly bodies, results of spectrum analysis applied to—W. HUGGINS. (R. 1866) 214
Heights, circular relative to—J. HENRY **236**
Heights of mountains in Colorado—G. ENGELMANN. (R. 1862) 150
Heights, quantity of rain at different—O. W. MORRIS; J. HENRY. (R. 1855.) 77
HEILPRIN, A. New species of eocene mollusca from southern United States. (P. 1880) 425
HEINEMANN, V. Lepidoptera 133
Helicinidæ—W. G. BINNEY 144
Heligoland, birds of—H. GÄRKE. (P. 1879) 333
HELLWALD, F. VON. American migration. (R. 1866) 214
HELMHOLTZ, H. Relation of physical sciences to science in general. (R. 1871.) 249
HELMHOLTZ, H.; MAXWELL, J. C. Later views of connection of electricity and magnetism. (R. 1873) 275
Hemiptera, instructions for collecting—P. R. UHLER. (R. 1858) 109
Hemirhamphus rosæ from coast of California, description of—D. S. JORDAN; C. H. GILBERT, (P. 1880) 425
Henry and the telegraph—W. B. TAYLOR. (R. 1878) 341, **405**
Henry as a discoverer—A. M. MAYER 356, **417**
HENRY, J.—
biographical memoir of, by A. GRAY. (R. 1878) 341, **407**
deposition of, in the case of Morse *vs.* O'Rielly, taken September, 1879 115
examination of, by English Scientific Commission 329
life and character of, by J. C. WELLING 356, **338**
memoir of, and sketch of his scientific work, by W. B. TAYLOR 356, **339**
memorial of, by United States Congress **356**
monument to, act of Congress for 356
report of Special Committee of Board of Regents on communication of—C. C. FELTON. (R. 1857) 107, **115**
statue of, proceedings of Congress relative to 356
statue of, report of Executive Committee on. (R. 1880) 442
HENRY, J., papers by:
Account of Priestley's lens. (R. 1859) 110
Acoustics applied to public buildings. (R. 1856) 91
Address on the Smithsonian Institution. (R. 1853) **E**, 67

HENRY, J., papers by:—Continued.
Annual reports, 1865–1877 (reprints) **343**
Annual reports, 1847–1877—*See* each annual report.
Appendix to notice of Schoenbein, the discoverer of ozone. (R. 1868).. 224
Aurora directions. (R. 1855) 77
Circular of instructions to observatories relative to telegraphic announcement of astronomical discoveries........ **263**
Circular relating to collections in archæology and ethnology........ **205**
Circular relative to ancient mining in Lake Superior copper region. (R. 1861)........ 149
Circular relative to collections of birds from Middle and South America. **168**
Circular relative to earthquakes 148
Circular relative to heights **236**
Circular respecting copyrights. (R. 1854) 75
Circular respecting new report on libraries. (R. 1854) 75
Circular sent with specimens presented. (R. 1872)........ 271
Circular to entomologists........ **178**
Circular to officers of Hudson's Bay Company **137**
Color-blindness. (R. 1877) 323
Communication relative to a publication by Prof. Morse. (R. 1857.) 107, 329, **115**
Currents of atmosphere and aerial navigation. (R. 1860)........ 147
Description of Smithsonian anemometer. (R. 1860)........ 147
Digest of act of organization of Smithsonian Institution........ **C**, 328
Directions for constructing lightning-rods **237**
Earthquake directions. (R. 1855) 77
Effect of the moon on the weather. (R. 1871)........ 249
Eulogy on A. D. Bache. (R. 1870) 244, **379**
Exposition of bequest of Smithson........ **E**
History of electro-magnetic telegraph. (R. 1857) 107, **115**
Instructions for observations of thunder storms **235**
Investigation of illuminating materials. (R. 1880) 442, **389**
Letter to Secretary of Treasury on payment of interest in coin. (R. 1865) 209
Memoir of W. W. Seaton. (R. 1866) 214
Meteorological stations, cost of establishing. (R. 1858) 109
Mode of testing building materials and account of the marble used in the extension of the United States Capitol. (R. 1856) 91
Notes relative to George Catlin. (R. 1872) 271
Notes to accounts of lightning discharges by G. W. Dodge and others. (R. 1867) 215
Notes to article on American migration by F. von Hellwald. (R. 1866.) 214
Notes to article on horary variations of barometer by M. Vaillant. (R. 1866) 214

HENRY, J., papers by :—Continued.
Notes to article on vitality by H. H. Higgins. (R. 1866) 214
Notes to articles on meteorology by G. Latimer and others. (R. 1871.) 249
Notice of Parker Cleaveland. (R. 1859) 110
On a physical observatory. (R. 1870) 244
On the "Moon hoax." (R. 1873) 275
Organization of local scientific societies. (R. 1875) 298
Programme of organization of Smithsonian **F**, 328
Queries relative to tornadoes **190**
Registration of periodical phenomena. (R. 1855) 77
Remarks appended to meteorological articles by W. C. Dennis and others. (R. 1866) 214
Reply to memorial on Lowe's aeronautic voyage. (R. 1860) 147
Report of Secretary, 1847–1877. (R. 1847–1877.) **H**, **I**, 21, 28, 51, 57, 67, 75, 77, 91, 107, 109, 110, 147, 149, 150, 187, 188, 209, 214, 215, 224, 228, 244, 249, 271, 275, 286, 298, 299, 323
Researches in sound. (R. 1878) 341, **406**
Statement in relation to the history of the electro-magnetic telegraph 115
Suggestions relative to objects of scientific investigation in Russian America **207**
Syllabus of course of lectures on physics. (R. 1856) 91
HENRY, J., and others. Scientific instructions to Captain Hall. (R. 1871) 249
HENRY, J.; DU PRÉ, W. Earthquakes in North Carolina, 1874. (R 1874) 286
HENRY, J.; GUYOT, A. Directions for meteorological observations. (R. 1855.) 77, **19**, **148**
HENRY, J.; KNIGHT, R. T. Connection of gales of wind and aurora. (R. 1871) 249
HENRY, J.; MORRIS, O. W. Quantity of rain at different heights. (R. 1855.) 77
HENRY, J.; RUSSELL, R. Lectures and notes on meteorology. (R. 1854) 75
HENRY, J.; WALLACH, R. Report of Committee of Regents on fire at the Smithsonian. (R. 1864) 188, 329
Henshall, J. A., notes on collection of fishes obtained by, from east Florida—D. S. JORDAN. (P. 1880) 425
Herbarium captured in Tennessee—H. R. WIRTZ. (R. 1862) 150
Herpetology of Hawaiian and Fanning Islands—T. H. STREETS 303
Herschel, Sir J. F. W., memoir of, by N. S. DODGE. (R. 1871) 249
HERSCHEL, Sir J. F. W. On atoms. (R. 1862) 150
Herschel, Sir W., eulogy on, by F. ARAGO. (R. 1870) 244
Herschel, Sir W., synopsis of scientific writings of, by E. S. HOLDEN; C. S. HASTINGS. (R. 1880) 442, **426**
Hexanchus corinus, new species of notidanoid shark, description of—D. S. JORDAN; C. H. GILBERT. (P. 1880) 425
HIGGINS, H. H. On vitality, with notes by J. Henry. (R. 1866) 214

High antiquity in Europe, study of—A. MORLOT. (R. 1862; R. 1864) 150, 188
HILDRETH, S. P. Meteorological observations, Marietta, Ohio 120
HILGARD, E. W. Geology of lower Louisiana and salt deposit on Petite Anse Island 248
HILGARD, J. E. Description of magnetic observatory at the Smithsonian Institution. (R. 1859) 110
HILGARD, J. E. Tides and tidal action in harbors. (R. 1874) 286, 390
HILGARD, J. E., and others. Scientific instructions to Capt. Hall. (R. 1871.) 249
HILL, A. J. Map of antiquities of United States. (R. 1861) 149
HILL, G. W. Ancient earthworks of Ashland county, Ohio. (R. 1877) 323
HILL, G. W. Antiquities of northern Ohio. (R. 1874) 286
HILL, T. Map of solar eclipse of March 15, 1858, and description of the occultator 101
HILLIER, S. L. Effect of lightning. (R. 1866) 214
HINCKS, W. On Smithsonian exchanges. (R. 1860) 147
Hints on public architecture—R. D. OWEN P
Hippocampus antiquorum, occurrence of, on St. George's Bank—G. B. GOODE. (P. 1878) 332
Hippoglossoides elassodon, new species of flounder, from Puget Sound, description of—D. S. JORDAN; C. H. GILBERT. (P. 1880) 425
Hippoglossoides exilis, new flounder, from coast of California, description of—D. S. JORDAN; C. H. GILBERT. (P. 1880) 425
Hippoglossus vulgaris, occurrence of, at Unalaska and St. Michael's, Alaska—T. H. BEAN. (P. 1879) 333
Historical documents in Guatemala—C. H. BERENDT. (R. 1876) 299
Historical manuscripts, catalogue of collection of—L. BERLANDIER. (R. 1854) 75
Historical sketch of Academy of Sciences of Paris—M. FLOURENS. (R. 1862.) 150
Historical sketch of Henry's contribution to electro-magnetic telegraph—W. B. TAYLOR. (R. 1878) 341, 405
Historical sketches of vestiges of antiquity in United States—S. F. HAVEN 71
Historical Society of Minnesota, grammar and dictionary of Dakota language. 40
Historical study of jade—S. BLONDEL. (R. 1876) 299
History—
ancient, of North America—M. MUCH. (R. 1871) 249
and antiquities of Santa Rosa Island, California—S. BOWERS. (R. 1877.) 323
and archæology, Mexican—B. MAYER 86
and climate of New Mexico—T. A. McPARLIN. (R. 1877) 323, 396
and geology, boundary line between—E. SUESS. (R. 1872) 271
and origin of Royal Society of London—C. A. ALEXANDER. (R. 1863.) 187
Indian, notes on—F. V. HAYDEN. (R. 1867) 215
of Chester county, Pennsylvania—W. DARLINGTON. (R. 1862) 150
of discovery of planet Neptune—B. A. GOULD 18
of discovery relative to magnetism. (R. 1863) 187

History—Continued.
of education in the United States—F. A. PACKARD. (R. 1863) 187
of electro-magnetic telegraph—J. HENRY. (R. 1857) 107
of fresh-water algæ of North America—H. C. WOOD 241
of marine algæ—W. H. HARVEY 32, 48, 95, 96
of my youth, an autobiography—F. ARAGO. (R. 1870) 244
of North American grasshoppers, circular in reference to **163**
of petroleum or rock-oil—T. S. HUNT. (R. 1861) 149
of Royal Institution of Great Britain—E. MAILLY. (R. 1867) 215
of Smithsonian Institution—W. J. RHEES **328**
of transactions of Anthropological Society of Paris, 1865–1867—P. BROCA. (R. 1868) 224
of works of Cuvier—M. FLOURENS. (R. 1868) 224
HITCHCOCK, E.—
Illustrations of surface geology **90**
On erosions of earth's surface 90
On geology of New England 90
Traces of glaciers in Massachusetts and Vermont 90
Hoax, the Moon—J. HENRY. (R. 1873) 275
HODGE, C. Prayer at funeral of Joseph Henry 356
HODGINS, J. G. Meteorological stations of Upper Canada. (R. 1858) 109
HODGINS, J. G. Meteorological system of Canada. (R. 1865) 209
Hodgkinson, Eaton, memoir of, by R. RAWSON. (R. 1868) 224
HODGSON, W. B., and others. On publication of Spanish works on New Mexico. (R. 1855) 77
HOEK, M. Letter in reference to meteoric shower of November 13, 1867 217
Holcodus, memoir on—R. W. GIBBES 14
HOLDEN, E. S.—
Index catalogue of books relating to nebulæ, clusters, etc **311**
Recent progress in astronomy 1879–1880. (R. 1880) 442, **427**
Reports of American and foreign observatories. (R. 1879) 345
Studies in Central American picture-writing. (E. 1879–'80) 476
HOLDEN, E. S.; BOEHMER, G. H. Report of observatories for 1880. (R. 1880) 442, **438**
HOLDEN, E. S.; HASTINGS, C. S. Synopsis of scientific writings of Sir William Herschel. (R. 1880) 442, **426**
Holland Society of Science, Harlem. Prize questions. (R. 1861, 1864, 1868, 1873) 149, 188, 224, 275
HOLMGREN, F. Color-blindness in relation to accidents by rail and sea. (R. 1877) 323, **399**
Horary variations of barometer—M. VAILLANT. (R. 1866) 214
HORNADAY, W. T. Classification of collections to illustrate taxidermy. (P. 1881) 467, **456**
HOTCHKISS, T. P. Indian remains in Caddo parish, Louisiana. (R. 1872) 271

HOUGH, F. B.—
Dates of blossoming of plants 182
Dates of defoliation or fall of leaf of plants 182
Dates of first appearance of birds 182
Dates of first appearance of fish 182
Dates of first appearance of insects 182
Dates of first appearance of reptiles 182
Dates of foliation of plants 182
Dates of opening and closing of lakes 182
Dates of opening and closing of rivers 182
Dates of ripening of fruits 182
Periodical phenomena, 1851 to 1859 182
HOUGH, J. Mounds in Washington county, Mississippi. (R. 1879) 345
Hours, best, to find mean temperature—C. DEWEY. (R. 1857) 107
Howgate Polar Expedition, natural history of Arctic America—L. KUMLIEN. **342**
HOY, P. R. Journal of an exploration of western Missouri. (R. 1864) 188
HOY, P. R. On *Amblystoma luridum*, a salamander of Wisconsin. (R. 1854.) 75
HUBBARD, J. S. Investigations of Biela's comet. (R. 1862) 150
Hudson's Bay, notes on fishes from—T. H. BEAN. (P. 1881) 467
HUDSON'S BAY COMPANY. Kennicott's explorations. (R. 1863) 187
Hudson's Bay Company, circular to officers of—J. HENRY **137**
Hudson's Bay Company, letter to officers of—G. SIMPSON 137
Hudson's Bay Territory, observations in—B. R. ROSS. (R. 1859) 110
Hudson's Bay Territory, Red river settlements, Indian remains in—D. GUNN. (R. 1867) 215
HUGGINS, W. Results of spectrum analysis applied to the heavenly bodies. (R. 1866) 214
Human race, probable future of the—A. DE CANDOLLE. (R. 1875) 298
Human remains from Patagonia—A. RIED. (R. 1862) 150
Humidity, relative, tables of—J. H. COFFIN **87**
Humming-bird, a new, (*Atthis Ellioti*), from Guatemala—R. RIDGWAY. (P. 1878) 332
Humming-birds, described, list of—D. G. ELLIOT **334**
Humming-birds, monograph of—D. G. ELLIOT **317**
HUMPHREYS, A. A. Method of ascertaining amount of water in rivers. (R. 1858) 109
Hungarian National Museum, acknowledgment for birds. (R. 1863) 187
Hungary, prehistoric antiquities of—F. F. ROMER. (R. 1876) 299, 440, **392**
HUNT, T. S. Chemistry of the earth. (R. 1869) 228, **376**
HUNT, T. S. History of petroleum or rock oil. (R. 1861) 149
HUNTINGTON, G. C. Climate of Kelley's Island, Ohio. (R. 1866) 214
Hurricane at Tortola, St. Thomas, and Porto Rico—G. A. LATIMER. (R. 1867.) 215
Hurricane in Island of St. Thomas. (R. 1867) 215

HUXLEY, T. H. Principles and methods of palæontology. (R. 1869) 228
Hydrobiinæ, researches upon the—W. STIMPSON **201**
Hydrogen as a gas and as a metal—J. E. REYNOLDS. (R. 1870) 244
Hygrometrical tables—A. GUYOT 153
Hymenoptera—
instructions for collecting—B. CLEMENS. (R. 1858) 109
letter relative to catalogue of—H. DE SAUSSURE. (R. 1862) 150
monograph of—H. DE SAUSSURE **254**
of Arctic regions—S. H. SCUDDER and others 342
Hypsometrical tables—A. GUYOT 153

I.

Ice—
disappearance of—R. H. GARDINER. (R. 1860) 147
formation of, at the bottom of water—M. ENGELHARDT. (R. 1866) 214
observations on—D. WALKER 146
Iceland, vegetable colonization of—C. MARTINS. (R. 1858) 109
Ichthyology—
Contributions to North American—
Part I. Review Rafinesque's memoirs—D. S. JORDAN **305**
Part II. A. Notes on *Cottidæ*, (etc.) B. Synopsis *Siluridæ*—D. S. JORDAN **306**
Part III. A. Distribution of fishes of Alleghany region, (etc.)—D. S. JORDAN; A. W. BRAYTON. B. Synopsis of family *Catostomidæ*—D. S. JORDAN **308**
of Hawaiian and Fanning Islands and California—T. H. STREETS 303
status of—T. GILL 247
Ichthyology—*See* Fishes.
Icichthys Lockingtoni, new species deep-water fish from coast of California—D. S. JORDAN; C. H. GILBERT. (P. 1880) 425
Icosteus ænigmaticus of California, description of—W. N. LOCKINGTON. (P. 1880) 425
Icterus, description of new species of, from West Indies—G. N. LAWRENCE. (P. 1880) 425
Idaho, distribution of forest trees in—W. W. JOHNSON. (R. 1870) 244
Identification of artisan and artist—N. WISEMAN. (R. 1870) 244
Illinois—
Adams county, mounds in, near Quincy—W. G. ANDERSON. (R. 1879.) 345
Albany, mounds near—R. J. FARQUHARSON. (R. 1874) 286

Illinois—Continued.
deposits of flint implements in—J. F. SNYDER. (R. 1876) 299
habits of the gopher of—J. B. PARVIN. (R. 1854) 75
Lawrence county, antiquities of—A. PATTON. (R. 1873) 275
Madison county, stone cists in, near Highland—A. OEHLER. (R. 1879.) 345
Mason county, antiquities of—J. COCHRANE. (R. 1877) 323
Mercer county, ancient mounds of—T. McWHORTER. (R. 1874) 286
Pike county, mounds in—B. MITCHELL. (R. 1879) 345
Rock Bluff, description of human skull from—J. A. MEIGS. (R. 1867.) 215
Rock Island, shell-bed skull from—A. S. TIFFANY. (R. 1874) 286
Rock Island county, mounds in—T. THOMPSON. (R. 1879) 345
Rock Island county, antiquities of—A. TOELLNER. (R. 1879) 345
Rock river valley, mound builders in—J. SHAW. (R. 1877) 323
Spoon river valley, mounds in—W. H. ADAMS. (R. 1879) 345
southern, agricultural flint implements in—C. RAU. (R. 1868.) 224, 440, **370**
Union county, antiquities of—T. M. PERRINE. (R. 1873) 275
Union county, mounds in, near Anna—T. M. PERRINE. (R. 1872) 271
Whitesides county, antiquities of—W. H. PRATT. (R. 1874) 286
Illinois Board of Education. Meteorological system for every State. (R. 1855.) 77
Illuminating materials, investigation of—J. HENRY. (R. 1880) 442, **389**
Illustrations of method of recording Indian languages—J. O. DORSEY; A. S. GATSCHET; S. R. RIGGS. (E. 1879-80) 476
Illustrations of surface geology—E. HITCHCOCK **90**
Image, stone, in Tennessee, account of discovery of—E. M. GRANT. (R. 1870.) 244
Imperial Academy of Sciences, Belles-lettres, and Arts, of Bordeaux. Prize questions. (R. 1868) 224
Imperial Academy of Sciences, Vienna. Prize questions. (R. 1864; R. 1865.) 188, 209
Imperial Geological Institute, Vienna, tertiary fossils presented by. (R. 1863.) 187
Imperial Library of Vienna, books presented by. (R. 1865) 209
Imperial Society of Natural Sciences of Cherbourg. Prize questions. (R. 1864.) 188
Imperial Society of Science, Agriculture, and Arts of Lille. Prize questions. (R. 1865) 209
Implement, wood, ancient, found in Connecticut—E. W. ELLSWORTH. (R. 1876) 299
Implements—
agricultural, North American stone period—C. RAU. (R. 1863) 187, 440
flint, agricultural, in southern Illinois—C. RAU. (R. 1868) 224, 440, **370**
flint, deposits of, in Illinois—J. F. SNYDER. (R. 1876) 299
flint, in Holmes county, Ohio—H. B. CASE. (R. 1877) 323
stone, North American—C. RAU. (R. 1872) 271, 440, **382**
Improvements, recent, in chemical arts—J. C. BOOTH; C. MORFIT **27**
Income, majority and minority reports on distribution of—J. A. PEARCE; J. MEACHAM. (R. 1853) 67, 329

Incorporation, act of, of Smithsonian Institution—*See* Congress.
Index-catalogue of books and memoirs on nebulæ and clusters—E. S. Holden. **311**
Index—
of genera of birds—S. F. Baird ---------- 108
of Smithsonian publications ---------- 478
systematic and alphabetical, of publications of the Smithsonian Institution to July, 1869. (R. 1868) ---------- 224
systematic, to list of foreign correspondents ---------- **257**
to genera of recent and fossil animals—S. H. Scudder ---------- **470**
to names applied to subdivisions of class *Brachiopoda*—W. H. Dall ---------- **304**
to North American botany—S. Watson ---------- **258**
to papers on anthropology published by Smithsonian Institution, 1847-1878—G. H. Boehmer. (R. 1879) ---------- 345, **421**
Indian—
boys and girls at Hampton Normal Institute, Va., catalogue of casts of heads of—R. H. Pratt. (P. 1879) ---------- 333
burial in California—W. M. King. (R. 1874) ---------- 286
conjurer's practice, details of—A. S. Gatschet. (E. 1879-80) ---------- 476
engravings on rocks along Green river valley—J. G. Bruff. (R. 1872.) 271
forts and dwellings, Indian Territory—W. E. Doyle. (R. 1876) ---------- 299
history, notes on—F. V. Hayden. (R. 1867) ---------- 215
languages—G. Flachenecker. (R. 1862) ---------- 150
languages, method of recording—J. O. Dorsey; A. S. Gatschet; S. R. Riggs. (E. 1879-80) ---------- 476
languages—*See* G. Gibbs, F. L. O. Roehrig, S. R. Riggs, J. G. Shea, W. L. Hardisty.
linguistics, account of library of—J. G. Shea. (R. 1861) ---------- 149
linguistics, recommendation of Shea's—G. Gibbs and others. (R. 1860.) 149
mode of making arrow-heads and obtaining fire—G. Crook. (R. 1871.) 249
mounds in southern Florida, explorations of—S. T. Walker. (R. 1879) 345
mounds near Fort Wadsworth, Dakota—A. J. Comfort. (R. 1871) ---------- 249
philology—W. W. Turner. (R. 1851) ---------- 51
photographs, catalogue of ---------- **216**
portraits and sketches of scenery, catalogue of—J. M. Stanley ---------- **53**
portraits, report of Committee of Regents on Stanley's gallery of. (R. 1857) 107
pottery—C. Rau. (R. 1866) ---------- 214, 440, **368**
prisoners at St. Augustine, Florida, catalogue of casts of heads of—R. H. Pratt. (P. 1878) ---------- 332
relics, catalogue of cabinet of, presented by J. H. Devereux. (R. 1872.) 271
relics from Schoharie, New York—F. D. Andrews. (R. 1879) ---------- 345
remains in Caddo parish, Louisiana—T. P. Hotchkiss. (R. 1872) ---------- 271
remains in Red River Settlement, Hudson's Bay Territory—D. Gunn. (R. 1867) ---------- 215

Indian—Continued.

remains near Prescott, Canada West—W. E. GUEST. (R. 1856) 91

tribes, cessions of land by, to United States—C. C. ROYCE. (E. 1879-80) 476

tribes of upper Missouri—T. A. CULBERTSON. (R. 1850) 28

village (Kushkushkee) near Newcastle, Pennsylvania.—E. M. MCCONNELL. (R. 1871) 249

vocabularies—G. GIBBS. (R. 1862) 150

vocabularies received from the Wheeler survey, list of—G. GIBBS. (R. 1874) 286

Indian Ocean, cyclone in the—N. PIKE. (R. 1867) 215

Indian Territory, Indian forts and dwellings in—W. E. DOYLE. (R. 1876) 299

Indiana—

Allen county, antiquities of—R. S. ROBERTSON. (R. 1874) 286

ancient burial mound in—W. PIDGEON. (R. 1867) 215

De Kalb county, antiquities of—R. S. ROBERTSON. (R. 1874) 286

Franklin county, mounds in—E. R. QUICK. (R. 1879) 345

Knox county, antiquities of—A. PATTON. (R. 1873) 275

La Porte county, antiquities of—R. S. ROBERTSON. (R. 1874) 286

Rush county, mounds in—F. JACKMAN. (R. 1879) 345

tornado in—J. CHAPPELSMITH **59**

Indians—

aboriginal, of America, language of—G. GIBBS. (R. 1870) 244

Cree, system of relationship of—E. A. WATKINS. (R. 1862) 150

Dakota or Sioux, language of—F. L. O. ROEHRIG. (R. 1871) 249

Haidah, of Queen Charlotte's Islands, British Columbia—J. G. SWAN **267**

Kutchin tribes—S. JONES. (R. 1866) 214, 365

Loucheux—W. L. HARDISTY. (R. 1866) 214, 365

Makah—J. G. SWAN **220**

mortuary customs of—H. C. YARROW. (E. 1879-80) 476

mythology of—J. W. POWELL. (E. 1879-80) 476

Navajo, sketch of the—J. LETTERMAN. (R. 1855) 77

of British America, account of—E. PETITOT. (R. 1865) 209

of Cape Flattery, Washington Territory—J. G. SWAN **220**

of Peru—F. L. GALT. (R. 1877) 323

of valley of Red River of the North, ethnology of—W. H. GARDNER. (R. 1870) 244

of western Nevada and California, Centennial mission to—S. POWERS. (R. 1876) 299

Pima, of Arizona—F. E. GROSSMAN. (R. 1871) 249

Quillehute. Method of taking surf smelt—J. G. SWAN. (P. 1880) 425

sign language of—G. MALLERY. (E. 1879-80) 476

Sioux or Dakota—A. G. BRACKETT. (R. 1876) 299

Sioux or Dakota, language of—F. L. O. ROEHRIG. (R. 1871) 249, **378**

Indians—Continued.
Tinneh or Chepewyan, of British and Russian America—G. GIBBS and others. (R. 1866) 214, **365**
uses of brain and marrow of animals by—T. R. PEALE. (R. 1870) 244
Indians—*See* California, Cape Flattery, Carib, Dakota, Haidah, Nevada, Kutchin, Loucheux, Makah, Mandan, Maya, Navajo, Peru, Portraits, Red River of the North, Shoshone, Sioux, Tinneh, Tonto.
Induction and deduction—J. VON LIEBIG. (R. 1870) 244
Induction, electricity of, in clouds—F. ZANTEDESCHI. (R. 1870) 244
Inflammation in arteries after ligature, acupressure, and torsion. Toner lecture No. VII—E. O. SHAKESPEARE **321**
Influence of aurora on the telegraph—W. D. SARGENT. (R. 1870) 244
Influence of rain upon the barometer—J. HANN. (R. 1877) 323, 398
Infusoria—J. W. BAILEY 23
Infusorial earths, examination of—A. M. EDWARDS 202
INGERSOLL, E. Fish mortality in Gulf of Mexico. (P. 1881) 467
Inquiries relative to crawfish and other crustacea 319
Inquiries relative to disease known as chorea—S. W. MITCHELL. (R. 1874) 286
Inquiry relative to food-fishes of United States—S. F. BAIRD **231**
Insect instincts and transformations, lecture on—J. G. MORRIS. (R. 1855) 77
Insects—
arsenic acid for protecting anatomical preparations from—J. B. S. JACKSON. (P. 1878) 332
circular concerning the department of—S. F. BAIRD **448**
classification of, from embryological data—L. AGASSIZ **16**
dates of first appearance of—F. B. HOUGH 182
directions for collecting and preserving—A. S. PACKARD **261**
instructions for collecting—S. F. BAIRD. (R. 1858) 109
of Arctic America—L. KUMLIEN 342
of Kerguelen Island—C. R. OSTEN SACKEN; H. A. HAGEN 294
Installation of collections in National Museum, plans for—G. B. GOODE. (P. 1881) 467, **472**
Instincts and transformations of insects, lecture on—J. G. MORRIS. (R 1855) 77
Institute of Bologna, Academy of Sciences of the. Prize questions. (R. 1862.) 150
Institute of France, historical sketch of, by M. FLOURENS. (R. 1862) 150
Institute of Rupert's Land, circular of. (R. 1861) 149
Institute, Royal Scientific and Literary, of Lombardy. Prize questions. (R. 1865) 209
Institution of Civil Engineers, London. Prize questions. (R. 1862) 150
Institutions—
domestic, in correspondence with Smithsonian Institution, list of. (R. 1853) 67, **69**, **238**
foreign, in correspondence with Smithsonian Institution, list of. (R. 1864; R. 1865) 188, 209, **64**, **154**, **225**, **243**, **309**, **469**

Institutions—Continued.

in United States and British Provinces of North America, list of—W. J. RHEES ---- **116**

in which phonography is taught. (R. 1856) ---- 91

scientific and literary, in United States, list of principal ---- **335**

Instructions—

for archæological investigations—G. GIBBS. (R. 1861) ---- 149

for collecting coleoptera—J. L. LE CONTE. (R. 1858) ---- 109

for collecting diatomacea—A. M. EDWARDS ---- **366**

for collecting diptera—H. LOEW; R. OSTEN SACKEN. (R. 1858) ---- 109

for collecting hemiptera—P. R. UHLER. (R. 1858) ---- 109

for collecting hymenoptera—B. CLEMENS. (R. 1858) ---- 109

for collecting insects—S. F. BAIRD. (R. 1858) ---- 109

for collecting land and fresh-water shells—J. LEWIS ---- **363**

for collecting lepidoptera—B. CLEMENS. (R. 1858) ---- 109

for collecting myriapods, phalangidæ, etc.—H. C. WOOD. (R. 1866) ---- 214

for collecting nests and eggs of North American birds. (R. 1858) ---- 139

for collecting neuroptera—P. R. UHLER. (R. 1858) ---- 109

for collecting orthoptera—P. R. UHLER. (R. 1858) ---- 109

for observations of thunder storms—J. HENRY ---- **235**

for research relative to ethnology and philology of America—G. GIBBS ---- **160**

in reference to collecting nests and eggs of North American birds—T. M. BREWER ---- 139

to Captain Hall for Arctic observation—J. HENRY and others. (R. 1871) 249

to observatories relative to telegraphic announcement of astronomical discoveries—J. HENRY ---- **263**

Instruments, meteorological,

articles on, in Smithsonian. (R. 1874) ---- 286

description of—L. CASELLA. (R. 1859) ---- 110

description of—A. GUYOT; J. HENRY. (R. 1855) ---- 77, **19**, **148**

Integrals, general, of planetary motion—S. NEWCOMB ---- **281**

Intensity of heat and light of the sun—L. W. MEECH. (R. 1856) ---- 91, **83**

Interest, letter to Secretary of Treasury on payment of, in coin—J. HENRY. (R. 1865) ---- 209

Intermixture of races—G. GIBBS. (R. 1864) ---- 188

Internal structure of the earth—J. G. BARNARD ---- **310**

International Archæological Congress, Antwerp, 1866. (R. 1866) ---- 214

International code of symbols of archæology—G. DE MORTILLET; E. CHANTRE. (R. 1875) ---- 298

International exchange, report on—G. H. BOEHMER ---- **477**

International Exhibition, Philadelphia—*See* Centennial.

International Fisheries Exhibition, Berlin, catalogue of United States exhibit at—G. B. GOODE ---- **413**

Interpolation, methods of, applicable to graduation of irregular series. Parts I, II.—E. L. DE FOREST. (R. 1871; R. 1873) 249, 275

Introduction, letters of. (R. 1865) 209

Introduction to study of Coptic language—M. KABIS. (R. 1867) 215

Invertebrata, marine, from New England coast distributed by United States Fish Commission, list of—A. E. VERRILL; R. RATHBUN. (P. 1879) 333

Invertebrata, marine, of Grand Manan—W. STIMPSON **50**

Invertebrata, marine, of northeastern coast of America, notice of recent additions to—A. E. VERRILL:

Part I. *Annelida*, etc. (P. 1879) 333

Part II. *Mollusca*, with notes on *Annelida*, etc. (P. 1880) 425

Part III. Catalogue of *Mollusca* recently added to fauna of southern New England. (P. 1880) 425

Invertebrate fossils—

check-list of—T. A. CONRAD **200**

from Arkansas, Wyoming, Colorado, and Utah, descriptions of new—C. A. WHITE. (P. 1880) 425

of North America, check-list of—F. B. MEEK **177**, **183**

report on—F. B. MEEK; F. V. HAYDEN 172

Invertebrates, marine, distributed by U. S. National Museum, list of—R RATHBUN. (P. 1881) 465, 467, **471**

Invertebrates—*See* Marine invertebrates.

Investigation of—

anatomy and physiology of the rattlesnake—S. W. MITCHELL **135**

disturbances of horizontal component of magnetic force—A. D. BACHE 162

disturbances of vertical component of magnetic force—A. D. BACHE **175**

eleven year period in amplitude of solar-diurnal variation and disturbances of magnetic declination—A. D. BACHE **113**

illuminating materials—J. HENRY. (R. 1880) 442, **389**

influence of moon on magnetic declination—A. D. BACHE **132**

orbit of Neptune and tables of its motion—S. NEWCOMB **199**

orbit of Uranus, with tables of its motion—S. NEWCOMB **262**

Investigations—

anthropological, in 1879—O. T. MASON. (R. 1879) 345, **420**

archæological, instructions for—G. GIBBS. (R. 1861) 149

chemical and physiological, relative to certain American vertebrata—J. JONES **82**

of Biela's comet—J. S. HUBBARD. (R. 1862) 150

scientific, in Russian America, suggestions relative to—J. HENRY **207**

Iowa—

ancient relics in—J. B. CUTTS. (R. 1872) 271

Delaware county, mounds in—M. W. MOULTON. (R. 1877) 328

Muscatine county, mounds in—T. THOMPSON. (R. 1879) 345

IRBY, J. R. McD. Works and character of Smithson 327

Iron and copper, preservation of, in salt water—A. E. BECQUEREL. (R. 1864.) 188
Ironclad Monadnock, deviation of compasses on—W. HARKNESS 239
Iron rust, destructive effect of. (R. 1861) 149
Irradiation—Abbé MOIGNO. (R. 1866) 214
Irritation of polarized nerve, effect of—B. F. LAUTENBACH. (R. 1878) .. 341, **411**
Irving, Washington, notice of, by C. C. FELTON. (R. 1859) 110
IRVING, W. On publication of Spanish works on New Mexico. (R. 1855) ... 77
IRWIN, B. J. D. Tucson meteorite. (R. 1863) 187
Island—
Petite Anse, salt deposit on—E. W. HILGARD 248
St. Thomas, hurricane in—G. A. LATIMER. (R. 1867) 215
Santa Rosa, history and antiquities of—S. BOWERS. (R. 1877) 323
Islands—
Fanning, natural history of—T. H. STREETS 303
Hawaiian, natural history of—T. H. STREETS 303
Kerguelen, natural history of—J. H. KIDDER and others............ 293, 294
North American, meteorological stations and observers in. (R. 1868) 224, 373
Pacific, natural history of—W. H. PEASE. (R. 1862) 150
Queen Charlotte's, Haidab Indians of—J. G. SWAN 267
St. Croix and Virgin, flora of—H. F. A. EGGERS 313
Shetland, Faroe, and Iceland, vegetable colonization of—C. MARTINS. (R. 1858) 109
Isle Jesus, Canada East, description of observatory on—C. SMALLWOOD. (R. 1856) 91
Isle Royale, Michigan, antiquities of—A. C. DAVIS. (R. 1874) 286
Isohyetal maps—*See* C A. Schott.
Isopoda of New England, notes on—O. HARGER. (P. 1879) 383
Isothermal charts—*See* Temperature.
Italy—*See* Prize questions.

J.

JACKMAN, F. Mounds and earthworks of Rush county, Indiana. (R. 1879.) 345
JACKSON, C. T. Catalogue of rocks, minerals, and ores collected on geological survey in Michigan. (R. 1854) 75
JACKSON, J. B. S. Arsenic acid for protecting anatomical preparations from insects. (P. 1878) 332
Jade. Study of the mineral called *yu* by the Chinese—S. BLONDEL. (R. 1876.) 299
JAMES, T. P. Mosses of Kerguelen Island 294
JAMIN, J. Photo-chemistry. (R. 1867) 215
JAMIN, J. Vegetation and the atmosphere. (R. 1864) 188
Japan—
analysis of coals from—J. A. MACDONALD 202
catalogue of Japanese woods from—L. F. WARD. (P. 1881) 467
examination of infusorial earth from—A. M. EDWARDS 202
geological researches in—R. PUMPELLY **202**
Government of, collection of cotton fibre presented by. (P. 1881) 467
Jargon, Chinook—
bibliography of—G. GIBBS 161
dictionary of—G. GIBBS; H. HALE **161**
vocabulary of—M. LIONNET; B. R. MITCHELL; W. W. TURNER **68**
JEFFERSON, J. P. Mortality of fishes in Gulf of Mexico. (P. 1878) 332
JEFFERSON, J. P.; PORTER, J. Y.; MOORE, T. Destruction of fish in vicinity of the Tortugas. (P. 1878) 332
JEVONS, W. S. On a national library. (R. 1873) 275
JEWETT, C. C.—
Construction of catalogues of libraries and their publication by separate stereotyped titles **47**
Copyright books from 1846 to 1849. (R. 1850) 28
General catalogue system for libraries. (R. 1850) 28
Report on catalogue system. (R. 1849) 21
Report on copyright system. (R. 1851) 51
Report on Halliwell manuscripts. (R. 1852) 57
Report on plan of library. (R. 1847) **H**
Report on public libraries of the United States. (R. 1849) 21, **25**
Reports on library. (R. 1848–1853) **I**, 21, 28, 51, 57, 67
Jewett, C. C., biographical notice of, by R. A. GUILD. (R. 1867) 215
Jewett, E., diagnoses of mollusca collected by—P. P. CARPENTER 252
Johns' (Bishop) library, deposit of—E. CANBY. (R. 1862) 150
JOHNSON, S. H. Notes on mortality among fishes of Gulf of Mexico. (P. 1881.) 467
JOHNSON, S. W. Lectures on agricultural chemistry. (R. 1859) 110
JOHNSON, W. R. Scientific character and researches of Smithson 327

JOHNSON, W. W. Distribution of forest trees in Montana, Idaho, and Washington. (R. 1870) 244
Joints, bibliography of diseases of the—W. W. KEEN 300
JONES, C. C., Jr. Aboriginal structures in Georgia. (R. 1877) 323, 400
JONES, C. C., Jr. Primitive manufacture of spear and arrow points on Savannah river. (R. 1879) 345
JONES, J.—
Analysis of blood 82
Chemical and physiological investigations relative to vertebrata 82
Explorations of aboriginal remains of Tennessee 259
Modes of burial 259
Observations on the liver, pancreas, spleen, kidney, etc 82
On burial caves 259
On earthworks 259
On mounds 259
On relics 259
JONES, J. M. Kjœkken-mœdding in Nova Scotia. (R. 1863) 187
JONES, S. The Kutchin Indians. (R. 1866) 214, 365
JORDAN, D. S.—
Contributions to North American ichthyology:
Part I. Review of Rafinesque's memoirs 305
Part II. Notes on *Cottidæ*, etc.; synopsis *Siluridæ* 306
Part III. Distribution of fishes of Alleghany region; synopsis of family *Catostomidæ* 308
Description of new species of *Caranx* (*Caranx Beani*) from Beaufort, North Carolina. (P. 1880) 425
Description of new species of North American fishes. (P. 1879) 333
Forgotten paper of Dr. Ayres and its bearing on nomenclature of cyprinoid fishes of San Francisco. (P. 1880) 425
Notes on collection of fishes from Clackamas river, Oregon. (P. 1878.) 332
Notes on *Cottidæ*, *Etheostomatidæ*, *Percidæ*, *Centrarchidæ*, *Aphododeridæ*, *Dorysomatidæ*, and *Cyprinidæ* 306
Notes on Curtiss' collection of fishes from Florida. (P. 1880) 425
Notes on Dugès' collection of fishes from Mexico. (P. 1879) 333
Notes on Henshall's collection of fishes from east Florida. (P. 1880) 425
Notes on *Sema* and *Dacentrus*. (P. 1880) 425
Notes on typical specimens of American fishes in British Museum and in Museum d'Histoire Naturelle, Paris. (P. 1879) 333
Review of Rafinesque's memoirs on North American fishes 305
Synopsis of *Catostomidæ* 308
Synopsis of *Siluridæ* of fresh waters of North America 306
JORDAN, D. S.; BRAYTON, A. W. Distribution of fishes of Alleghany region of South Carolina, Georgia, and Tennessee 308

JORDAN, D. S.; GILBERT, C. H.—

Description of new agonoid fish (*Agonus vulsus*) from California. (P. 1880) 425

Description of new agonoid fish (*Brachiopsis xyosternus*) from California. (P. 1880) 425

Description of new embiotocoid fish (*Abeona aurora*) from Monterey, California, with notes on a related species. (P. 1880) 425

Description of new embiotocoid fish (*Cymatogaster rosaceus*) from coast of California. (P. 1880) 425

Description of new embiotocoid fish (*Ditrema atripes*) from coast of California. (P. 1880) 425

Description of new flounder (*Hippoglossoides exilis*) from coast of California. (P. 1880) 425

Description of new flounder (*Platysomatichthys stomias*) from coast of California. (P. 1880) 425

Description of new flounder (*Pleuronichthys verticalis*) from California, with notes on other species. (P. 1880) 425

Description of new flounder (*Xystreurys liolepis*) from Santa Catalina Island, California. (P. 1880) 425

Description of new ray (*Platyrhina triseriata*) from coast of California. (P. 1880) 425

Description of new scorpænoid fish (*Sebastichthys maliger*) from coast of California. (P. 1880) 425

Description of new scorpænoid fish (*Sebastichthys proriger*) from Monterey Bay, California. (P. 1880) 425

Description of new species of deep-water fish (*Icichthys Lockingtoni*) from coast of California. (P. 1880) 425

Description of new species of *Hemirhampus* (*Hemirhampus Rosæ*) from coast of California. (P. 1880) 425

Description of new species of *Nemichthys* (*Nemichthys avocetta*) from Puget Sound. (P. 1880) 425

Description of new species of notidanoid shark (*Hexanchus corinus*) from Pacific coast of United States. (P. 1880) 425

Description of new species of *Paralepis* (*Paralepis coruscans*) from Straits of Juan de Fuca. (P. 1880) 425

Description of new species of *Pomadosys* from Mazatlan. (P. 1881) 467

Description of new species of *Ptychochilus* (*Ptychochilus Harfordii*) from Sacramento river. (P. 1881) 467

Description of new species of ray (*Raia rhina*) from coast of California. (P. 1880) 425

Description of new species of ray (*Raia stellulata*) from Monterey, California. (P. 1880) 425

Description of new species of rock cod (*Sebastichthys serriceps*) from coast of California. (P. 1880) 425

Description of new species of rockfish (*Sebastichthys carnatus*) from coast of California. (P. 1880) 425

JORDAN, D. S.; GILBERT, C. H.—Continued.
Description of new species of rockfish (*Sebastichthys chrysomelas*) from coast of California. (P. 1880) 425
Description of new species of *Sebastichthys* (*Sebastichthys miniatus*) from Monterey bay, California. (P. 1880) 425
Description of new species of *Xenichthys* (*Xenichthys ocyurus*) from west coast of Central America. (P. 1881) 467
Description of new species of *Xiphister* and *Apodichthys* from Monterey, California. (P. 1880) 425
Description of *Sebastichthys mystinus*. (P. 1881) 467
Description of seven new species of sebastoid fishes from coast of California. (P. 1880) 425
Description of two new species of fishes (*Ascelicthys rhodorus* and *Scytalina cerdale*) from Neah bay, Washington Territory. (P. 1880) 425
Description of two new species of flounders (*Parophrys ischyurus* and *Hippoglossoides elassodon*) from Puget Sound. (P. 1880) 425
Description of two new species of *Sebastichthys* (*Sebastichthys entomelas* and *Sebastichthys rhodochloris*) from Monterey bay, Cal. (P. 1880.) 425
Description of two new species of scopeloid fishes (*Sudis ringens* and *Myctophum crenulare*) from Santa Barbara channel, Cal. (P. 1880.) 425
Descriptions of five new species of fishes from Mazatlan, Mexico. (P. 1881) 467
Descriptions of thirty-three new species of fish from Mazatlan, Mexico. (P. 1881) 467
Generic relations of *Belone exilis*. (P. 1880) 425
Generic relations of *Platyrhina exasperata*. (P. 1880) 425
List of fishes collected by Lt. H. E. Nichols in Gulf of California and on west coast of Lower California, with descriptions of four new species. (P. 1881) 467
List of fishes of Pacific coast of United States, with table showing distribution of species. (P. 1880) 425
Note on *Raia inornata*. (P. 1881) 467
Notes on collection of fishes from San Diego, California. (P. 1880) 425
Notes on collection of fishes from Utah Lake. (P. 1880) 425
Notes on collection of fishes made by Lt. H. E. Nichols on west coast of Mexico, with descriptions of new species. (P. 1881) 467
Notes on fishes of Beaufort Harbor, North Carolina. (P. 1878) 332
Notes on fishes of Pacific coast of United States. (P. 1881) 467
Notes on sharks from coast of California. (P. 1880) 425
Occurrence of *Cephaloscyllium laticeps* (Duméril), Gill, in California. (P. 1880) 425
Oil shark of southern California (*Galeorhinus galeus*). (P. 1880) 425
JORDAN, D. S.; JOUY, P. L. Check-list of duplicate fishes of Pacific, distributed by Smithsonian Institution in 1881. (P. 1881) 467
Journal of exploration of western Missouri in 1854—P. R. HOY. (R. 1864) 188

Journals of Board of Regents—*See* Regents.
Journey to the Yukon, Russian America—W. W. KIRBY. (R. 1864) 188
JOUY, P. L. Description of new species of *Squalius* (*Squalius aliciæ*) from Utah Lake. (P. 1881) 467
JOUY, P. L.; JORDAN, D. S. Check-list of duplicates of fishes of Pacific, distributed by Smithsonian Institution in 1881. (P. 1881) 467
Judiciary Committee, Senate, report of, on management of Smithsonian Institution—A. P. BUTLER. (R. 1855) 77
Jupiter, orbit and tables of—J. N. STOCKWELL 232
Jupiter, small planets between Mars and—Prof. LESPIAULT. (R. 1861) 149
Jurassic fossils, check-list of—F. B. MEEK **177**
Jussieus, the, and the natural method—M. FLOURENS. (R. 1867) 215

K.

KABIS, M. Introduction to study of Coptic language. (R. 1867) 215
KÄMTZ; DUFOUR, C. Scintillation of the stars. (R. 1861) 149
KANE, E. K.—
Astronomical observations in the Arctic Seas **129**
Magnetic observations in the Arctic Seas **97**
Meteorological observations in the Arctic Seas **104**
Physical observations in the Arctic Seas **198**
Tidal observations in the Arctic Seas **130**
Kansas—
Butler county, account of storm in—W. HARRISON. (R. 1871) 249
climate of—R. S. ELLIOTT. (R. 1870) 244
coleoptera of—J. L. LE CONTE **126**
new cretaceous invertebrate fossils from—C. A. WHITE. (P. 1879) 333
Kansas City, Missouri, antiquities of—W. H. R. LYKINS. (R. 1877) 323
Karif or Carib language and people—C. H. BERENDT. (R. 1873) 275
KAROLYI, Lieut. VON; CRAIG, B. F. Products of combustion of gun-cotton and gunpowder. (R. 1864) 188
KEEN, W. W. Bibliography of works on diseases 300
KEEN, W. W. Surgical complications and sequels of continued fevers. Toner lecture No. V **300**
Keller, Dr., abstract of report of, on settlements in Switzerland—A. MORLOT. (R. 1863) 187
KELLEY, O. H. Ancient town in Minnesota. (R. 1863) 187
Kelley's Island, Ohio, climate of—G. C. HUNTINGTON. (R. 1866) 214

Kennebec river, Maine, opening and closing of—R. H. GARDINER. (R. 1858.) 109

KENNEDY, J. P. Authority to naval officers to receive and transmit specimens to the Smithsonian Institution 34

Kennicott's explorations—HUDSON'S BAY COMPANY. (R. 1863) 187

Kentucky—

ancient mounds in—R. PETER. (R. 1872) 271

antiquities from—S. S. LYON. (R. 1858) 109

Breckinridge county, age of stone and troglodytes of—R. S. ROBERTSON. (R. 1874) 286

Hancock county, antiquities of—J. FRIEL. (R. 1877) 323

Lexington, ancient mound near—R. PETER. (R. 1871) 249

Union county, exploration of ancient mounds in—S. S. LYON. (R. 1870.) 244

Kepler, his life and works, by M. BERTHRAND. (R. 1869) 228

Kerguelen Island, contributions to natural history of—

I. Ornithology—J. H. KIDDER; E. COUES **293**

II. Oölogy, botany, etc.—J. H. KIDDER and others **294**

Kershner collection from Kerguelen Island 294

Kew Observatory, apparatus and processes employed in verification of barometers at—J. WELSH. (R. 1859) 110

Kew Observatory, experiments on aneroid barometers made at—B. STEWART. (R. 1868) 224

KIDDER, J. H. Experiments on animal heat of fishes. (P. 1879) 333

KIDDER, J. H. Mammals of Kerguelen Island 294

KIDDER, J. H., and others. Natural history of Kerguelen Island **294**

KIDDER, J. H.; COUES, E. Birds of Kerguelen Island **293**

Kidney, observations on—J. JONES 82

Kinetic theories of gravitation—W. B. TAYLOR. (R. 1876) 299, **395**

KING, C. B. Catalogue of engravings presented to Smithsonian. (R. 1861) 149

KING, W. M. Account of Indian burial in California. (R. 1874) 286

KIPP, J. Accuracy of Catlin's account of Mandan ceremonies. (R. 1872) 271

KIRBY, W. W. Journey to the Yukon, Russian America. (R. 1864) 188

KIRKWOOD, D. Asteroids between Mars and Jupiter. (R. 1876) 299

Kitchen-midden in Costa Rica, note on shells from—W. H. DALL. (P. 1878.) 332

Kitchen-midden—*See* Kjœkken-mœddings.

Kjœkken-mœddings in Nova Scotia—J. M. JONES. (R. 1863) 187

Kjœkken-mœddings on northwest coast of America—P. SCHUMACHER. (R. 1873; R. 1874) 275, 286

Klamath lake dialect, details of Indian conjurer's practice in—A. S. GATSCHET. (E. 1879-80) 476

Klamath lake dialect, "The Relapse" in—A. S. GATSCHET. (E. 1879-80) 476

KLETZINSKY, Prof. Nitrogen bodies of modern chemistry. (R. 1872) 271

KNAPP, G. Earthworks on Arkansas river. (R. 1877) 323

KNIGHT, E. H. Study of savage weapons at Centennial Exhibition. (R. 1879) 345, **415**

KNIGHT, G. H. New system of weights and measures. (R. 1867) ---------- 215

KNIGHT, R. T.; HENRY, J. Connection of gales of wind and appearance of aurora. (R. 1871) ---------- 249

Knowledge of cryptogamous plants, present state of—W. REICHARDT. (R. 1871) 249

KOHL, J. G. On collection of charts and maps of America. (R. 1856) ------ 91

KORNHUBER, G. A. Alternate generation and parthenogenesis in the animal kingdom. (R. 1871) ---------- 249

KRON, F. J. Antiquities of Stanley and Montgomery counties, North Carolina. (R. 1874) ---------- 286

KRON, H. J. Lightning discharges. (R. 1867) ---------- 215

KUMLIEN, L.—

Ethnology, mammals, and birds of Arctic America ---------- 342

Howgate Polar Expedition, natural history of Arctic America ---------- 342

Report on explorations in Greenland. (R. 1878) ---------- 341

KUNHARDT AND COMPANY. Free freight to Smithsonian Institution between United States and Germany. (R. 1861) ---------- 149

Kushkushkee, Indian village near Newcastle, Penn., account of—E. M. McCONNELL. (R. 1871) ---------- 249

Kutchin Indians—S. JONES. (R. 1866) ---------- 214, 365

L.

Labels for collections, etc. ---------- 164

LABOULAYE, E. Acknowledgment for books on education. (R. 1867) ---------- 215

Lacustrian cities of Switzerland—F. TROYON. (R. 1861) ---------- 149

Lacustrian constructions or palafittes of the lake of Neuchâtel—E. DESOR. (R. 1865) ---------- 209, **360**

Lacustrian habitations of Switzerland—F. TROYON. (R. 1861) ---------- 149

Lacustrian settlements in Switzerland, abstract of Dr. Keller's report on—A. MORLOT. (R. 1863) ---------- 187

La Have Banks, occurrence of *Lycodes vahlii* on—G. B. GOODE; T. H. BEAN. (P. 1879) ---------- 333

Lake Neuchâtel, lacustrian constructions of—E. DESOR. (R. 1865) ---------- 209

Lake Pepin, antiquities on banks of—L. C. ESTES. (R. 1866) ---------- 214

Lake Superior, ancient mining on shores of—C. WHITTLESEY ---------- **155**

Lake Superior copper region, circular relative to ancient mining in—J. HENRY. (R. 1861) ---------- 149

Lake Superior, Isle Royale, antiquities of—A. C. DAVIS. (R. 1874) ---------- 286

Lake Winnipeg, notes on egging expedition to—D. GUNN. (R. 1867) 215
Lakes, dates of opening and closing of—F. B. HOUGH 182
Lakes, North American, fluctuations of level in—C. WHITTLESEY **119**
Lakes, Norwegian, statistics relative to—O. E. DREUTZER. (R. 1866) 214
Lalande observations, 1795—S. C. WALKER 5
LAMARCK, J. B. Distinction between tornadoes and tempests. (R. 1871) 249
LAMONT, J. The solar eclipse of July 18, 1860. (R. 1864) 188
Land and fresh-water shells—*See* Shells.
Land, cessions of, by Indian tribes to United States—C. C. ROYCE. (E. 1879-80.) 476
Land, gradual approach of sea upon—S. P. MAYBERRY. (R. 1867) 215
Language—
Carib or Karif—C. H. BERENDT. (R. 1873) 275
Coptic, introduction to the study of—M. KABIS. (R. 1867) 215
Dakota, grammar and dictionary of—S. R. RIGGS **40**
dominant, for science—A. DE CANDOLLE; J. E. GRAY. (R. 1874) 286
evolution of—J. W. POWELL. (E. 1879-80) 476
of aboriginal Indians of America—G. GIBBS. (R. 1870) 244
of Dakota or Sioux Indians—F. L. O. ROEHRIG. (R. 1871) 249, **378**
of Navajos, said to resemble the Welsh—S. Y. MCMASTERS. (R. 1865.) 209
phonetic, vocal sounds of L. Bridgman compared with elements of—F. LIEBER 12
sign, among North American Indians compared with that among other peoples and deaf mutes—G. MALLERY. (E. 1879-80) 476
trade, of Oregon, dictionary of—G. GIBBS **161**
trade, of Oregon, vocabulary of—B. R. MITCHELL; W. W. TURNER **68**
Yoruba, of Africa, grammar and dictionary of—T. J. BOWEN **98**
Languages—
Indian—G. FLACHENECKER. (R. 1862) 150
Indian—G. GIBBS. (R. 1865) 209
Indian, method of recording—J. O. DORSEY; A. S. GATSCHET; S. R. RIGGS. (E. 1879-80) 476
LAPHAM, I. A. Antiquities of Wisconsin **70**
Lapidary, aboriginal, stock-in-trade of—C. RAU. (R. 1877) 323, 440, **402**
La Place, eulogy on, by F. ARAGO. (R. 1874) 286
La Rive—*See* De La Rive.
Lartet, E., scientific labors of, by F. FISHER. (R. 1872) 271
Larynx, bibliography of diseases of the—W. W. KEEN 300
Latiloid genera, note on—T. GILL. (P. 1881) 467
Latimer collection of antiquities from Porto Rico—O. T. MASON. (R. 1876.) 299, **397**
LATIMER, G. A.—
Earthquakes in St. Thomas. (R. 1867) 215
Hurricane at Tortola, St. Thomas, and Porto Rico. (R. 1867) 215
Meteorology of Porto Rico. (R. 1871) 249

Latin vocabulary with comparative words in English, Spanish, and French --- **170**

Latitudes and longitudes, Arctic—E. K. Kane---------- **129**

Laugel, A. The sun, its chemical analysis. (R. 1861)---------- 149

Lausanne, report on ethnological collections of Museum at—F. Troyon. (R. 1861)---------- 149

Lautenbach, B. F. Effect of irritation of a polarized nerve. (R. 1878.) 341, **411**

Law, A. E. Antiquities of Blount county, Tennessee. (R. 1874)---------- 286

Law of deposit of flood-tide—C. H. Davis ---------- **33**

Law of variation of temperature in ascending currents of air—J. Hann. (R. 1877)---------- 323, **398**

Law of variation of temperature in ascending moist currents—L. Sohncke. (R. 1877) ---------- 323, **398**

Lawrence, G. N.—

- Birds of southwestern Mexico collected by F. E. Sumichrast ---------- **295**
- Catalogue of Ober's collection of birds of Antigua and Barbuda, with his notes. (P. 1878)---------- 332
- Catalogue of Ober's collection of birds of Dominica, with his notes and observations. (P. 1878) ---------- 332
- Catalogue of Ober's collection of birds of Grenada, including others seen, but not obtained. (P. 1878) ---------- 332
- Catalogue of Ober's collection of birds of Guadeloupe. (P. 1878)------ 332
- Catalogue of Ober's collection of birds of Lesser Antilles, with table showing distribution. (P. 1878)---------- 332
- Catalogue of Ober's collection of birds of Martinique. (P. 1878) ------ 332
- Catalogue of Ober's collection of birds of St. Vincent, with his notes. (P. 1878) ---------- 332
- Description of new species of bird of family *Turdidæ* from Dominica, W. I. (P. 1880)---------- 425
- Description of new species of *Icterus* from West Indies. (P. 1880) ---- 425
- Description of new species of parrot, of genus *Chrysotis*, from Dominica. (P. 1880) ---------- 425
- Description of new subspecies of *Loxigilla* from West Indies. (P. 1881.) 467

Laws of atmospheric circulation over the earth—J. H. Coffin ---------- 268

Lea, I. Check-list of the shells of North America ---------- **128**

Le Conte, John. Constants of nature. (R. 1878) ---------- 341

Le Conte, J. L.—

- Classification of coleoptera of North America. Parts I, II-------- **136, 265**
- Coleoptera of Kansas and eastern New Mexico---------- **126**
- Instructions for collecting coleoptera. (R. 1858)---------- 109
- List of coleoptera of North America. Part I---------- **140**
- New species of North American coleoptera. Parts I, II---------- **167, 264**
- Revision of Melsheimer's catalogue of coleoptera---------- **62**

Le Conte, Joseph. Lecture on coal. (R. 1857)---------- 107

Lecture on American fire-alarm telegraph—W. F. Channing. (R. 1854) ---- 75

Lectures on—
agricultural chemistry—S. W. Johnson. (R. 1859) 110
Arctic explorations—I. I. Hayes. (R. 1861) 149
astronomy—A. Caswell. (R. 1858) 109
bridges—F. Rogers. (R. 1861) 149
bridges and roads—F. Rogers. (R. 1860) 147
the camel—G. P. Marsh. (R. 1854) 75
cancerous tumors. Toner lecture No. I—J. J. Woodward **266**
coal—J. Le Conte. (R. 1857) 107
dual character of the brain. Toner lecture No. II—C. E. Brown-Séquard. **291**
electro-physiology—C. Matteucci. (R. 1865) 209
insect instincts and transformations—J. G. Morris. (R. 1855) 77
marine algæ—W. H. Harvey. (R. 1855) 77
meteoric stones—J. L. Smith. (R. 1855) 77
meteorology—R. Russell, with notes by J. Henry. (R. 1854) 75
mollusca, or shell-fish and their allies—P. P. Carpenter. (R. 1860.) 147, **152**
natural history as applied to farming and gardening—J. G. Morris. (R. 1855) 77
nature and cure of bites of serpents and wounds of poisoned arrows—D. Brainard. (R. 1854) 75
nature of reparatory inflammation in arteries after ligature, etc. Toner lecture No. VII—E. O. Shakespeare **321**
oxygen and its combinations—G. I. Chace. (R. 1855) 77
physical ethnology—D. Wilson. (R. 1862) 150
planetary disturbances—E. S. Snell. (R. 1855) 77
principles of linguistic science—W. D. Whitney. (R. 1863) 187, **352**
relations of time and space—S. Alexander. (R. 1861) 149
sanitary drainage of Washington. Toner lecture No. VIII—G. E. Waring, Jr. **349**
shells of Gulf of California—P. P. Carpenter. (R. 1859) 110
strain and over-action of the heart. Toner lecture No. III—J. M. Da Costa **279**
study of high antiquity in Europe—A. Morlot. (R. 1862; R. 1864.) 150, 188
study of nature and mechanism of fever. Toner lecture No. IV—H. C. Wood **282**
surgical complications and sequels of fevers. Toner lecture No. V—W. W. Keen **300**
Switzerland—A. D. Bache. (R. 1870) 244
syllabus of a course of, on physics—J. Henry. (R. 1856) 91
undulatory theory of light—F. A. P. Barnard. (R. 1862) 150
the Union—H. Reed. (R. 1854) 75
vastness of visible creation—S. Alexander. (R. 1857) 107
zone of small planets between Mars and Jupiter—E. Loomis. (R. 1854.) 75

Lectures, Toner—
No. I. Cancerous tumors—Woodward 266
II. Dual character of brain—Brown-Séquard 291
III. Over-action of heart—Da Costa 279
IV. Study of fever—Wood 282
V. Continued fevers—Keen 300
VI. Sub-cutaneous surgery—Adams 302
VII. Reparatory inflammation—Shakespeare 321
VIII. Sanitary drainage of Washington—Waring 349
Lee, Dr. Progress of astronomical photography. (R. 1861) 149
Lee, J. C. Y. Ancient ruin in Arizona. (R. 1872) 271
Legacy—*See* Bequest.
Legendre, memoir of, by E. De Beaumont. (R. 1867) 215
Leidy, J.—
Ancient fauna of Nebraska 58
Cretaceous reptiles of the United States 192
Extinct sloth tribe of North America 72
Extinct species of American ox 41
Fauna and flora within living animals 44
On parasites 44
Report on fossils from Nebraska. (R. 1851) 51
Review of cretaceous reptiles of United States. (R. 1864) 188
Leidy, J.; Tryon, G. W. Report on shells presented to Academy of Natural Sciences. (R. 1865) 209
Leipsic Museum of Ethnology—A. Schott; O. T. Mason. (R. 1873) 275
Lemström, S.; De La Rive, A. A. Electricity of the atmosphere and the aurora borealis. (R. 1874) 286
Lens, account of Priestley's—J. Henry. (R. 1859) 110
Lepidopsetta isolepis, new flat fish, found in markets of San Francisco, note on—W. N. Lockington. (P. 1880) 425
Lepidoptera—
appendix to Morris' synopsis of—B. Clemens 133
described, of North America, catalogue of—J. G. Morris 118
described, of North America, synopsis of. Part I—J. G. Morris 133
diurnal, of Arctic America—W. H. Edwards 342
instructions for collecting—B. Clemens. (R. 1858) 109
introduction to Morris' synopsis of—V. Heinemann 133
method of preserving—T. R. Peale. (R. 1863) 187
nocturnal, of Arctic America—S. H. Scudder 342
notes to Morris' synopsis of—W. H. Edwards 133
Lepsius, R. Presentation of books on Egypt. (R. 1860) 147
Leptocardii, arrangement of families of—T. Gill 247
Lesley, J. P. On the classification of books. (R. 1862) 150

LESPIAULT, Prof. Small planets between Mars and Jupiter. (R. 1861) 149
Lesser Antilles, catalogue of Ober's collection of birds of—G. N. LAWRENCE. (P. 1878) 332
Letter—
by M. Hoek in reference to meteoric shower of November 13, 1867 ...... **217**
from Robert Hare relative to gift of apparatus ...... **I**, 329
from Joseph Henry to Secretary Treasury on payment of interest in coin. (R. 1865) 209
from Richard Rush relative to Smithson. (R. 1853) 67, 328
LETTERMAN, J. Sketch of the Navajo Indians. (R. 1855) 77
Letters—
of introduction. (R. 1865) 209
on work of the Museum—B. PHILLIPS. (P. 1881) 467, **454**
relative to programme of organization of Smithsonian Institution 328
relative to Smithson's bequest 328
Leurynnis, Lockington, identity of, with *Lycodopsis*, Collet—T. GILL. (P. 1880) 425
Level, fluctuations of, in North American lakes—C. WHITTLESEY **119**
LEWIS, J. Instructions for collecting land and fresh-water shells. (R. 1866.) 214, **363**
Lewis, J., letter of, to G. W. Tryon, Jr., on shells 253
LEWIS; QUALE. Account of cryolite of Greenland. (R. 1866) 214
Lexington, Kentucky, ancient mound near—R. PETER. (R. 1871) 249
Liberia, mixed races in—E. D. BLYDEN. (R. 1870) 244
Liberia College, facts respecting—A. CRUMMELL. (R. 1861) 149
Libraries—
circular respecting new report on—J. HENRY. (R. 1854) 75
construction of catalogues of, and their publication by means of separate stereotyped titles—C. C. JEWETT **47**
general catalogue system for—C. C. JEWETT. (R. 1850) 28
general catalogue system for, report of Commission on. (R. 1850) 28
public, in United States and British Provinces, list of—W. J. RHEES. **116**, **238**
public of United States, notices of—C. C. JEWETT. (R. 1849) 21, **25**
report of Commission on stereotype catalogue of **47**
rules for cataloguing—C. C. JEWETT **47**
Library—
Beaufort, deposit of—E. M. STANTON. (R. 1862) 150
Bishop Johns', deposit of—E. CANBY. (R. 1862) 150
Imperial, of Vienna, books presented by. (R. 1865) 209
of Bureau of Ethnology, catalogue of linguistic manuscripts in—J. C. PILLING. (E. 1879–80) 476
of Indian linguistics, account of—J. G. SHEA. (R. 1861) 149
of National Museum, circular asking contributions to. (P. 1881) ... 467, **458**
on a national—W. S. JEVONS. (R. 1873) 275

Library of Congress—
act of Congress to transfer Smithsonian library to. (R. 1865) ------ 209, 328
catalogue of publications of societies and of periodical works belonging to the Smithsonian Institution deposited in ---------------------------- **179**
meteorological articles received by the Smithsonian Institution and deposited in. (R. 1871; R. 1873) ---------------------------- 249, 275
Library of Smithsonian Institution—
act of Congress to transfer, to Library of Congress. (R. 1865) ------ 209, 328
additions to—*See* each annual report.
and copyright system—C. C. JEWETT. (R. 1851) -------------------- 51
and Halliwell manuscripts, report on—C. C. JEWETT. (R. 1852) ------ 57
catalogue of publications of societies and other periodical works in, **117**, **179**
donations to, from foreign institutions. (R. 1864) -------------------- 188
publications of learned societies and periodicals in. Parts I, II ------ **73**, **85**
report on—C. C. JEWETT. (R. 1848, 1849, 1853) ---------------- I, 21, 67
report on plan of—C. C. JEWETT. (R. 1847) ------------------------ **H**
statistics of, 1846–1877 -- 329
Lichens of Arctic America—E. TUCKERMAN ---------------------------- 342
Lichens of Kerguelen Island—E. TUCKERMAN ---------------------------- 294
LIEBER, F. Vocal sounds of Laura Bridgman compared with elements of phonetic language -- **12**
LIEBIG, J. VON. Induction and deduction. (R. 1870) -------------------- 244
Life—
and character of Joseph Henry—J. C. WELLING ---------------- 356, **338**
and labors of Henry Gustavus Magnus. (R. 1870) -------------------- 244
and scientific labors of Stefano Marianini—C. MATTEUCCI. (R. 1869) -- 228
and works of Michael Faraday—A. A. DE LA RIVE. (R. 1867) ------- 215
and works of Kepler—M. BERTHRAND. (R. 1869) -------------------- 228
of George Catlin—J. HENRY. (R. 1872) ---------------------------- 271
of Prof. Chester Dewey—M. B. ANDERSON. (R. 1870) -------------- 244
Life—*See* Biography, Eulogy, Memoirs.
Light—
and heat of sun, relative intensity of—L. W. MEECH. (R. 1856) ---- 91, **83**
polar, or aurora borealis, its phenomena and laws—E. LOOMIS. (R. 1865.) 209
undulatory theory of, lectures on—F. A. P. BARNARD. (R. 1862) ----- 150
velocity of, essay on—C. DELAUNAY. (R. 1864) ---------------- 188, **354**
Light-House Board—
investigations by, relative to illuminating materials—J. HENRY. (R. 1880) -- 442, **389**
proceedings of, on death of J. Henry ---------------------------- 356
researches by, in sound—J. HENRY. (R. 1878) ---------------- 341, **406**
Lighting, architecture in relation to—D. B. REID. (R. 1856) -------------- 91

Lightning—
and thunder, observations on—S. MASTERMAN. (R. 1855) 77
discharges, accounts of—G. W. DODGE and others. (R. 1867) 215
effect of—S. L. HILLIER. (R. 1866) 214
Lightning-rods, directions for constructing—J. HENRY **237**
Lille, Imperial Society of Science, Agriculture, and Arts of. Prize questions. (R. 1865) 209
LILLJEBORG, W. Outline of systematic review of the classification of birds. (R. 1865) 209, **364**
Limitations to use of some anthropological data—J. W. POWELL. (E. 1879-80.) 476
Limpets from deep waters off eastern coast of U. S.—W. H. DALL. (P. 1881.) 467
Limpets of Alaska and Arctic region, report on—W. H. DALL. (P. 1878) 332
Lindheimer's botanical exploration in New Mexico and California, account of—A. GRAY. (R. 1849) 21
Linguistic manuscripts in library of Bureau of Ethnology, catalogue of—J. C. PILLING. (E. 1879-80) 476
Linguistic science, lectures on principles of—W. D. WHITNEY. (R. 1863.) 187, **352**
Linguistics, Indian, account of library of—J. G. SHEA. (R. 1861) 149
Linguistics, Indian, recommendation of Shea's—G. GIBBS and others. (R. 1861.) 149
LIONNET, M. Vocabulary of the Chinook jargon 68
Liparis ranula, new species of, obtained by U. S. Fish Commission off Halifax, Nova Scotia—G. B. GOODE; T. H. BEAN. (P. 1879) 333
Liquids, expansion of, by heat—F. W. CLARKE 289
Liquids, specific heats of—F. W. CLARKE 276
Lisboa, M. M., books on Brazil, presented by. (R. 1865) 209
List of—
additions to Museum—*See* each annual report.
addresses of foreign institutions, 1862-1865. (R. 1865) 209
algæ of Rhode Island—S. T. OLNEY 241
American correspondents **69**
American libraries and public institutions—W. J. RHEES **238**
anthropological publications of Charles Rau. (P. 1881) 467
apparatus available for scientific research. (R. 1878) 341
articles deposited by Smithsonian Institution in Corcoran Gallery of Art. (R. 1874) 286
birds and mammalia of Missouri river—E. HARRIS. (R. 1850) 28
birds of central California, partial—L. BELDING. (P. 1878) 332
birds of District of Columbia—E. COUES; S. S. PRENTISS. (R. 1861) 149
casts of heads of Indian boys and girls at Hampton, Va.—R. H. PRATT. (P. 1879) 333
coleoptera of North America. Part I—J. L. LE CONTE **140**
collections presented by foreign Centennial commissioners. (R. 1876) 299

List of—Continued.
described birds of Mexico, Central America, and West Indies not in Smithsonian Institution ---- **185**
described species of humming-birds—D. G. Elliot ---- **334**
desiderata among North American birds—R. Ridgway. (P. 1881) ---- **467**
domestic institutions in correspondence with Smithsonian Institution. **69**, **238**
duplicates of fishes of Pacific coast distributed by Smithsonian Institution in 1881—D. S. Jordan; P. L. Jouy. (P. 1881) ---- 467
European fishes in National Museum—T. H. Bean. (P. 1879) ---- 383
expeditions from which specimens in Museum have been derived—S. F. Baird. (R. 1867) ---- 215
fishes collected by Lieut. H. E. Nichols in Gulf of California—D. S. Jordan; C. H. Gilbert. (P. 1881) ---- 467
fishes of Pacific coast of United States—D. S. Jordan; C. H. Gilbert. (P. 1880) ---- 425
foreign agents of Smithsonian Institution in 1876. (*See also* annual reports) ---- 290
foreign correspondents of Smithsonian Institution. **64**, **154**, **225**, **243**, **309**, **469**
foreign correspondents of Smithsonian Institution, systematic index to ---- **257**
generic names of animals—S. H. Scudder ---- **470**
Indian vocabularies received from the Wheeler Expedition. (R. 1874.) 286
institutions, libraries, colleges, and other establishments in correspondence with the Smithsonian Institution—W. J. Rhees ---- **238**
invertebrate fossils of North America—
Cretaceous and jurassic—F. B. Meek ---- **177**
Eocene and oligocene—T. A. Conrad ---- **200**
Miocene—F. B. Meek ---- **183**
marine invertebrata of New England distributed by United States Fish Commission—A. E. Verrill; R. Rathbun. (P. 1879) ---- 383
marine invertebrates, mainly from New England, distributed by U. S. National Museum—R. Rathbun. (P. 1881) ---- 467, **465**, **471**
meteorological material contributed to Smithsonian Institution. (R. 1860–1865, 1867–1871) ---- 147, 149, 150, 187, 188, 209, 215, 224, 228, 244, 249
meteorological stations and observers. (R. 1849; R. 1853–1873) ---- 21, 67, 75, 77, 91, 107, 109, 110, 147, 149, 150, 187, 188, 209, 214, 215, 224, 228, 244, 249, 271, 275.
minerals in United States National Museum—F. M. Endlich. (R. 1873; P. 1880) ---- 275, 425
North American batrachia and reptilia—E. D. Cope ---- **292**
North American species of myriapods of family *Lysiopetalidæ*—J. A. Ryder. (P. 1880) ---- 425
official publications of the United States Government between 1868 and 1881—G. H. Boehmer ---- 447
papers presented to Royal Society by James Smithson. (R. 1853) ---- 67, 330
periodicals received by the Institution. (R. 1880) ---- **Q**, 442, **436**

List of—Continued.

photographic portraits of North American Indians in Smithsonian Institution **216**

plants of the upper Missouri—T. C. PORTER. (R. 1850) 28

plants of Washington and vicinity—L. F. WARD **460**

principal literary and scientific institutions in United States, 1879 .... **335**

public libraries, institutions, and societies in United States and British Provinces of North America—W. J. RHEES **116**

publications of the Smithsonian Institution. (R. 1868) 74, 203, 224, 226, 245, 278, 290, 301, 344, 437, 478

publications of the United States National Museum. (P. 1881) 467, **474**

Regents, officers, and assistants of the Smithsonian Institution and U. S. National Museum. (*See also* each annual report) 466, **290**

scientific papers of A. D. Bache—B. A. GOULD. (R. 1870) 244, 329, 379

shells of exploring expedition **193**

shells of North America—I. LEA; P. P. CARPENTER; W. STIMPSON; W. G. BINNEY; T. PRIME **128**

species of Middle and South American birds not in United States National Museum—R. RIDGWAY. (P. 1881) 467

substances derived from animal kingdom—G. B. GOODE 297

Literary exchanges—*See* Exchanges.

Literary study of jade—S. BLONDEL. (R. 1876) 299

Littoral marine fauna of Provincetown, Mass.—R. RATHBUN. (P. 1880) 425

Liver, observations on the—J. JONES 82

LIVERMORE, G. Report on Jewett's general stereotype catalogue of public libraries 47

Living animals, flora and fauna within—J. LEIDY **44**

Lloyd, North German, free freight between Germany and the United States. (R. 1858) 109

LLOYD, W. A. Exchange of specimens. (R. 1867) 215

LLOYD, W. A. Sparrows sent to the United States. (R. 1867) 215

LOCKE, J. Catalogue of rocks, minerals, ores, and fossils. (R. 1854) 75

LOCKE, J. Observations on terrestrial magnetism **35**

LOCKETT, S. H. Mounds in Louisiana. (R. 1872) 271

LOCKINGTON, W. N.—

Description of new chiroid fish (*Myriolepis zonifer*) from Monterey Bay, California. (P. 1880) 425

Description of new fish from Alaska (*Uranidea microstoma*). (P. 1880.) 425

Description of new genus and some new species of California fishes (*Icosteus ænigmaticus* and *Osmerus attenuatus*). (P. 1880) 425

Description of new genus and species of *Cottidæ*. (P. 1881) 467

Description of new sparoid fish (*Sparus brachysomus*) from Lower California. (P. 1880) 425

LOCKINGTON, W. N.—Continued.
Description of new species of *Agonidæ* (*Brachyopsis verrucosus*) from coast of California. (P. 1880) 425
Description of new species of *Prionotus* (*Prionotus stephanophyrs*) from coast of California. (P. 1880) 425
Descriptions of new genera and species of fishes from coast of California. (P. 1879) 333
Note on new flat fish (*Lepidopsetta isolepis*) found in markets of San Francisco. (P. 1880) 425
Remarks on species of genus *Chirus* found in San Francisco market. (P. 1880) 425
Review of the *Pleuronectidæ* of San Francisco. (P. 1879) 333
Locusts and grasshoppers of America—A. S. TAYLOR. (R. 1858) 109
LOEW, H.—
Monographs of the diptera of North America—
Part I. Edited by R. OSTEN SACKEN **141**
Part II. Edited by R. OSTEN SACKEN **171**
Part III **256**
Review of North American *Trypetina* 256
LOEW, H.; OSTEN SACKEN, R. Instructions for collecting diptera. (R. 1858.) 109
LOGAN, T. M.—
Climate of California. (R. 1855) 77
Meteorological observations at Sacramento, California. (R. 1854) 75
Meteorology of Sacramento, California. (R. 1857) 107
LOGAN, W. E. Request for duplicate shells. (R. 1859) 110
LOMBARD, H. C. Report on the transactions of Society of Physics and Natural History of Geneva, July, 1868, to June, 1869. (R. 1869) 228
Lombardy, Royal Scientific and Literary Institute of. Prize questions. (R. 1865.) 209
London Institution of Civil Engineers. Prize questions. (R. 1862) 150
London Royal Horticultural Society. Exchange of publications. (R. 1861) 149
London, Royal Society of, origin and history of—C. A. ALEXANDER. (R. 1863.) 187
LONGFELLOW, H. W., and others. Report of American Academy of Arts and Sciences on organization of Smithsonian Institution. (R. 1853) 67
Long Island, fishes on coast of New Jersey and—S. F. BAIRD. (R. 1854.) 75, **348**
Longitude, transatlantic—B. A. GOULD **223**
Longitudes, Arctic—E. K. KANE 129
LOOMIS, E.—
Aurora borealis, or polar light, its phenomena and laws. (R. 1865) 209
Lecture on zone of small planets between Mars and Jupiter. (R. 1854.) 75
On certain storms in Europe and America, December, 1836 **127**
Report on meteorology of the United States. (R. 1847) **H**
Lopholatilus chamæleonticeps, new genus and species of fish from New England, description of—G. B. GOODE; T. H. BEAN. (P. 1879) 333
Loucheux Indians—W. L. HARDISTY. (R. 1866) 214, 365

LOUD, F. H. Discussion of Prof. Snell's barometric observations. (R. 1880.) 442, **435**
Louisiana, Caddo parish, Indian remains in—T. P. HOTCHKISS. (R. 1872) --- 271
Louisiana, lower, geology of, and salt deposit of Petite Anse Island—E. W. HILGARD ---- **248**
Louisiana, mounds in—S. H. LOCKETT. (R. 1872) ---- 271
LOVERING, J. Memorial of J. Henry ---- 356
Lowe, T. S. C., aeronautic voyage of, reply to memorial on—J. HENRY. (R. 1860) ---- 147
Lowe, T. S. C., memorial of citizens of Philadelphia relative to aeronautic voyage of, across the Atlantic. (R. 1860) ---- 147
Loxigilla, description of new subspecies of, from West Indies—G. N. LAWRENCE. (P. 1881) ---- 467
LUBBOCK, J. North American archæology. (R. 1862) ---- 150
LUBBOCK, J. Social and religious condition of lower races of man. (R. 1869.) 228
Lucernariæ, and their allies, anatomy and physiology of—H. J. CLARK ---- **242**
LUDEWIG, H. E., and others. On publication of Spanish works on New Mexico. (R. 1855) ---- 77
LUGGER, O. Occurrence of Canada porcupine in Maryland. (P. 1881) ---- 467
Lunar effect on magnetic force—A. D. BACHE ---- 195
LUPTON, N. T. Breeding habits of sea catfish (*Ariopsis milberti*). (P. 1878.) 332
Luray cavern, blind form of *Lysiopetalidæ* from—J. A. RYDER. (P. 1880) --- 425
Luray cavern, report of visit to—O. T. MASON and others. (R. 1880) ---- 442, **433**
Lussac, Gay, eulogy on, by F. ARAGO. (R. 1876) ---- 299
Lutjanus Blackfordii, from coast of Florida, description of—G. B. GOODE; T. H. BEAN. (P. 1878) ---- 332
Lutjanus Stearnsii, from coast of Florida, description of—G. B. GOODE; T. H. BEAN. (P. 1878) ---- 332
Lycodes paxillus, description of species of—G. B. GOODE; T. H. BEAN. (P. 1879) 333
Lycodes Turneri, from Alaska, description of—T. H. BEAN. (P. 1878) ---- 33
Lycodes Vahlii, occurrence of, on La Have and Grand Banks—G. B. GOODE; T. H. BEAN. (P. 1879) ---- 333
Lycodopsis, Collett, identity of, with *Leurynnis*, Lockington—T. GILL. (P. 1880) ---- 425
Lycopodiaceæ of Kerguelen Island—A. GRAY ---- 294
LYKINS, W. H. R. Antiquities of Kansas City, Missouri. (R. 1877) ---- 323
LYMAN, T. Ethnographical collections. (R. 1862) ---- 150
LYON, S. S. Antiquities from Kentucky. (R. 1858) ---- 109
LYON, S. S. Mounds in Union county, Kentucky. (R. 1870) ---- 244
LYON, W. B. Antiquities in New Mexico. (R. 1871) ---- 249
Lysiopetalidæ, North American species of—J. A. RYDER. (P. 1880) ---- 425

M.

McClintock, F. L. Meteorological observations in the Arctic Seas ---------- **146**
McConnell, E. M. Account of old Indian village, Kushkushkee, near Newcastle, Pennsylvania. (R. 1871) ---------- 249
McCosh, J. Prayer at memorial service of Prof. Joseph Henry ---------- 356
Macdonald, J. A. Analyses of Chinese and Japanese coals ---------- 202
McHenry, J. W.; Haile, J. Antiquities of Jackson Co., Tenn. (R. 1874.) 286
McKay, C. L. Review of *Centrarchidæ*. (P. 1881) ---------- 467
McKinley, W. Mounds in McIntosh and Early counties, Georgia. (R. 1872.) 271
McMasters, S. Y. Language of Navajos said to resemble the Welsh. (R. 1865.) 209
McParlin, T. A. Notes on history and climate of New Mexico. (R. 1877.) 323, **396**
McWhorter, T. Ancient mounds of Mercer county, Illinois. (R. 1874) --- 286
Mackerel, the frigate, (*Auxis Rochei*,) on New England coast—G. B. Goode. (P. 1880) ---------- 425
Madrid Royal Academy of Science. Exchanges. (R. 1861) ---------- 149
Maedler, J. H. Movement of the stars around a central point. (R. 1859) -- 110
Magendie, F., memoir of, by M. Flourens. (R. 1866) ---------- 214
Magnetic—
observations at Girard College, discussion of—A. D. Bache:
Part I. Eleven year period in amplitude of solar diurnal variation -- **113**
Part II. Solar diurnal variation in magnetic declination ---------- **121**
Part III. Influence of moon on magnetic declination ---------- **132**
Parts IV, V, VI. Horizontal force ---------- **162**
Parts VII, VIII, IX. Vertical force ---------- **175**
Parts X, XI, XII. Dip and total force ---------- **186**
Parts I–XII. Complete ---------- **195**
observations in the Arctic Seas—E. K. Kane ---------- **97**
observations in the Arctic Seas—I. I. Hayes ---------- 196
observations, on continuance of—E. Sabine. (R. 1858) ---------- 109
observations on the iron-clad "Monadnock"—W. Harkness ---------- **239**
observatory at the Smithsonian Institution, description of—J. E. Hilgard. (R. 1859) ---------- 110
storms—E. Sabine. (R. 1860) ---------- 147
survey of Pennsylvania, (etc.)—A. D. Bache ---------- **166**
telegraph—*See* Telegraph.
Magnetism—
history of discovery relative to. (R. 1863) ---------- 187
later views of connection of electricity and—H. Helmholtz; J. C. Maxwell. (R. 1873) ---------- 275
terrestrial, observations on—W. Harkness ---------- **239**
terrestrial, observations on—J. Locke ---------- **35**
terrestrial, observations on, in Mexico—Baron von Müller; A. Sonntag. **114**

Magnus, Henry Gustavus, life and labors of. (R. 1870) 244

MAGRINI, L. Continuous vibratory movement of all matter. (R. 1868) 224

MAILLY, E.—

Estimate of population of the world. (R. 1873) 275

Eulogy on Quetelet. (R. 1874) 286

History of Royal Institution of Great Britain. (R. 1867) 215

Maine—

Brunswick, results of meteorological observations at—P. CLEAVELAND. **204**

Schoodic lakes, description of apparently new species of *Gasterosteus* from—T. H. BEAN. (P. 1879) 333

Kennebec river, opening and closing of—R. H. GARDINER. (R. 1858.) 109

Portland Society of Natural History, account of—E. C. BOLLES. (R. 1867) 215

remains of walrus (?) in—C. H. BOYD. (P. 1881) 467

Makah Indians, account of the—G. GIBBS 220

Makah Indians, memoir on the—J. G. SWAN **220**

Makah vocabulary—J. G. SWAN 220

MALLERY, G. Sign language among North American Indians compared with that among other peoples and deaf-mutes. (E. 1879–80) 476

MALLET, R. On observations of earthquake phenomena. (R. 1859) 110

MALLINKROOT, C. Changes of wind. (R. 1866) 214

Maltheidæ, note on the—T. GILL. (P. 1878) 332

Mammals—

and birds of Missouri river, list of—E. HARRIS. (R. 1850) 28

arrangement of families of—T. GILL **230**

bibliography of—T. GILL 230

extinct, of Nebraska—J. LEIDY 58

North American, catalogue of—S. F. BAIRD **105**

of Arctic America—L. KUMLIEN 342

of Kerguelen Island—J. H. KIDDER 294

synoptical tables of—T. GILL 230

Man—

as the contemporary of the mammoth and reindeer in middle Europe. (R. 1867) 215

ancient, in Michigan, characteristics pertaining to—H. GILLMAN. (R. 1875) 298, **393**

later prehistoric, remains of, from caves in Alaska—W. H. DALL **318**

on traces of the early mental condition of—E. B. TAYLOR. (R. 1867) 215

social and religious condition of the lower races of—J. LUBBOCK. (R. 1869.) 228

Management of the Smithsonian Institution, report of Senate Judiciary Committee on—A. P. BUTLER. (R. 1855) 77

Mandan ceremonies, accuracy of Catlin's account of—J. KIPP. (R. 1872) 271

MANN, C. Habits of a species of salamander. (R. 1854) 75

Manners of Shoshone Indians—A. G. BRACKETT. (R. 1879) 345

Manufacture of spear and arrow points along Savannah river—C. C. JONES, Jr. (R. 1879) 345
Manuscripts, Halliwell, report on—C. C. JEWETT. (R. 1852) 57
Manuscripts, etc., historical and geographical, catalogue of collection of—L. BERLANDIER. (R. 1854) 75
Manuscripts, linguistic, in library of Bureau of Ethnology, catalogue of—J. C. PILLING. (E. 1879-80) 476
Map of—
antiquities of United States, proposed—A. J. HILL. (R. 1861) 149
solar eclipse of March 15, 1858—T. HILL 101
stars for observations on meteorites 359
stars near North Pole for observations on auroras 350
United States, ethnological, proposed—G. GIBBS. (R. 1862) 150
Maps—
and charts of America, on a collection of—J. G. KOHL. (R. 1856) 91
catalogue of collection of—L. BERLANDIER. (R. 1854) 75
ethnological, of North America, suggestions relative to—L. H. MORGAN. (R. 1861) 149
of winds of the globe—S. J. COFFIN 268
Marble used in extension of U. S. Capitol, account of—J. HENRY. (R. 1856.) 91
MARCET, Prof. Report on transactions of Society of Physics and Natural History of Geneva, July, 1862, to June, 1863. (R. 1863) 187
MAREY, E. J. Natural history of organized bodies. (R. 1867) 215
MAREY, E. J. Phenomena of flight in the animal kingdom. (R. 1869) 228
Marianini, Stefano, life and scientific labors of, by C. MATTEUCCI. (R. 1869.) 228
Marietta, Ohio, meteorological observations at—S. P. HILDRETH; J. WOOD 120
Marine algæ, lecture on—W. H. HARVEY. (R. 1855) 77
Marine algæ of North America—W. H. HARVEY:
Part I. *Melanospermeæ* 32
Part II. *Rhodospermeæ* 43
Part III. *Chlorospermeæ* 95
Parts I, II, III, complete 96
Marine invertebrates—
distributed by U. S. National Museum—R. RATHBUN. (P. 1881.) 465, 467
of Grand Manan—W. STIMPSON 50
of New England coast distributed by United States Fish Commission—A. E. VERRILL; R. RATHBUN. (P. 1879) 383
of northeastern coast of America, notice of recent additions to, with descriptions of new genera and species—A. E. VERRILL:
Part I. *Annelida*, etc. (P. 1879) 333
Part II. *Mollusca*, with notes on *Annelida*, etc. (P. 1880) 425
Part III. Catalogue of *Mollusca* recently added to fauna of southern New England. (P. 1880) 425
on collection and preservation of—W. STIMPSON 34

Maritime disasters of the Antilles. (R. 1867) ---- 215
Marrow of animals, uses of, among Indians—T. R. PEALE. (R. 1870) ---- 244
Mars, secular variations of elements of orbit of—J. N. STOCKWELL ---- 232
Mars, small planets between Jupiter and—Prof. LESPIAULT. (R. 1861) ---- 149
Marschall, A., list of generic names supplemental to those catalogued by—S. H. SCUDDER ---- 470
MARSH, G. P. Lecture on the camel. (R. 1854) ---- 75
MARSH, G. P., and others. On publication of Squier and Davis' ancient monuments. (R. 1847) ---- **H, K**
Marsipobranchii, arrangement of families of—T. GILL ---- 247
MARTIN, S. D. Account of lightning discharges. (R. 1867) ---- 215
Martinique, catalogue of Ober's collection of birds of—G. N. LAWRENCE. (P. 1878) ---- 332
MARTINS, C. Vegetable colonization of the British Isles of Shetland, Faroe, and Iceland. (R. 1858) ---- 109
Martius, C. F. P. von, honorary medal to—W. HAIDINGER. (R. 1863) ---- 187
Martius, C. F. P. von, memoir of, by C. RAU. (R. 1869) ---- 440, **251**
Maryland, Charles county, antiquities of—O. N. BRYAN. (R. 1874) ---- 286
Maryland, occurrence of Canada porcupine in—O. LUGGER. (P. 1881) ---- 467
MASON, C. Statement relative to the telegraph. (R. 1857) ---- 107
MASON, O. T.—
- Abstracts of anthropological correspondence, 1880. (R. 1880) ---- 442
- Anthropological investigations in 1879. (R. 1879) ---- 345, **420**
- Anthropological investigations in 1880. (R. 1880) ---- 442, **432**
- Bibliography of anthropology. (R. 1879; R. 1880) ---- 345, 442
- Latimer collection of antiquities from Porto Rico. (R. 1876) ---- 299, **397**
- Leipsic Museum of Ethnology. (R. 1873) ---- 275
- Record of progress in anthropology, 1879, 1880. (R. 1880) ---- 442, **432**
- Report on Luray Cavern. (R. 1880) ---- 442, **433**
- Summary of anthropological correspondence, 1879. (R. 1879) ---- 345, **420**

Massachusetts—
- Buzzards' Bay, occurrence of *Belone latimanus* in—G. B. GOODE. (P. 1878) ---- 332
- Provincetown, Cape Cod, littoral marine fauna of—R. RATHBUN. (P. 1880) ---- 425
- Vineyard Sound, occurrence of oceanic bonito in—V. N. EDWARDS. (P. 1878) ---- 332

MASTERMAN, S. Observations on natural phenomena, shooting stars, aurora, etc. (R. 1857) ---- 107
MASTERMAN, S. Observations on thunder and lightning. (R. 1855) ---- 77
Materia medica collection, classification and arrangement of—J. M. FLINT. (P. 1881) ---- 467, **450**
Materia medica section of the U. S. National Museum, memoranda for collectors of drugs for the—J. M. FLINT. (P. 1881) ---- 467, **452**

Matter, continuous vibratory movement of—L. MAGRINI. (R. 1868) 224

MATTEUCCI, C.—

Electrical currents of the earth. (R. 1867; R. 1869) 215, 228

Lectures on electro-physiology. (R. 1865) 209

Life and scientific labors of Stefano Marianini. (R. 1869) 228

Mauvaises Terres, expedition to the upper Missouri and the—T. A. CULBERTSON. (R. 1850) 28

Mauvaises Terres of Nebraska, extinct mammalia and chelonia from the—J. LEIDY 58

MAXWELL, J. C.; HELMHOLTZ, H. Later views of connection of electricity and magnetism. (R. 1873) 275

Maya sculpture, remarks on ancient relic of—A. SCHOTT. (R. 1871) 249

MAYBERRY, S. P. Gradual approach of sea upon land. (R. 1867) 215

MAYBERRY, S. P. Shell heaps at mouth of St. John's river, Florida. (R. 1877) 323

MAYER, A. M. Henry as a discoverer. Memorial address 356, **417**

MAYER, A. M., translation by, of Delaunay's essay on velocity of light. (R. 1864) 188, **354**

MAYER, B. Observations on Mexican history and archæology **86**

Mazatlan, descriptions of new fishes from—D. S. JORDAN; C. H. GILBERT. (P. 1881) 467

MEACHAM, J. Minority report of Committee of Regents on distribution of Smithson income. (R. 1853) 67

MEADS, O. Memorial of Joseph Henry 356

Means available for correcting measures of sun's distance—G. B. AIRY. (R. 1859) 110

Means of destroying the grasshopper—V. MOTSCHULSKY. (R. 1858) 109

Measurements, anthropological, table of—SCHERZER; SCHWARZ. (R. 1866) 214

Measurements, mountain—A. GUYOT. (R. 1862) 150

Measures—

and weights, English and French, tables of. (R. 1863; R. 1864) 187, 188

and weights, metric system of, with tables—H. A. NEWTON. (R. 1865.) 209, **371**

and weights, new system of, with 8 as the metrical number—G. H. KNIGHT. (R. 1867) 215

of sun's distance—G. B. AIRY. (R. 1859) 110

Measuring instrument, use of galvanometer as—J. C. POGGENDORFF. (R. 1859.) 110

Mechanics and artisans, scientific education of—A. P. PEABODY. (R. 1872.) 271, **380**

Mechanism of fever, study of. Toner lecture No. IV—H. C. WOOD **282**

Medal to Von Martius—W. HAIDINGER. (R. 1863) 187

Medical practice, relation of food to work and its bearing on—S. HAUGHTON. (R. 1870) 244

Medicines, classification of forms in which drugs and, appear and are administered—J. M. FLINT. (P. 1881) 467, **451**

Medulla oblongata and trapezium, gray substance of the—J. DEAN **173**

MEECH, L. W. Relative intensity of heat and light of the sun. (R. 1856.) 91, **83**
MEEK, F. B. Check-list of invertebrate fossils of North America. Cretaceous and jurassic **177**
MEEK, F. B. Check-list of invertebrate fossils of North America. Miocene. **183**
MEEK, F. B, and others. Scientific instructions to Capt. Hall. (R. 1871) 249
MEEK, F. B.; HAYDEN, F. V. Palæontology of upper Missouri. Part I **172**
MEEK, J. B. Account of tornado in Spruce Creek valley, Centre county, Penn. (R. 1871) 249
MEIGS, J. A. Description of human skull from Rock Bluff, Illinois. (R. 1867.) 215
Melanians of North America—G. W. TRYON, Jr. 253
Melanospermeæ of North America, descriptions of—W. H. HARVEY **32**
Melbourne Mining Department. Exchange system. (R. 1865) 209
MELSHEIMER, F. E. Catalogue of described coleoptera of the United States **62**
Melting points, bibliography of—F. W. CLARKE 255
Melting points, tables of. Part I—F. W. CLARKE 255
Melting points, tables of. First supplement—F. W. CLARKE 288
Memoir—*See* Biography, Life, Eulogy.
Memoir of—
Agassiz, Louis, by R. P. STEBBINS. (R. 1873) 275
Babbage, Charles, by N. S. DODGE. (R. 1873) 275
Beautemps-Beaupré, C. F, by E. DE BEAUMONT. (R. 1863) 187
Blainville, Ducrotay de, by M. FLOURENS. (R. 1865) 209
Bravais, Auguste, by E. DE BEAUMONT. (R. 1869) 228
Buch, Leopold von, by M. FLOURENS. (R. 1862) 150
Candolle, Pyramus de, by M. FLOURENS (R. 1859) 110
Clark, H. J., by A. S. PACKARD 242
Cuvier, G., by M. FLOURENS. (R. 1868) 224
Delambre, J. B., by J. FOURIER. (R. 1864) 188
Encke, J. F., by G. HAGEN. (R. 1868) 224
Gibbs, George, by J. A. STEVENS. (R. 1873) 275
Haüy, René Just, by G. CUVIER. (R. 1860) 147
Henry, Joseph, by A. GRAY. (R. 1878) 341, 356, **407**
Henry, Joseph, by J. LOVERING 356
Henry, Joseph, by S. NEWCOMB 356
Henry, Joseph, by W. B. TAYLOR 356, **339**
Herschel, Sir John Frederick William, by N. S. DODGE. (R. 1871) 249
Hodgkinson, Eaton, by R. RAWSON. (R. 1868) 224
Legendre, A. M., by E. DE BEAUMONT. (R. 1867) 215
Magendie, F., by M. FLOURENS. (R. 1866) 214
Martius, C F. P. von, by C. RAU. (R. 1869) 228, 440, **251**
Oersted, H. C., by E. DE BEAUMONT. (R. 1868) 224
Peltier, J. C. A., by F. A. PELTIER. (R. 1867) 215

Memoir of—Continued.
Priestley, J., by G. CUVIER. (R. 1858) 109
Saint-Hilaire, Isidore Geoffroy, by J. L. QUATREFAGES. (R. 1862) 150
Saint-Hilaire, Geoffroy, by M. FLOURENS. (R. 1861) 149
Seaton, W. W., by J. HENRY. (R. 1866) 214
Thénard, Louis Jacques, by M. FLOURENS. (R. 1862) 150
Torrey, John, by A. GRAY. (R. 1873) 275
Memoir on—
anatomy and physiology of lucernariæ—H. J. CLARK **242**
explosiveness of nitre—R. HARE **17**
extinct sloth tribe of North America—J. LEIDY **72**
extinct species of American ox—J. LEIDY **41**
meteorological subjects, by J. Hann and others. Translated by C. ABBE. (R. 1877) 323, **398**
methods of interpolation—E. L. DE FOREST. (R. 1871, 1873) 249, 275
mosasaurus—R. W. GIBBES **14**
Memoranda for collectors of drugs for materia medica section of the U. S. National Museum—J. M. FLINT. (P. 1881) 467, **452**
Memoranda of inquiry relative to food fishes of United States **231**
Memorial—
address on Joseph Henry—A. M. MAYER 356, **417**
of citizens of Philadelphia relative to Lowe's aeronautic voyage across the Atlantic. (R. 1860) 147, 329
of Joseph Henry. (Published by Congress) 356
of Regents to Congress asking appropriations for Museum. (R. 1867.) 215, 329
of Regents to Congress relative to Smithson fund. (R. 1850; R. 1866.) 28, 214, 329
to Congress in behalf of Regents relative to new museum building—G. BANCROFT. (R. 1876) 299, 329
Menhaden, gulf, (*Brevoortia patronus*), note on—S. STEARNS. (P. 1878) 332
Mental condition of man, early traces of—E. B. TYLOR. (R. 1867) 215
Mercury, secular variations of elements of orbit of, with tables—J. N. STOCKWELL 232
MERINO, ST. M. Figure of the earth. (R. 1863) 187
Merlucius, diagnosis of genus of fish related to—G. B. GOODE. (P. 1880) 425
MERRILL, J. C. Habits of Rocky Mountain goat. (P. 1879) 333
MERRILL, J. C. List of birds observed near Fort Brown, Texas, 1876-1878. (P. 1878) 332
Mesozoic rocks of Arkansas, Wyoming, Colorado, and Utah, descriptions of new invertebrate fossils from—C. A. WHITE. (P. 1880) 425
Metal, hydrogen as gas and—J. E. REYNOLDS. (R. 1870) 244
Metallic castings of delicate natural objects. (P. 1881) 467
Metamorphism and formation of crystalline rocks—G. A. DAUBRÉE. (R. 1861.) 149
Meteoric fire-ball, orbit and phenomena of—J. H. COFFIN **221**

Meteoric shower of November 13, 1867, letter of M. Hoek, relative to **217**
Meteoric stones, lectures on—J. L. SMITH. (R. 1855) 77
Meteorite—
in Mexico—A. WOODWORTH. (R. 1867)............................ 215
in Mexico, account of—R. SIMSON. (R. 1867)...................... 215
in Mexico, discovery of large—W. M. PIERSON. (R. 1873) 275
Tucson, account of—S. AINSA. (R. 1863)............................ 187
Tucson, account of—B. J. D. IRWIN. (R. 1863)...................... 187
Meteorites—
extract from discourse on—F. BRENNDECKE. (R. 1869) 228
in Mexico—J. H. CARLETON. (R. 1865)............................ 209
in mineralogical collection of Yale College, catalogue of—G. J. BRUSH. (R. 1868) 224
Synthetic experiments relative to—G. A. DAUBRÉE. (R. 1868)........ 224
Meteorograph, universal, for detached observatories—E. H. VON BAUMHAUER. (R. 1879) 345
Meteorological—
articles in periodicals received by Smithsonian Institution and deposited in Library of Congress. (R. 1871; R. 1873).................. 249, 275
correspondence of the Institution, extracts from. (R. 1866) 214
discovery—F. L. CAPEN. (R. 1866) 214
instruments, description of—L. CASELLA. (R. 1859).................. 110
material contributed to the Smithsonian Institution. (R. 1860–1866, 1868, 1871, 1874) 147, 149, 150, 187, 188, 209, 214, 224, 228, 244, 249, 286
memoirs—J. HANN; L. SOHNCKE; T. REYE; W. FERREL; A. COLDING; M. PESLIN; C. ABBE. (R. 1877) 323, **398**
publications deposited in Library of Congress, classified list of. (R. 1873.) 275
reports preserved in Smithsonian Institution, classified list of. (R. 1873.) 275
stations, cost of establishment of—J. HENRY. (R. 1858) 109
stations and observers, list of. (R. 1849, 1853–1872.) 21, 67, 75, 77, 91, 107, 109, 110, 147, 149, 150, 157, 187, 188, 209, 214, 215, 224, 228, 244, 249, 271, **373**
subjects, short memoirs on, by J. Hann and others. Translated by C. ABBE. (R. 1877).. 323, **398**
suggestions for Russian America—J. HENRY 207
system for every State—ILLINOIS STATE BOARD OF EDUCATION. (R. 1855.) 77
system of Canada—J. G. HODGINS. (R. 1865) 209
system of Smithsonian Institution, report on—E. FOREMAN. (R. 1851; R. 1852).. 51, 57
tables—A. GUYOT.. **31**, **153**
telegrams by Western Union Telegraph Company—H. SIBLEY. (R. 1862) 150
Meteorological observations—
at Brunswick, Maine—P. CLEAVELAND.............................. **204**
at Marietta, Ohio—S. P. HILDRETH; J. WOOD **120**

Meteorological observations—Continued.
at Philadelphia, Girard College, discussion of—A. D. BACHE. **113, 121, 132, 162, 175, 186, 195**
at Providence, Rhode Island, 1831-1860—A. CASWELL **103**
at Providence, Rhode Island, 1831-1876—A. CASWELL **443**
at Sacramento, California—F. W. HATCH. (R. 1854) 75
at Sacramento, California—T. M. LOGAN. (R. 1854) 75
at San Francisco, California—H. GIBBONS. (R. 1854) 75
at Washington, Arkansas—N. D. SMITH **131**
combined, report of American Association for Advancement of Science on system of. (R. 1851) 51
directions for—A. GUYOT; J. HENRY. (R. 1855) 77, **19**, **148**
in the Arctic Seas—I. I. HAYES 196
in the Arctic Seas—E. K. KANE **104**
in the Arctic Seas—F. L. MCCLINTOCK **146**
results of, from 1854 to 1859. Vols. I, II **157**, **182**
Smithsonian, for the year 1855 .... **93**

Meteorology—
articles on. (R. 1867; R. 1870) 215, 244
articles on, with notes by J. Henry. (R. 1871) 249
communication relative to—J. P. ESPY. (R. 1847) .... **H**
lectures and notes on—R. RUSSELL; J. HENRY. (R. 1854) 75
of Caracas, South America—G. A. ERNST. (R. 1867) 215
of Colonia Tovar, Venezuela—A. FENDLER. (R. 1857) 107
of District of Columbia—J. WISSNER. (R. 1857) 107
of Green river country, Utah—Col. COLLINS. (R. 1871) 249
of Porto Rico—G. LATIMER. (R. 1871) 249
of Russia—A. WOEIKOFF. (R. 1872) 271
of Sacramento, California—T. M. LOGAN. (R. 1857) 107
of the United States, report on—E. LOOMIS. (R. 1847) .... **H**

Meteorology—*See* Atmospheric pressure, Temperature, Rain, Winds, etc.

Meteors—
articles on, preserved in Smithsonian. (R. 1874) 286
observation of—L. ANDREWS. (R. 1866) 214
of November 13, 1867 .... **217**
planisphere of the heavens for observations of **359**

Method of—
ascertaining amount of water in rivers—A. A. HUMPHREYS. (R. 1858.) 109
forming small weights—R. HARE. (R. 1858) 109
preserving lepidoptera—T. R. PEALE. (R. 1863) 187

Methods of—
capture and utilization of animals—G. B. GOODE 297
installation in the National Museum—G. B. GOODE. (P. 1881) 467, **472**

Methods of—Continued.
interpolation applicable to graduation of irregular series—E. L. DE FOREST. (R. 1871) 249
interpolation, additions to memoir on—E. L. DE FOREST. (R. 1873) 275
making and preserving plaster casts—A. PIRZ. (P. 1881) 467
Metric system for scientific observation—A. GUYOT. (R. 1848) I
Metric system of weights and measures with tables—H. A. NEWTON. (R. 1865.) 209, **371**
Metric system with 8 as base—G. H. KNIGHT. (R. 1867) 215
METTENIUS, G. Acknowledgment for ferns. (R. 1862) 150
Mexican axolotl, change of, to an amblystoma—A WEISMANN. (R. 1877.) 323, **401**
Mexican boundary, forests and trees of Florida and the—J. G. COOPER. (R. 1860.) 147
Mexican history and archæology, observations on—B. MAYER **86**
Mexican Society of Geography and Statistics. Exchanges. (R. 1861; R. 1865.) 149, 209
Mexico—
description of large fossil gasteropod from—C. A. WHITE. (P. 1880) 425
description of new fishes from—D. S. JORDAN; C. H. GILBERT. (P. 1881.) 467
description of new species of genus *Brevoortia* from—G. B. GOODE. (P. 1878) 332
eastern, earthquake in, January, 1866—C. SARTORIUS. (R. 1866) 214
explorations of John Xantus in—M. ROMERO. (R. 1862) 150
Guanajuato and Chapala lake, notes on Dugès' collection of fishes from—D. S. JORDAN. (P. 1879) 333
list of described birds of, not in Smithsonian collection **185**
magnetic observations in—Baron VON MÜLLER; A. SONNTAG 114
meteorite in—R. SIMSON. (R. 1867) 215
meteorite in—A. WOODWORTH. (R. 1867) 215
meteorite in, discovery of—W. M. PIERSON. (R. 1873) 275
meteorites in—J. H. CARLETON. (R. 1865) 209
notes on fishes from, collected by Lieut. H. E. Nichols—D. S. JORDAN; C. H. GILBERT. (P. 1881) 467
scientific expedition to, report addressed to Emperor of France by Minister of Public Instruction. (R. 1864) 188
southwestern, birds of, collected by F. E. Sumichrast—G. N. LAWRENCE. 295
Vera Cruz, account of antiquities in—H. FINCK. (R. 1870) 244
Mexico, Gulf of, catalogue of fishes collected in, by J. W. Velie—G. B. GOODE; T. H. BEAN. (P. 1879) 333
Mexico, Gulf of, mortality of fishes in—J. P. JEFFERSON. (P. 1878) 332
Mica beds in Alabama—W. GESNER. (R. 1879) 345
Mica mines, ancient, in North Carolina—C. D. SMITH. (R. 1876) 299
Michigan—
ancient mining in—C. WHITTLESEY 155
Beaver Island, natural history of—J. J. STRANG. (R. 1854) 75

Michigan—Continued.
catalogue of rocks, minerals, and ores collected on geological survey in—C. T. Jackson. (R. 1854) 75
characteristics pertaining to ancient man in—H. Gillman. (R. 1875.) 298, **393**
Isle Royale, Lake Superior, antiquities of—A. C. Davis. (R. 1874) 286
mound-builders and platycnemism in—H. Gillman. (R. 1873) 275, **393**
Microscope, the. (R. 1860) 147
Microscopic organisms—
directions for collecting 65
directions for collecting, preserving, and transporting—A. M. Edwards. **366**
notes on new species and localities of—J. W. Bailey **63**
Microscopical examination of Japanese infusorial earths—A. M. Edwards 202
Microscopical examination of soundings made by U. S. Coast Survey off Atlantic coast of United States—J. W. Bailey **20**
Microscopical observations in South Carolina, Georgia, and Florida—J. W. Bailey **23**
Middle America—
birds of—S. F. Baird 181
birds of, circular for collecting 168
birds of, not in National Museum—R. Ridgway. (P. 1881) 467
(explanation of term) 181
Migration, the American—F. von Hellwald. (R. 1866) 214
Migrations and nesting habits of west coast birds—J. G. Cooper. (P. 1879) 333
Milan Agricultural Association. Exchange of publications. (R. 1863) 187
Milky way, bibliography of works relating to—E. S. Holden 311
Miller, F. Mound in Trumbull county, Ohio. (R. 1877) 323
Mills, Clark, casts of heads of Indian boys and girls at Hampton, Virginia, taken by. (P. 1879) 333
Mills, Clark, casts of heads of Indian prisoners in Florida taken by. (P. 1878.) 332
Mineral, jade, study of—S. Blondel. (R. 1876) 299
Mineralogical collection, arrangement of—C. U. Shepard. (R. 1861) 149
Mineralogical collection of Yale College, catalogue of meteorites in the—G. J. Brush. (R. 1868) 224
Mineralogical composition of the normal mesozoic diabase upon Atlantic border—G. W. Hawes. (P. 1881) 467
Mineralogy, progress in, in 1879 and 1880—G. W. Hawes. (R. 1880) 442, **428**
Minerals—
and ores collected on geological survey in Michigan, catalogue of—C. T. Jackson. (R. 1854) 75
and rocks, catalogue of—J. W. Foster. (R. 1854) 75
and rocks, catalogue of—J. D. Whitney. (R. 1854) 75
catalogue of, with their formulas, etc.—T. Egleston **156**
in U. S. National Museum in 1873, list of—F. M. Endlich. (R. 1873.) 275

Minerals—Continued.
in U. S. National Museum in 1879, list of—F. M. ENDLICH. (P. 1880.) 425
rocks, ores, and fossils, catalogue of—J. LOCKE. (R. 1854) 75
Mines, ancient mica, in North Carolina—C. D. SMITH. (R. 1876) 299
Mining, ancient, in Lake Superior copper region, circular relative to—J. HENRY. (R. 1861) 149
Mining, ancient, on shores of Lake Superior—C. WHITTLESEY **155**
Mining Department, Melbourne. Exchange system. (R. 1865) 209
Minnesota—
ancient town in, account of—O. H. KELLEY. (R. 1863) 187
Fort Ripley, natural history of country about—J. E. HEAD. (R. 1854.) 75
Hennepin county, mounds on Gideon's farm near Excelsior—F. H. NUTTER. (R. 1879) 345
Lake Pepin and Mississippi river, antiquities on banks of—L. C. ESTES. (R. 1866) 214
Red river of the North, ethnology of Indians of—W. H. GARDNER. (R. 1870) 244
Minnesota Historical Society. Dakota grammar 40
Miocene fossils, check list of—F. B. MEEK **183**
Miscellanea, Museum, labels, etc.—S. F. BAIRD **164**
Miscellaneous Collections, Smithsonian. Vols. I-XXIII. 122, 123, 124, 125, 158, 169, 191, 212, 213, 250, 273, 274, 312, 314, 315, 322, 336, 337, 416, 423, 424, 468, 475
Miscellaneous Collections, Smithsonian, catalogue and index of 478
Miscellaneous tables—A. GUYOT **153**
Missionary Society, Southern. Yoruba grammar and dictionary 98
Missions—*See* American Board of Commissioners.
Mississippi—
aboriginal lapidary in—C. RAU. (R. 1877) 323, **402**
eastern, collection of fishes from—O. P. HAY. (P. 1880) 425
mounds in—S. A. AGNEW. (R. 1867) 215
Washington county, mounds in—J. HOUGH. (R. 1879) 345
Yazoo county, antiquities of—J. W. C. SMITH. (R. 1874) 286
Mississippi river and Lake Pepin, antiquities on banks of—L. C. ESTES. (R. 1866) 214
Mississippi river, description of new species of fishes from—T. H. BEAN. (P. 1879) 333
Mississippi valley, ancient monuments of—E. G. SQUIER; E. H. DAVIS **1**
Mississippi valley, physical geography of—C. ELLET, Jr **13**
Missouri—
ancient relics in—J. W. FOSTER. (R. 1863) 187
antiquities in—I. DILLE. (R. 1862) 150
Kansas City, antiquities of—W. H. R. LYKINS. (R. 1877) 323
New Madrid, earthquake at—T. DUDLEY. (R. 1858) 109

Missouri—Continued.
prehistoric evidences in—G. C. BROADHEAD. (R. 1879) 345
St. Louis, ancient mound at—T. R. PEALE. (R. 1861) 149
St. Louis, temperature of—A. FENDLER. (R. 1860) 147
upper, expedition to Mauvaises Terres and—A. CULBERTSON. (R. 1850.) 28
upper, list of plants of—T. C. PORTER. (R. 1850) 28
upper, palæontology of—F. B. MEEK; F. V. HAYDEN 172
western, exploration of—P. R. HOY. (R. 1864) 188
Missouri river, ancient earthworks on—A. BARRANDT. (R. 1870) 244
Missouri river, list of birds and mammalia of—E. HARRIS. (R. 1850) 28
MITCHELL, A. Antiquities of Florida. (R. 1874) 286
MITCHELL, B. Mounds in Pike county, Illinois. (R. 1879) 345
MITCHELL, B. R.; TURNER, W. W. Vocabulary of the jargon of Oregon 68
MITCHELL, S. S. Funeral sermon of Joseph Henry 356
MITCHELL, S. W. Inquiries relative to disease known as chorea. (R. 1874) 286
MITCHELL, S. W. Researches upon the venom of the rattlesnake 135
MITCHELL, S. W.; MOREHOUSE, G. R. Researches upon anatomy and physiology of respiration in chelonia 159
Mitla, drawings of—J. G. SAWKINS 86
Mixed races in Liberia—E. D. BLYDEN. (R. 1870) 244
Mobile river, shell-heaps on—A. S. GAINES; K. M. CUNNINGHAM. (R. 1877.) 323
Modern theory of chemical types—C. M. WETHERILL. (R. 1863) 187
Modes of flight in relation to aeronautics—J. B. PETTIGREW. (R. 1867) 215
MOIGNO, F. N. Accidental or subjective colors. (R. 1866) 214
MOLINA, L., Costa Rican minister, recommending Dr. Berendt. (R. 1865) 209
Mollusca of Northeastern coast of America. Parts I, II, III—A E. VERRILL. (P. 1879; P. 1880) 333, 425
Mollusca, or shellfish, and their allies, lectures on—P. P. CARPENTER. (R. 1860) 147, 152
Molluscoids of Arctic America—A. E. VERRILL 342
Mollusks—
arrangement of families of—T. GILL 227
bibliography of—T. GILL 227
eocene, some new species of, from southern United States—A. HEILPRIN. (P. 1880) 425
new forms of, from Alaska—W. H. DALL. (P. 1878) 332
of Arctic America—W. H. DALL 342
of Kerguelen Island—W. H. DALL 294
of western North America—P. P. CARPENTER 252
Monadnock, ironclad, deviation of compasses on—W. HARKNESS 239
Mongolia, geological researches in—R. PUMPELLY 202
Monograph of—
American corbiculadæ, recent and fossil—T. PRIME 145

Monograph of—Continued.
bats of North America—H. ALLEN 165
cottoids of North America—C. GIRARD 30
dolichopodidæ—H. LOEW 171
ortalidæ—H. LOEW 256
strepomatidæ, (American melanians)—G. W. TRYON 253
tipulidæ—C. R. OSTEN SACKEN 219
wasps—H. DE SAUSSURE 254
Monographs of diptera of North America—
Part I—H. LOEW; R. OSTEN SACKEN 141
Part II—H. LOEW; R. OSTEN SACKEN 171
Part III—H. LOEW 256
Part IV—R. OSTEN SACKEN 219
Montana, distribution of forest trees in—W. W. JOHNSON. (R. 1870) 244
Montana, prehistoric remains in—P. W. NORRIS. (R. 1879) 345
Monterey Bay, California, new fishes from—D. S. JORDAN; C. H. GILBERT. (P. 1880) 425
Monument to Joseph Henry, proceedings of Congress relative to 356
Monuments—
aboriginal, of State of New York—E. G. SQUIER 15
ancient, of the Mississippi valley—E. G. SQUIER; E. H. DAVIS 1
and antiquities of Denmark, preservation of—J. J. A. WORSAAE. (R. 1879.) 345
Moon—
effect of, on the magnetic force—A. D. BACHE 162, 175
effect of, on the weather—J. HENRY. (R. 1871) 249
influence of, on magnetic declination—A. D. BACHE 132
occultations of planets by—*See* Downes, J.
Moon-hoax, on the—J. HENRY. (R. 1873) 275
MOORE, M. A. Fish mortality in the Gulf of Mexico. (P. 1881) 467
MOORE, T., and others. Destruction of fish near the Tortugas. (P. 1878) 332
MOREHOUSE, G. W.; MITCHELL, S. W. Anatomy and physiology of respiration in chelonia 159
MORFIT, C; BOOTH, J. C. Recent improvements in chemical arts 27
MORGAN, L. H.—
Circular in reference to degrees of relationship among different nations 138
Proposed ethnological map of North America. (R. 1861) 149
Systems of consanguinity and affinity of the human family 218
Morgan, L. H., circular to diplomatic agents by State Department relative to research of 138
MORIN, A. Warming and ventilating buildings. Parts I, II. (R. 1873; R. 1874) 275, 286, 439
MORLOT, A.—
Abstract of Dr. Keller's report on lacustrian settlements in Switzerland. (R. 1863) 187

MORLOT, A.—Continued.
Archæology. (R. 1861) 149
General views on archæology. (R. 1860) 147
Lecture on study of high antiquity in Europe. (R. 1862; R. 1864.) 150, 188
MORRIS, J. G.—
Catalogue of described lepidoptera of North America........ **118**
Lecture on insect instincts and transformations. (R. 1855) 77
Lecture on natural history as applied to farming and gardening. (R. 1855.) 77
Synopsis of described lepidoptera **133**
MORRIS, O. W.; HENRY, J. Quantity of rain at different heights. (R. 1855.) 77
Morse, S. F. B., account of origin and development of invention of—W. B. TAYLOR. (R. 1878)........ 341, **405**
Morse, S. F. B., communication relative to a publication of—J. HENRY. (R. 1857) 107, 115, 329
Mortality—
of fishes in Gulf of Mexico—E. INGERSOLL. (P. 1881)........ 467
of fishes in Gulf of Mexico—J. P. JEFFERSON. (P. 1878) 332
of fishes in Gulf of Mexico—S. H. JOHNSON. (P. 1881) 467
of fishes in Gulf of Mexico—M. A. MOORE. (P. 1881) 467
of fishes in vicinity of Tortugas—J. P. JEFFERSON; T. MOORE; J. Y. PORTER. (P. 1878) 332
tables of, methods of interpolation applied to graduation of—E. L. DE FOREST. (R. 1871; R. 1873) 249, 275
MORTILLET, G. DE; CHANTRE, E. International code of symbols for charts of prehistoric archæology. (R. 1875)........ 298
MORTON, S. G., and others. On publication of Squier and Davis' ancient monuments. (R. 1847)........ **H**
Mortuary customs of North American Indians—H. C. YARROW. (E. 1879-80.) 476
Mosasaurus and the three allied genera, *Holcodus*, *Conosaurus*, and *Amphorosteus*, memoir on—R. W. GIBBES........ **14**
Motion, planetary, general integrals of—S. NEWCOMB........ **281**
Motion, rotary, problems of, presented by gyroscope, precession of equinoxes, and pendulum—J. G. BARNARD........ **240**
MOTSCHULSKY, V. On means of destroying the grasshopper. (R. 1858) 109
MOULTON, M. W. Mounds in Delaware county, Iowa. (R. 1877)........ 323
Mound in—
Dakota, Lincoln county—A. BARRANDT. (R. 1872) 271
Florida, colored bead from—A. M. HARRISON. (R. 1877)........ 323
Florida, gold ornament from—C. RAU. (R. 1877) 323, 440, **403**
Indiana—W. PIDGEON. (R. 1867) 215
Kentucky, near Lexington—R. PETER. (R. 1871) 249
Missouri, St. Louis—T. R. PEALE. (R. 1861)........ 149
Ohio, Trumbull county—F. MILLER. (R. 1877)........ 323
Pennsylvania, western—W. M. TAYLOR. (R. 1877) 323

Mound in—Continued.
Tennessee, near Chattanooga—M. C. READ. (R. 1867) ... 215
Tennessee, east—A. F. DANILSEN. (R. 1863) ... 187
Wisconsin—C. K. DEAN. (R. 1872) ... 271
Wisconsin, Grant county—J. WARNER. (R. 1872) ... 271
Mound-builders—
and platycnemism in Michigan—H. GILLMAN. (R. 1873) ... 275, **393**
in Rock river valley, Illinois—J. SHAW. (R. 1877) ... 323
of Wisconsin, mounds and osteology of—J. N. DE HART. (R. 1877) ... 323
Mounds and osteology of the mound-builders of Wisconsin—J. N. DE HART. (R. 1877) ... 323
Mounds in—
Dakota, Fort Wadsworth—A. J. COMFORT. (R. 1871) ... 249
Florida, (southern,) explorations among—S. T. WALKER. (R. 1879) ... 345
Georgia—M. F. STEPHENSON. (R. 1870) ... 244
Georgia, Bartow county—M. F. STEPHENSON. (R. 1872) ... 271
Georgia, McIntosh and Early counties—W. MCKINLEY. (R. 1872) ... 271
Illinois, Mercer county—T. MCWHORTER. (R. 1874) ... 286
Illinois, near Albany, skull and bones from—R. J. FARQUHARSON. (R. 1874) ... 286
Illinois, Pike county—B. MITCHELL. (R. 1879) ... 345
Illinois, Rock Island county—T. THOMPSON. (R. 1879) ... 345
Illinois, Spoon river valley—W. H. ADAMS. (R. 1879) ... 345
Illinois, Union county, near Anna—T. M. PERRINE. (R. 1872) ... 271
Indiana, Franklin county—E. R. QUICK. (R. 1879) ... 345
Indiana, Rush county—F. JACKMAN. (R. 1879) ... 345
Iowa, Delaware county—M. W. MOULTON. (R. 1877) ... 323
Iowa, Des Moines valley, notes on—S. B. EVANS. (R. 1879) ... 345
Iowa, Muscatine county—T. THOMPSON. (R. 1879) ... 345
Kentucky—R. PETER. (R. 1872) ... 271
Kentucky, exploration of—S. S. LYON. (R. 1870) ... 244
Kentucky, Union county, exploration of—S. S. LYON. (R. 1870) ... 244
Louisiana—S. H. LOCKETT. (R. 1872) ... 271
Louisiana, Moorehouse parish—B. H. BRODNAX. (R. 1879) ... 345
Minnesota, Hennepin county, on Gideon's farm—F. H. NUTTER. (R. 1879) 345
Mississippi—S. A. AGNEW. (R. 1867) ... 215
Mississippi, Washington county—J. HOUGH. (R. 1879) ... 345
New Brunswick and New England, notes on—S. F. BAIRD. (P. 1881.) 467
Ohio, Trumbull county—F. MILLER. (R. 1877) ... 323
Pennsylvania, (western)—W. M. TAYLOR. (R. 1877) ... 323
Tennessee—J. JONES ... 259
Wisconsin, Grant county—M. STRONG. (R. 1879) ... 299
Wisconsin, Winnebago county—T. ARMSTRONG. (R. 1879) ... 345

Mountain, Black, North Carolina, topography of—T. L. CLINGMAN. (R. 1855.) 77
Mountain measurements—A. GUYOT. (R. 1862) 150
Mountains, electric resonance of—H. DE SAUSSURE. (R. 1868) 224
Mountains in Colorado, heights of—G. ENGELMANN. (R. 1862) 150
Mountains, lakes, and the snow-line, Norwegian—O. E. DREUTZER. (R. 1866.) 214
Movement of the stars around a central point—J. H. MAEDLER. (R. 1859) 110
MUCH, M. Ancient history of North America. (R. 1871) 249
MUDGE, B. F. Account of lightning discharges. (R. 1867) 215
MÜLLER, Baron VON. Observations on terrestrial magnetism in Mexico 114
MÜLLER, F. Smithsonian exchanges. (R. 1860) 147
MÜLLER, J.—
Principles of the mechanical theory of heat. (R. 1868) 224
Report on recent progress in physics—electricity. (R. 1856; R. 1857.) 91, 107
Report on recent progress in physics—galvanism. (R. 1855; R. 1857; R. 1858) 77, 107, 109
Report on transactions of Geneva Society of Physics and Natural History, June, 1875, to July, 1876. (R. 1877) 323
Mummy and skulls from Patagonia—A. REID. (R. 1862) 150
Mummy case, Gliddon—C. PICKERING 208
MURPHEY, H. C., and others. On publication of Spanish works on New Mexico. (R. 1855) 77
Musci of Kerguelen Island—T. P. JAMES 294
Museum—
at Lausanne, ethnological collections of—F. TROYON. (R. 1861) 149
Blackmore, Salisbury, England, notice of. (R. 1868) 224
British, statistics of—S. F. BAIRD. (R. 1850) 28
d'Histoire Naturelle, Paris, notes on typical American fishes in—D. S. JORDAN. (P. 1879) 333
Hungarian National. Acknowledgment for birds. (R. 1863) 187
miscellanea—S. F. BAIRD 164
of ethnology, Leipsic—A. SCHOTT; O. T. MASON. (R. 1873) 275
of National University of Greece. Exchange of specimens. (R. 1867.) 215
of Norway, Ethnological—L. K. DAA. (R. 1862) 150
of Toronto University, objects of. (R. 1865) 209
on formation of a—L. AGASSIZ. (R. 1849) 21
Smithsonian—*See* Museum, U. S. National.
Museum, U. S. National—
acts and resolutions of Congress relative to—*See* Congress.
additions to, list of—*See* each annual report.
birds of Middle and South America not in—R. RIDGWAY. (P. 1881) 467
Bulletins of—*See* Bulletins.
catalogue and index of the Proceedings and Bulletins of 478
catalogue of collection of Japanese cotton fibre presented to. (P. 1881.) 467

Museum, U. S. National—Continued.

catalogue of collection of Japanese woods presented to—L. F. WARD. (P. 1881) 467

catalogue of Old World birds in—R. RIDGWAY. (P. 1881) 467, **462**

circular asking contributions to library of. (P. 1881) 467, **458**

circulars of—*See* Circulars.

classification of collections of—G. B. GOODE. (P. 1881) 467, **457**

classification of collections of, to illustrate taxidermy—W. T. HORNADAY. (P. 1881) 467, **456**

collections furnished to, by explorations, 1838 to 1877—S. F. BAIRD. (R. 1877) 323

contributions to, and their acknowledgment. (P. 1881) 467, **473**

directory of officers, collaborators, and employés of 466

distribution by, of marine invertebrates—R. RATHBUN. (P. 1881.) 467, **465**, **471**

establishment and officers of Smithsonian Institution and. (P. 1881.) 467, **449**

letters on work of—B. PHILLIPS. (P. 1881) 467, **454**

list of publications of. (P. 1881) 467 478, **474**

memorial of Regents of Smithsonian Institution to Congress asking appropriations for. (R. 1867) 215, 329

memorial to Congress in behalf of Regents of Smithsonian Institution for new building for—G. BANCROFT. (R. 1876) 299, 329

organization and objects of—G. B. GOODE. (P. 1881) 467, **459**

outline of scheme of classification for collections in—G. B. GOODE. (P. 1881) 467, **457**

plan of organization and regulations of—G. B. GOODE. (P. 1881) 467, **445**

plans for installation of collections in—G. B. GOODE. (P. 1881) 467, **472**

proceedings in Congress relative to 328

Proceedings of. Vols. I-IV, 1878-1881 .... **332**, **333**, **425**, **467**

report of Committee of Regents on—A. GRAY; H. COPPÉE. (R. 1874.) 286

report of Committee of Regents on—A. GRAY; A. A. SARGENT; H. CLYMER. (R. 1876) 299

report on, and statistics of British Museum—S. F. BAIRD. (R. 1850) 28

reports of Building Commission of, for 1879, 1880. (R. 1879; R. 1880.) 345, 442, **409**, **434**

reports on, 1853-1867, 1873-1877—S. F. BAIRD. (R. 1853-1867, 1873-1877) 67, 75, 77, 91, 107, 109, 110, 147, 149, 150, 187, 188, 209, 214, 215, 275, 286, 298, 299, 323

Myadestes obscurus, description of two new races of—L. STEJNEGER. (P. 1881.) 467

Myctophum crenulare, description of—T. H. BEAN. (P. 1881) 467

Myctophum crenulare from Santa Barbara channel, California, description of—D. S. JORDAN; C. H. GILBERT. (P. 1880) 425

Myological specimens, rapid preparation of—F. PLATEAU. (P. 1881) 467

Myriapods, list of North American species of, belonging to family of *Lysiopetalidæ*—J. A. Ryder. (P. 1880) ---- 425

Myriapods, phalangidæ, etc., instructions for collecting—H. C. Wood. (R. 1866) ---- 214

Myriolepis zonifer, a new chiroid fish from Monterey Bay, Calfornia, description of—W. N. Lockington. (P. 1880) ---- 425

Mythology of North American Indians—J. W. Powell. (E. 1879-80) ---- 476

Myths, Indian. (E. 1879-80) ---- 476

N.

Naill, D. W. Dispersion of a cloud by electrical discharge. (R. 1858) ---- **109**

Naples, Italy, Royal Institute for Encouragement of Natural, Economical, and Technological Sciences. Prize questions. (R. 1873) ---- 275

Narrative of the Hassler expedition—L. Agassiz. (R. 1872) ---- 271, 329

National Academy of Sciences, bequest to—A. D. Bache. (R. 1872) ---- 271, 329

National library, on a—W. S. Jevons. (R. 1873) ---- 275

National Museum—*See* Museum, U. S. National.

Natural history—

- applied to farming and gardening, lecture on—J. G. Morris. (R. 1855.) 77
- bibliography of American—C. Girard ---- **48**
- directions for collecting, preserving, and transporting specimens of—S. F. Baird. (R. 1856) ---- 91, **34**
- explorations in, in the United States, 1851—S. F. Baird. (R. 1851) ---- 51
- of Arctic America—L. Kumlien ---- **342**
- of Beaver Island, Michigan—J. J. Strang. (R. 1854) ---- 75
- of country about Fort Ripley, Minnesota—J. E. Head. (R. 1854) ---- 75
- of Fanning Islands—T. H. Streets ---- 303
- of fresh-water fishes of North America—C. Girard ---- **30**
- of Hawaiian Islands, etc.—T. H. Streets ---- **303**
- of Kerguelen Island—J. H. Kidder and others ---- **294**
- of lower California—T. H. Streets ---- 303
- of organized bodies—E. J. Marey. (R. 1867) ---- 215
- of Pacific Islands—W. H. Pease. (R. 1862) ---- 150
- suggestions relative to investigations in, in Russian America—S. F. Baird ---- 207

Natural History Society—*See* Geneva.

Natural method, the Jussieus and the—M. Flourens. (R. 1867) ---- 215

Naturalists, generic names of animals employed by—S. H. Scudder ---- **470**

Nature—
and art, on tables of the constants of—C. BABBAGE. (R. 1856) 91
and mechanism of fever. Toner lecture No. IV—H. C. WOOD.......... **282**
and origin of force—W. B. TAYLOR. (R. 1870) 244, 375
of reparatory inflammation in arteries after ligature. Toner lecture No. VII—E. O. SHAKESPEARE **321**
Nature—*See* Constants of Nature.
Navajo Indians, language of, said to resemble Welsh—S. Y. McMASTERS. (R. 1865) 209
Navajo Indians, sketch of the—J. LETTERMAN. (R. 1855) 77
Naval officers, authority to, to receive and transmit specimens to Smithsonian... 34
Navigation of Ohio and other rivers, improvement of—C. ELLET **13**
Navy Department, authority given by, to naval officers to receive and transmit specimens to the Smithsonian Institution 34
Neah Bay, Washington Territory, description of two new species of fishes from—D. S. JORDAN; C. H. GILBERT. (P. 1880) 425
Nebraska—
ancient fauna of—J. LEIDY **58**
palæontology of—F. B. MEEK; F. V. HAYDEN **172**
report on fossils from—J. LEIDY. (R. 1851) 51
Nebulæ, index-catalogue of books relative to—E. S. HOLDEN **311**
Nebulæ, researches relative to the—Prof. GAUTIER. (R. 1863) 187
Nebular hypothesis, bibliography of the—E. S. HOLDEN 311
Nematoda of northeast coast of North America—A. E. VERRILL. (P. 1879).. 333
Nemertina of northeast coast of America—A. E. VERRILL. (P. 1879) 333
Nemichthys avocetta, new species of Nemichthys, description of—D. S. JORDAN; C. H. GILBERT. (P. 1880) 425
Neptune—
ephemerides of, 1848, 1846–49, 1850, 1851, 1852—S. C. WALKER. **4, 5, 6, 7, 24**
history of discovery of—B. A. GOULD **18**
investigation of orbit of, with tables of its motion—S. NEWCOMB....... **199**
researches relative to—S. C. WALKER **3**
secular variations of elements of orbit of—J. N. STOCKWELL **232**
Nereis-Boreali-Americana—W. H. HARVEY:
Part I. *Melanospermeæ* **32**
Part II. *Rhodospermeæ* **43**
Part III. *Chlorospermeæ* **95**
Parts I, II, III, complete **96**
Neritidæ, fresh-water—W. G. BINNEY 144
Nerve, polarized, effect of irritation of—B. F. LAUTENBACH. (R. 1878).. 341, **411**
Nervous system of *Rana pipiens*, anatomy of—J. WYMAN **45**
Nests—
and eggs of American birds, instructions for collecting—S. F. BAIRD. (R. 1858) 109, **139**

Nests—Continued.
and eggs of the eight North American species of empidonaces—T. M. Brewer. (P. 1879) ... 333
instructions for collecting and preserving—T. M. Brewer ... 139
of west coast birds—J. G. Cooper. (P. 1879) ... 333
Netherlands, the, Royal Academy of. Prize questions. (R. 1861) ... 149
Neuchâtel, lake of, palafittes or lacustrian constructions of—E. Desor. (R. 1865) ... 209, **360**
Neuroptera—
instructions for collecting—P. R. Uhler. (R. 1858) ... 109
North American, synopsis of—H. Hagen. (R. 1861) ... 149, **134**
of Arctic America—S. H. Scudder ... 342
of North America, synopsis of—H. Hagen ... **134**
of North America, synopsis of—P. R. Uhler ... 134
pseudo-, of Kerguelen Island—H. A. Hagen ... 294
Nevada, western, Centennial mission to Indians of—S. Powers. (R. 1876) ... 299
New—
classification of clouds—A. Poëy. (R. 1870) ... 244
species and localities of microscopical organisms, notes on—J. W. Bailey. **63**
species of North American coleoptera. Parts I, II—J. L. Le Conte. **167**, **264**
system of weights and measures, with 8 as metrical number—G. H. Knight. (R. 1867) ... 215
tables for determining values of coefficients in perturbative function of planetary motion—J. D. Runkle ... **79**
New Brunswick—
Bay of Fundy, marine invertebrata of region about mouth of—W. Stimpson ... 50
shell heaps in—J. Fowler. (R. 1870) ... 244
shell mounds of—S. F. Baird. (P. 1881) ... 467
New England—
crustacea dredged off south coast of—S. I. Smith. (P. 1880) ... 425
fishes from south coast of, descriptions of new genera and species of—G. B. Goode. (P. 1880) ... 425
frigate mackerel (*Auxis Rochei*) on coast of—G. B. Goode. (P. 1880) ... 425
geology of—E. Hitchcock ... 90
marine invertebrata from, distributed by U. S. Fish Commission—A. E. Verrill; R. Rathbun. (P. 1879) ... 333
marine invertebrates from, distributed by U. S. National Museum—R. Rathbun. (P. 1881) ... 467, **465**, **471**
mollusca added to fauna of—A. E. Verrill. (P. 1880) ... 425
shell mounds on coast of—S. F. Baird. (P. 1881) ... 467
New Harmony, Indiana, account of tornado near, April 30, 1852—J. Chappelsmith ... **59**
New Haven Journal. Account of lightning discharges. (R. 1867) ... 215

New Jersey—
artificial shell deposits in—C. RAU. (R. 1864) 188, 440, **362**
fishes on the coast of Long Island and—S. F. BAIRD. (R. 1854) 75, **348**
stone age in—C. C. ABBOTT. (R. 1875) 298, **394**
New Jersey Historical Society, address of Prof. Henry before the **E**
New Madrid, Missouri, earthquake at—T. DUDLEY. (R. 1858) 109
New Mexico—
account of Lindheimer's, Fendler's, and Wright's botanical explorations in—A. GRAY. (R. 1849) 21
antiquities in—W. B. LYON. (R. 1871) 249
communications relative to publication of Spanish works on—E. ROBINSON; H. E. LUDEWIG; E. G. SQUIER; H. C. MURPHEY; W. B. HODGSON; W. IRVING; W. H. PRESCOTT; J. SPARKS; G. BANCROFT; F. L. HAWKS. (R. 1855) 77
description of new cretaceous *Pinna* from—C. A. WHITE. (P. 1880) 425
diary of excursion in—J. H. CARLETON. (R. 1854) 75
eastern, coleoptera of Kansas and—J. L. LE CONTE **126**
notes on the history and climate of—T. A. MCPARLIN. (R. 1877) 323, **396**
plants of, collected by C. Wright. Parts I, II—A. GRAY 22, 42
report of explorations in Arizona and—J. STEVENSON. (R. 1880) 442
New York—
aboriginal monuments of—E. G. SQUIER **15**
Clinton, Hamilton College. Exchange of specimens. (R. 1861) 149
fishes of—T. GILL. (R. 1856) 91
Fishkill, deposit of arrow-heads near—E. M. SHEPARD. (R. 1877) 323
New York, explosion of nitre in, July, 1845—R. HARE 17
Orleans county, antiquities of—F. H. CUSHING. (R. 1874) 286
Schoharie, Indian relics from—F. D. ANDREWS. (R. 1879) 345
Tompkins county, ancient fort and burial ground in—D. TROWBRIDGE. (R. 1863) 187
University of State of, Regents of. Acknowledgment of specimens. (R. 1865) 209
NEWBERRY, J. S. Description of fossil plants from Chinese coal-bearing rocks. 202
Newcastle, Pennsylvania, account of old Indian village near—E. M. MCCONNELL. (R. 1871) 249
NEWCOMB, S.—
General integrals of planetary motion **281**
Investigation of orbit of Neptune, with tables of its motion **199**
Investigation of orbit of Uranus, with tables of its motion **262**
Memorial address on Joseph Henry 356
NEWCOMB, S., and others. Scientific instructions to Capt. Hall. (R. 1871) 249
Newfoundland, new species of fishes from Grand Banks of—G. B. GOODE. (P. 1880) 425
NEWTON, A. Suggestions for forming collections of birds' eggs 139

NEWTON, A. Suggestions for saving parts of skeletons of birds. (R. 1860) -- 147

NEWTON, H. A. Metric system of weights and measures, with tables. (R. 1865) ---- 209, **371**

Nicaragua—

antiquities of—E. G. SQUIER. (R. 1850) ---- 28

archæological researches in—J. F. BRANSFORD ---- **383**

eruption of volcano in—A. B. DICKINSON. (R. 1867) ---- 215

Nichols, Lieut. H. E.—

list of fishes collected by, in Gulf of California and on west coast of lower California—D. S. JORDAN; C. H. GILBERT. (P. 1881) ---- 467

notes on fishes collected by, in British Columbia and southern Alaska—T. H. BEAN. (P. 1881) ---- 467

notes on fishes collected by, on west coast of Mexico—D. S. JORDAN; C. H. GILBERT. (P. 1881) ---- 467

NICKLÉS, F. J. Scientific Congress of Carlsruhe, 1858. (R. 1860) ---- 147

Nile, explorations of the—C. HALE. (R. 1865) ---- 209

Nitre, memoir on explosiveness of—R. HARE ---- **17**

Nitrification—B. F. CRAIG. (R. 1861) ---- 149

Nitrogen bodies of modern chemistry—Prof. KLETZINSKY. (R. 1872) ---- 271

Nomenclator zoölogicus. Alphabetical list of generic names employed by naturalists. Part I—S. H. SCUDDER ---- **470**

Nomenclature of—

certain North American birds, revisions of—R. RIDGWAY. (P. 1880) -- 425

clouds ---- **347**

North American birds—R. RIDGWAY ---- **422**

NORRIS, P. W. Prehistoric remains in Montana. (R. 1879) ---- 345

North America—

abbreviations of names of States and Territories of ---- **164**

algæ of, fresh-water, history of—H. C. WOOD, Jr ---- **241**

algæ of, marine—*See* W. H. Harvey.

ancient aboriginal trade in—C. RAU. (R. 1872) ---- 271, 440, **385**

ancient history of—M. MUCH. (R. 1871) ---- 249

atlas of, physical, proposed—G. GIBBS. (R. 1866) ---- 214

batrachia and reptiles of, check-list of—E. D. COPE ---- **292**

bats of, monograph of—H. ALLEN ---- **165**

birds added by L. Belding to fauna of—R. RIDGWAY. (P. 1881) ---- 467

birds of, catalogue of—S F. BAIRD ---- **106**

birds of, instructions for collecting nests and eggs of ---- **139**

birds of, nomenclature and catalogue of—R. RIDGWAY ---- **422**

birds of, review of. Part I—S. F. BAIRD ---- **181**

botany of, bibliographical index to—S. WATSON ---- **258**

coleoptera of, classification of. Parts I, II—J. L. LE CONTE ---- **136**, **265**

coleoptera of, list of—J. L. LE CONTE ---- **140**

North America—Continued.
coleoptera of, new species of. Parts I, II—J. L. Le Conte **167, 264**
combined meteorological system for, report of Committee of American Association for Advancement of Science on. (R. 1851) 51
conchology of, bibliography of. Parts I, II—W. G. Binney **142, 174**
contributions to natural history of fresh-water fishes of. Part I. Monograph of cottoids—C. Girard **30**
diptera of, catalogue of—C. R. Osten Sacken **102, 270**
diptera of, monographs of—H. Loew; R. Osten Sacken. **141, 171, 219, 256**
duck new to fauna of—R. Ridgway. (P. 1881) 467
explorations on western coast of—W. H. Dall. (R. 1873) 275
extinct sloth tribe of—J. Leidy **72**
fishes of east coast of, catalogue of—T. Gill **283**
fishes of Pacific coast of, duplicates of, distributed in 1881—D. S. Jordan; P. L. Jouy. (P. 1881) 467
forests and trees of, distribution of—J. G. Cooper. (R. 1858) 109, **351**
grasshoppers of, circular relative to history of **163**
Indians of, uses of brain and marrow of animals among—T. R. Peale. (R. 1870) 244
lakes of, fluctuations of level of—C. Whittlesey **119**
lepidoptera of, catalogue of—J. G. Morris **118**
lepidoptera of, synopsis of—J. G. Morris **133**
libraries, public, in, list of—W. J. Rhees **116**
mammals of, catalogue of—S. F. Baird **105**
map of, ethnological, suggestions relative to—L. H. Morgan. (R. 1861.) 149
meteorological stations and observers in. (R. 1868) 224, **373**
mollusks of western—P. P. Carpenter **252**
myriapods of, belonging to family *Lysiopetalidæ*—J. A. Ryder. (P. 1880) 425
neuroptera of, synopsis of—H. Hagen **134**
orthoptera of, catalogue of—S. H. Scudder **189**
rain and snow fall of, tables of—C. A. Schott **222, 353**
reptiles of, catalogue of—S. F. Baird; C. Girard **49**
shells of, catalogue of—I. Lea; P. P. Carpenter; W. Stimpson; W. G. Binney; T. Prime **128**
shells of, circular in reference to collecting **176**
shells of, land and fresh-water. Parts I–IV—W. G. Binney; T. Bland. **143, 144, 194, 253**
siluridæ of, synopsis of—D. S. Jordan 306
stone implements of—C. Rau. (R. 1872) 271, **382**
North American—
archæology—J. Lubbock. (R. 1862) 150
birds, catalogue of—S. F. Baird **108**

North American—Continued.
birds, catalogue of—R. RIDGWAY. (P. 1880) 425, **422**
birds, desiderata among—R. RIDGWAY. (P. 1881) 467
Continent, physical geography of—J. FROEBEL. (R. 1854) 75
fishes, duplicates of, distributed by Smithsonian Institution—T. H. BEAN. (P. 1880) 425
Indians, catalogue of portraits of—J. M. STANLEY **53**
Indians, list of photographic portraits of **216**
stone implements—C. RAU. (R. 1872) 271, **382**
stone period, agricultural implements of—C. RAU. (R. 1863) 187, **382**
tortoises, land, of genus *Xerobates*—F. W. TRUE. (P. 1881) 467
North American Ichthyology, contributions to—
Part I. Review Rafinesque's memoirs—D. S. JORDAN **305**
Part II. *A.* Notes on *Cottidæ*, (etc.) *B.* Synopsis *Siluridæ*—D. S. JORDAN **306**
Part III. *A.* Distribution of fishes of Alleghany region, (etc.)—D. S. JORDAN; A. W. BRAYTON. *B.* Synopsis of family *Catostomidæ*—D. S. JORDAN **308**
North American Oölogy. Part I. Raptores and fissirostres—T. M. BREWER **89**
North Carolina—
ancient mica mines in—C. D. SMITH. (R. 1876) 299
Beaufort, description of new species of fish (*Caranx Beani*) from—D. S. JORDAN. (P. 1880) 425
Beaufort, notes on fishes of—D. S. JORDAN; C. H GILBERT. (P. 1878.) 332
Black Mountain, topography of—T. L. CLINGMAN. (R 1855) 77
earthquakes in, in 1874—W. DU PRÉ; J. HENRY. (R. 1874) 286
Lenoir county, antiquities in—J. M. SPAINHOUR. (R. 1871) 249
Montgomery county, antiquities of—F. J. KRON. (R. 1874) 286
occurrence of *Phycis regius* in—T. H. BEAN. (P. 1880) 425
Stanley county, antiquities of—F. J. KRON. (R. 1874) 286
North German Lloyd, free freight between Germany and United States by—R. SCHLEIDEN. (R. 1858) 109
North Pacific Surveying Expedition, contributions to natural history made in connection with—T. H. STREETS 303
North Pole, expedition toward the, scientific instructions to—J. HENRY; J. E. HILGARD; S. NEWCOMB; S. F. BAIRD; F. B. MEEK; L. AGASSIZ. (R. 1871) 249
North Pole, map of stars near the, for observations on the aurora **350**
Northern Hemisphere, winds of the—J. H COFFIN **52**
Northern latitudes, record of auroral phenomena observed in—P. FORCE **84**
Northern seas, the—J. BABINET. (R. 1869) 228
Northumberland, Duke of, account of the 330
Northumberland, Duke of, presentation of books by. (R. 1859) 110

Northwest coast of America, kjökken-möddings on the—P. SCHUMACHER. (R. 1873) ---- 275
NORTON, E. On wasps ---- 254
Norway, Ethnological Museum of—L. K. DAA. (R. 1862) ---- 150
Norway, University of Christiania, ethnological specimens from. (R. 1863) -- 187
Norwegian mountains, lakes, and the snow-line—O. E. DREUTZER. (R. 1866.) 214
Notacanthus phasganorus from Newfoundland—G. B. GOODE. (P. 1880) ---- 425
Note on occurrence of *Phycis regius* in South Carolina—T. H. BEAN. (P. 1880.) 425
Note on the latiloid genera—T. GILL. (P. 1881) ---- 467
Notes—
of egging expedition to Shoal Lake, Lake Winnipeg—D. GUNN. (R. 1867) ---- 215
on aboriginal shell mounds of New Brunswick and New England—S. F. BAIRD. (P. 1881) ---- 467
on American migration—F. VON HELLWALD. (R. 1866) ---- 214
on fishes—*See* D. S. Jordan; C. H. Gilbert; *also*, Proceedings National Museum.
on fishes of Pacific coast of United States—D. S. JORDAN; C. H. GILBERT. (P. 1881) ---- 467
on history and climate of New Mexico—T. A. MCPARLIN. (R. 1877.) 323, **396**
on horary variations of barometer—M. VAILLANT; J. HENRY. (R. 1866.) 214
on Indian history—F. V. HAYDEN. (R. 1867) ---- 215
on life and character of Joseph Henry—J. C. WELLING ---- 356, **338**
on mortality among fishes of Gulf of Mexico—S. H. JOHNSON. (P. 1881.) 467
on new species and localities of microscopical organisms—J W. BAILEY. **63**
on physical geography of North America—J. G. COOPER. (R. 1858.) 109, **351**
on *Salmonidæ* of upper Columbia—C. BENDIRE. (P. 1881) ---- 467
on some Costa Rican birds—R. RIDGWAY. (P. 1881) ---- 467
on Tinneh or Chepewyan Indians of British and Russian America—G. GIBBS and others. (R. 1866) ---- 214, **365**
on Tonto Apaches—C. SMART. (R. 1867) ---- 215
relative to George Catlin—J. HENRY. (R. 1872) ---- 271
to accounts of lightning discharges, by G. W. Dodge and others—J. HENRY. (R. 1867) ---- 215
to article on vitality, by H. H. Higgins—J. HENRY. (R 1866) ---- 214
to articles on meteorology, by G. Latimer and others—J. HENRY. (R. 1871) ---- 249
to lectures on meteorology, by R. Russell—J. HENRY. (R. 1854) ---- 75
Notice, biographical, of—
Agassiz, L., by J. A. GARFIELD. (R. 1873) ---- 275
Agassiz, L., by P. PARKER. (R. 1873) ---- 275
Blackmore Museum, Salisbury, England. (R. 1868) ---- 224
Chase, S. P., by J. A. GARFIELD. (R. 1873) ---- 275

Notice, biographical, of—Continued.
Chase, S. P., by H. HAMLIN. (R. 1873) 275
Cleaveland, Parker, by J. HENRY. (R. 1859) 110
Espy, James P., by A. D. BACHE. (R. 1859) 110
Harvey, W. H., by A. GRAY. (R. 1867) 215
Irving, Washington, by C. C. FELTON. (R. 1859) 110
Jewett, C. C., by R. A. GUILD. (R. 1867) 215
Rush, Richard, by J. A. PEARCE. (R. 1859) 110
Schoenbein, Christian Frederic, the discoverer of ozone. (R. 1868) 224
Smithson, James, by D. GILBERT, President of the Royal Society. (R. 1853) 67, 330
Smithson, James, by W. R. JOHNSON; J. R. McD. IRBY 327
Smithson, James, by W. J. RHEES. (R. 1879) 349, **330**
Turner, W. W., by C. C. FELTON. (R. 1859) 110
Würdemann, G, by A. D. BACHE. (R. 1859) 110
Notice of recent additions to marine invertebrates of northeast coast of America—A. E. VERRILL. (P. 1880) 425
Notices of public libraries in the United States—C. C. JEWETT **25**
Nova Scotia—
birds of—BLACKISTON; T. BLAND; J. R. WILLIS. (R. 1858) 109
fishes obtained at—*See* G. B. Goode; T. H. Bean.
kjökken-möddings in—J. M. JONES. (R. 1863) 187
Numeration, report on improved system of—W. B. TAYLOR. (R. 1867) 215
Nuovi Lincei, Pontifical Academy of the. Prize questions. (R. 1865; R. 1867) 209, 215
Nutation, phenomena of—J. G. BARNARD 310
NUTTER, F. H. Mounds on Gideon's farm, near Excelsior, Hennepin county, Minnesota. (R. 1879) 345

O.

Ober, F. A.—
birds of Antigua and Barbuda collected by, catalogue of—G. N. LAWRENCE. (P. 1878) 332
birds of Dominica collected by, catalogue of—G. N. LAWRENCE. (P. 1878.) 332
birds of Grenada collected by, catalogue of—G. N. LAWRENCE. (P. 1878.) 332
birds of Guadeloupe collected by, catalogue of—G. N. LAWRENCE. (P. 1878) 332
birds of Lesser Antilles collected by, catalogue of—G. N. LAWRENCE. (P. 1878) 332
birds of Martinique collected by, catalogue of—G. N. LAWRENCE. (P. 1878) 332
birds of St. Vincent collected by, catalogue of—G. N. LAWRENCE. (P. 1878) 332
OBER, F. A. Ornithology of the Caribbee Islands. (R. 1878) 341
Obsequies of Joseph Henry 356
Observations—
astronomical—W. HARKNESS 239
astronomical, discussion of Piazzi's—B. A. GOULD. (R. 1863) 187
astronomical, in Arctic Seas—E. K. KANE **129**
in Hudson's Bay Territory—B. R. Ross. (R. 1859) 110
magnetic, in the Arctic Seas—E. K. KANE **97**
physical, in Arctic Seas—I. I. HAYES **196**
physical, in Arctic Seas. Parts I–IV—E. K. KANE **198**
scientific, metric system for—A. GUYOT. (R 1848) I
Observations—*See* Magnetic, Meteorological, Physical, Tidal.
Observations, meteorological—
at Brunswick, Maine—P. CLEAVELAND **204**
at Providence, Rhode Island—A. CASWELL **103**, **443**
at Sacramento, California—F. W. HATCH. (R. 1854) 75
at Sacramento, California—T. M. LOGAN. (R. 1854) 75
at Washington, Arkansas—N. D. SMITH **131**
combined, report of committee of American Association for Advancement of Science on system of. (R. 1851) 51
directions for—A. GUYOT **19**
for year 1855 **93**
in the Arctic Seas—E. K. KANE **104**
Observations of—
earthquake phenomena—R. MALLET. (R. 1859) 110
Siredon lichenoides—W. E. CARLIN. (P. 1881) 467
temperature, best hours for—C. DEWEY. (R. 1860) 147
thunder storm, John Wise's—R. HARE. (R. 1854) 75
thunder storms, instructions for—J. HENRY **235**

Observations on—
auroras, map of stars near North Pole for ---- **350**
Batis maritima of Linnæus—J. Torrey ---- **60**
electric resonance of mountains—H. De Saussure. (R. 1868) ---- 224
gold ornament from mound in Florida—C. Rau. (R. 1877) ---- 323, 440, **403**
ice—D. Walker ---- 146
Mexican history and archæology—B. Mayer ---- **86**
natural phenomena, shooting stars, aurora, etc.—S. Masterman. (R. 1857) ---- 107
prehistoric mounds of Grant county, Wisconsin—M. Strong. (R. 1876.) 299
terrestrial magnetism—J. Locke ---- **35**
terrestrial magnetism and deviation of compasses of iron-clad "Monadnock"—W. Harkness ---- **239**
terrestrial magnetism in Mexico—Baron von Müller; A. Sonntag ---- **114**
thunder and lightning—S. Masterman. (R. 1855) ---- 77
Observatories—
at Dorpat and Poulkova, description of—C. Abbe. (R. 1867) ---- 215, **369**
detached, universal meteorograph for—E. H. von Baumhauer. (R. 1879.) 345
instructions to, relative to telegraphic announcements of astronomical discoveries—J. Henry ---- 263
reports of, 1879—E. S. Holden. (R. 1879) ---- 345, **410**
reports of, 1880—E. S. Holden; G. H. Boehmer. (R. 1880) ---- 442, **438**
Observatory—
at Cordova, Argentine Republic, account of—B. A. Gould. (R. 1873.) 275
at St. Martin, Isle Jesus, Canada East, description of—C. Smallwood. (R. 1856) ---- 91
Girard College—*See* Bache, A. D.
Kew, verification of barometers at—J. Welsh. (R. 1859) ---- 110
magnetic, at Smithsonian Institution, description of—J. E Hilgard. (R. 1859) ---- 110
physical, on a—J. Henry. (R. 1870) ---- 244
Toronto, instructions by, for aurora observations ---- 148
Observers, meteorological, of Smithsonian Institution, list of. (R. 1868) ---- 224, **373**
Observers—*See* Meteorological stations and observers.
Occultations—
in 1852—C. H. Davis ---- 29
of planets and stars by the moon, 1853—J. Downes ---- **54**
visible in the United States during the years 1848-1852—J. Downes. **8, 9, 10, 11**, 29
Occultator, account of—T. Hill ---- 101
Ocean, fresh water in the—W. C. Dennis. (R. 1866) ---- 214
Ocean, Indian, cyclone in the—N. Pike (R. 1867) ---- 215
Oceanic bonito on coast of United States—G. B. Goode; T. H. Bean. (P. 1878.) 332

Oceanic bonito (*Orcynus pelamys*), occurrence of, in Vineyard Sound—V. N. EDWARDS. (P 1878) 332
ODLING, W. Scientific work of Thomas Graham. (R. 1871) 249
OEHLER, A. Stone cists near Highland, Madison county, Illinois. (R. 1879.) 345
Oersted, H. C., memoir of, by E. DE BEAUMONT. (R. 1868) 224
Officers—
and establishment of the Smithsonian Institution and National Museum. **449**
collaborators, employés, etc., of Smithsonian Institution, National Museum, Geological Survey, Bureau of Ethnology, and Fish Commission, directory of **466**
and Regents of Smithsonian Institution, 1846, list of .... **N**
Ohio—
ancient earthworks in, sketch of—I. DILLE. (R. 1866) 214
ancient works in, descriptions of—C. WHITTLESEY **37**
Ashland county, earthworks in—G. W. HILL. (R. 1877) 323
Ashtabula county, double-walled earthwork in—S. D. PEET. (R. 1876.) 299
Holmes county, flint instruments in—H. B. CASE. (R. 1877) 323
Kelley's Island, climate of—G. C. HUNTINGTON. (R. 1866) 214
Marietta, meteorological observations at—S. P. HILDRETH; J. WOOD .. **120**
northern, antiquities of—G. W. HILL. (R. 1874) 286
Perry county, antiquities of—W. ANDERSON. (R. 1874) 286
Trumbull county, mound in—F. MILLER. (R. 1877) 323
Ohio river, habits of black bass of the—J. EOFF. (R. 1854) 75
Ohio river, suggestions for improvement of navigation of—C. ELLET, Jr. 13
Oil—
coal, explosibility of—Z. ALLEN. (R. 1861) 149
porpoise, manufacture of—C. COOK. (P. 1878) 332
rock, or petroleum, history of—T. S. HUNT. (R. 1861) 149
Oil-shark of southern California—D. S. JORDAN; C. H. GILBERT. (P. 1880.) 425
Old-World birds in National Museum, catalogue of—R. RIDGWAY. (P. 1881.) 467
Oligocene fossils, check-list of—T. A. CONRAD 200
Olmos, Peru, account of solar eclipse at—J. M. GILLISS **100**
OLMSTED, D. Aurora borealis, recent secular period of **81**
OLNEY, S. T. List of Rhode Island algæ 241
Omaha myth—J. O. DORSEY. (E. 1879-80) 476
Oölogy, North American. Part I. Raptores and fissirostres—T. M. BREWER.. **89**
Oölogy of Kerguelen Island—J. H. KIDDER; E. COUES 294
Opening and closing of Kennebec river, Maine—R. H. GARDINER. (R. 1858.) 109
Opheosaurus ventralis, remarks on osteology of—R. W. SHUFELDT. (P. 1881.) 467
Orbit—
and phenomena of meteoric fire-ball—J. H. COFFIN **221**
of Neptune, investigation of, with tables of its motion—S. NEWCOMB .. **199**
of Uranus, investigation of, with tables of its motion—S. NEWCOMB **262**

Orbits, planetary, secular variations of—J. N. STOCKWELL. (R. 1871) ... 249, **232**
Orcynus pelamys (oceanic bonito), occurrence of, in Vineyard Sound, Massachusetts—V. N. EDWARDS. (P. 1878) ... 332
Oregon—
fishes of, notes on collection of—D. S. JORDAN. (P. 1878) ... 332
jargon of—B. R. MITCHELL; W. W. TURNER ... **68**
trade-language of—G. GIBBS ... 161
Ores collected on geological survey in Michigan, catalogue of—C. T. JACKSON. (R. 1854) ... 75
Ores, rocks, minerals, and fossils, catalogue of—J. LOCKE. (R. 1854) ... 75
Organic bases—A. BAUER. (R. 1872) ... 271
Organisms—*See* Microscopic.
Organization and objects of the United States National Museum—G. B. GOODE. (P. 1881) ... 467, **459**
Organization, plan of, and regulations of the U. S. National Museum—G. B. GOODE. (P. 1881) ... 467, **445**
Organization of—
local scientific societies—J. HENRY. (R. 1875) ... 298
Smithsonian Institution, programme of ... **F**, **J**, 328
Smithsonian Institution, report of American Academy of Arts and Sciences on—E. EVERETT; J. SPARKS; B. PEIRCE; H. W. LONGFELLOW; A. GRAY. (R. 1853) ... 67
Smithsonian Institution, report of committee of Regents on ... **B**, **L**, 328
Organized bodies, natural history of—E. J. MAREY. (R. 1867) ... 215
O'Rielly, Henry, deposition of J. Henry in case of S. F. B. Morse *versus* ... 115
Origin—
and history of the Smithsonian Institution—W. J. RHEES ... **328**
and propagation of disease—J. C. DALTON. (R. 1873) ... 275
of force—W. B. TAYLOR. (R. 1870) ... 244, **375**
Ornament, gold, from a mound in Florida, observations on—C. RAU. (R. 1877.) 323, 440, **403**
Ornithology—
of Caribbee Islands—F. A. OBER. (R. 1878) ... 341
of Hawaiian and Fanning Islands and California—T. H. STREETS ... 303
of Kerguelen Islands—J. H. KIDDER; E. COUES ... 293
Ortalidæ, monograph of—H. LOEW ... 256
Orthoptera—
bibliography of—S. H. SCUDDER ... 189
instructions for collecting—P. R. UHLER. (R. 1858) ... 109
of North America, catalogue of—S. H. SCUDDER ... **189**
OSBORNE, J. A. Account of lightning discharges. (R. 1867) ... 215
Osmerus attenuatus, new species of California fish, description of—W. N. LOCKINGTON. (P. 1880) ... 425

OSTEN SACKEN, R.—
Bibliography of diptera 270
Catalogue of described diptera of North America **102**, **270**
Diptera of Kerguelen Island 294
Directions for collecting and preserving diptera 102
Monograph of *Tipulidæ* 219
Monographs of diptera of North America. Part IV **219**
OSTEN SACKEN, R.; LOEW, H. Instructions for collecting diptera. (R. 1858.) 109
OSTEN SACKEN, R.; LOEW, H. Monographs of diptera of North America. Parts I, II **141**, **171**
Osteology and mounds of the mound-builders of Wisconsin—J. N. DE HART. (R. 1877) 323
Osteology of *Opheosaurus ventralis*—R. W. SHUFELDT. (P. 1881) 467
Ostraciontidæ (trunk fishes), a study of, with notes on American species—G. B. GOODE. (P. 1879) 333
Othonops eos, a new gobioid fish from San Diego, Cal.—R. SMITH. (P. 1881.) 467
Outline of scheme of classification of collections in U. S. National Museum—G. B. GOODE. (P. 1881) 467, **457**
Outline of systematic review of the class of birds—W. LILLJEBORG **364**
OWEN, D. D. Catalogue of geological specimens. (R. 1854) 75
OWEN, D. D. Report on building stones. (R. 1847) .... **H**, 329
OWEN, R. D. Hints on public architecture .... **P**
Owl, description of a new, from Porto Rico—R. RIDGWAY. (P. 1881) 467
Ox, American, extinct species of—J. LEIDY **41**
Oxygen and its combinations, lecture on—G. I. CHACE. (R. 1855) 77
Ozone and antozone—C. M. WETHERILL. (R. 1864) 188, **355**
Ozone, notice of C. F. Schoenbein, the discoverer of. (R. 1868) 224

P.

Pacific coast—
fishes from, descriptions of new—D. S. JORDAN; C. H. GILBERT. (P. 1881) ---- 467
fishes from, distributed in 1881—D. S. JORDAN; P. L. JOUY. (P. 1881.) 467
fishes of—*See* D. S. Jordan; C. H. Gilbert.
fishes of, bibliography of—T. H. BEAN. (P. 1881) ---- 467
fishes of, bibliography of—T. GILL ---- 463
fishes of, notes on—D. S. JORDAN; C. H. GILBERT. (P. 1881) ---- 467
Pacific Islands, natural history of—W. H. PEASE. (R. 1862) ---- 150
PACKARD, A. S. Directions for collecting and preserving insects ---- **261**
PACKARD, A. S. Memoir of H. J. Clark ---- 242
PACKARD, F. A. Project of outline history of education in the United States. (R. 1863) ---- 187
PAGE, C. G. Report on effect of frost on building stones. (R. 1847) ---- **H**, 329
Palæontology—
list of generic names employed in—S. H. SCUDDER ---- 470
of the upper Missouri—F. B. MEEK; F. V. HAYDEN ---- **172**
principles and methods of—T. H. HUXLEY. (R. 1869) ---- 228
Palafittes or lacustrian constructions of the lake of Neuchâtel—E. DESOR. (R. 1865) ---- 209, **360**
Palenque tablet in the U. S. National Museum—C. RAU ---- **331**
Palermo, evaporation observed at, in 1865, 1866—P. TACCHINI. (R. 1870) ---- 244
PALMIERI, Prof. Electro-magnetic seismograph. (R. 1870) ---- 244
PALMIERI, Prof. Presence of electricity during fall of rain. (R. 1870) ---- 244
Panama, shells of, review of C. B. Adams' catalogue of—P. P. CARPENTER ---- 252
Pancreas, observations on the—J. JONES ---- 82
Pandoridæ, contributions towards a monograph of the—P. P. CARPENTER ---- 252
Paralepis coruscans, new species of *Paralepis*, description of—D. S. JORDAN; C. H. GILBERT. (P. 1880) ---- 425
Parasites—J. LEIDY ---- 44
Paris—
Academy of Sciences, historical sketch of the—M. FLOURENS. (R. 1862.) 150
Anthropological Society of, history of transactions of, 1865 to 1867—P. BROCA. (R. 1868) ---- 224
Exposition—*See* French Exposition.
Muséum d'Histoire Naturelle, typical specimens of American fishes in the—D. S. JORDAN. (P. 1879) ---- 333
PARKER, P. Biographical notice of L. Agassiz. (R. 1873) ---- 275, 329
PARKER, P. Eulogy on Henry Wilson. (R. 1875) ---- 298, 329
Parophrys ischyurus, new species of flounders from Puget Sound, description of—D. S. JORDAN; C. H. GILBERT. (P. 1880) ---- 425

Parrot, new species of, of genus *Chirus*, from Dominica—G. N. LAWRENCE. (P. 1880) 425
Parthenogenesis in the animal kingdom—G. A. KORNHUBER. (R. 1871) 249
PARVIN, J. B. Habits of the gopher of Illinois. (R. 1854) 75
Past and future of geology—J. PRESTWICH. (R. 1875) 298
Patagonia, human remains from—A. RIED. (R. 1862) 150
Patent Office, U. S., meteorological observations under the direction of. Vols. I, II **157, 182**
PATTERSON, R.; SHARPLESS, T. Phonography. (R. 1856) 91
PATTON, A. Antiquities of Knox county, Indiana. (R. 1873) 275
PATTON, A. Antiquities of Lawrence county, Illinois. (R. 1873) 275
PEABODY, A. P. Scientific education of mechanics and artisans. (R. 1872.) 271, **380**
PEALE, T. R.—
Ancient mound in St. Louis, Missouri. (R. 1861) 149
Method of preserving lepidoptera. (R. 1863) 187
Prehistoric remains in vicinity of city of Washington, D. C. (R. 1872.) 271
Uses of brain and marrow of animals among Indians of North America. (R. 1870) 244
Pearce, J. A., eulogy on, by A. D. BACHE. (R. 1862) 150, 329
PEARCE, J. A. Notice of Richard Rush. (R. 1859) 110, 329
PEARCE, J. A. Report of Committee of Regents on distribution of Smithsonian income. (R 1853) 67
PEASE, W. H. Acknowledgment for shells, etc. (R. 1861) 149
PEASE, W. H. Natural history of Pacific Islands. (R. 1862) 150
Pedro II, Dom, biographical sketch of, by A. FIALHO. (R. 1876) 299
PEET, S. D. Double-walled earthwork in Ashtabula county, Ohio. (R. 1876.) 299
PEIRCE, B., and others. Report of American Academy of Arts and Sciences on organization of Smithsonian Institution. (R. 1853) 67
PELTIER, F. A. Memoir of J. C. A. Peltier. (R. 1867) 215
Peltier, J. C. A., memoir of, by F. A. PELTIER. (R. 1867) 215
Peltier, J. C. A., scientific researches of. (R. 1867) 215
Pendulum, problems of rotary motion presented by the—J. G. BARNARD 240
Pennsylvania—
Centre county, Spruce creek valley, account of a tornado in—J. B. MEEK. (R. 1871) 249
Chester county, birds of—V. BARNARD. (R. 1860) 147
Chester county, history of—W. DARLINGTON. (R. 1862) 150
magnetic survey of—A. D. BACHE **166**
Newcastle, old Indian village, Kushkushkee, near—E. M. MCCONNELL. (R. 1871) 249
western, ancient mound in—W. M. TAYLOR. (R. 1877) 323
Pensacola, Florida, description of new species of amber fish (*Seriola Stearnsii*) from—G. B. GOODE. (P. 1879) 333

Pepin, Lake, antiquities on the banks of—L. C. ESTES. (R. 1866) 214
Perca flavescens, notes on—F. STEINDACHNER. (P. 1878) 332
Percidæ, notes on—D. S. JORDAN 306
Perennibranchiates, acknowledgment of—J. G. FISHER. (R. 1863) 187
Periodical phenomena—
directions for registry of 148
observations on, 1851 to 1859—F. B. HOUGH 182
registration of—J. HENRY. (R. 1855) 77
registry of 65, **148**
Periodicals—
deposited in Library of Congress, meteorological articles in. (R. 1873) 275
in Library of Smithsonian Institution. Parts I, II; foreign works; 1866. **73, 85, 117, 179**
received by the Institution, list of. (R. 1880) 442, **436**
received in reading-room of Smithsonian Institution in 1853, check-list of. **Q**
PERRINE, T. M. Antiquities of Union county, Illinois. (R. 1873) 275
PERRINE, T. M. Mounds near Anna, Union county, Illinois. (R. 1872) 271
Persistence of images—F. N. MOIGNO. (R. 1866) 214
Perspiration and respiration, apparatus for testing results of—M. PETTENKOFER. (R. 1864) 188
Peru—
earthquake in, August 13, 1868—J. V. CAMPBELL. (R. 1870) 244
Indians of—F. L. GALT. (R. 1877) 323
Olmos, total eclipse of sun, September 7, 1858, observed near—J. M. GILLISS **100**
PESLIN, M. Relation between barometric variations and general atmospheric currents. (R. 1877) 323, 398
PETER, R. Ancient mounds in Kentucky. (R. 1872) 271
PETER, R. Ancient mound near Lexington, Kentucky. (R. 1871) 249
Petite Anse Island, salt deposit on—E. W. HILGARD 248
PETITOT, E. Account of the Indians of British America. (R. 1865) 209
Petrel, supposed new, from Sandwich Islands, description of—R. RIDGWAY. (P. 1881) 467
Petroleum collections, circular in reference to—S. F. BAIRD. (P. 1881) 467, **447**
Petroleum or rock oil, history of—T. S. HUNT. (R. 1861) 149
PETTENKOFER, M. Apparatus for testing the results of perspiration and respiration. (R. 1864) 188
PETTIGREW, J. B. Modes of flight in relation to aeronautics. (R. 1867) 215
Phænogamia of Kerguelen Island—A. GRAY 294
Phalangidæ, instructions for collecting—H. C. WOOD. (R. 1866) 214
Phenomena—
accompanying the propagation of electricity in highly rarefied elastic fluids—A. DE LA RIVE. (R. 1863) 187
in telegraphic lines during the aurora borealis—G. B. DONATI. (R. 1872.) 271

Phenomena—Continued.
natural, observations on—S. MASTERMAN. (R. 1857) 107
of contact, studies on—T. L. PHIPSON. (R. 1862) 150
of flight in animal kingdom—E. J. MAREY. (R. 1869) 228
of meteoric fire-ball—J. H. COFFIN **221**
of precession and nutation—J. G. BARNARD 310
periodical registration of—J. HENRY. (R. 1855) 77
Philadelphia—
exhibit at—*See* Centennial.
magnetic and meteorological observations at—*See* A. D. Bache.
memorial of citizens of, relative to Lowe's aeronautic voyages across Atlantic. (R. 1860) 147
Philadelphia Academy of Natural Sciences, report on shells presented to—J. LEIDY; G. W. TRYON. (R. 1865) 209
PHILLIPS, B. Two letters on work of the Museum. (P. 1881) 467, **454**
Philological circular—G. GIBBS. (R. 1862) 150
Philology, Indian—W. W. TURNER. (R. 1851) 51
Philology, instructions for research relative to—G. GIBBS **160**
Philosophical Society of Washington—
Bulletins of. Vols. I–III. March, 1871, to June, 1880 **423**
memoir of Joseph Henry read before the—W. B. TAYLOR 356, **339**
notes on life and character of Joseph Henry read before the—J. C. WELLING 356, **338**
proceedings of, on death of Joseph Henry 356
Philosophy, annals of, contributions to, by J. Smithson. (R. 1853) 67, 330
Philosophy, Batavian Society of Experimental, of Rotterdam. Prize questions. (R. 1861) 149
PHIPSON, T. L. The catalytic force or studies on the phenomena of contact. (R. 1862) 150
Phlegmasia, disease of, bibliography of works on—W. W. KEEN 300
Phonetic language, vocal sounds of L. Bridgman compared with elements of—F. LIEBER 12
Phonography—T. SHARPLESS; R. PATTERSON. (R. 1856) 91
Phonography, institutions in which, is taught. (R. 1856) 91
Photo-chemistry—J. JAMIN. (R. 1867) 215
Photographs of Indians, list of **216**
Photography, astronomical, progress in—Dr. LEE. (R. 1861) 149
Photography, celestial, use of silvered-glass telescope in—H. DRAPER **180**
Phycis Chesteri from deep-sea fauna of northwestern Atlantic, description of—G. B. GOODE; T. H. BEAN. (P. 1878) 332
Phycis Earlii, new hake, from South Carolina, description of—T. H. BEAN. (P. 1880) 425
Phycis regius from North Carolina, note on occurrence of—T. H. BEAN. (P. 1880) 425

Physical—
atlas of North America, proposed—G. GIBBS. (R. 1866) 214
ethnology, lectures on—D. WILSON. (R. 1862) 150
geography of Mississippi valley—C. ELLET, Jr. **13**
geography of North America—J. G. COOPER. (R. 1858) 109, **351**
geography of North American Continent—J. FROEBEL. (R. 1854) 75
observations in the Arctic Seas—I. I. HAYES **196**
observations in the Arctic Seas—E. K. KANE **198**
observations in the Arctic Seas—F. L. McCLINTOCK **146**
observatory, on a—J. HENRY. (R. 1870) 244
sciences, on the relation of, to science in general—H. HELMHOLTZ. (R. 1871) 249
tables—A. GUYOT **153**
Physics—
present fundamental principles of—F. J. PISKO. (R. 1879) 345
recent progress in, 1879 and 1880—G. F. BARKER. (R. 1880) 442, **429**
report on recent progress in, electricity, galvanism—J. MÜLLER. (R. 1855–1858) 77, 91, 107, 109
syllabus of a course of lectures on—J. HENRY. (R. 1856) 91
terrestrial, articles on—J. V. CAMPBELL; Prof. PALMIERI; W. W. JOHNSON; W. D. SARGENT. (R. 1870) 244
Physics and Natural History, Geneva Society of—*See* Geneva.
Physiological investigations of vertebrata—J. JONES **82**
Physiology—
electro-, lectures on—C. MATTEUCCI. (R. 1865) 209
of fever—H. C. WOOD **357**
of lucernarians—H. J. CLARK 242
of rattlesnake—S. W. MITCHELL 135
of respiration in chelonia—S. W. MITCHELL; G. R. MOREHOUSE **159**
Piazzi's astronomical observations, discussion of—B. A. GOULD. (R. 1863) 187
PICKERING, C. Gliddon mummy case in Museum of Smithsonian Institution. **208**
Picture writing, Central American, studies in—E. S. HOLDEN. (E. 1879–80.) 476
PIDGEON, W. Ancient burial mound in Indiana. (R. 1867) 215
PIERSON, W. M. Discovery of large meteorite in Mexico. (R. 1873) 275
PIKE, N. Cyclone in Indian Ocean. (R. 1867) 215
PILAR, G. Revolutions of crust of the earth. (R. 1876) 299
Pile work antiquities of Olmutz. (R. 1866) 214
PILLING, J. C. Catalogue of linguistic manuscripts in library of Bureau of Ethnology. (E. 1879–80) 476
Pima Indians of Arizona—F. E. GROSSMAN. (R. 1871) 249
Pinna, cretaceous, from New Mexico, description of new—C. A. WHITE. (P. 1880) 425
PIRZ, A. Methods of making and preserving plaster casts. (P. 1881) 467
Pisces, class, arrangement of—T. GILL 247

PISKO, F. J. Present fundamental principles of physics. (R. 1879) ---------- 345
Pitcher plant, new, (*Darlingtonia Californica*,) from California—J. TORREY -- 61
Pits at Embarrass, Wisconsin—E. E. BREED. (R. 1877) ---------- 323
Pittsburg, on Des Moines river, composition of ancient pottery found at—R. N. DAHLBERG; C. DAHLBERG. (R. 1879) ---------- 345
Plan of—
a bibliography—J. FRIEDLÄNDER. (R. 1858) ---------- 109
organization and regulations of U. S. National Museum—G. B. GOODE. (P. 1881) ---------- 467, **445**
research upon the atmosphere—C. M. WETHERILL. (R. 1866) ---------- 214
Smithsonian exhibit at Centennial—S. F. BAIRD. (R. 1875) ---------- 298
Planet—*See* Neptune, Uranus.
Planetary—
disturbances, lecture on—E. S. SNELL. (R. 1855) ---------- 77
motion, general integrals of—S. NEWCOMB ---------- **281**
motion, perturbative function of, tables for determining values of coefficients in—J. D. RUNKLE ---------- **79**, **94**
orbits, secular variations of elements of—J. N. STOCKWELL. (R. 1871.) 249, **232**
Planetoids—*See* Asteroids.
Planets—
between Mars and Jupiter—Prof. LESPIAULT. (R. 1861) ---------- 149
between Mars and Jupiter, lecture on—E. LOOMIS. (R. 1854) ---------- 75
occultations of—*See* Downes, J.
Planisphere of the visible heavens for observations of meteoric displays ---------- **359**
Plans for the installation of collections in the U. S. National Museum—G. B. GOODE. (P. 1881) ---------- 467, **472**
Plans of the Smithsonian building—R. D. OWEN ---------- **P**
Plantæ Frémontianæ—J. TORREY ---------- **46**
Plantæ Wrightianæ Texano-Neo-Mexicanæ. Parts I, II—A. GRAY ---------- **22**, **42**
PLANTAMOUR, E. Report on transactions of the Society of Physics and Natural History of Geneva, July, 1864, to June, 1865; July, 1874, to June, 1875. (R. 1865; R. 1877) ---------- 209, 323
Plants—
collected by J. C. Frémont in California—J. TORREY ---------- 46
cryptogamous, present state of knowledge of—W. REICHARDT. (R. 1871.) 249
dates of blossoming of—F. B. HOUGH ---------- 182
dates of defoliation or fall of leaf of—F. B. HOUGH ---------- 182
dates of foliation of—F. B. HOUGH ---------- 182
directions for collecting and preserving—L. F. WARD ---------- **460**
of Arctic America, descriptions of—A. GRAY ---------- 342
of Texas, New Mexico, and Mexico, collected by C. Wright—A. GRAY. **22**
of upper Missouri, list of—T. C. PORTER. (R. 1850) ---------- 28
of Washington, check-list of—L. F. WARD ---------- **461**

Plants—*See* Torrey, J., Gray, A.

Plaster casts—

methods of making and preserving—A. PIRZ. (P. 1881) 467

of antique and modern statues—W. J. STONE. (R. 1855) 77

of heads of Indian boys and girls at Hampton, Virginia—R. H. PRATT. (P. 1879) 333

of heads of Indian prisoners at St. Augustine, Florida—R. H. PRATT. (P. 1878) 332

PLATEAU, F. Rapid preparation of myological specimens. (P. 1881) 467

PLATEAU, J. Experimental and theoretical researches on the figures of equilibrium of a liquid mass withdrawn from the action of gravity. Parts I–VI. (R. 1863–1866) 187, 188, 209, 214

Platessa ferruginea, note on—G. B. GOODE; T. H. BEAN. (P. 1878) 332

Platessa rostrata, note on—G. B. GOODE; T. H. BEAN. (P. 1878) 332

Platycnemism in Michigan—H. GILLMAN. (R. 1873) 275, **393**

Platyrhina exasperata, generic relations of—D. S. JORDAN; C. H. GILBERT. (P. 1880) 425

Platyrhina triseriata, new ray from coast of California, description of—D. S. JORDAN; C. H. GILBERT. (P. 1880) 425

Platysomatichthys stomias, new flounder from coast of California, description of—D. S. JORDAN; C. H. GILBERT. (P. 1880) 425

Pleuronectes glaber, identity of, with *Euchalarodus Putnami*—T. H. BEAN. (P. 1878) 332

Pleuronectidæ of San Francisco, review of—W. N. LOCKINGTON. (P. 1879) 333

Pleuronichthys verticalis, new flounder from coast of California, description of—D. S. JORDAN; C. H. GILBERT. (P. 1880) 425

POE, O. M. Account of lightning discharges. (R. 1867) 215

POËY, A. New classification of clouds. (R. 1870) 244

POEY, F. Notes on American species of genus *Cybium*. (P. 1878) 332

POGGENDORFF, J. C. Use of galvanometer as measuring instrument. (R. 1859.) 110

Points, boiling and melting—F. W. CLARKE 255, 288

Points, spear and arrow, primitive manufacture of, along line of Savannah river—C. C. JONES, Jr. (R. 1879) 345

Poison—*See* Venom.

Poisoned arrows, lecture on nature and cure of wounds of—D. BRAINARD. (R. 1854) 75

Poisonous water in Gulf of Mexico, destruction of fish by—J. Y. PORTER. (P. 1881) 467

Polar expedition—*See* Hall, Capt.

Polar expedition, the Howgate, contributions to natural history of Arctic America made in connection with—L. KUMLIEN **342**

Polar light, or aurora borealis, its phenomena and laws—E. LOOMIS. (R. 1865.) 209

Polaris expedition, scientific instructions for—J. HENRY; J. E. HILGARD; S. NEWCOMB; S. F. BAIRD; F. B. MEEK; L. AGASSIZ. (R. 1871) 249

Polarized nerve, effect of irritation of—B. F. LAUTENBACH. (R. 1878) 341, **411**

POLLOCK, J. Assay of coins at the Mint of the United States. (R. 1868) 224

Polychrome bead from Florida—S. S. HALDEMAN. (R. 1877) 323, **404**

Polypetalæ, bibliographical index of—S. WATSON 258

Polypi, relations of lucernarians to—H. J. CLARK 242

Polyzoa of northeastern coast of America, notice of recent additions to—A. E. VERRILL. (P. 1879) 333

Pomadasys, description of new species of, from Mazatlan, Mexico—D. S. JORDAN; C. H. GILBERT. (P. 1881) 467

Pontifical Academy of the Nuovi Lincei, Rome. Prize questions. (R. 1865; R. 1867) 209, 215

POOLE, H. Cone-in-cone. (R. 1863) 187

Popocatepetl, examination of—Baron VON MÜLLER; A. SONNTAG **114**

Population of the world, estimate of the—E. MAILLY. (R. 1873) 275

Porcupine, Canada, occurrence of, in Maryland—O. LUGGER. (P. 1881) 467

Porcupine, Canada, occurrence of, in West Virginia—G. B. GOODE. (P. 1878.) 332

Porifera of northeast coast of America—A. E. VERRILL. (P. 1879) 333

Porpoise oil, manufacture of—C. COOK. (P. 1878) 332

PORTER, Commodore. Account of hail storm on the Bosphorus. (R. 1870) 244

PORTER, J. Y. Destruction of fish by poisonous water in Gulf of Mexico. (P. 1881) 467

PORTER, J. Y.; JEFFERSON, J. P.; MOORE, T. Destruction of fish near the Tortugas. (P. 1878) 332

PORTER, T. C. List of plants of upper Missouri. (R. 1850) 28

Portland Society of Natural History, account of—E. C. BOLLES. (R. 1867) 215

Porto Rico—
- description of new owl from—R. RIDGWAY. (P. 1881) 467
- great hurricane at—G. A. LATIMER. (R. 1867) 215
- Latimer collection of antiquities from—O. T. MASON. (R. 1876) **397**
- meteorology of—G. LATIMER. (R. 1871) 249

Portraits—
- of North American Indians, catalogue of—J. M. STANLEY **53**
- of North American Indians, Stanley, report of Committee of Regents on. (R. 1857) 107
- photographic, of North American Indians, in gallery of Smithsonian Institution, list of **216**

Potamocottus Bendirei, description of—T. H. BEAN. (P. 1881) 467

Pottery—
- ancient, from Phillips county, Arkansas—J. H. DEVEREUX. (R. 1872.) 271
- ancient, from Pittsburg, on Des Moines river—R. N. DAHLBERG; C. DAHLBERG. (R. 1879) 345
- Indian—C. RAU. (R. 1866) 214, 440, **368**

Pouched rat, or salamander of Georgia, habits of—W. GESNER. (R. 1860) 147

Poulkova and Dorpat, description of observatories at—C. ABBE. (R. 1867.) 215, **369**

POWELL, B. Reports on state of knowledge of radiant heat. (R. 1859) 110
POWELL, J. W.—
Evolution of language. (E. 1879-80) 476
Limitations to use of some anthropological data. (E. 1879-80) 476
Mythology of North American Indians. (E. 1879-80) 476
Report of Director of Bureau of Ethnology. (E. 1879-80) **476**
Wyandot government. (E. 1879-80) 476
POWERS, S. Centennial mission to Indians of western Nevada and California. (R. 1876) 299
PRATT, R. H. Catalogue of casts of heads of Indian boys and girls at Hampton Institute, Virginia. (P. 1879) 333
PRATT, R. H. Catalogue of casts of heads of Indian prisoners at St. Augustine, Florida. (P. 1878) 332
PRATT, W. H. Antiquities of Whiteside county, Illinois. (R. 1874) 286
Prayer at funeral of Joseph Henry—C. HODGE 356
Prayer at memorial of Joseph Henry—J. MCCOSH 356
Prayer at memorial of Joseph Henry—B. SUNDERLAND 356
Precession of the equinoxes—J. N. STOCKWELL 232
Precession of the equinoxes, problems presented by—J. G. BARNARD 240, 310
Precious stones—J. BABINET. (R. 1870) 244
Precipitation—
influence of rain upon the formation of—J. HANN. (R. 1877) 323, 398
of rain and snow in the United States, charts of—C. A. SCHOTT **374**
of rain and snow in the United States, tables of—C. A. SCHOTT **222, 353**
Prehistoric—
antiquities of Hungary—F. F. ROMER. (R. 1876) 299, 440, **392**
archæology, international code of symbols for charts of—G. DE MORTILLET; E. CHANTRE. (R. 1875) 298
evidences in Missouri—G. C. BROADHEAD. (R. 1879) 345
man, remains of, from caves in Alaska—W. H. DALL **318**
mounds of Grant county, Wisconsin—M. STRONG. (R. 1876) 299
remains in vicinity of city of Washington, D. C.—T. R. PEALE. (R. 1872) 271
PRENTISS, S. S.; COUES, E. List of birds of the District of Columbia. (R. 1861) 149
Preparation of large myological specimens—F. J. PLATEAU. (P. 1881) 467
Preparations, dry, on Semper's method of making—J. A. RYDER. (P. 1881.) 467
Prescott, Canada West, ancient Indian remains near—W. E. GUEST. (R. 1856) 91
PRESCOTT, W. H., and others. On publication of Spanish works on New Mexico. (R 1855) 77
Present state of ethnology in relation to form of human skull—A. RETZIUS. (R. 1859) 110

Presentation of—
books—DUKE OF NORTHUMBERLAND. (R. 1859) ---------- 110
books—IMPERIAL LIBRARY OF VIENNA. (R. 1865) ---------- 209
books on Brazil—M. M. LISBOA. (R. 1865) ---------- 209
books on Egypt—R. LEPSIUS. (R. 1860) ---------- 147
collections by foreign governments. (R. 1876) ---------- 299
engravings—C. B. KING. (R. 1861) ---------- 149
specimens—UNIVERSITY OF CHRISTIANIA, NORWAY. (R. 1863) ---------- 187
Preservation—
and collection of marine invertebrates—W. STIMPSON ---------- 34
of antiquities and national monuments in Denmark—J. J. A. WORSAAE. (R. 1879) ---------- 345
of copper and iron in salt water—A. E. BECQUEREL. (R. 1864) ---------- 188
of wood. (R. 1864) ---------- 188
Preserving—
diptera, directions for—R. OSTEN SACKEN ---------- 102
fish, directions for—T. H. BEAN. (P. 1881) ---------- 467, **464**
insects, directions for—A. S. PACKARD ---------- **261**
lepidoptera, method of—T. R. PEALE. (R. 1863) ---------- 187
nests and eggs, instructions for—T. M. BREWER ---------- 189
plants, directions for—L. F. WARD ---------- **460**
specimens of diatomacea—A. M. EDWARDS ---------- **366**
specimens of natural history—S. F. BAIRD. (R. 1856) ---------- 91, **34**
Pressure and velocity of the wind—J. HANN. (R. 1877) ---------- 323, 398
Pressure of the air—J. HANN and others. (R. 1877) ---------- 323, 398
PRESTWICH, J. Past and future of geology. (R. 1875) ---------- 298
Priestley, J., memoir of, by G. CUVIER. (R. 1858) ---------- 109
Priestley's lens, account of—J. HENRY. (R. 1859) ---------- 110
PRIME, T. Monograph of American corbiculadæ ---------- **145**
PRIME, T., and others. Check-list of shells of North America ---------- **128**
Primitive manufacture of spear and arrow points along line of Savannah river—C. C. JONES, Jr. (R. 1879) ---------- 345
Prince Regent's Inlet, meteorological observations in—F. L. McCLINTOCK ---------- 146
Princeton, New Jersey, address at, by J. HENRY ---------- **E**
Principles—
and methods of palæontology—T. H. HUXLEY. (R. 1869) ---------- 228
of crystallography and crystallophysics, explanation of—A. BREZINA. (R. 1872) ---------- 271, **386**
of mechanical theory of heat—J. MÜLLER. (R. 1868) ---------- 224
of physics, present fundamental—F. J. PISKO. (R. 1879) ---------- 345
of subcutaneous surgery—W. ADAMS ---------- **302**
Prionotus stephanophrys, new species of *Prionotus* from coast of California, description of—W. N. LOCKINGTON. (P. 1880) ---------- 425

Prize questions—
Academy of Sciences of the Institute of Bologna. (R. 1862) 150
Batavian Society of Experimental Philosophy of Rotterdam. (R. 1861.) 149
Dunkirk Society for Encouragement of Sciences, Letters, and Arts. (R. 1865) 209
Holland Society of Science, Harlem. (R. 1861, 1864, 1867, 1873) 149, 188, 224, 275
Imperial Academy of Sciences of Vienna. (R. 1864; R. 1865) 188, 209
Imperial Society of Natural Sciences of Cherbourg. (R. 1864) 188
Imperial Society of Science, Agriculture, and Arts of Lille. (R. 1865.) 209
London Institution of Civil Engineers. (R. 1862) 150
Pontifical Academy of Nuovi Lincei, Rome. (R. 1865; R. 1867) 209, 215
Royal Academy of Netherlands. (R. 1861) 149
Royal Academy of Science, Literature, and Fine Arts, Brussels. (R. 1873.) 275
Royal Danish Society of Sciences. (R. 1862, 1865, 1867) 150, 209, 215
Royal Institute for Encouragement of Natural, Economical, and Technological Science, Naples. (R. 1873) 275
Royal Prussian Academy of Sciences. (R. 1864) 188
Royal Scientific and Literary Institute of Lombardy. (R. 1865) 209
Society for Encouragement of Science, Literature, and Art, Dunkirk, France. (R. 1873) 275
Society of Arts and Sciences of Utrecht. (R. 1861; R. 1862) 149, 150
Society of Science, Art, and Literature of Hainaut, Mons, Belgium. (R. 1873) 275
Problems of rotary motion, presented by gyroscope, precession of equinoxes, and pendulum—J. G. Barnard **240**
Proceedings of—
Board of Regents—*See* Regents.
Establishment, 1853–1854. (R. 1853) 67, **329**
U. S. National Museum. Vols. I–IV, 1878–1881 **332**, **333**, **425**, **467**
U. S. National Museum, catalogue and index of 478
Products of combustion of gun-cotton and gunpowder—Lieut. von Karolyi; B. F. Craig. (R. 1864) 188
Productus giganteus, note on occurrence of, in California—C. A. White. (P. 1880) 425
Programme of organization of Smithsonian Institution **F**, **J**, 328
Progress—
in physics—*See* J. Müller.
in science, record of—*See* Record.
of astronomical photography—Dr. Lee. (R. 1861) **149**
Project of outline history of education in United States—F. A. Packard. (R. 1863) 187
Promotion of science in the United States, Tyndall trust for the. (R. 1872) 271
Propagation of disease—J. C. Dalton. (R. 1873) 275
Prospectus of a Bibliographia Americana—H. Stevens. (R. 1848) **I**

Providence, Rhode Island, meteorological observations at—A. CASWELL:
1831 to 1860 ---- **103**
1831 to 1876 ---- **443**

Provincetown, Massachusetts, experiments made at, upon animal heat of fishes—J. H. KIDDER. (P. 1879) ---- 333

Provincetown, Massachusetts, littoral marine fauna of—R. RATHBUN. (P. 1880.) 425

Provincial Society of Arts and Sciences, Utrecht. Prize questions. (R. 1862.) 150

Provisional classification of the food collections—G. B. GOODE. (P. 1881.) 467, **455**

Prussian Royal Academy of Sciences. Prize questions. (R. 1864) ---- 188

Psychrometric observations ---- 157

Psychrometrical tables—J. H. COFFIN ---- **87**

Pterophryne, on proper specific name of—T. GILL. (P. 1878) ---- 332

Ptychochilus Harfordi, new species of *Ptychochilus*, description of—D. S. JORDAN; C. H. GILBERT. (P. 1881) ---- 467

Public—
architecture, hints on—R. D. OWEN ---- **P**
buildings, acoustics applied to—J. HENRY. (R. 1856) ---- 91
instruction, minister of, report to Emperor of France by, on scientific expedition to Mexico. (R. 1864) ---- 188
libraries of the United States, notices of—C. C. JEWETT. (R. 1849) -- 21, **25**
libraries—*See* Libraries.

Publications—
exchange of—AGRICULTURAL ASSOCIATION OF MILAN. (R. 1863) ---- 187
exchange of—CHAMBER OF COMMERCE OF BORDEAUX. (R. 1863) ---- 187
of learned societies and periodicals in Smithsonian library. **73, 85, 117, 179**
of Smithsonian Institution, list of. (R. 1866.) 74, 203, 226, 245, 278, 290, 301, 344, 437, 478
of U. S. Government, 1868-1881—G. H. BOEHMER ---- 477
of U. S. National Museum, list of. (P. 1881) ---- 467, **474**
periodical received in reading-room of Smithsonian Institution ---- **Q**
report on, 1853-1866—S. F. BAIRD. (R. 1853-1866.) 67, 75, 77, 91, 107, 109, 110, 147, 149, 150, 187, 188, 209, 214

Puebla, Mexico, description of large fossil gasteropod from—C. A. WHITE. (P. 1880) ---- 425

Puget Sound, description of two new species of flounders (*Parophrys ischyurus* and *Hippoglossoides elassodon*) from—D. S. JORDAN; C. H. GILBERT. (P. 1880) ---- 425

Pulmonata geophila, monograph of—W. G. BINNEY; T. BLAND ---- **194**

Pulmonata limnophila, monograph of—W. G. BINNEY ---- **143**

PUMPELLY, R. Geological researches in China, Japan, and Mongolia ---- **202**

Purple dyeing, ancient and modern. (R. 1863) ---- 187

Q.

QUALE; LEWIS. Account of the cryolite of Greenland. (R. 1866) 214
Qualitative determinations by the blow-pipe—T. EGLESTON. (R. 1872) 271
Quartermasters, authority to, to receive and transmit specimens to Smithsonian. 34
QUATREFAGES, J. L. Memoir of Isidore Geoffroy St. Hilaire. (R. 1862) 150
Queen Charlotte's Islands, Haidah Indians of—J. G. SWAN 267
Queries about expression for anthropological inquiry—C. DARWIN. (R. 1867.) 215
Queries relative to tornadoes—J. HENRY **190**
Questions relative to the food fishes of the United States—S. F. BAIRD **234**
Questions—*See* Prize questions.
Quetelet, L. A. J., eulogy on, by E. MAILLY. (R. 1874) 286
QUICK, E. R. Mounds in Franklin county, Indiana. (R. 1879) 345
Quillehute Indians of west coast of Washington Territory, method of taking surf smelt by—J. G. SWAN. (P. 1880) 425
Quincy, Illinois, mounds near—W. G. ARMSTRONG. (R. 1879) 345

R.

Rabbit catching the sun in a trap (Omaha myth)—J. O. DORSEY. (E. 1879-80.) 476
Race, the human, probable future of—A. DE CANDOLLE. (R. 1875) 298
Races—
intermixture of—G. GIBBS. (R. 1864) 188
lower, social and religious condition of the—J. LUBBOCK. (R. 1869) 228
mixed, in Liberia—E. D. BLYDEN. (R. 1870) 244
Radiant heat, reports on state of knowledge of—B. POWELL. (R. 1859) 110
Radiates of Arctic America—A. E. VERRILL 342
Radiation, lecture on—J. TYNDALL. (R. 1868) 224
Rafinesque's memoirs on North American fishes, review of—D. S. JORDAN 305
Raia inornata, note on—D. S. JORDAN; C. H. GILBERT. (P. 1881) 467
Raia rhina, new species of ray from coast of California, description of—D. S. JORDAN; C. H. GILBERT. (P. 1880) 425
Raia stellulata, new species of ray from Monterey, California, description of—D. S. JORDAN; C. H. GILBERT. (P. 1880) 425
Rain—
and atmospheric pressure—J. HANN. (R. 1877) 323, 398
and barometric minima—T. REYE. (R. 1877) 323, 398
and snow, tables of precipitation in—C. A. SCHOTT **222, 353**

Rain—Continued.

articles on, preserved in Smithsonian. (R. 1874) 286, **353**

gauges—R. H. GARDINER. (R. 1858) 109

influence of, upon the barometer—J. HANN. (R. 1877) 323, 398

observations 157

presence of electricity during fall of—Prof. PALMIERI. (R. 1870) 244

quantity of, at different heights—O. W. MORRIS; J. HENRY. (R. 1855.) 77

snow, or hail, electricity of induction in strata of atmosphere surrounding cloud resolving into—F. ZANTEDESCHI. (R. 1870) 244

Rain-charts of United States, 1, 2, 3: summer, winter, and year—C. A. SCHOTT. **374**

Rana pipiens, anatomy of nervous system of—J. WYMAN **45**

Raptores, oology of—T. M. BREWER 89

Rat, pouched, of Georgia, habits of—W. GESNER. (R. 1860) 147

RATHBUN, R. Littoral marine fauna of Provincetown, Cape Cod, Massachusetts. (P. 1880) 425

RATHBUN, R. Marine invertebrates from New England, distributed by U. S. National Museum, list of. (P. 1881) 467, **465**, **471**

RATHBUN, R.; VERRILL, A. E. Marine invertebrata of New England, distributed by Fish Commission. (P. 1879) 333

Ratio between diameter and circumference of a circle—W. FERREL **233**

Rattlesnake, researches upon venom of—S. W. MITCHELL **135**

Rattlesnakes, bibliography of—S. W. MITCHELL 135

Rattlesnakes, genera and species of—E. D. COPE 135

RAU, C.—

Agricultural flint implements in southern Illinois. (R. 1868.) 224, 440, **370**

Agricultural implements of North American stone period. (R. 1863.) 187, 440

Ancient aboriginal trade in North America. (R. 1872) 271, 440, **385**

Anthropological publications, list of. (P. 1881) 467

Archæological collection of the U. S. National Museum **287**

Artificial shell-deposits in New Jersey. (R. 1864) 188, 440, **362**

Drilling in stone without metal. (R. 1868) 224, 440, **372**

Gold ornament from mound in Florida, observations on. (R. 1877.) 323, 440, **403**

Indian pottery. (R. 1866) 214, 440, **368**

Memoir of C. F. P. Von Martius. (R. 1869) 228, 440, **251**

North American stone implements. (R. 1872) 271, 440, **382**

Palenque tablet in the U. S. National Museum **331**

Stock-in-trade of an aboriginal lapidary. (R. 1877) 323, 440, **402**

Translation of Baegert's account of the Indians of southern California. (R. 1863; R. 1864) 187, 188, 440, **361**

Translation of Romer's antiquities of Hungary. (R. 1876) 299, 440, **392**

RAWSON, R. Memoir of Eaton Hodgkinson. (R. 1868) 224

READ, M. C. Ancient mound near Chattanooga, Tennessee. (R. 1867) 215

Reading-room of Smithsonian Institution, periodicals received in, 1853 ------- Q
Recalculation of atomic weights. Constants of Nature Part v—F. W. CLARKE. **441**
Receipts of specimens—*See* annual reports.
Recent—
improvements in the chemical arts—J. C. BOOTH; C. MORFIT --------- 27
progress in physics—J. MÜLLER. (R. 1855–1858) ---------- 77, 91, 107, 109
progress in relation to the theory of heat—A. CAZIN. (R. 1868)------- 224
progress in science, reports on—*See* Record of recent progress.
researches on secular variations of planetary orbits—J. N. STOCKWELL. (R. 1871) ---------- 249
Recommendation of Shea's Indian linguistics—G. GIBBS and others. (R. 1861.) 149
Record of—
auroras in higher northern latitudes—P. FORCE ---------- **84**
meteorological material preserved in Smithsonian. (R. 1874)---------- 286
monthly meteorological reports preserved in Smithsonian Institution. (R. 1873) ---------- 275
Record of recent progress in science, 1879 and 1880—
Anthropology—O. T. MASON. (R. 1880) ---------- 442, **432**
Astronomy—E. S. HOLDEN. (R. 1880)---------- 442, **427**
Botany—W. G. FARLOW. (R. 1880) ---------- 442, **430**
Chemistry—G. F. BARKER. (R. 1880) ---------- 442, **429**
Geology—G. W. HAWES. (R. 1880) ---------- 442, **428**
Mineralogy—G. W. HAWES. (R. 1880) ---------- 442, **428**
Physics—G. F. BARKER. (R. 1880)---------- 442, **429**
Zoölogy—T. GILL. (R. 1880)---------- 442, **431**
Recording Indian languages, method of—J. O. DORSEY; A. S. GATSCHET; S. R. RIGGS. (E. 1879–80) ---------- 476
Records and results of magnetic survey of Pennsylvania—A. D. BACHE------ 166
Red river of the North, ethnology of Indians of valley of—W. H. GARDNER. (R. 1870) ---------- 244
Red river settlement, Hudson's Bay Territory, Indian remains in—D. GUNN. (R. 1867) ---------- 215
REED, H. Lecture on "the Union." (R. 1854) ---------- 75
Refraction of sound—W. B. TAYLOR. (R. 1875) ---------- 298
Regents of Smithsonian Institution—
list of, 1846 ---------- N
list of, 1846–1879. (*See also* each annual report) ---------- 329
memorial of Board of, relative to Smithson fund. (R. 1850; R. 1866.) 28, 214, 329
memorial of Board of, to Congress asking appropriations for museum. (R. 1867)---------- 215, 329
memorial to Congress in behalf of, relative to new museum building—G. BANCROFT. (R. 1876) ---------- 299, 329
proceedings of Board of. (*See also* each annual report)-- **A, G, H, I, M**, 329
proceedings of Board of, on death of Joseph Henry---------- 356

Regents of Smithsonian Institution—Continued.
proceedings of Board of, relative to the electro-magnetic telegraph.. **115**, 329
report of Committee of, on Corcoran Art Gallery. (R. 1872) 271, 329
report of Committee of, on fire at Smithsonian—R. WALLACH; J. HENRY. (R. 1864) 188, 329
report of Committee of, on Museum—A. GRAY; H. COPPÉE. (R. 1874) 286, 329
report of Committee of, on Museum—A. GRAY; A. A. SARGENT; H. CLYMER. (R. 1876) 299, 329
report of Committee of, on Stanley's gallery of Indian portraits. (R. 1857) 107, 329
report of Committee of, on communication of J. Henry relative to electro-magnetic telegraph—C. C. FELTON. (R. 1857) 107, 329
reports of Committee of, on distribution of Smithsonian income. J. A. PEARCE; J. MEACHAM. (R. 1853) 67, 329
Regents of University of State of New York. Acknowledgment for specimens. (R. 1865) 209, 329
Registration of periodical phenomena—J. HENRY. (R. 1855) 77
Registry of periodical phenomena 148, **65**
Regulations of the Smithsonian Institution, 1872 260
Regulations of the U. S. National Museum—G. B. GOODE. (P. 1881) ... 467, **445**
REICHARDT, W. Present state of knowledge of cryptogamous plants. (R. 1871.) 249
REID, D. B. Architecture in relation to ventilation, warming, lighting, fire-proofing, acoustics, and health. (R. 1856) 91
Reigen Mazatlan collection of mollusks—P. P. CARPENTER 252
Reindeer, man as the contemporary of, in middle Europe. (R. 1867) 215
Relation—
between barometric variations and atmospheric currents—M. PESLIN. (R. 1877) 323, 398
of food to work, and its bearing on medical practice—S. HAUGHTON. (R. 1870) 244
of physical sciences to science in general—H. HELMHOLTZ. (R. 1871).. 249
of time and space, lecture on—S. ALEXANDER. (R. 1861) 149
Relationship—
circular respecting degrees of—L. H. MORGAN **138**
system of, of Cree Indians—E. A. WATKINS. (R. 1862) 150
systems of—L. H. MORGAN **218**
Relative intensity of heat and light of sun—L. W. MEECH. (R. 1856)..... 91, **83**
Relic, ancient, of Maya sculpture, remarks on—A. SCHOTT. (R. 1871) 249
Relics—
ancient, in Missouri—J. W. FOSTER. (R. 1863) 187
ancient Indian—J. JONES 259
ancient, of northwestern Iowa—J. B. CUTTS. (R. 1872) 271
presented by J. H. Devereux. (R. 1872) 271

Religion of Shoshone Indians—A. G. BRACKETT. (R. 1879) 345

Religious condition of lower races of man—J. LUBBOCK. (R. 1869) 228

Remains—

aboriginal, of Tennessee—J. JONES 259

ancient, in Colorado—E. L. BERTHOUD. (R. 1867) 215

human, from Patagonia—A. RIED. (R. 1862) 150

Indian, in Caddo parish, Louisiana—T. P. HOTCHKISS. (R. 1872) 271

of later prehistoric man from caves in Alaska—W. H. DALL 318

of walrus (?) in Maine—C. H. BOYD. (P. 1881) 467

prehistoric, in Montana—P. W. NORRIS. (R. 1879) 345

prehistoric, in vicinity of city of Washington, D. C.—T. R. PEALE. (R. 1872) 271

Zapotec, account of—J. G. SAWKINS; B. MAYER 86

Remains—*See* Ancient remains.

Remarkable forms of hail-stones in Georgia—S. ABICH. (R. 1869) 228

Remarks—

concerning nature of currents of air—A. COLDING. (R. 1877) 323, 398

on ancient relic of Maya sculpture—A. SCHOTT. (R. 1871) 249

on *Cara gigantesca* of Yzamal in Yucatan—A. SCHOTT. (R. 1869) 228

on kjökken-möddings on northwest coast of America—P. SCHUMACHER. (R. 1873) 275

on osteology of *Opheosaurus ventralis*—R. W. SHUFELDT. (P. 1881) 467

on physical geography of North America—J. FROEBEL. (R. 1854) 75

on species of genus *Chiurus*—W. N. LOCKINGTON. (P. 1880) 425

Reminiscences of Joseph Henry by S. B. DOD 356

Reparatory inflammation in arteries after ligature, etc., nature of. Toner lecture No. VII—E. O. SHAKESPEARE 321

Reply to criticisms of J. Hann by W. FERREL. (R. 1877) 323, 398

Report—*See* Henry, J., Baird, S. F., Regents.

Report of—

American Academy of Arts and Sciences on organization of Smithsonian—E. EVERETT; J. SPARKS; B. PIERCE; H. W. LONGFELLOW; A. GRAY. (R. 1853) 67

architect—B. S. ALEXANDER. (R. 1854) 75

architects, 1879, 1880—CLUSS and SCHULZE. (R. 1879; R. 1880) 345, 442, **409**, **434**

Board of Regents of Smithsonian Institution, 1847-1880 **G**, **H**, **I**, 21, 28, 51, 57, 67, 75, 77, 91, 107, 109, 110, 147, 149, 150, 187, 188, 209, 214, 215, 224, 228, 244, 249, 271, 275, 286, 298, 299, 323, 341, 345, 442

Bureau of Ethnology, first—J. W. POWELL. (E. 1879-80) **476**

chemist—F. W. TAYLOR. (R. 1880) 442

Commission on general stereotype catalogue of public libraries. (R. 1850.) 28, 47

Committee of American Association on system of combined meteorological observations. (R. 1851) 51

Report of—Continued.
Executive Committee (*See also* each annual report) 329
Executive Committee on Henry statue. (R. 1880) 442
experiments on animal heat of fishes—J. H. KIDDER. (P. 1879) 333
explorations in New Mexico and Arizona—J. STEVENSON. (R. 1880) 442
Government explorations and surveys. (R. 1878) 341
National Museum Building Commission for 1879. (R. 1879) 345, **409**
National Museum Building Commission for 1880. (R. 1880) 442, **434**
Secretary of Smithsonian Institution, 1847–1877—J. HENRY. (R. 1847–1877) **F**, **H**, **I**, 21, 28, 51, 57, 67, 75, 77, 91, 107, 109, 110, 147, 149, 150, 187, 188, 209, 214, 215, 224, 228, 244, 249, 271, 275, 286, 298, 299, 323
Secretary of Smithsonian Institution, 1878–1880—S. F. BAIRD. (R. 1878–1880) 341, 345, 442, **408**, **418**, **419**
Senate Judiciary Committee on management of Smithsonian—A. P. BUTLER. (R. 1855) 77
Smithsonian Institution—*See* Report of Board of Regents.
visit to Luray Cavern—O. T. MASON. (R. 1880) 442, **433**
Report of Committee of Regents of Smithsonian Institution on—
best use of new hall of the Institution—L. AGASSIZ. (R. 1867) 215, 329
communication from S. F. B. Morse—C. C. FELTON. (R. 1857) 107, 329
Corcoran Art Gallery. (R. 1872) 271, 329
electro-magnetic telegraph—C. C. FELTON. (R. 1857) 107, 329
fire of January, 1865—R. WALLACH; J. HENRY. (R. 1864) 188, 329
Greek album 329
Museum—A. GRAY; H. COPPÉE. (R. 1874) 286, 329
Museum—A. GRAY; A. A. SARGENT; H. CLYMER. (R. 1876) 299
organization of Institution **B**, **L**, 328
Stanley's gallery of Indian portraits. (R. 1857) 107, 329
system of accounts. (R. 1866) 214
Washington canal—R. DELAFIELD. (R. 1868) 224, 329
Report on—
building stones—D. D. OWEN 329
catalogue system—C. C. JEWETT. (R. 1849) 21
Centennial Exhibition—S. F. BAIRD. (R. 1876) 299, **307**
contents of bottles of water from Gulf of Mexico—W. G. FARLOW. (P. 1881) 467
copyright system—C. C. JEWETT. (R. 1851) 51
effect of frost on stones—C. G. PAGE 329
ethnological collections of Museum of Lausanne—F. TROYON. (R. 1861) 149
exploration of ancient mounds in Union county, Kentucky—S. S. LYON. (R. 1870) 244
fishes of New Jersey coast, as observed in 1854—S. F. BAIRD. (R. 1854) 75, **348**
fossils from Nebraska—J. LEIDY. (R. 1851) 51

Report on—Continued.
Halliwell manuscripts—C. C. JEWETT. (R. 1852) ---------- 57
history of discovery of Neptune—B. A. GOULD ---------- **18**
improved system of numeration—W. B. TAYLOR. (R. 1867) ---------- 215
international exchanges—G. H. BOEHMER ---------- 477
lacustrian settlements—A. MORLOT. (R. 1863) ---------- 187
library—C. C. JEWETT. (R. 1848–1853) ---------- I, 21, 28, 51, 57, 67
limpets and chitons of Alaskan and Arctic regions—W. H. DALL. (P. 1878) ---------- 332
magnetic telegraph ---------- **115**
meteorological system—E. FOREMAN. (R. 1852) ---------- 57
meteorology of the United States—E. LOOMIS. (R. 1847) ---------- **H**
mollusca of west coast of North America—P. P. CAPENTER ---------- **252**
Museum and statistics of British Museum—S. F. BAIRD. (R. 1850) ---------- 28
paleontological collections made by Lieut. G. K. Warren—F. B. MEEK; F. V. HAYDEN ---------- 172
plan of library—C. C. JEWETT. (R. 1847) ---------- **H**
proposed exhibit by Smithsonian Institution at the Centennial Exhibition—S. F. BAIRD. (R. 1875) ---------- 298
public libraries of United States—C. C. JEWETT. (R. 1849) ---------- 21
publications, exchanges, explorations, and Museum, 1851–1877—S. F. BAIRD. (R. 1851–1877) ---------- 51, 57, 67, 75, 77, 91, 107, 109, 110, 147, 149, 150, 187, 188, 209, 214, 215, 224, 228, 244, 249, 271, 275, 286, 298, 299, 323
recent progress in physics: electricity, galvanism—J. MÜLLER. (R. 1855–1857) ---------- 77, 91, 107
shell heaps of Tampa Bay, Florida—S. T. WALKER. (R. 1879) ---------- 345
shells presented to Academy of Natural Sciences—J. LEIDY; G. W. TRYON. (R. 1865) ---------- 209
state of knowledge of radiant heat—B. POWELL. (R. 1859) ---------- 110
survey of economic geology of Trinidad—G. P. WALL; J. G. SAWKINS. (R. 1856) ---------- 91
system of accounts. (R. 1866) ---------- 214
use of new hall in Smithsonian building—L. AGASSIZ. (R. 1867) ---------- 215
Report to Emperor of France by Minister of Public Instruction on scientific expedition to Mexico. (R. 1864) ---------- 188
Reports, meteorological, preserved in Smithsonian Institution, list of. (R. 1873.) 275
Reports of—
astronomical observatories, 1879—E. S. HOLDEN. (R. 1879) ---------- 345, **410**
astronomical observatories, 1880—E. S. HOLDEN; G. H. BOEHMER. (R. 1880) ---------- 442, **438**
Committees of Regents, 1846–1877 ---------- 329
Secretary of Smithsonian Institution, J. Henry, 1865–1877 ---------- **343**
Smithsonian Institution, catalogue and index of ---------- 478

Reports on transactions of Geneva Society of Physics—*See* Geneva.
Reptiles—
circular relating to collections of living ---- **320**
cretaceous—J. LEIDY ---- **192**
cretaceous, review of—J. LEIDY. (R. 1864) ---- 188
dates of first appearance of—F. B. HOUGH ---- 182
extinct—J. LEIDY ---- 192
North American, catalogue of. Part I. Serpents—S. F. BAIRD; C. GIRARD ---- **49**
Reptilia, check-list of North American—E. D. COPE ---- **292**
Request for bison by Bern Museum. (R. 1865) ---- 209
Request for shells—W. E. LOGAN. (R. 1859) ---- 110
Research—
ethnological—E. H. DAVIS. (R. 1866) ---- 214
relative to ethnology and philology of America, instructions for—G. GIBBS ---- **160**
upon the atmosphere, plan of a—C. M. WETHERILL. (R. 1866) ---- 214
Researches—
archæological, at Concise—F. TROYON. (R. 1861) ---- 149
archæological, in Nicaragua—J. F. BRANSFORD ---- **383**
by officers of Hudson's Bay Company, letter of Sir G. Simpson ---- 137
geological, in China, Mongolia, and Japan—R. PUMPELLY ---- **202**
in sound—J. HENRY. (R. 1878) ---- 341, **406**
on ammonia-cobalt bases—W. GIBBS; F. A. GENTH ---- **88**
on electrical rheometry—A. SECCHI ---- **36**
on figure of equilibrium of a liquid mass withdrawn from action of gravity—*See* J. Plateau.
on secular variations of planetary orbits—J. N. STOCKWELL. (R. 1871.) 249
relative to nebulæ—Prof. GAUTIER. (R. 1863) ---- 187
relative to planet Neptune—S. C. WALKER ---- **3**
scientific, list of apparatus available for. (R. 1878) ---- 341
scientific, of Peltier—F. A. PELTIER. (R. 1867) ---- 215
upon anatomy and physiology of Chelonia—S. W. MITCHELL; G. R. MOREHOUSE ---- **159**
upon fever—H. C. WOOD ---- 357
upon *Hydrobiinæ* and allied forms—W. STIMPSON ---- **201**
upon venom of the rattlesnake—S. W. MITCHELL ---- **135**
Residuary legacy—*See* Smithson.
Resolutions of Congress—*See* Congress.
Resolutions of Regents—*See* each annual report.
Resonance, electric, of mountains, observations on the—H. DE SAUSSURE. (R. 1868) ---- 224
Respiration, apparatus for testing results of—M. PETTENKOFER. (R. 1864) ---- 188

Respiration in the Chelonia, researches on—S. W. MITCHELL; G. R. MOREHOUSE ---- 159
Results of—
magnetic survey of Pennsylvania—A. D. BACHE ---- 166
meteorological observations at Brunswick, Maine—P. CLEAVELAND ---- **204**
meteorological observations at Marietta, Ohio—S. P. HILDRETH; J. WOOD ---- **120**
meteorological observations at Providence, Rhode Island, 1831-1860, 1831-1876—A. CASWELL ---- **103**, **443**
meteorological observations in the United States, 1854-1859 ---- 157, 182
precipitation in rain and snow in United States—C. A. SCHOTT ---- **222**, **353**
spectrum analysis applied to heavenly bodies—W. HUGGINS. (R. 1866.) 214
RETZIUS, A. Present state of ethnology in relation to form of the skull. (R. 1859) ---- 110
Review of—
American birds. Part I. North and Middle America—S. F. BAIRD ---- **181**
American species of genus *Scops*—R. RIDGWAY. (P. 1878) ---- 332
classification of birds—W. LILLJEBORG. (R. 1865) ---- 209, **364**
cretaceous reptiles of the United States—J. LEIDY. (R. 1864) ---- 188
genera and species of family *Centrarchidæ*—C. L. MCKAY. (P. 1881) ---- 467
genus *Centurus*—R. RIDGWAY. (P. 1881) ---- 467
pleuronectidæ of San Francisco—W. N. LOCKINGTON. (P. 1879) ---- 333
Rafinesque's memoirs on North American fishes—D. S. JORDAN ---- 305
Revisions of nomenclature of North American birds—R. RIDGWAY. (P. 1880.) 425
Revolutions of crust of the earth—G. PILAR. (R. 1876) ---- 299
REYE, T. Rain-fall and barometric minima. (R. 1877) ---- 323, 398
REYNOLDS, J. E. Hydrogen as gas and metal. (R. 1870) ---- 244
RHEES, W. J.—
Catalogue and index of publications of the Smithsonian Institution, U. S. National Museum, etc., 1846-1881 ---- **478**
James Smithson and his bequest. (R. 1879) ---- 345, **330**
Journals of Board of Regents, reports, statistics, etc., of Smithsonian Institution ---- 329
List of public libraries, institutions, and societies in United States and British Provinces ---- **116**
List of public libraries, institutions, and societies in United States in correspondence with Smithsonian Institution ---- **238**
Origin and history of Smithsonian Institution ---- **328**
Scientific writings of James Smithson, (edited by) ---- 327
Rheometry, electrical, researches on—A. SECCHI ---- **36**
Rhinobatidæ, American, synopsis and descriptions of—S. GARMAN. (P. 1880.) 425
Rhinonemus caudacuta, identity of with *Gadus cimbrius*—G. B. GOODE; T. H. BEAN. (P. 1878) ---- 332

Rhode Island, list of algæ of—S. T. OLNEY 241
Rhode Island, Providence, meteorological observations at, 1831-1860, 1831-1876—A. CASWELL **103**, **443**
Rhodospermeæ—W. H. HARVEY 43
RIDGWAY, R.—
Catalogue of birds of North America. (P. 1880) 425
Catalogue of Old World birds in U. S. National Museum. (P. 1881) 467
Catalogue of *Trochilidæ* in U. S. National Museum. (P. 1880) 425
Description of new fly-catcher and new petrel from Sandwich Islands. (P. 1881) 467
Description of new owl from Porto Rico. (P. 1881) 467
Description of new species of birds from Costa Rica and notes on rare species. (P. 1878) 332
Descriptions of new species and races of American birds and synopsis of genus *Tyrannus*. (P. 1878) 332
Descriptions of new species and races of birds in U. S. National Museum. (P. 1878) 332
Descriptions of two new thrushes from the United States. (P. 1881) 467
List of special desiderata among North American birds. (P. 1881) 467
List of species of Middle and South American birds not in National Museum. (P. 1881) 467
Nomenclature of North American birds chiefly in National Museum **422**
Notes on some Costa Rican birds. (P. 1881) 467
On *Amazilia Yucatanensis* and *Amazilia cerviniventris*. (P. 1881) 467
On duck new to American fauna. (P. 1881) 467
On new humming bird, *Atthis Elliotti*, from Guatemala. (P. 1878) 332
On two recent additions to North American bird fauna by L. Belding. (P. 1881) 467
Review of American species of genus *Scops*. (P. 1878) 332
Review of genus *Centurus*. (P. 1881.) 467
RIED, A. Human remains from Patagonia. (R. 1862) 150
RIGGS, S. R. A dog's revenge (Dakota fable.) (E. 1879-80) 476
RIGGS, S. R. Grammar and dictionary of Dakota language **40**
Ripley, Fort, Minnesota, natural history of the country about—J. E. HEAD. (R. 1854) 75
Rissoidæ, fresh-water—W. G. BINNEY 144
River, Kennebec, opening and closing of the—R. H. GARDINER. (R. 1858) 109
Rivers—
dates of opening and closing of—F. B. HOUGH 182
diminution of water in—H. G. WEX. (R. 1875) 298
improvement of navigation of—C. ELLET, Jr. 13
method of ascertaining amount of water in—A. A. HUMPHREYS. (R. 1858) 109
Roads and bridges, lectures on—F. ROGERS. (R. 1860; R. 1861) 147, 149

ROBERTSON, R. S.—
Age of stone and troglodytes of Breckenridge county, Kentucky. (R. 1874) 286
Antiquities of Allen and De Kalb counties, Indiana. (R. 1874) 286
Antiquities of La Porte county, Indiana. (R. 1874) *286
Antiquities of Nashville, Tennessee. (R. 1877) 323
ROBINSON, E., and others. On publication of Spanish works on New Mexico. (R. 1855) 77
ROBINSON, E., and others. On publication of Squier and Davis' ancient monuments K
Rock Bluff, Illinois, description of human skull from—J. A. MEIGS. (R. 1867.) 215
Rock-oil, or petroleum, history of—T. S. HUNT. (R. 1861) 149
Rock river valley, Illinois, mound builders in—J. SHAW. (R. 1877) 323
Rocks—
catalogue of—J. W. FOSTER. (R. 1854) 75
catalogue of—C. T. JACKSON. (R. 1854) 75
catalogue of—J. LOCKE. (R. 1854) 75
catalogue of—J. D. WHITNEY. (R. 1854) 75
crystalline, metamorphism, and formation of—G. A. DAUBRÉE. (R. 1861.) 149
in Green river valley, Indian engravings on face of—J. G. BRUFF. (R. 1872) 271
Rocky Mountain goat, habits of the—J. C. MERRILL. (P. 1879) 333
Rodent, rare, (*Cricetodipus parvus*)—F. W. TRUE. (P. 1881) 467
ROEHRIG, F. L. O. Language of Dakota or Sioux Indians. (R. 1871) 249, **378**
ROGERS, F. Lectures on roads and bridges. (R. 1860; R. 1861) 147, 149
ROGERS, W. B. Memorial address on Joseph Henry 356
Rome, Pontifical Academy—*See* Prize questions.
ROMER, F. F. Prehistoric antiquities of Hungary. (R. 1876) 299, 440, **392**
ROMERO, M. Explorations of John Xantus in Mexico. (R. 1862) 150
ROSING, J. Exchange system. (R. 1865) 209
ROSS, B. R. Eastern Tinneh Indians. (R. 1866) 214, 365
ROSS, B. R. Observations in Hudson's Bay Territory. (R. 1859) 110
Rotary motion, problems of—J. G. BARNARD **240**
ROTHROCK, J. T. Sketch of flora of Alaska. (R. 1867) 215, 367
Rotterdam, Batavian Society of Experimental Philosophy of. Prize questions. (R. 1861) 149
Royal—
Academy of Netherlands. Prize questions. (R. 1861) 149
Academy of Science, Madrid. On exchanges. (R. 1861) 149
Danish Society of Sciences. Prize questions. (R. 1862, 1865, 1867.) 150, 209, 215
Horticultural Society, London. Exchange of publications. (R. 1861) 149
Institution of Great Britain, history of—E. MAILLY. (R. 1867) 215
Prussian Academy of Sciences. Prize questions. (R. 1864) 188

Royal—Continued.
Scientific and Literary Institute of Lombardy. Prize questions. (R. 1865.) 209
Society of London, list of Smithson's papers presented to. (R. 1853.) 67, 330
Society of London, notice of Smithson, by D. Gilbert, president of. (R. 1853) 67, 330
Society of London, origin and history of—C. A. ALEXANDER. (R. 1863.) 187
Society of Victoria, address of president of—R. L. J. ELLERY. (R. 1868.) 224
ROYCE, C. C. Cessions of land by Indian tribes to United States. (E. 1879–80.) 476
Ruin, ancient, in Arizona—J. C. Y. LEE. (R. 1872) 271
Ruins—
at Savannah, Tennessee—J. P. STELLE. (R. 1870) 244
in Hardin county, Tennessee—J. P. STELLE. (R. 1870) 244
in White river cañon, Pima county, Arizona—R. T. BURR. (R. 1879.) 345
Rules—
for cataloguing libraries—C. C. JEWETT 47
for examination of specimens. (R. 1880) 442
of distribution of Smithsonian publications 290
RUNKLE, J. D. New tables for determining perturbation of planets 79
RUNKLE, J. D. Supplement for asteroid perturbations 94
Rupert's Land, Institute of, circular of the. (R. 1861) 149
Rush, R.—
correspondence of, relative to Smithson 328
letter from, relative to James Smithson. (R. 1853) 67, 328
notice of, by J. A. PEARCE. (R. 1859) 110
RUSSELL, R. Lectures on meteorology, with notes by J. HENRY. (R. 1854) .. 75
Russia, meteorology in—A. WOEIKOFF. (R. 1872) 271
Russian America—
ethnological investigations in, suggestions for—G. GIBBS 207
suggestions relative to objects of scientific investigation in—J. HENRY .. **207**
Tinneh Indians of—G. GIBBS; B. ROSS; W. L. HARDISTY; S. JONES. (R. 1866) 214, **365**
Yukon, journey to the—W. W. KIRBY. (R. 1864) 188
RÜTIMEYER, L. Fauna of middle Europe during the stone age. (R. 1861) .. 149
RYDER, J. A.—
Camaraphysema, a new type of sponge, (P. 1880) 425
List of North American species of myriapods belonging to family of *Lysiopetalidæ*, with description of blind form from Luray Cave, Virginia. (P. 1880) 425
On Semper's method of making dry preparations. (P. 1881) 467

S.

SABINE, E. Magnetic storms. (R. 1860) 147
SABINE, E. On continuance of magnetic observations. (R. 1858) 109
Sable Island Bank, description of *Argentina syrtensium*, new deep-sea fish from—G. B. GOODE; T. H. BEAN. (P. 1878) 332
Sacken, Osten—*See* Osten Sacken.
Sacramento, California—
meteorological observations at—F. W. HATCH. (R. 1854) 75
meteorological observations at—T. M. LOGAN. (R. 1854) 75
meteorology of—T. M. LOGAN. (R. 1857) 107
Sacramento river, description of new species of *Ptychochilus* (*Ptychochilus Harfordi*) from—D. S. JORDAN; C. H. GILBERT. (P. 1881) 467
Saint Augustine, Florida, catalogue of casts of heads of Indian prisoners at—R. H. PRATT. (P. 1878) 332
Saint Christopher, West Indies, description of new subspecies of saxigilla from—G. N. LAWRENCE. (P. 1881) 467
Saint Croix Island, flora of—H. F. A. EGGERS 318
Saint George's Banks, occurrence of *Hippocampus antiquorum* on—G. B. GOODE. (P. 1878) 332
Saint Hilaire, Etienne Geoffroy, memoir of, by M. FLOURENS. (R. 1861) 149
Saint Hilaire, Isidore Geoffroy, memoir of—J. L. QUATREFAGES. (R. 1862) 150
Saint John's river, Florida, catalogue of fishes of—G. B. GOODE. (P. 1879) 333
Saint John's river, Florida, shell-heaps at mouth of—S. P. MAYBERRY. (R. 1877) 323
Saint Louis, Missouri, ancient mound in—T. R. PEALE. (R. 1861) 149
Saint Louis, Missouri, temperature of—A. FENDLER. (R. 1860) 147
Saint Martin, Isle Jesus, Canada East, description of observatory at—C. SMALLWOOD. (R. 1856) 91
Saint Michael's, Alaska, occurrence of *Hippoglossus vulgaris* at—T. H. BEAN. (P. 1879) 333
Saint Michael's, Alaska, occurrence of *Stichæus punctatus* at—T. H. BEAN. (P. 1878) 332
Saint Petersburg Academy of Sciences. Exchange system. (R. 1867) 215
Saint Thomas—
earthquakes in—G. A. LATIMER. (R. 1867) 215
hurricane in the island of—G. A. LATIMER. (R. 1867) 215
whirlwind at, August 21, 1871—A. COLDING. (R. 1877) 323, 398
Saint Vincent, catalogue of Ober's collection of birds of—G. N. LAWRENCE. (P. 1878) 332
Salamander—
habits of a species of—C. MANN. (R. 1854) 75
inhabiting Wisconsin—P. R. HOY. (R. 1854) 75
or pouched rat, of Georgia, habits of—W. GESNER. (R. 1860) 147

Salisbury, England, notice of Blackmore Museum at. (R. 1868) ---- 224
Salmon in Columbia river, Chinook names of—S. B. SMITH. (P. 1881) ---- 467
Salmonidæ of upper Columbia, notes on the—C. BENDIRE. (P. 1881) ---- 467
Salt deposit on Petite Anse Island—E. W. HILGARD ---- 248
Salt water, preservation of copper and iron in—A. E. BECQUEREL. (R. 1864.) 188
Samoan Islands, fishes from the—T. H. STREETS ---- 303
San Diego, California—
description of new gobioid fish (*Othonops eos*) from—R. SMITH. (P. 1881.) 467
description of new species of *Gobiesox* (*Gobiesox rhessodon*) from—R. SMITH. (P. 1881) ---- 467
notes on collection of fishes from—D. S. JORDAN; C. H. GILBERT. (P. 1880) ---- 425
occurrence of species of cremnobates at—R. SMITH. (P. 1880) ---- 425
San Francisco, California—
climate of—H. GIBBONS. (R. 1854) ---- 75
fishes of—*See* Jordan, D. S., Gilbert, C. H., Lockington, W. N.
review of *Pleuronectidæ* of—W. N. LOCKINGTON. (P. 1879) ---- 333
Sandwich Islands, description of new fly-catcher and new petrel from—R. RIDGWAY. (P. 1881) ---- 467
Sanitary drainage of Washington, suggestions for the. Toner lecture No. VIII—G. E. WARING ---- **349**
Santa Barbara, California, pleistocene fossils collected at, by E. Jewett—P. P. CARPENTER ---- 252
Santa Barbara channel, California, description of two new species of scopeloid fishes (*Sudis ringens* and *Myctophum crenulare*) from—D. S. JORDAN; C. H. GILBERT. (P. 1880) ---- 425
Santa Catalina Island, California, description of new flounder (*Xystreurys liolepis*) from—D. S. JORDAN; C. H. GILBERT. (P. 1880) ---- 425
Santa Lucia Cosumalwhuapa, Guatemala, sculptures of—S. HABEL ---- **269**
Santa Rosa Island, history and antiquities of—S. BOWERS. (R. 1877) ---- 323
Sarcophagus from Beirut, Syria, account of—A. A. HARWOOD. (R. 1870) ---- 244
SARGENT, A. A., and others. Report on Museum. (R. 1876) ---- 299
SARGENT, W. D. Influence of aurora on the telegraph. (R. 1870) ---- 244
Sargus Holbrookii, a new sparoid fish from Savannah Bank, description of—T. H. BEAN. (P. 1878) ---- 332
SARTORIUS, C. Earthquakes in eastern Mexico, January, 1866. (R. 1866) ---- 214
SARTORIUS, C. Eruption of volcano of Colima. (R. 1869) ---- 228
Saturn, secular variations of elements of orbit of, with tables—J. N. STOCKWELL ---- 232
SAUNDERS, Commander. Tidal record at Wolstenholm Sound, 1849, 1850 ---- 180
Saussure—*See* De Saussure.
Savage weapons at Centennial Exhibition, study of—E. H. KNIGHT. (R. 1879) ---- 345, **415**
Savannah, Tennessee, account of aboriginal ruins at—J. P. STELLE. (R. 1870.) 244

Savannah Bank, description of new sparoid fish (*Sargus Holbrookii*) from—T. H. Bean. (P. 1878) ---------- 332
Savannah river, primitive manufacture of spear and arrow points along line of—C. C. Jones, Jr. (R. 1879) ---------- 345
Sawkins, J. G., drawings of Zapotec remains by ---------- 86
Sawkins, J. G.; Wall, G. P. Economic geology of Trinidad. (R. 1856) -- 91
Scenery, catalogue of sketches of—J. M. Stanley ---------- 53
Scheme for qualitative determinations by the blow-pipe—T. Egleston. (R. 1872) ---------- 271
Scheme of classification for collections of U. S. National Museum—G. B. Goode. (P. 1881) ---------- 467, 457
Scherzer; Schwarz. Table of anthropological measurements. (R. 1866) -- 214
Schlagintweit, H. De. Ethnographical collections. (R. 1862) ---------- 150
Schlagintweit ethnographic collection, account of the—H. Zisgenbals. (R. 1867) ---------- 215
Schleiden, R. Free freight between Germany and United States by North German Lloyd. (R. 1858) ---------- 109
Schoenbein, C. F., notice of, by J. Henry. (R. 1868) ---------- 224
Schoharie, New York, Indian relics from—F. D Andrews. (R. 1879) ------ 345
Schoodic Lakes, Maine, description of new species of *Gasterosteus* from—T. H. Bean. (P. 1879) ---------- 333
Schott, A. Remarks on ancient relic of Maya sculpture. (R. 1871) -------- 249
Schott, A. Remarks on the *Cara gigantesca* in Yucatan. (R. 1869) -------- 228
Schott, A.; Mason, O. T. Leipsic Museum of Ethnology. (R. 1873) ------ 275
Schott, C. A.—
Base-chart of the United States ---------- **414**
Discussion of Caswell's meteorological observations at Providence, Rhode Island ---------- **103**
Discussion of Cleaveland's meteorological observations at Brunswick, Maine ---------- **204**
Discussion of Hayes' physical observations in the Arctic Seas ---------- **196**
Discussion of Hildreth's and Wood's meteorological observations at Marietta, Ohio ---------- **120**
Discussion of Kane's astronomical observations in the Arctic Seas ------ **129**
Discussion of Kane's magnetic observations in the Arctic Seas -------- **97**
Discussion of Kane's meteorological observations in the Arctic Seas ---- **104**
Discussion of Kane's physical observations in the Arctic Seas ---------- **198**
Discussion of Kane's tidal observations in the Arctic Seas ---------- **130**
Discussion of McClintock's meteorological observations in the Arctic Seas ---------- **146**
Discussion of Smith's meteorological observations made near Washington, Arkansas ---------- **131**
Tables, distribution, and variation of atmospheric temperature ---------- **277**
Tables of rain and snow in the United States ---------- **222**, **353**

SCHOTT, C. A.; EVERETT, J. D. Underground temperature. (R. 1874) 286
Schulze—*See* Cluss & Schulze.
SCHUMACHER, P. Ancient graves and shell-heaps of California. (R. 1874) 286
SCHUMACHER, P. Kjökken-möddings on the northwest coast of North America. (R. 1873) 275
SCHWARZ; SCHERZER. Table of anthropological measurements. (R. 1866) 214
Science—
on a dominant language for—A. DE CANDOLLE; J. E. GRAY. (R. 1874.) 286
in general, relation of the physical sciences to—H. HELMHOLTZ. (R. 1871.) 249
recent progress in—*See* Record.
trust fund for promotion of, in the United States—J. TYNDALL. (R. 1872) 271
Science, Agriculture, and Arts, Society of, Lille—*See* Prize questions.
Science, Art, and Literature, Society of, Hainaut—*See* Prize questions.
Sciences, Harlem Society of—*See* Prize questions.
Sciences, Letters, and Arts, Society of, Dunkirk—*See* Prize questions.
Sciences, Natural, Society of, Cherbourg—*See* Prize questions.
Sciences, Royal Danish Society of—*See* Prize questions.
Scientific—
character and researches of Smithson—W. R. JOHNSON 327
Congress of Carlsruhe, 1858—F. J. NICKLÈS. (R. 1860) 147
coöperation—UNIVERSITY OF TORONTO. (R. 1861) 149
education of mechanics and artisans—A. P. PEABODY. (R. 1872) 271, **380**
exchanges—*See* Exchanges.
expedition to Mexico by French Government. (R. 1864) 188
instructions to Capt. Hall—J. HENRY; J. E. HILGARD; S. NEWCOMB; S. F. BAIRD; F. B. MEEK; L. AGASSIZ. (R. 1871) 249
investigation in Russian America, suggestions relative to—J. HENRY **207**
labors of Edward Lartet—F. FISCHER. (R. 1872.) 271
observations, on metric system for—A. GUYOT. (R. 1848) I
progress, reports of. (R. 1880) 442, **427, 428, 429, 430, 431, 432**
researches of J. C. A. Peltier—F. A. PELTIER. (R. 1867) 215
societies, local, organization of—J. HENRY. (R. 1875) 298
writings of Sir William Herschel—E. S. HOLDEN; C. S. HASTINGS. (R. 1880) 442, **426**
writings of James Smithson 327
Scientific and Literary Institute of Lombardy—*See* Prize questions.
Scintillation of the stars—C. DUFOUR; KÄMTZ. (R. 1861) 149
Scops, review of American species of genus—R. RIDGWAY. (P. 1878) 332
SCUDDER, S. H.—
Bibliography of orthoptera 189
Catalogue of orthoptera of North America **189**
Nomenclator zoölogicus. An alphabetical list of generic names of recent and fossil animals **470**

SCUDDER, S. H., and others. Insects of Arctic America ---------- 342

Sculpture, Maya, remarks on ancient relic of—A. SCHOTT. (R. 1871) -------- 249

Sculptures of Santa Lucia Cosumalwhuapa in Guatemala—S. HABEL -------- **269**

Scytalina cerdale, new species of fish from Neah Bay, Washington Territory, description of—D. S. JORDAN; C. H. GILBERT. (P. 1880) ---------- 425

Sea, gradual approach of, upon land—S. P. MAYBERRY. (R. 1867) ---------- 215

Seas, the northern—J. BABINET. (R. 1869) ---------- 228

Seaton, W. W., memoir of, by J. HENRY. (R. 1866) ---------- 214

Sebastichthys carnatus, new species of rockfish from coast of California, description of—D. S. JORDAN; C. H. GILBERT. (P. 1880) ---------- 425

Sebastichthys chrysomelas, new species of rockfish from coast of California, description of—D. S. JORDAN; C. H. GILBERT. (P. 1880) ---------- 425

Sebastichthys entomelas, new species of *Sebastichthys* from Monterey Bay, California, description of—D. S. JORDAN; C. H. GILBERT. (P. 1880) ----- 425

Sebastichthys maliger, new scorpænoid fish from coast of California, description of—D. S. JORDAN; C. H. GILBERT. (P. 1880) ---------- 425

Sebastichthys miniatus, new species of *Sebastichthys* from Monterey Bay, California, description of—D. S. JORDAN; C. H. GILBERT. (P. 1880) ----- 425

Sebastichthys mystinus, description of—D. S. JORDAN; C. H. GILBERT. (P. 1881) 467

Sebastichthys proriger, new scorpænoid fish from Monterey Bay, California, description of—D. S. JORDAN; C. H. GILBERT. (P. 1880) ---------- 425

Sebastichthys rhodochloris, new species of *Sebastichthys* from Monterey Bay, California, description of—D. S. JORDAN; C. H. GILBERT. (P. 1880) -- 425

Sebastichthys serriceps, new species of rock cod from coast of California, description of—D. S. JORDAN; C. H. GILBERT. (P. 1880) ---------- 425

Sebastoid fishes, description of seven new species of—D. S. JORDAN; C. H. GILBERT. (P. 1880) ---------- 425

SECCHI, A. Researches on electrical rheometry ---------- **36**

Secretary of Smithsonian Institution, report of—*See* Henry, J., Baird, S. F.

Secretary of Treasury, letter to, on payment of interest in coin—J. HENRY. (R. 1865) ---------- 209

Secular period of aurora borealis—D. OLMSTED ---------- **81**

Secular variations of elements of planetary orbits—J. N. STOCKWELL. (R. 1871) ---------- 249, **232**

Seismograph, electro-magnetic—Prof. PALMIERI. (R. 1870) ---------- 244

Sema, note on—D. S. JORDAN. (P. 1880) ---------- 425

Semper's method of making dry preparations—J. A. RYDER. (P. 1881) ----- 467

Senate Judiciary Committee, report of, on management of Smithsonian—A. P. BUTLER. (R. 1855) ---------- 77

Senses, the. Sense of feeling, sense of smell. (R. 1865) ---------- 209

Senses, the. Sense of taste, sense of hearing, sense of sight. (R. 1866) ------- 214

Séquard—*See* Brown-Séquard.

Series, converging, expressing ratio of diameter and circumference of a circle—W. FERREL ---------- **233**

Seriola Stearnsii, new species of amber fish from Pensacola, Florida, description of—G. B. GOODE. (P. 1879) ---- 333
Sermon at funeral of Joseph Henry—S. S. MITCHELL ---- 356
Serpent venom, bibliography of—S. W. MITCHELL ---- 135
Serpents, catalogue of—S. F. BAIRD; C. GIRARD ---- **49**
Serpents, lecture on nature and cure of bites of—D. BRAINARD. (R. 1854) ---- 75
Seven cities of Cibola, Coronado's march in search of the—J. H. SIMPSON. (R. 1869) ---- 228
Sexual characters of eels—S. T. CATTIE. (P. 1880) ---- 425
Shad, western gizzard, *Dorosoma cepedianum heterurum*, notes on—S. WILMOT. (P. 1878) ---- 332
SHAKESPEARE, E. O. The nature of reparatory inflammation in arteries after ligature, etc. Toner lecture No. VII ---- **321**
Shark, the oil, of southern California, (*Galeorhinus galeus*)—D. S. JORDAN; C. H. GILBERT. (P. 1880) ---- 425
SHARPLESS, T.; PATTERSON, R. Phonography. (R. 1856) ---- 91
SHAW, J. Mound-builders in Rock river valley, Illinois. (R. 1877) ---- 323
SHEA, J. G. Account of library of Indian linguistics. (R. 1861) ---- 149
Shea's Indian linguistics, recommendation of—G. GIBBS and others. (R. 1861.) 149
Shell-bed skull—A. S. TIFFANY. (R. 1874) ---- 286
Shell-deposits, artificial, of the United States—D. G. BRINTON. (R. 1866.) 214, 440
Shell-deposits, artificial, in New Jersey—C. RAU. (R. 1864) ---- 188, 362
Shell engravings granted by British Museum. (R. 1863) ---- 187
Shellfish and their allies, lectures on—P. P. CARPENTER. (R. 1860) ---- 147, **152**
Shell-heap in Georgia—D. BROWN. (R. 1871) ---- 249
Shell-heaps—
  and ancient graves of California—P. SCHUMACHER. (R. 1874) ---- 286
  at mouth of St. John's river, Florida—S. P. MAYBERRY. (R. 1877) ---- 323
  in New Brunswick—J. FOWLER. (R. 1870) ---- 244
  of Tampa Bay, Florida—S. T. WALKER. (R. 1879) ---- 345
  on Mobile river, Alabama—A. S. GAINES; K. M. CUNNINGHAM. (R. 1877) ---- 323
Shell-mounds—*See* Mounds.
Shells—
  acknowledgment for—W. H. PEASE. (R. 1861) ---- 149
  bibliography of. Parts I, II—W. G. BINNEY ---- **142**, **174**
  duplicate, collected by United States exploring expedition—C. WILKES. **193**
  from California, description of new species of, in U. S. National Museum—W. H. DALL. (P. 1878) ---- 332
  from Costa Rica kitchen-midden—W. H. DALL. (P. 1878) ---- 332
  land and fresh-water, instructions for collecting—J. LEWIS. (R. 1866) 214, **363**
  land and fresh-water, of North America:
    Part I. *Pulmonata geophila*—W. G. BINNEY; T. BLAND ---- **194**

Shells—Continued.
land and fresh-water, of North America:
Part II. *Pulmonata limnophila* and *Thallasophila*—W. G. BINNEY. **143**
Part III. *Ampullariidæ*, *Valvatidæ*, (etc.)—W. G. BINNEY **144**
Part IV. *Strepomatidæ* (American melanians)—G. W. TRYON, Jr. **253**
letter on—J. LEWIS 253
North American, check-list of—I. LEA; P. P. CARPENTER; W. STIMPSON; W. G. BINNEY; T. PRIME **128**
North American, circular in reference to collecting **176**
of Gulf of California, lectures on the—P. P. CARPENTER. (R. 1859) 110
of Panama, collected by C. B. Adams, descriptions of new species and varieties of *Chitonidæ* and *Acmæidæ* in—P. P. CARPENTER 252
presented to Academy of Natural Sciences, report on—J. LEIDY; G. W. TRYON. (R. 1865) 209
request for duplicate—W. E. LOGAN. (R. 1859) 110
Shells—*See* Mollusca.
SHEPARD, C. U. Arrangement of mineralogical collection. (R. 1861) 149
SHEPARD, E. M. Deposit of arrow-heads near Fishkill, New York. (R. 1877.) 323
SHERMAN, W. T. Memorial address on J. Henry 356
SHERMAN, W. T. Report of National Museum Building Commission, 1879, 1880. (R. 1879; R. 1880) 345, 442, **409**, **434**
Shetland, vegetable colonization of—C. MARTINS. (R. 1858) 109
Shipping fresh fish and other animals, circular relative to—S. F. BAIRD **384**
Shoal Lake, Lake Winnipeg, egging expedition to—D. GUNN. (R. 1867) 215
Shooting stars, observations on—S. MASTERMAN. (R. 1857) 107
Short memoirs on meteorological subjects, translated by C. ABBE. (R. 1877.) 323, 398
Shoshone Indians, religion, superstitions, and manners of—A. G. BRACKETT. (R. 1879) 345
SHUFELDT, R. W. Remarks upon osteology of *Opheosaurus ventralis*. (P. 1881.) 467
Siberia, descriptions of new fishes from—T. H. BEAN. (P. 1881) 467
SIBLEY, H. Meteorological telegrams by Western Union Telegraph Company. (R. 1862) 150
Sight, sense of. (R. 1866) 214
Sign language among North American Indians—G. MALLERY. (E. 1879–80.) 476
Sign language of deaf mutes—G. MALLERY. (E. 1879–80) 476
Siluridæ of fresh waters of North America, synopsis of—D. S. JORDAN 306
Silver coins, assay of, at United States Mint—J. POLLOCK. (R. 1868) 224
Silver coins, foreign, table of. (R. 1868) 224
Silvered-glass telescope, on construction of—H. DRAPER **180**
SIMPSON, G. Letter to officers of Hudson's Bay Company relative to scientific researches 137
SIMPSON, J. H. Coronado's march in search of the seven cities of Cibola. (R. 1869) 228

SIMSON, R. Meteorite in Mexico. (R. 1867) ---------- 215
Sioux Indians—A. G. BRACKETT. (R. 1876) ---------- 299
Sioux Indians, language of the—F. L. O. ROEHRIG. (R. 1871) ---------- 249, 378
Sioux nation of the upper Missouri—T. A. CULBERTSON. (R. 1850) ---------- 28
Sioux—*See* Dakota.
Siredon lichenoides, observations on—W. E. CARLIN. (P. 1881) ---------- 467
Six Nations, wampum belts of the—W. M. BEAUCHAMP. (R. 1879) ---------- 345
Skeletons of birds, suggestions for saving parts of—A. NEWTON. (R. 1860) ---------- 147
Sketch of—
Academy of Science of Paris—M. FLOURENS. (R. 1862) ---------- 150
ancient earthworks of Ohio—I. DILLE. (R. 1866) ---------- 214
ancient earthworks on upper Missouri—A. BARRANDT. (R. 1870) ---------- 244
flora of Alaska—J. T. ROTHROCK. (R. 1867) ---------- 215, 367
Navajo Indians—J. LETTERMAN. (R. 1855) ---------- 77
scientific work of Joseph Henry—W. B. TAYLOR ---------- 356, **339**
Sketches, historical and bibliographical, of archæology of United States—S. F. HAVEN ---------- 71
Sketches of scenery, catalogue of—J. M. STANLEY ---------- 53
Skull—
and long bones from mounds near Albany, Illinois—R. J. FARQUHARSON. (R. 1874) ---------- 286
human, from Rock Bluff, Illinois, description of—J. A. MEIGS. (R. 1867.) 215
human, present state of ethnology in relation to form of the—A. RETZIUS. (R. 1859) ---------- 110
shell-bed, from Rock Island, Illinois—A. S. TIFFANY. (R. 1874) ---------- 286
Skulls and mummy from Patagonia—A. RIED. (R. 1862) ---------- 150
Sloth tribe of North America, extinct—J. LEIDY ---------- **72**
SMALLWOOD, C. Description of observatory at St. Martin, Isle Jesus, Canada East. (R. 1856) ---------- 91
SMART, C. Notes on the Tonto Apaches. (R. 1867) ---------- 215
Smell, sense of. (R. 1865) ---------- 209
Smelt, surf, of northwest coast, and method of taking by Indians—J. G. SWAN. (P. 1880) ---------- 425
SMITH, B. Spanish works on New Mexico. (R. 1855) ---------- 77
SMITH, C. D. Ancient mica mines in North Carolina. (R. 1876) ---------- 299
SMITH, J. L. Lecture on meteoric stones. (R. 1855) ---------- 77
SMITH, J. W. C. Antiquities of Yazoo county, Mississippi. (R. 1874) ---------- 286
SMITH, N. D. Meteorological observations made near Washington, Arkansas. **131**
SMITH, R.—
Description of new gobioid fish (*Othonops eos*) from San Diego, California. (P. 1881) ---------- 467
Description of new species of gobiesox (*Gobiesox rhessodon*) from San Diego, California. (P. 1881) ---------- 467
Occurrence of species of cremnobates at San Diego, California. (P. 1880.) 425

SMITH, S. B. On the Chinook names of salmon in Columbia river. (P. 1881.) 467
SMITH, S. I.—
Crustaceans of Kerguelen Island ... 294
Notice of crustacea dredged off south coast of New England in 1880. (P. 1880) ... 425
Notice of new species of *Willemœsia* group of crustacea (recent *Eryontidæ*.) (P. 1879) ... 333
Occurrence of *Chelura terebrans* (crustacean destructive to timber) on coast of United States. (P. 1879) ... 333
Smithson fund, memorial of Regents to Congress relative to the. (R. 1850) ... 28
Smithson, James—
act of Congress to receive residuary legacy of. (R. 1866) ... 214, 329
catalogue of library of ... 330
character and researches of—W. R. JOHNSON ... 327
contributions to Annals of Philosophy by. (R. 1853) ... 67, 330
exposition of bequest of—J. HENRY ... E
letter from Richard Rush relative to. (R. 1853) ... 67, 328
letters from Fladgate, Clark, and Finch, relative to. (R. 1861) ... 149, 328
life of, by W. J. RHEES. (R. 1879) ... 345, **330**
list of papers presented to Royal Society by. (R. 1853) ... 67, 330
notice of, by D. Gilbert, president of the Royal Society. (R. 1853) ... 67, 330
personal effects of ... 328, 330
scientific writings of ... 327
will of. (R. 1853) ... 67, 328, 330
will of, *fac-similé* of ... 330
works and character of—J. R. McD. IRBY ... 327
Smithson, James, and his bequest—W. J. RHEES. (R. 1879) ... 345, **330**
Smithsonian—
building, report on use of new hall in—L. AGASSIZ. (R. 1867) ... 215
Bulletin No. I. Vocabulary of the jargon ... 68
Contributions to Knowledge—*See* Contributions.
Miscellaneous Collections—*See* Miscellaneous Collections.
publications—*See* Publications.
publications, catalogue and index of—W. J. RHEES ... **478**
Reports—*See* Reports.
Smithsonian Institution—
act to establish—*See* Congress.
address on the—J. HENRY. (R. 1853) ... E, 67
business arrangements of the ... **325**
directory of officers, collaborators, and employés of the ... **466**
establishment and officers of the ... **449**
Journals of Regents, reports of committees, statistics, etc.—W. J. RHEES. **329**
magnetic observatory at, description of—J. E. HILGARD. (R. 1859) ... 110

Smithsonian Institution—Continued.
origin and history of—W. J. RHEES **328**
report of American Academy of Arts and Sciences, on the. (R. 1853) .. 67
report of Senate Judiciary Committee on management of—A. P. BUTLER. (R. 1855) 77
views and plans of the—R. D. OWEN .... P
Snake Indians, religion, superstition, and manners of—A. G. BRACKETT. (R. 1879) 345
SNELL, E. S. Lecture on planetary disturbances. (R. 1855) 77
Snell's barometric observations, discussion of—F. H. LOUD. (R. 1880) ... 442, **435**
Snow—
charts—*See* Rain.
electricity during fall of—F. ZANTEDESCHI. (R. 1870) 244
gauge—W. E. GUEST. (R. 1858) 109
gauges—R. H. GARDINER. (R. 1858) 109
line, Norwegian—O. E. DREUTZER. (R. 1866) 214
observations of 157
tables of precipitation in—C. A. SCHOTT **222**, **353**
SNYDER, J. F. Deposit of stone implements in Illinois. (R. 1876) 299
Social and religious condition of the lower races of man—J. LUBBOCK. (R. 1869.) 228
Societies—
list of, in United States and British Provinces—W. J. RHEES 116
local scientific, organization of—J. HENRY. (R. 1875) 298
proceedings of, relative to Joseph Henry 356
publications of, in Smithsonian library, 1854, 1856, 1858, 1866. **73**, **85**, **117**, **179**
Societies—*See* Holland, Belgium, Publications.
Society—
Batavian, of Experimental Philosophy, Rotterdam. Prize questions. (R. 1861) 149
Bath and West of England, for Encouragement of Agricultural Arts, etc. Exchange system. (R. 1867) 215
for Encouragement of Science, Dunkirk—*See* Prize questions.
Society of—
Arts and Sciences, Utrecht. Prize questions. (R. 1861) 149
Natural History, Portland, Maine, account of—E. C. BOLLES. (R. 1867.) 215
Natural Sciences, Cherbourg—*See* Prize questions.
Physics and Natural History of Geneva—*See* Geneva.
Science, Agriculture, and Arts of Lille—*See* Prize questions.
Science, Art, and Literature, Hainaut—*See* Prize questions.
Sciences, Harlem—*See* Prize questions.
Sciences, Letters, and Arts, Dunkirk—*See* Prize questions.
Sciences, Royal Danish—*See* Prize questions.
Victoria, address of president—R. L. J. ELLERY. (R. 1868) 224

SOHNCKE, L. Law of variation of temperature in ascending moist currents of air. (R. 1877) ---- 323, 398
Solar—
diurnal variation in magnetic declination—A. D. BACHE ---- 113, 121
diurnal variation in vertical component of magnetic force—A. D. BACHE. 175
eclipse of April 25, 1865—Baron DE PRADOS. (R. 1864) ---- 188
eclipse of July 18, 1860—J. LAMONT. (R. 1864) ---- 188
system, harmonies of the—S. ALEXANDER ---- **280**
Solids, specific heat of—F. W. CLARKE ---- 276
Solids, tables of expansion of, by heat—F. W. CLARKE ---- 289
Solitary wasps, synopsis of—H. DE SAUSSURE ---- 254
SONNTAG, A. Observations on terrestrial magnetism in Mexico ---- **114**
Sonora, plants collected in, by C. Wright—A. GRAY ---- 22
Sound, refraction of—W. B. TAYLOR. (R. 1875) ---- 298
Sound, researches in—J. HENRY. (R. 1878) ---- 341, **406**
Soundings, microscopical examination of—J. W. BAILEY ---- **20**, **23**
Sounds, vocal, of Laura Bridgman—F. LIEBER ---- **12**
South America—
birds of, not in U. S. National Museum—R. RIDGWAY. (P. 1881) ---- 467
Caracas, meteorology of—G. A. ERNST. (R. 1867) ---- 215
circular relative to collections of birds from ---- 168
rain-fall in—C. A. SCHOTT ---- 222, 353
travels in—S. HABEL ---- 269
South Carolina—
description of new hake from—T. H. BEAN. (P. 1880) ---- 425
fishes of—D. S. JORDAN; A. W. BRAYTON ---- **308**
microscopical observations in—J. W. BAILEY ---- 23
Southern Baptist Missionary Society. Yoruba grammar and dictionary ---- 98
Southern States, antiquities in the—H. C. WILLIAMS. (R. 1880) ---- 244
Southern States, microscopical observations in the—J. W. BAILEY ---- 23
Space and time, lecture on the relations of—S. ALEXANDER. (R. 1861) ---- 149
SPAINHOUR, J. Antiquities in Lenoir county, North Carolina. (R. 1871) ---- 249
Spanish vocabulary, with comparative words in English, French, and Latin ---- 170
Spanish works on New Mexico, by Buckingham Smith, communications relative to publication of. (R. 1855) ---- 77
SPARKS, J., and others. On publication of Spanish works on New Mexico. (R. 1855) ---- 77
SPARKS, J., and others. Report of American Academy of Art and Sciences on organization of Smithsonian Institution. (R. 1853) ---- 67
Sparoid fish, new, (*Sparus brachysomus*,) from lower California—W. N. LOCKINGTON. (P. 1880) ---- 425
Sparrows sent to United States—W. A. LLOYD. (R. 1867) ---- 215

Sparus brachysomus, new sparoid fish, from lower California, description of—W. N. LOCKINGTON. (P. 1880) 425
Specific gravity—
bibliography of—F. W. CLARKE 255
of sea water—D. WALKER 146
tables. Constants of Nature, Part I—F. W. CLARKE **255**
tables. First supplement to Constants of Nature, Part I—F. W. CLARKE. **288**
Specific heat, bibliography of—F. W. CLARKE 276
Specific heat tables. Constants of Nature, Part II—F. W. CLARKE **276**
Specimens—
acknowledged by British Museum. (R. 1865) 209
acknowledged by Chicago Academy of Sciences. (R. 1867) 215
authority to collectors of customs to receive and transmit to Smithsonian Institution 34
authority to naval officers to receive and transmit to Smithsonian Institution 34
authority to quartermasters of War Department to receive and transmit to Smithsonian Institution 34
derived from expeditions—S. F. BAIRD. (R. 1867) 215
exchange of—Hamburg Zoölogical Gardens. (R. 1867) 215
exchange of—W. A. LLOYD. (R. 1867) 215
exchange of—University of Costa Rica. (R. 1867) 215
exchange of—University of Greece. (R. 1867) 215
from Brazil, presented—M. M. LISBOA. (R. 1865) 209
large myological, rapid preparation of—F. PLATEAU. (P. 1881) 467
of flamingo from south Florida, presented—G. WURDEMAN. (R. 1860.) 147
of natural history, directions for collecting, preserving, and transporting—S. F. BAIRD. (R. 1856) 91, **34**
presented, circular sent with—J. HENRY. (R. 1872) 271
receipts and distribution of. (R. 1880) 442
rules for examination of. (R. 1880) 442
Spectrum analysis applied to the heavenly bodies—W. HUGGINS. (R. 1866) 214
Spencer's telescope, examination of, for Hamilton College. (R. 1855) 77
Spheres, tangencies of—B. ALVORD 80
Spleen, observations on—J. JONES 82
Sponge, a new type of, (*Camaraphysema*)—J. A. RYDER. (P. 1880) 425
Spruce Creek valley, Pennsylvania, account of tornado in—J. B. MEEK. (R. 1871) 249
Squalius aliciæ from Utah Lake—P. L. JOUY. (P. 1881) 467
SQUIER, E. G. Aboriginal monuments of State of New York **15**
SQUIER, E. G. Antiquities of Nicaragua. (R. 1850) 28
SQUIER, E. G., and others. On publication of Spanish works on New Mexico. (R. 1855) 77

SQUIER, E. G.; DAVIS, C. H. Ancient monuments of the Mississippi valley. **1**
Squier, E. G.; Davis, C. H., correspondence relative to memoir by. (R. 1847.) **H, K**
Stanley's gallery of Indian portraits, report of Committee of Regents on the. (R. 1857) 107
STANLEY, J. M. Catalogue of portraits of North American Indians **53**
STANTON, E. M. Deposit of Beaufort Library. (R. 1862) 150
Star clusters, bibliography of—E. S. HOLDEN 311
Stars—
 index-catalogue of—E. S. HOLDEN 311
 movement of, around a central point—J. H. MAEDLER. (R. 1859) 110
 near the North Pole, map of, for observations on auroras **350**
 scintillation of the—C. DUFOUR; KÄMTZ. (R. 1861) 149
State Department. Circular to diplomatic agents relative to Morgan's research. 138
Statement and exposition of harmonies of the solar system—S. ALEXANDER **280**
Stations, meteorological, of Smithsonian Institution (*See, also*, List) **373**
Statistics of—
 British Museum—S. F. BAIRD. (R. 1850) 28
 Norwegian mountains, lakes, and snow line—O. E. DREUTZER. (R. 1866.) 214
 Smithsonian Institution, finances, exchanges, etc., 1846–1877 329
Statue of Joseph Henry, proceedings of Congress relative to 856
Statues, on plaster casts of—W. J. STONE. (R. 1855) 77
STEARNS, J. Translation of Babinet on diamonds and precious stones. (R. 1870) 244, **377**
Stearns, S., catalogue of fishes from Pensacola, collected by—G. B. GOODE; T. H. BEAN. (P. 1879) 333
Stearns, S., description of new species of amber fish (*Seriola Stearnsii*) obtained near Pensacola, by—G. B. GOODE; T. H. BEAN. (P. 1879) 333
STEARNS, S. Note on Gulf menhaden, *Brevoortia patronus*. (P. 1878) 332
STEBBINS, R. P. Memoir of Louis Agassiz. (R. 1873) 275
STEINDACHNER, F. Note on *Perca flavescens*. (P. 1878) 332
STEJNEGER, L. Description of two new races of *Myadestes obscurus*. (P. 1881.) 467
STELLE, J. P. Account of aboriginal ruins in Hardin Co., Tennessee. (R. 1870.) 244
STELLE, J. P. Account of aboriginal ruins at Savannah, Tennessee. (R. 1870.) 244
STEPHENSON, M. F. Account of ancient mounds in Georgia. (R. 1870) 244
STEPHENSON, M. F. Mounds in Bartow county, Georgia. (R. 1872) 271
Stereotype catalogue of public libraries, report of Commissioners on. (R. 1850.) 28, 47
Stereotyped titles for library catalogues—C. C. JEWETT **47**
STEVENS, H. Prospectus of a bibliographia Americana. (R. 1848) **I**
STEVENS, J. A. Memoir of George Gibbs. (R. 1873) 275
STEVENSON, J. Report of explorations in New Mexico and Arizona. (R. 1880.) 442
STEWART, B. Experiments on aneroid barometers at Kew Observatory. (R. 1868.) 224
Stichæus punctatus, occurrence of, at St. Michael's, Alaska—T. H. BEAN. (P. 1878) 332

STIMPSON, W.—
Check-list of the shells of North America ---- 128
On collection and preservation of marine invertebrates ---- 34
Researches upon the *Hydrobiinæ* and allied forms ---- **201**
Synopsis of the marine invertebrata of Grand Manan ---- **50**
Stock-in-trade of an aboriginal lapidary—C. RAU. (R. 1877) ---- 323, 440, **402**
Stockholm Academy of Sciences. Acknowledgment of birds. (R. 1867) ---- 215
STOCKWELL, J. N. Secular variations of elements of orbits of the eight principal planets. (R. 1871) ---- 249, **232**
STONE, W. J. On plaster casts of statues. (R. 1855) ---- 77
Stone—
celts in the West Indies and Africa—G. J. GIBBS. (R. 1877) ---- 323
cists near Highland, Madison county, Illinois—A. OEHLER. (R. 1879.) 345
drilling in, without metal—C. RAU. (R. 1868) ---- 224, 440, **372**
image in Tennessee, account of discovery of—E. M. GRANT. (R. 1870.) 244
implements, North American—C. RAU. (R. 1872) ---- 271, 440, **382**
Stone age—
and the troglodytes of Breckinridge county, Kentucky—R. S. ROBERTSON. (R. 1874) ---- 286
fauna of middle Europe during the—L. RÜTIMEYER. (R. 1861) ---- 149
in New Jersey—C. C. ABBOTT. (R. 1875) ---- 298, **394**
Stone period, North American, agricultural implements of the—C. RAU. (R. 1863) ---- 187, 440
Stones, precious—J. BABINET. (R. 1870) ---- 244, 377
Storm in Butler county, Kansas, June 23, 1871—W. HARRISON. (R. 1871) ---- 249
Storms—
in Europe and America, December, 1836—E. LOOMIS ---- **127**
magnetic—E. SABINE. (R. 1860) ---- 147
of 1859—J. H. COFFIN ---- 182
thunder, instructions for observations of—J. HENRY ---- 235
Strain and over-action of the heart. Toner lecture No. III—J. M. DA COSTA. 279
Strait of Juan de Fuca, Indians of—J. G. SWAN ---- 220
Strait of Juan de Fuca, description of new species of *Paralepis* (*Paralepis coruscans*) from—D. S. JORDAN; C. H. GILBERT. (P. 1880) ---- 425
STRANG, J. J. Natural History of Beaver Island, Michigan. (R. 1854) ---- 75
STREETS, T. N. Contributions to natural history of Hawaiian Islands, Fanning Islands, and lower California ---- 303
Strepomatidæ (American melanians)—G. W. TRYON ---- **253**
Stricklandia Davidsoni, note on the occurrence of, in Georgia—C. A. WHITE. (P. 1880) ---- 425
Stricklandia Salteri, note on the occurrence of, in Georgia—C. A. WHITE. (P. 1880) ---- 425
STRONG, M. Antiquities in Wisconsin. (R. 1877) ---- 323

STRONG, M. Observations on the prehistoric mounds of Grant county, Wisconsin. (R. 1876) 299
Structure, internal, of the earth—J. G. BARNARD **310**
Structure of cancerous tumors. Toner lecture No. I—J. J. WOODWARD 266
Structures, aboriginal, in Georgia—C. C. JONES, Jr. (R. 1877) 323, 400
Study of—
chionis minor—J. H. KIDDER; E. COUES 294
high antiquity in Europe, lecture on—A. MORLOT. (R. 1862; R. 1864.) 150, 188
jade—S. BLONDEL. (R. 1876) 299
mortuary customs of North American Indians—H. C. YARROW. (E. 1879–80) 476
nature and mechanism of fever. Toner lecture No. IV—H. C. WOOD 282
phenomena of contact—T. L. PHIPSON. (R. 1862) 150
physiology of fever—H. C. WOOD **357**
savage weapons at the Centennial—E. H. KNIGHT. (R. 1879) 345, **415**
skulls and long bones from mounds in Illinois—R. J. FARQUHARSON. (R. 1874) 286
trunk fishes, *Ostraciontidæ*—G. B. GOODE. (P. 1879) 333
Studies in Central American picture writing—E. S. HOLDEN. (E. 1879–80) 476
Subcutaneous surgery. Toner lecture No. VI—W. ADAMS **302**
Sudis ringens, new species of scopeloid fish from Santa Barbara channel, California, description of—D. S. JORDAN; C. H. GILBERT. (P. 1880) 425
SUESS, E. Boundary line between geology and history. (R. 1872) 271
Suggestions—
for ethnological researches in Russian America—G. GIBBS 207
for forming collections of birds' eggs—A. NEWTON 139
for meteorological observations in Russian America—J. HENRY 207
for sanitary drainage of Washington city—G. E. WARING **349**
for saving parts of the skeletons of birds—A. NEWTON. (R. 1860) 147
relative to ethnological map of North America—L. H. MORGAN. (R. 1861.) 149
relative to objects of scientific investigations in Russian America—J. HENRY; S. F. BAIRD 207
to beginners in botany—L. F. WARD **460**
Sulphurous acid, action of, upon putrefactive bacteria. (P. 1881) 467
Sumichrast, F., birds of Mexico, collected by—G. N. LAWRENCE **295**
Summary of anthropological correspondence previous to 1880—O. T. MASON. (R. 1879) 345
Sun—
chemical analysis of the—A. LAUGEL. (R. 1861) 149
disk of the, external appearance of. (R. 1866) 214
eclipse of the, September 7, 1858—J. M. GILLISS 100
eclipse of the, March 15, 1868—T. HILL 101
eclipse of the, April 25, 1865—M. DE PRADOS. (R. 1864) 188
relative intensity of heat and light of the—L. W. MEECH. (R. 1856.) 91, **83**

SUNDERLAND, B. Prayer at memorial of Joseph Henry 356
Sun's distance, means available for correcting measures of the—G. B. AIRY. (R. 1859) 110
Superstitions of Shoshone Indians—A. G. BRACKETT (R. 1879) 345
Supplement, asteroid, to new tables of planetary motion—J. D. RUNKLE **94**
Surgery, subcutaneous. Toner lecture No. VI—W. ADAMS **302**
Surgical complications and sequels of continued fevers. Toner lecture No. V—W. W. KEEN **300**
Survey—
in Michigan, catalogue of rocks, minerals, and ores collected in the—C. T. JACKSON. (R. 1854) 75
magnetic, of Pennsylvania and parts of adjacent States—A. D. BACHE. 166
of economic geology of Trinidad—G. P. WALL; J. G. SAWKINS. (R. 1856) 91
of State of New York—E. G. SQUIER 15
Surveying expedition, North Pacific, natural history of—T. H. STREETS **303**
Surveys, Government—*See* Explorations.
SWAN, J. G.—
Eulachon, or candlefish of northwest coast. (P. 1880) 425
Haidah Indians of Queen Charlotte's Islands, British Columbia **267**
Makah Indians of Cape Flattery, Strait of Fuca **220**
Makah vocabulary 220
Surf smelt of the northwest coast, and mode of taking them by the Quillehute Indians of west coast of Washington Territory. (P. 1880.) 425
Sweden, Stockholm, Academy of Sciences. Acknowledgment of birds. (R. 1867.) 215
Switzerland—
Concise, archæological researches made at—F. TROYON. (R. 1861) 149
Crania helvetica—F. TROYON. (R. 1864) 188
lacustrian cities of—F. TROYON. (R. 1861) 149
lacustrian settlements in, abstract of Dr. Keller's report on—A. MORLOT. (R. 1863) 187
Lake of Neuchâtel, palafittes or lacustrian constructions of—E. DESOR. (R. 1865) 209, **360**
Lausanne, Cantonal Museum at, antiquarian and ethnological collections of the—F. TROYON. (R. 1861) 149
lecture on—A. D. BACHE. (R. 1870) 244
Syllabus of a course of lectures on physics—J. HENRY. (R. 1856) 91
Symbols for charts of prehistoric archæology, international code of—G. DE MORTILLET; E. CHANTRE. (R. 1875) 298
Symbols used by James Smithson 327
Synopsis of—
American *Rhinobatidæ*—S. GARMAN. (P. 1880) 425
American wasps, solitary wasps—H. DE SAUSSURE **254**
catostomidæ—D. S. JORDAN 308

Synopsis of—Continued.
marine invertebrata of Grand Manan—W. STIMPSON **50**
North American lepidoptera—J. G. MORRIS **133**
North American neuroptera—H. HAGEN; P. R. UHLER **134**
pediculate fishes of east coast of extra tropical North America—T. GILL. (P. 1878) 332
scientific writings of Sir William Herschel—E. S. HOLDEN; C. S. HASTINGS. (R. 1880) 442, **426**
siluridæ of fresh waters of North America—D. S. JORDAN 306
trochilidæ—D. G. ELLIOTT **317**
useful and injurious animals—G. B. GOODE 297
Synoptical tables of characters of mammals—T. GILL 230
Synthetic experiments relative to meteorites—G. A. DAUBRÉE. (R. 1868) 224
Syria, Beirut, sarcophagus from—A. A. HARWOOD. (R. 1870) 244
System—
meteorological, of Smithsonian Institution—E. FOREMAN. (R. 1851; R. 1852) 51, 57
of accounts adopted by Board of Regents. (R. 1866) 214
of combined meteorological observations, report on, by committee of American Association for Advancement of Science. (R. 1851) 51
of numeration, improved, report on—W. B. TAYLOR. (R. 1867) 215
of weights and measures, new—G. H. KNIGHT. (R. 1867) 215
solar, harmonies of the—S. ALEXANDER 280
Systematic—
index of Smithsonian publications. (R. 1868) 224, 478
index to list of foreign correspondents **257**
list of batrachia and reptilia—E. D. COPE 292
review of classification of birds—W. LILLJEBORG. (R. 1865) 209, 364
Systems of consanguinity and affinity of the human family—L. H. MORGAN **218**
Systems of relationship of Cree Indians—E. A. WATKINS. (R. 1862) 150

T.

Table of—

anthropological measurements—SCHERZER; SCHWARZ. (R. 1866) 214

chemical equivalents of sixty-three elements. (R. 1864) 188

distribution of birds—G. N. LAWRENCE. (P. 1878) 332

foreign gold and silver coins. (R. 1868) 224

Tables—

asteroid—J. D. RUNKLE **94**

barometrical—A. GUYOT 153

for conversion of centigrade degrees to Fahrenheit's scale. (R. 1863) .. 187

for determining values of coefficients in perturbative function of planetary motion which depend on ratio of mean distances—J. D. RUNKLE .. **79**

hygrometrical—A. GUYOT 153

hypsometrical—A. GUYOT 153

meteorological—A. GUYOT **31**, **153**

metric—H. A. NEWTON. (R. 1865) 209, **371**

miscellaneous—A. GUYOT 153

mortality, methods of interpolation applied to. Parts I, II—E. L. DE FOREST. (R. 1871; R. 1873) 249, 275

of atmospheric temperature—C. A. SCHOTT **277**

of constants of nature and art—C. BABBAGE. (R. 1856) 91

of expansion by heat. Constants of Nature, Part III—F. W. CLARKE. **289**

of meteorological corrections—A. GUYOT 153

of motion of Neptune—S. NEWCOMB 199

of motion of Uranus—S. NEWCOMB 262

of precipitation in rain and snow—C. A. SCHOTT **222**, **353**

of variations of elements of orbits of the eight principal planets—J. N. STOCKWELL 232

of weights and measures, English and French. (R. 1863-1865.) 187, 188, 209

of winds of the globe—J. H. COFFIN; S. J. COFFIN **268**

physical—A. GUYOT **153**

psychrometrical—J. H. COFFIN **87**

specific gravity. Constants of Nature, Part I, and supplement—F. W. CLARKE **255**, **288**

specific heat. Constants of Nature, Part II—F. W. CLARKE **276**

thermometrical—A. GUYOT 153

Tablet, Palenque—C. RAU **331**

TACCHINI, P. Evaporation observed at Palermo in 1865 and 1866. (R. 1870.) 244

Tampa Bay, Florida, shell-heaps of—S. T. WALKER. (R. 1879) 345

Tangencies of circles and of spheres—B. ALVORD **80**

Taste, sense of. (R. 1866) 214

Taxidermy, classification of collections of U. S. National Museum to illustrate art of—W. T. HORNADAY. (P. 1881) ---------------------------- 467, **456**
TAYLOR, A. S. Grasshoppers and locusts of America. (R. 1858)------------ 109
TAYLOR, F. W. Report of chemist of Smithsonian Institution. (R. 1880)--- 442
TAYLOR, W. B.—
Henry and the telegraph. (R. 1878)------------------------------ 341, **405**
Kinetic theories of gravitation. (R. 1876) ---------------------- 299, **395**
Memoir on the scientific work of Joseph Henry---------------------- 356, **339**
Refraction of sound. (R. 1875) ------------------------------------ 298
Report on improved system of numeration. (R. 1867) ----------------- 215
Thoughts on the nature and origin of force. (R. 1870)------------ 244, **375**
TAYLOR, W. M. Ancient mound in western Pennsylvania. (R. 1877) ------ 323
Telegrams, astronomical, circular relative to—J. HENRY ------------------- **263**
Telegrams, meteorological, by Western Union Telegraph Company—H. SIBLEY. (R. 1862) -- 150
Telegrams read at memorial of Joseph Henry--------------------------------- 356
Telegraph—
American fire-alarm, lecture on the—W. F. CHANNING. (R. 1854) ---- 75
electro-magnetic, deposition of J. Henry in relation to. (R. 1857)-- 107, 115
electro-magnetic, Henry's contribution to—W. B. TAYLOR. (R. 1878.) 341, **405**
electro-magnetic, Morse's invention—W. B. TAYLOR. (R. 1878) -- 341, **405**
electro-magnetic, proceedings of Board of Regents in relation to. (R. 1857)-- 107, **115**
Henry and the—W. B. TAYLOR. (R. 1878)--------------------------- **405**
history of the—J. HENRY. (R. 1857) ------------------------------ 107, 115
influence of aurora on the—W. D. SARGENT. (R. 1870) -------------- 244
lines, phenomena in, during auroras—G. B. DONATI. (R. 1872) ------- 271
report of Committee of Regents on the. (R. 1857) ------------ 107, 115, 329
statement of S. P. Chase relative to the. (R. 1857)------------ 107, 115, 329
statement of L. D. Gale relative to the. (R. 1857) ------------ 107, 115, 329
statement of James Hall relative to the. (R. 1857)------------ 107, 115, 329
statement of J. Henry relative to history of. (R. 1857) ------- 107, 115, 329
statement of Charles Mason relative to the. (R. 1857) -------- 107, 115, 329
Telegraphic announcements of astronomical discoveries—J. HENRY----------- **263**
Telescope—
Henry Draper's, account of—T. W. WEBB. (R. 1864) --------------- 188
silvered-glass, construction of, and its use in celestial photography—H. DRAPER --- **180**
Spencer's, examination of, for Hamilton College, Clinton, N.Y. (R. 1855.) 77
Temperature—
chart of United States for the year—C. A. SCHOTT ---------------- **381, 388**
charts of United States, summer, winter, and year—C. A. SCHOTT ----- **387**

Temperature—Continued.
in ascending currents of air, laws of variation of—J. HANN. (R. 1877.) 323, 398
in ascending moist currents of air, laws of variation of—L. SOHNCKE. (R. 1877) 323, 398
mean, best hours to find—C. DEWEY. (R. 1857; R. 1860) 107, 147
observations in the Arctic Seas—I. I. HAYES 196
observations in the Arctic Seas—E. K. KANE 104
observations in the Arctic Seas—F. L. McCLINTOCK 146
of St. Louis, Missouri—A. FENDLER. (R. 1860) 147
tables for United States and adjacent parts of America—C. A. SCHOTT **277**
underground—C. A. SCHOTT; J. D. EVERETT. (R. 1874) 286
Temperature—*See* Kane, Hayes, Meteorology, etc.
Tempests and tornadoes, distinction between—J. B. LAMARCK. (R. 1871) 249
Tennessee—
aboriginal remains of—J. JONES 259
Alleghany region of, fishes of—D. S. JORDAN; A. W. BRAYTON 308
antiquities in—I. DILLE. (R. 1862) 150
antiquities in—E. O. DUNNING. (R. 1870) 244
antiquities of—W. M. CLARK. (R. 1877) 323
antiquities of—J. JONES **259**
antiquities of—D. F. WRIGHT. (R. 1874) 286
Blount county, antiquities of—A. E. LAW. (R. 1874) 286
Chattanooga, ancient mound near—M. C. READ. (R. 1867) 215
East, mound in—A. F. DANILSEN. (R. 1863) 187
explorations in—E. A. DAYTON. (R. 1870) 244
Hardin county, aboriginal ruins in—J. P. STELLE. (R. 1870) 244
herbarium captured in—H. R. WIRTZ. (R. 1862) 150
Jackson county, antiquities of—J. HAILE; J. W. McHENRY. (R. 1874.) 286
Nashville, antiquities of—R. S. ROBERTSON. (R. 1877) 323
Savannah, aboriginal ruins at—J. P. STELLE. (R. 1870) 244
stone image in, discovery of—E. M. GRANT. (R. 1870) 244
Terrestrial magnetism—
observations on—W. HARKNESS 239
observations on—J. LOCKE **35**
observations on—Baron VON MÜLLER; A. SONNTAG 114
Terrestrial magnetism—*See* Bache, A. D.
Terrestrial physics, articles on. (R. 1870) 244
Tertiary fossils, presented—IMPERIAL GEOLOGICAL INSTITUTE, VIENNA. (R. 1863) 187
Testing building materials, on mode of—J. HENRY. (R. 1856) 91
Testing results of perspiration and respiration, apparatus for—M. PETTENKOFER. (R. 1864) 188

Texas—
hail storm in—G. M. BACHE. (R. 1870) 244
new cretaceous invertebrate fossils from, descriptions of—C. A. WHITE. (P. 1879) 333
ornithology of, notes on—J. C. MERRILL. (P. 1878) 332
plants of, collected by C. Wright. Parts I, II—A. GRAY 22, 42
zoölogical position of—E. D. COPE **412**
Thalassophila—W. G. BINNEY **143**
Thénard, L. J., memoir of, by M. FLOURENS. (R. 1862) 150
Theoretical researches—*See* Plateau, J.
Theories, kinetic, of gravitation—W. B. TAYLOR. (R. 1876) 299, **395**
Theory—
mechanical, of heat, principles of—J. MÜLLER. (R. 1868) 224
modern, of chemical types—C. M. WETHERILL. (R. 1863) 187
of heat, recent progress in relation to—A. CAZIN. (R. 1868) 224
Thermometer scales, table for conversion of centigrade to Fahrenheit. (R. 1863.) 187
Thermometer, wet and dry bulb, tables for—J. H. COFFIN **87**
Thermometric observations 157
Thermometrical tables—A. GUYOT **153**
THOMPSON, T. Mounds in Iowa and Illinois. (R. 1879) 345
Thoughts on the nature and origin of force—W. B. TAYLOR. (R. 1870) 244, **375**
Thrushes, description of two new, from United States—R. RIDGWAY. (P. 1881.) 467
Thunder—
and lightning, observations on—S. MASTERMAN. (R. 1855) 77
storm, on John Wise's observation of a—R. HARE. (R. 1854) 75
storms, instructions for observations of—J. HENRY **235**
Tidal observations—
at Wolstenholm Sound—Com. SAUNDERS 130
in the Arctic Seas—I. I. HAYES 196
in the Arctic Seas—E. K. KANE **130**
Tide, flood, law of deposit of the—C. H. DAVIS **33**
Tides and tidal action in harbors—J. E. HILGARD. (R. 1874) 286, **390**
TIFFANY, A. S. Shell-bed skull from Illinois. (R. 1874) 286
Timber of submarine structures, occurrence of *Chelura terebrans*, a crustacean destructive to—S. I. SMITH. (P. 1879) 333
Time and space, lecture on relations of—S. ALEXANDER. (R. 1861) 149
Tinneh or Chepewyan Indians of British America—G. GIBBS; W. L. HARDISTY; S. JONES; B. R. ROSS. (R. 1866) 214, **365**
Tipulidæ, monograph of—R. OSTEN SACKEN 219
TOELLNER, A. Antiquities of Rock Island county, Illinois. (R. 1879) 345
Tokio, University of, catalogue of Japanese woods presented by—L. F. WARD. (P. 1881) 467

Tompkins county, New York, ancient fort and burial ground in—D. TROWBRIDGE. (R. 1863) 187
TONER, J. M. Deed of foundation of Toner lectures. (R. 1872) 271, 329
Toner lectures—
No. I. On the structure of cancerous tumors and the mode in which adjacent parts are invaded—J. J. WOODWARD 266
II. Dual character of the brain—C. E. BROWN-SÉQUARD 291
III. On strain and over-action of the heart—J. M. DA COSTA 279
IV. A study of the nature and mechanism of fever—H. C. WOOD 282
V. On the surgical complications and sequels of the continued fevers, with a bibliography of works on diseases of the joints, bones, larynx, the eye, gangrene, hæmatoma, phlegmasia, etc.—W. W. KEEN 300
VI. Subcutaneous surgery, its principles, and its recent extension in practice—W. ADAMS 302
VII. The nature of reparatory inflammation in arteries after ligature, acupressure, and torsion—E. O. SHAKESPEARE 321
VIII. Suggestions for the sanitary drainage of Washington city—G. E. WARING, Jr. 349
Tonto Apaches, notes on the—C. SMART. (R. 1867) 215
Topography of Black Mountain, North Carolina—T. L. CLINGMAN. (R. 1855.) 77
Tornado in Spruce creek valley, Centre county, Pennsylvania—J. B. MEEK. (R. 1871) 249
Tornado near New Harmony, Indiana, April 30, 1852—J. CHAPPELSMITH 59
Tornadoes and tempests, distinction between—J. B. LAMARCK. (R. 1871) 249
Tornadoes, queries relative to—J. HENRY 190
Toronto—
Observatory, instructions by, for observations of aurora 148
Observatory, map of stars near North Pole used by 350
University. Objects of the museum. (R. 1865) 209
University. Scientific coöperation. (R. 1861) 149
Torrey, John, memoir of, by A. GRAY. (R. 1873) 275
TORREY, J.—
Observations on the *Batis maritima* 60
On the *Darlingtonia Californica*, a new pitcher plant from northern California 61
Plantæ Frémontianæ, or descriptions of plants collected by J. C. Frémont in California 46
Tortoises, North American land, of genus *Xerobates*—F. W. TRUE. (P. 1881.) 467
Tortola, great hurricane at—G. A. LATIMER. (R. 1867) 215
Tortugas, destruction of fish in vicinity of the—J. P. JEFFERSON; J. Y. PORTER; T. MOORE. (P. 1878) 332
Totten, Gen. J. G., eulogy on, by J. G. BARNARD. (R. 1865) 209
Traces of early mental condition of man—E. B. TYLOR. (R. 1867) 215

Trade—
ancient aboriginal—C. RAU. (R. 1872) 271, 440, **385**
language of Oregon, dictionary of the—G. GIBBS 161
language of Oregon, vocabulary of the—B. R. MITCHELL; W. W. TURNER **68**
Transactions—*See* Geneva Society, Paris Anthropological Society.
Transatlantic longitude—B. A. GOULD **223**
Transfer of Smithsonian library to Library of Congress, act of Congress to authorize. (R. 1865) 209, 328, 329
Transformations, lecture on insect instincts and—J. G. MORRIS. (R. 1855) 77
Transit of Venus expedition to Kerguelen Island—J. H. KIDDER and others. 293, 294
Transporting specimens of *Diatomaceæ*, directions for—A. M. EDWARDS 366
Transporting specimens of natural history, directions for—S. F. BAIRD. (R. 1856) 91, 34
Trapezium, gray substance of the—J. DEAN 173
Travels in Central and South America—S. HABEL 269
Treasury Department, authority given by, to collectors of customs and others to receive and transmit specimens to the Smithsonian 34
Treasury, Secretary of, letter to, on payment of interest in coin—J. HENRY. (R. 1865) 209, 329
Treasury of United States, account of, with Smithson fund 328, 329
Trees—
forest, distribution of, in Montana, Idaho, and Washington—W. W. JOHNSON. (R. 1870) 244
of Florida and the Mexican boundary—J. G. COOPER. (R. 1860) 147
of North America, distribution of—J. G. COOPER. (R. 1858) 109, **351**
Trinidad, economic geology of—G. P. WALL; J. G. SAWKINS. (R. 1856) 91
Trochilidæ—
classification and synopsis of—D. G. ELLIOT **317**
in collection of U. S. National Museum, catalogue of—R. RIDGWAY. (P. 1880) 425
list of—D. G. ELLIOT **334**
Troglodytes of Breckinridge county, Kentucky—R. S. ROBERTSON. (R. 1874.) 286
Troglodytes or cave dwellers of the valley of the Vézère—P. BROCA. (R. 1872.) 271
TROWBRIDGE, D. Ancient fort and burial ground in Tompkins county, New York. (R. 1863) 187
TROYON, F.—
Archæological researches made at Concise. (R. 1861) 149
Lacustrian cities of Switzerland. (R. 1861) 149
On the *Crania helvetica*. (R. 1864) 188
Report on ethnological collection of Museum at Lausanne, Switzerland. (R. 1861) 149
TRUE, F. W. On North American land tortoises of genus *Xerobates*. (P. 1881.) 467
TRUE, F. W. On the rare rodent, *Cricetodipus parvus*. (P. 1881) 467

Truncatellidæ—W. G. BINNEY ---- 144
Trust fund for the promotion of science in the United States—J. TYNDALL. (R. 1872) ---- 271
Tryon, G. W., letter to, on shells—J. LEWIS ---- 253
TRYON, G. W. Report on shells presented to Philadelphia Academy of Natural Sciences. (R. 1865) ---- 209
TRYON, G. W. Strepomatidæ or American melanians ---- **253**
Trypetina, review of—H. LOEW ---- 256
TUCKERMAN, E. Lichens of Arctic America ---- 342
TUCKERMAN, E. Lichens of Kerguelen Island ---- 294
TUCKETT, F. F. On barometer tables. (R. 1867) ---- 215
Tucson meteorite, account of—S. AINSA. (R. 1863) ---- 187
Tucson meteorite, account of—B. J. D. IRWIN. (R. 1863) ---- 187
Tumors, cancerous, structure of—J. J. WOODWARD ---- 266
Tunicata of northeast coast of America—A. E. VERRILL. (P. 1879) ---- 333
Turdidæ, description of new species of, from Dominica—G. N. LAWRENCE. (P. 1880) ---- 425
Turner, W. W., notice of, by C. C. FELTON. (R. 1859) ---- 110
TURNER, W. W. Indian philology. (R. 1851) ---- 51
TURNER, W. W., and others. On publication of Squier and Davis' Ancient Monuments of the Mississippi valley. (R. 1847) ---- **H, K**
TURNER, W. W.; BOWEN, T. J. Yoruba grammar and dictionary ---- 98
TURNER, W. W.; MITCHELL, B. R. Vocabulary of the jargon of Oregon ---- **68**
TYLOR, E. B. On traces of the early mental condition of man. (R. 1867) ---- 215
TYNDALL, J. Radiation. (R. 1868) ---- 224
TYNDALL, J. Trust fund for the promotion of science in the United States. (R. 1872) ---- 271, 329
Tyrannus, synopsis of genus—R. RIDGWAY. (P. 1878) ---- 332

U.

UHLER, P. R.—
Circular in reference to the history of North American grasshoppers 163
Instructions for collecting hemiptera. (R. 1858) 109
Instructions for collecting neuroptera. (R. 1858) 109
Instructions for collecting orthoptera. (R. 1858) 109
Synopsis of neuroptera of North America 134
Underground temperature—C. A. SCHOTT; J. D. EVERETT. (R. 1874) 286
Union, lectures on the—H. REED. (R. 1854) 75
United States—
animal resources and fisheries of the, catalogue of collection to illustrate the—G. B. GOODE **326**
animal resources of the, catalogue of collection to illustrate the—G. B. GOODE **297**
antiquities of the, proposed map of—A. J. HILL. (R. 1861) 149
archæology of the—S. F. HAVEN **71**
base chart of the—C. A. SCHOTT **414**
chalk found in the—T. A. CONRAD. (R. 1865) 209
coleoptera of the, catalogue of the—F. E. MELSHEIMER **62**
collections presented to the, by foreign commissioners, list of. (R. 1876.) 299
education in the, project of outline history of—F. A. PACKARD. (R. 1863.) 187
ethnological map of the, proposed—G. GIBBS. (R. 1862) 150
exhibit of fisheries and fish culture of the, at Berlin, 1880—G. B. GOODE. **413**
explorations in the—*See* Baird, S. F.
fishes, food, of the—*See* Baird, S. F.
fishes of Pacific coast of the—D. S. JORDAN; C. H. GILBERT. (P. 1880.) 425
fishes of Pacific coast of the, bibliography of—T. H. BEAN. (P. 1881.) 467
fishes of Pacific coast of the, bibliography of—T. GILL 463
fishes of Pacific coast of the, notes on—D. S. JORDAN; C. H. GILBERT. (P. 1881) 467
free freight between England and the—E. CUNARD. (R. 1859) 110
free freight between Germany and the—KUNHARDT & Co. (R. 1861) 149
free freight between Germany and the, by North German Lloyd—R. SCHLEIDEN. (R. 1858) 109
fund for promotion of science in the—J. TYNDALL. (R. 1872) 271
institutions, scientific and literary, in the, list of the principal **335**
libraries, institutions, and societies in the, list of—W. J. RHEES **116**, **238**
libraries, public, in the, notices of—C. C. JEWETT **25**
libraries, public, of the, report on—C. C. JEWETT. (R. 1849) 21
limpets and chitons from deep waters off eastern coast of the—W. H. DALL. (P. 1881) 467

United States—Continued.
meteorology of the, report on—E. LOOMIS. (R. 1847) ---------------- **H**
microscopic examinations of soundings off Atlantic coast of the—J. W. BAILEY ---------------- **20**
mollusca of the southern, some new species of eocene—A. HEILPRIN. (P. 1880) ---------------- 425
occultations visible in the—*See* Downes, J.
physical geography of the—C. ELLET, Jr. ---------------- 13
rain and snow fall in the, tables of—C. A. SCHOTT ---------------- **222**, **353**
rain charts of the, 1, 2, 3: summer, winter, year—C. A. SCHOTT ---------------- **374**
reptiles, cretaceous, of the—J. LEIDY ---------------- **192**
reptiles, cretaceous, of the, review of—J. LEIDY. (R. 1864) ---------------- 188
shell-deposits, artificial, of the—D. G. BRINTON. (R. 1866) ---------------- 214
sparrows sent to the—W. A. LLOYD. (R. 1867) ---------------- 215
temperature chart of the, for the year—C. A. SCHOTT ---------------- **381**, **388**
temperature charts of the, 1, 2, 3: summer, winter, year—C. A. SCHOTT. **387**
temperature tables of the—C. A. SCHOTT ---------------- **277**
thrushes from the, description of two new—R. RIDGWAY. (P. 1881) --- 467
trees of the, catalogue of—J. G. COOPER. (R. 1858) ---------------- 109, 351
United States Exploring Expedition, duplicate shells collected by the ---------------- 193
United States Fish Commission—*See* Fish Commission.
United States Government, list of publications of, 1868-1881—G. H. BOEHMER. 477
United States National Museum—*See* Museum, U. S. National.
United States Patent Office, results of meteorological observations under the direction of the. Vols. I, II ---------------- **157**, **182**
United States Treasury—*See* Treasury.
Universal meteorograph for detached observatories—E. H. VON BAUMHAUER. (R. 1879) ---------------- 345
University—
National, of Greece, Museum of. Exchange of specimens. (R. 1867.) 215
of Christiania, Norway, ethnological specimens presented by. (R. 1863.) 187
of Costa Rica. Exchange of specimens. (R. 1867) ---------------- 215
of State of New York, Regents of the. Acknowledgment for specimens. (R. 1865) ---------------- 209
of Tokio, catalogue of Japanese woods presented by—L. F. WARD. (P. 1881) ---------------- 467
of Toronto, objects of museum of. (R. 1865) ---------------- 209
of Toronto, scientific coöperation. (R. 1861) ---------------- 149
Uranidea marginata, new species of fish, description of—T. H. BEAN. (P. 1881.) 467
Uranidea microstoma, new fish from Alaska, description of—W. N. LOOKINGTON. (P. 1880) ---------------- 425
Uranus, investigation of orbit of, with tables of its motion—S. NEWCOMB ----- 262
Uranus, secular variation of elements of orbit of—J. N. STOCKWELL ---------------- 232

Urine, observations on the—J. JONES ---- 82
Use of galvanometer as a measuring instrument—J. C. POGGENDORFF. (R. 1859.) 110
Uses of brain and marrow of animals among Indians—T. R. PEALE. (R. 1870.) 244
Utah, descriptions of new invertebrate fossils from—C. A. WHITE. (P. 1880.) 425
Utah lake, description of new species of *Squalius* (*Squalius aliciæ*) from—P. L. JOUY. (P. 1881) ---- 467
Utah lake, notes on collection of fishes from—D. S. JORDAN; C. H. GILBERT. (P. 1880) ---- 425
Utrecht, Provincial Society of Arts and Sciences. Prize questions. (R. 1861; R. 1862) ---- 149, 150

V.

VAILLANT, M.; HENRY, J. Horary variations of the barometer. (R. 1866) ---- 214
Values of $b_s^{(i)}$ and its derivatives—J. D. RUNKLE ---- 94
Values of coefficients in perturbative function of planetary motion depending on ratio of mean distances—J. D. RUNKLE ---- 79
Valvatidæ—W. G. BINNEY ---- 144
Van Rensselaer harbor, Arctic Seas, observations at—*See* Kane.
Vapor, aqueous, on the diminution of, with increasing altitude in the atmosphere—J. HANN. (R. 1877) ---- 323, 398
Vapor, aqueous, table for determining elastic force of—J. H. COFFIN ---- 87
Vastness of the visible creation, lectures on—S. ALEXANDER. (R. 1857) ---- 107
Vegetable colonization of Shetland Islands, Faroe Islands, and Iceland—C. MARTINS. (R. 1858) ---- 109
Vegetable species, causes which limit, towards the north—A. DE CANDOLLE. (R. 1858) ---- 109
Vegetation and the atmosphere—J. JAMIN. (R. 1864) ---- 188
Velie, J. W., catalogue and description of fishes collected by, in Gulf of Mexico—G. B. GOODE; T. H. BEAN. (P. 1879) ---- 333
Velocity of light, essay on the—C. DELAUNAY. (R. 1864) ---- 188, **354**
Velocity of the wind—J. HANN and others. (R. 1877) ---- 323, 398
Venezuela, Colonia Tovar, meteorology and ethnology of—A. FENDLER. (R. 1857; R. 1866) ---- 107, 214
Venom of rattlesnake, researches on the—S. W. MITCHELL ---- **135**
Venom of serpents, bibliography of—S. W. MITCHELL ---- 135
Ventilating and warming buildings. Parts I, II—A. MORIN. (R. 1873; R. 1874) ---- 275, 286, **439**
Ventilation, architecture in relation to—D. B. REID. (R. 1856) ---- 91
Venus, secular variations of elements of orbit of—J. N. STOCKWELL ---- 232

Venus—*See* Transit of Venus.
Vera Cruz, Mexico, antiquities in—H. FINCK. (R. 1870) 244
Verification of barometers at the Kew Observatory—J. WELSH. (R. 1859) 110
VERRILL, A. E.—
Annelids, echinoderms, and anthozoa of Kerguelen Island 294
Annelids, molluscoids, and radiates of Arctic America 342
Marine invertebrata of New England. (P. 1879) 333
Mollusca recently added to fauna of southern New England, catalogue of. (P. 1880) 425
Mollusca, with notes on annelida, echinodermata, etc. (P. 1880) 425
Recent additions to marine invertebrata of northeast coast of America, with new genera and species. Parts I, II, III. (P. 1879; P. 1880.) 333, 425
VERRILL, A. E.; RATHBUN, R. Marine invertebrata of northeast coast of America distributed by Fish Commission. (P. 1879) 333
Vertebrata, chemical and physiological investigations relative to—J. JONES 82
Vespidæ, synopsis of—H. DE SAUSSURE 254
Vestiges of antiquity in the United States—S. F. HAVEN 71
Vézère, valley of the, cave-dwellers of the—P. BROCA. (R. 1872) 271
Vibratory movement of matter—L. MAGRINI. (R. 1868) 224
Victoria Royal Society, address of the president—R. L. J. ELLERY. (R. 1868.) 224
Vienna—
Imperial Academy of Sciences of. Prize questions. (R. 1864; R. 1865.) 188, 209
Imperial Geological Institute, tertiary fossils presented by. (R. 1863) 187
Imperial Library of, books presented. (R. 1865) 209
Views and plans of Smithsonian Institution—R. D. OWEN P
Vineyard Sound, Massachusetts, occurrence of oceanic bonito in—V. N. EDWARDS. (P. 1878) 332
Virgin Islands, flora of the—H. F. A. EGGERS 313
Virginia—
Hampton, catalogue of casts of heads of Indian boys and girls at—R. H. PRATT. (P. 1879) 333
Luray Cave, blind myriapod from—J. A. RYDER. (P. 1880) 425
Luray Cave, report of visit to—O. T. MASON and others. (R. 1880.) 442, **433**
Vitality—H. H. HIGGINS; J. HENRY. (R. 1866) 214
Viviparidæ—W. G. BINNEY 144
Vocabularies, Indian—G. GIBBS. (R. 1862) 150
Vocabularies, Indian, received from the Wheeler expedition, list of. (R. 1874.) 286
Vocabulary—
comparative—A. GALLATIN 160
comparative, English, Spanish, French, Latin 170
Makah—J. G. SWAN 220
of Chinook jargon, or trade language of Oregon—G. GIBBS **161**
of Chinook jargon, or trade language of Oregon—B. R. MITCHELL; W. W. TURNER; G. GIBBS **68**

Vocal sounds of Laura Bridgman—F. LIEBER ---- 12
Voices of crustaceans—G. B. GOODE. (P. 1878) ---- 332
Volcano—
in Nicaragua, eruption of—A. B. DICKINSON. (R. 1867) ---- 215
of Colima, eruption of—C. SARTORIUS. (R. 1869) ---- 228
of Popocatepetl, examination of—Baron VON MÜLLER; A. SONNTAG ---- 114
VOLLUM, E. P. On the wingless grasshopper of California. (R. 1860) ---- 147
Volta, Alexander, eulogy on, by F. ARAGO. (R. 1875) ---- 298
VON BAUMHAUER, E. H. Universal meteorograph for detached observatories. (R. 1879) ---- 345
Von Buch, Leopold, memoir of, by M. FLOURENS. (R. 1862) ---- 150
VON HELLWALD, F. The American migration. (R. 1866) ---- 214
VON KAROLYI, Lieut.; CRAIG, B. F. Products of combustion of gun-cotton and gunpowder. (R. 1864) ---- 188
VON LIEBIG, J. Induction and deduction. (R. 1870) ---- 244
Von Martius, C. F. P., honorary medal to—W. HAIDINGER. (R. 1863) ---- 187
Von Martius, C. F. P., memoir of, by C. RAU. (R. 1869) ---- 228, 440, **251**
VON MÜLLER, Baron. Observations on terrestrial magnetism in Mexico ---- 114

W.

WAITE, M. R. Memorial of Joseph Henry ---- 856
WALE; HAWKINS. Blow-pipe apparatus. (R. 1872) ---- 271
WALKER, D. Observations on Arctic auroras and specific gravity of sea water. 146
WALKER, D. Observations on ice ---- 146
WALKER, S. C. Ephemerides of planet Neptune, 1848, 1846–1849, 1850, 1851, 1852 ---- **4, 5, 6, 7, 24**
WALKER, S. C. Researches relative to planet Neptune ---- **3**
WALKER, S. T. Explorations among Indian mounds in southern Florida. (R. 1879) ---- 345
WALKER, S. T. Shell-heaps of Tampa Bay, Florida. (R. 1879) ---- 345
WALL, G. P.; SAWKINS, J. G. Report on survey of economic geology of Trinidad. (R. 1856) ---- 91
WALLACH, R.; HENRY, J. Report of Committee of Regents on the fire at Smithsonian. (R. 1864) ---- 188
Walrus, remains of, in Maine—C. H. BOYD. (P. 1881) ---- 467
Wampum belts of the six nations—W. M. BEAUCHAMP. (R. 1879) ---- 345
War Department, authority given by, to officers of Quartermaster's Department to receive and transmit specimens to Smithsonian ---- 84

WARD, L. F.—
Barometer tube breaking suddenly. (R. 1866) 214
Catalogue of collection of Japanese woods presented by University of Tokio, Japan. (P. 1881) 467
Check-list of plants of Washington and vicinity **461**
Directions for collecting and preserving plants **460**
Guide to flora of Washington and vicinity **444**
WARING, G. E., Jr. Suggestions for sanitary drainage of Washington city. Toner lecture No. VIII 349
Warming and ventilating buildings. Parts I, II—A. MORIN. (R. 1873; R. 1874) 275, 286, **439**
Warming, architecture in relation to—D. B. REID. (R. 1856) 91
WARNER, J. Big elephant mound in Grant county, Wisconsin. (R. 1872) 271
Warren, G. K., report on collections made by—F. B. MEEK; F. V. HAYDEN. 172
WARTMANN, E. Report on transactions of the Society of Physics and Natural History of Geneva, July, 1867, to June, 1868. (R. 1868) 224
Washington, Arkansas, meteorological observations near—N. D. SMITH **131**
Washington, D. C.—
canal of, report of Committee of Regents on—R. DELAFIELD. (R. 1868.) 224
flora of, and vicinity, guide to the—L. F. WARD **444**
notice of, in Harriot's travels 330
notice of, in Isaac Weld's travels 330
prehistoric remains in vicinity of—T. R. PEALE. (R. 1872) 271
sanitary drainage of. Toner lecture No. VIII—G. E. WARING, Jr. **349**
Washington Philosophical Society, bulletin of. Vols. I-III; March, 1871, to June, 1880 423
Washington Territory—
fishes of—T. H. BEAN. (P. 1881) 467
forest trees in, distribution of—W. W. JOHNSON. (R. 1870) 244
Indians of—J. G. SWAN 220
method of taking surf smelt by Indians of—J. G. SWAN. (P. 1880) 425
Neah Bay, description of two new species of fishes (*Ascelicthys rhodorus* and *Scytalina cerdale*) from—D. S. JORDAN; C. H. GILBERT. (P. 1880) 425
Wasps, American solitary, synopsis of—H. DE SAUSSURE **254**
Wasps, translation of De Saussure's monograph of—E. NORTON 254
Water—
formation of ice at bottom of—M. ENGELHARDT. (R. 1866) 214
from Gulf of Mexico, report on—W. G. FARLOW. (P. 1881) 467
in rivers, diminution of—H. G. WEX. (R. 1875) 298
in rivers, method of ascertaining the amount of—A. A. HUMPHREYS. (R. 1858) 109
polluted, in Gulf of Mexico, destruction of fish by—W. C. W. GLAZIER. (P. 1881) 467

Water—Continued.
salt, preservation of copper and iron in—A. E. Becquerel. (R. 1864.) 188
sea, specific gravity of—D. Walker 146
Watkins, E. A. System of relationship of Cree Indians. (R. 1862) 150
Watson, S. Bibliographical index to North American botany. Part I. *Polypetalæ* **258**
Weapons, savage, at Centennial Exhibition, study of—E. H. Knight. (R. 1879) 345, **415**
Weather, effect of moon on the—J. Henry. (R. 1871) 249
Webb, T. W. Account of Henry Draper's telescope. (R. 1864) 188
Weights, atomic, recalculation of. Constants of Nature, Part V—F. W. Clarke. 441
Weights, small, method of forming—R. Hare. (R. 1858) 109
Weights and measures—
English and French, tables of. (R. 1863; R. 1864) 187, 188
metric system of, with tables—H. A. Newton. (R. 1865) 209, **371**
new system of, with 8 as the metrical number—G. H. Knight. (R. 1867.) 215
Weismann, A. Change of Mexican axolotl to amblystoma. (R. 1877) 323, **401**
Weld, I. Account of city of Washington, 1807 330
Welling, J. C. Notes on the life and character of Joseph Henry 356, **338**
Welsh, language of Navajos said to resemble—S. Y. McMasters. (R. 1865.) 209
Welsh, J. Construction and verification of standard barometers. (R. 1859.) 110
West Indies—
birds of the—*See* Lawrence, G. N., Ober, F. A.
list of described birds of the, not in Smithsonian collection **185**
loxigilla from, description of new subspecies of—G. N. Lawrence. (P. 1881) **467**
stone celts in the—G. J. Gibbs. (R. 1877) 323
West Virginia, occurrence of Canada porcupine in—G. B. Goode. (P. 1878.) 332
Wet and dry bulb thermometer, tables for—J. H. Coffin 87
Wetherill, C. M.—
Modern theory of chemical types. (R. 1863) 187
Ozone and antozone. (R. 1864) 188, **355**
Plan of a research upon the atmosphere. (R. 1866) 214
Wex, H. G. Diminution of the water of rivers and streams. (R. 1875) 298
Wheeler expedition, list of Indian vocabularies received from the. (R. 1874.) 286
Wheeler expedition—*See* Explorations.
Whirlwind at St. Thomas, August 21, 1871—A. Colding. (R. 1877) 323, 398
White, C. A.—
Description of new cretaceous pinna from New Mexico. (P. 1880) **425**
Description of very large fossil gasteropod from State of Puebla, Mexico. (P. 1880) **425**
Descriptions of new cretaceous invertebrate fossils from Kansas and Texas. (P. 1879) **333**

WHITE, C. A.—Continued.
Descriptions of new invertebrate fossils from the mesozoic and cenozoic rocks of Arkansas, Wyoming, Colorado, and Utah. (P. 1880) 425
Descriptions of new species of carboniferous invertebrate fossils. (P. 1879.) 333
Note on acrothele. (P. 1880) 425
Note on *Criocardium* and *Ethmocardium*. (P. 1879) 333
Note on *Endothyra ornata*. (P. 1879) 333
Note on occurrence of *Productus giganteus* in California. (P. 1880) 425
Note on occurrence of *Stricklandia salteri* and *Stricklandia Davidsoni* in Georgia. (P. 1880) 425
On certain cretaceous fossils from Arkansas and Colorado. (P. 1881) 467
White river cañon, Pima county, Arizona, ruins in—R. T. BURR. (R. 1879.) 345
WHITNEY, J. D. Catalogue of rocks, minerals, etc. (R. 1854) 75
WHITNEY, J. D. Cave in Calaveras county, California. (R. 1867) 215
WHITNEY, W. D. Lectures on principles of linguistic science. (R. 1863.) 187, **352**
WHITTLESEY, C.—
Ancient mining on shores of Lake Superior **155**
Descriptions of ancient works in Ohio **37**
On fluctuations of level in North American lakes **119**
On fresh-water glacial drift of the northwestern States **197**
Wilkes, C., duplicate shells of exploring expedition under **193**
Will of Smithson. (R. 1853) **B**, 67, 328, 330
Willemœsia group of crustacea, (recent *Eryontidæ*,) notice of new species of the—S. I. SMITH. (P. 1879) 333
WILLIAMS, H. C. On antiquities in some of the southern States. (R. 1870.) 244
WILLIAMSON, G. Antiquities in Guatemala. (R. 1876) 299
WILLIS, J. R.; BLACKISTON; BLAND. Birds of Nova Scotia. (R. 1858) 109
WILLIS, J. R.; BLAND. Birds of Bermuda. (R. 1858) 109
WILMOT, S. Notes on western gizzard shad, *Dorosoma cepedianum heterurum*. (P. 1878) 332
WILSON, D. Lectures on physical ethnology. (R. 1862) 150
Wilson, Henry, eulogy on, by P. PARKER. (R. 1875) 298
Wind—
and fog—J. BALFOUR. (R. 1866) 214
articles on, preserved in Smithsonian. (R. 1874) 286
changes of—C. MALLINIKROOT. (R. 1866) 214
connection of gales of, and appearance of aurora—R. T. KNIGHT; J. HENRY. (R. 1871) 249
observations of, in the Arctic Seas—I. I. HAYES 196
observations of, in the Arctic Seas—E. K. KANE 104
observations of, in the Arctic Seas—F. L. MCCLINTOCK 146
observations of, in the United States 157
relation between difference of pressure and velocity of—J. HANN. (R. 1877) 323, 398

Winds—
in Florida—J. BALTZELL. (R. 1866) 214
of the globe—J. H. COFFIN 268
of the northern hemisphere—J. H. COFFIN 52
upper, importance of attention to the—C. DEWEY. (R. 1866) 214
Winnipeg Lake, egging expedition to—D. GUNN. (R. 1867) 215
WIRTZ, H. R. Herbarium captured in Tennessee. (R. 1862) 150
Wisconsin—
antiquities in—M. STRONG. (R. 1877) 323
antiquities of—I. LAPHAM 70
earthworks in—E. E. BREED. (R. 1872) 271
Grant county, elephant mound in—J. WARNER. (R. 1872) 271
Grant county, observations on prehistoric mounds of—M. STRONG. (R. 1876) 299
mound in—C. K. DEAN. (R. 1872) 271
mounds and osteology of mound-builders of—J. N. DE HART. (R. 1877.) 323
mounds in—W. G. ANDERSON. (R. 1879) 345
salamander of—P. R. HOY. (R. 1854) 75
Winnebago county, mounds in—T. ARMSTRONG. (R. 1879) 345
Wise, J., on observation by, of a thunder storm—R. HARE. (R. 1854) 75
WISEMAN, N. Identification of the artisan and artist. (R. 1870) 244
WISSNER, J. Meteorology of the District of Columbia. (R. 1857) 107
WITHERS, R. E. Memorial address on Joseph Henry 356
WOEIKOFF, A. Discussion of winds of the globe 268
WOEIKOFF, A. Meteorology in Russia. (R. 1872) 271
Wolstenholm Sound, tidal record at—Com. SAUNDERS 130
Wood, ancient implement of, from Connecticut—E. W. ELLSWORTH. (R. 1876) 299
Wood, preservation of. (R. 1864) 188
WOOD, H. C.—
Bibliography of algæ 241
Contribution to the history of the fresh-water algæ of North America 241
Fever. A study in morbid and normal physiology. (R. 1878) 341, 357
Instructions for collecting myriapods, phalangidæ, etc. (R. 1866) 214
Study of nature and mechanism of fever. Toner lecture No. IV 282
WOOD, J. Meteorological observations at Marietta, Ohio 120
Woods of Japan, collection of, presented to U. S. National Museum, catalogue of—L. F. WARD. (P. 1881) 467
WOODWARD, J. J. Structure of cancerous tumors and mode in which adjacent parts are invaded 266
WOODWORTH, A. Meteorite in Mexico. (R. 1867) 215
WOOLSEY, T. D. Eulogy on C. C. Felton. (R. 1861) 149
Work, relation of food to, and its bearing on medical practice—S. HAUGHTON. (R. 1870) 244

Works published by Smithsonian Institution to January, 1866 ---- 203
World, estimate of population of the—E. MAILLY. (R. 1873) ---- 275
WORSAAE, J. J. A. Preservation of antiquities and national monuments in Denmark. (R. 1879) ---- 345
Wounds of poisoned arrows, lecture on nature and cure of—D. BRAINARD. (R. 1854) ---- 75
Wright, C., account of botanical explorations of, in New Mexico and California—A. GRAY. (R. 1849) ---- 21
Wright, C., account of plants collected by, in Texas and New Mexico. Parts I, II—A. GRAY ---- 22, 42
WRIGHT, D. F. Antiquities of Tennessee. (R. 1874) ---- 286
WRIGHT, G. Account of lightning discharges. (R. 1867) ---- 215
Writings, scientific, of Sir William Herschel, synopsis of—E. S. HOLDEN; C. S. HASTINGS. (R. 1880) ---- 442, **426**
Writings, scientific, of James Smithson ---- 327
Würdemann, G., notice of, by A. D. BACHE. (R. 1859) ---- 110
WÜRDEMANN, G. Specimens of flamingo, etc., from south Florida. (R. 1860.) 147
WÜRDEMANN, W.; GREEN, J. On filling barometer tubes. (R. 1859) ---- 110
Wyandot government—J. W. POWELL. (E. 1879-80) ---- 476
WYMAN, J. Anatomy of nervous system of *Rana pipiens* ---- **45**
Wyoming, new invertebrate fossils from—C. A. WHITE. (P. 1880) ---- 425

X.

Xantus, John, explorations of, in Mexico—M. ROMERO. (R. 1862) ---- 150
Xenichthys ocyurus, new species of *Xenichthys* from west coast of Central America, description of—D. S. JORDAN; C. H. GILBERT. (P. 1881) ---- 467
Xerobates, land tortoises of genus—F. W. TRUE. (P. 1881) ---- 467
Xiphister, description of new species of, from Monterey, California—D. S. JORDAN; C. H. GILBERT. (P. 1880) ---- 425
Xystreurys liolepis, new flounder from Santa Catalina Island, California, description of—D. S. JORDAN; C. H. GILBERT. (P. 1880) ---- 425

Y.

Yacht "Fox," meteorological observations made on—F. L. McClintock...... 146

Yale College, catalogue of meteorites in—G. J. Brush. (R. 1868) 224

Yarrow, H. C. Study of mortuary customs of the North American Indians. (E. 1879-80) 476

Yellowstone river, prehistoric remains near the—P. W. Norris. (R. 1879) .. 345

Yoruba, Africa—

country and people of, description of—T. J. Bowen.......... **98**

language of, bibliography of.......... 98

language of, grammar and dictionary of—T. J. Bowen; W. W. Turner. **98**

language of, grammar and dictionary of—Southern Baptist Missionary Society.......... 98

Young, C. B. Translation of Morin on warming and ventilating buildings. (R. 1873; R. 1874) 275, 286, **439**

Young, C. B. Translation of Von Baumbauer on a universal meteorograph. (R. 1879) 345

Young, Thomas, eulogy on, by F. Arago. (R. 1869) 228

Young, W. J. Cloud bursts. (R. 1867) 215

Yu, (Chinese name of jade,) study of—S. Blondel. (R. 1876).......... 299

Yucatan, remarks on *Cara gigantesca* of Yzamal in—A. Schott. (R. 1869) .. 228

Yukon, Russian America, journey to the—W. W. Kirby. (R. 1864) 188

Yzamal, Yucatan, remarks on *Cara gigantesca* of—A. Schott. (R. 1869)..... 228

Z.

Zantedeschi, F. R. Electricity of induction in aerial strata of atmosphere surrounding cloud resolving into rain, etc. (R. 1870).......... 244

Zapotec remains, notice of—B. Mayer; J. G. Sawkins 86

Zisgenbals, H. Schlagintweit ethnographic collection. (R. 1867) 215

Zone of small planets between Mars and Jupiter, lecture on the—E. Loomis. (R. 1854) 75

Zoölogical—

Gardens, Hamburg. Exchange of specimens. (R. 1867).......... 215

position of Texas—E. D. Cope.......... **412**

Record, list of generic names supplemental to those indexed in—S. H. Scudder 470

Zoölogicus, Nomenclator. A list of generic names of recent and fossil animals—S. H. Scudder 470

Zoölogy, list of generic names employed in—S. H. Scudder.......... 470

Zoölogy, record of recent progress in, 1879, 1880—T. Gill. (R. 1880)... 442, **431**

[illegible]

[illegible]

[illegible]

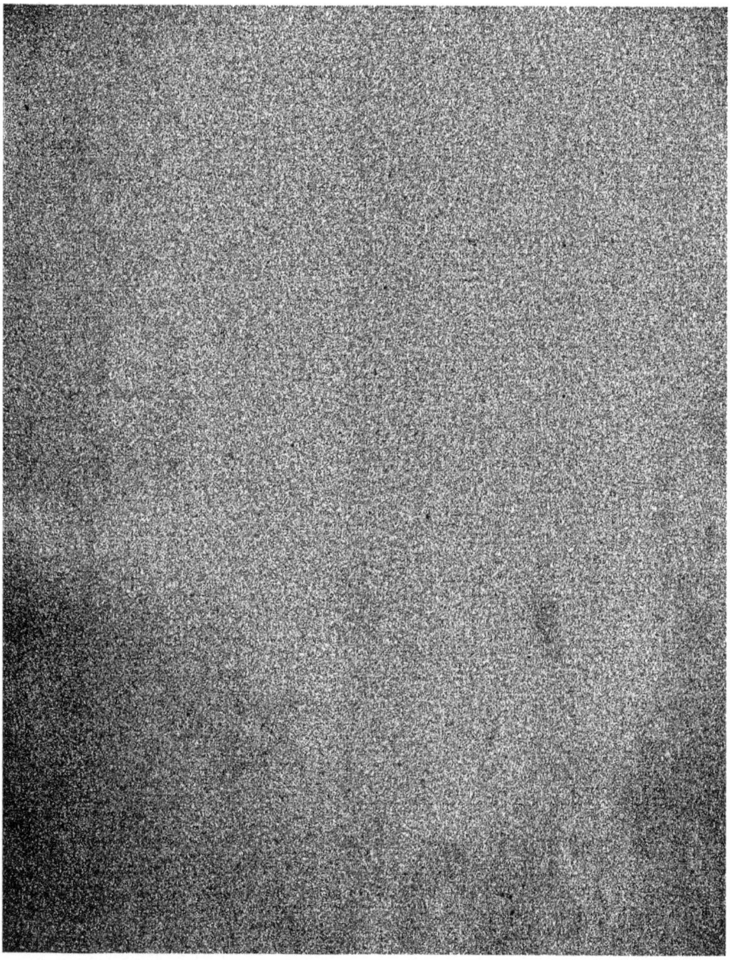

Lightning Source UK Ltd.
Milton Keynes UK
UKHW011201240219
337912UK00010B/599/P

9 781397 305671